MIDI POWER!

Robert Guérin

MIDI Power!

Library of Congress Catalog Number 2002112024

ISBN 1-929685-66-1

5 4 3 2 1

Educational facilities, companies, and organizations interested in multiple copies or licensing of this book should contact the publisher for quantity discount information. Training manuals, CD-ROMs, and portions of this book are also available individually or can be tailored for specific needs.

Muska & Lipman Publishing
2645 Erie Avenue, Suite 41
Cincinnati, Ohio 45208
www.muskalipman.com
publisher@muskalipman.com

About the Author

Robert Guerin

Websites: zerodb.ca or www.wavedesigners.com, Email: rguerin@zerodb.ca

A composer for the past fourteen years and a music enthusiast since 1976, Robert has worked on a variety of personal and commercial projects, such as feature and short films, television themes, and educational and corporate videos. Composing, arranging, playing, recording, and mixing most of his own material, he has developed working habits that allow him to be creative without losing the sense of efficiency.

As a professor, Robert has put together five courses covering a wide range of topics, such as: computer software for musicians, digital audio technologies, sound on the web, sound in multimedia productions, how musicians can get job interviews, hard disk recording, and many more topics. He has been program coordinator at Trebas Institute in Montreal and a part time professor at Vanier College also in Montreal. Robert has developed online courses on sound integration in webpages and has written articles for audio- and music-related online magazines.

As an entrepreneur, he has developed many skills necessary in today's world. Robert has expanded his knowledge and expertise to ensure his business survival by adopting new multimedia and web-related technologies.

Robert is the author of two other books published by Muska & Lipman: Cubase VST Power! (in stores now) and Cubase SX Power! (coming to stores later in 2002).

Dedications

I would like to dedicate this book to all the people on this earth, who help make this a better place to live in through the harmony of their music. It is after all, one of the rare forms of human expression where cultural diversities enrich its language and bring these cultures together for a common purpose.

Acknowledgements

I would like to give thanks to the following people for their help and support throughout the writing process, and for putting up with my caffeine-induced personality at times: Andy Shafran and his team at Muska & Lipman (especially Mark and Sherri); Christopher Hawkins at www.streamworksaudio.com for his input; Stefane "the Mac guy" Richard for his Mac tips and screenshots; all the technical editors that worked really hard to make this book what it is; everyone I've contacted throughout the writing process, including manufacturers and software developers—your help is appreciated and this book would not have been possible without your support. I would also like to thank my friends (Sang Hee, Patricia, Pierre, Liz and Steve) for your continuous encouragement. Mom and Dad, thanks for being there.

Finally, I would like to thank the community of web masters, web mistresses, and content providers who create, edit, and update valuable information about MIDI and other audio-related topics on their websites for all to use and benefit from. Your work helps us all to be better at what we do and keeps knowledge where it should be: accessible to everyone.

Merci à tous!

Contents

Appendix A: Understanding Binary, Decimal, and Hexadecimal 265

Appendix B: MIDI 1.0 Specification 275

Appendix C: The Standard MIDI File Format 299

Appendix D: Understanding Timing Concepts 315

Appendix E: The MIDI Troubleshooting Checklist 321

Introduction

Since its release on the market in the early 80s, MIDI has played a significant role in the music industry. But more importantly, it has given musicians and enthusiasts alike a tool that enables them to bridge the gap that existed before. MIDI provided, for the first time, a means of communicating musical information from one device to another in a way that was accepted and adopted by an entire industry. This is, in itself, a big deal.

Since its inception, MIDI has taken an important place in professional and project studios. It has also played an important role in live performance and has influenced the types of music composers create. With the rise of music-based computer applications, it then provided an even more important way for musicians to create music using these highly versatile devices. Over the years, MIDI and digital audio became so intertwined as a way to create music, that it became difficult to understand where one left off and the other picked up.

In the mid 90s, some believed that MIDI had no future. Digital audio workstations were becoming so affordable and computers were offering so much processing power, that using MIDI was almost considered to be a thing of the past. But as usually happens, things evolve in cycles. Now, with software synthesizers, samplers, and drum machines, MIDI and Audio multi-track applications and hundreds of MIDI applications making their way into the market, MIDI has reclaimed its place in our creative process once again.

As you probably know, there are a good number of books that discuss MIDI. However, while all these books offer information on the subject, I found that very few of them deal strictly with an in-depth look at MIDI itself. Many of these books discuss digital audio applications, or hardware devices such as mixers, monitors, or microphones. This book, on the other hand, is meant as a reference guide to MIDI and MIDI alone. From how it works to how you can connect devices together using MIDI, to how it integrates into a computer environment and how it has evolved since it was created.

This book will discuss different types of MIDI software, but not how to use the software in step-by-step instructions. It will also discuss how to set up your MIDI studio, but it will not tell you which buttons to press on your synthesizer. It will, however, point you in the right direction and give you the necessary information to deal with issues that might arise as you are working with MIDI. MIDI Power! also provides an in-depth look at MIDI and its messages and protocols. You'll learn to make sense of the MIDI language and appreciate its potential.

Is This Book for You?

This book is for you if you want to learn about MIDI—how to use it, how to make it work, how to edit it, why you should use it, when you should use it, and how to take advantage of it with your computer.

This book is not for you if you are looking for a book on how to use a specific device, such as a synthesizer, sampler, hardware sequencer, or patch bay—or how to use a specific software application, such as a sequencer, software instrument, or patch editor.

If you are new to MIDI and would like to learn what all the fuss is about, or if you're a veteran MIDI user looking to find out where MIDI is going or how it integrates in today's computer world, you will definitely find answers in these pages. This book is meant as a reference book: something to come back to when you need it.

How This Book Is Organized

Let's take a look at what you will find in the pages that follow. At the end of this book, you will also find seven appendices that will come in handy once you have a firm understanding of what MIDI is all about.

▶ Chapter 1, The Basics covers the history of MIDI as well as a definition of MIDI itself. This will give you the foundation you need to understand the different components involved in MIDI, its vocabulary, and hierarchical organization.

▶ Chapter 2, Basic MIDI Messages looks at the information contained in a MIDI communication. As in any language, understanding how sentences are created allows you to better control your communication. For example, in a sentence, you could have a subject, verb, and a noun, "John eats chocolate." In a MIDI message you have the same kind of structure "Play note on channel 1, C3 softly." This chapter looks at the different types of messages and how, when, and why they are used.

▶ Chapter 3, Control Change Messages is an extension of what was covered in the previous chapter. It looks at a specific type of MIDI message called control changes. You will learn how to use those messages to control certain aspects of your musical performance.

▶ Chapter 4, General MIDI and Standard MIDI Files are two major additions made to the MIDI specification since it was introduced. These additions address compatibility issues when sharing MIDI files with others. This chapter will discuss what General MIDI is and how to use it. It will also address the standard MIDI file format as well as extensions made to the General MIDI specification through the GS and XG standards.

▶ Chapter 5, MIDI Hardware Devices takes a look at MIDI-enabled devices from sound modules to MIDI patch bays, passing through a wide range of audio devices that support MIDI. It will also look at some basic and more complex MIDI setups, without the use of a computer.

▶ Chapter 6, MIDI and the Computer looks at what you need to start using your computer with your external MIDI devices. For example, we'll discuss MIDI interfaces and sound cards with MIDI integration for gamers, musicians, and laptop and network users. We'll also look at some basic and more complex MIDI setups, this time integrating the computer into the setups.

▶ Chapter 7, MIDI Inside Your Computer discusses one of the newer issues with

MIDI: how to get it to work inside your computer and how to set up your computer for optimal MIDI as well as audio performance.

▶ Chapter 8, Sequencing With MIDI takes a look at the most popular type of MIDI application inside your computer—covering its configuration, the recording process, and editing environments. You will also find information about converting MIDI to music notation through specialized software as well as integrated features in sequencers.

▶ Chapter 9, MIDI Software: A Sound Creation Environment brings you into the world of software instruments, which are taking MIDI to a new level by giving a new meaning to the term Virtual Studio. Patch editors and librarians are also covered in this chapter. Keeping track of your synthesizer patch settings, editing your synthesizer's sounds through your computer, and saving them for later use has never been easier than it is now, thanks to these applications.

▶ Chapter 10, MIDI Software: A Toolbox Filled With Toys is an extension of the two previous chapters, giving you an overview of the different ways programmers have used their skills to make MIDI more versatile than ever. This chapter will also look at MIDI and the web, offering solutions for a variety of needs and giving tips on how to create MIDI-enabled web pages.

▶ Chapter 11, Deeper Into MIDI: System Exclusive and Synchronization is for those of you who always wondered about these two advanced MIDI feature—you'll be surprised at how easy and useful they can be. Learn how SysEx (System Exclusive) works, when you can use it creatively, and why you would want to bother with it in the first place. Along with SysEx, we will look at how you can synchronize different devices, software, and video using MIDI's own synchronization options.

▶ Appendix A, Understanding Binary, Decimal, and Hexadecimal will help you understand these three common numbering systems that are part of MIDI. MIDI is transmitted using binary codes, which are usually represented in hexadecimals in technical documents, which, in turn, are displayed as decimal values inside your MIDI applications. To get the whole picture, you will need to understand how to convert from one to another easily.

▶ Appendix B, MIDI 1.0 Specification is a reference guide to the MIDI specification, giving you a table view of MIDI and how it works, as defined by the organization that oversees the dissemination of this standard.

▶ Appendix C, The Standard MIDI File Format looks at the construction of a MIDI file, its parameters, and the values within those parameters. This is where you find out how to repair a corrupted MIDI file!

▶ Appendix D, Understanding Timing Concepts sheds light on the different ways MIDI deals with time as defined by musicians and also as defined by the applications that use it, such as sequencers.

▶ Appendix E, The MIDI Troubleshooting Checklist offers a series of questions you should ask yourself when you are confronted with MIDI problems, with or without a computer involved.

▶ Appendix F, MIDI Arrangements: Tips and Tricks offers you ideas for making better use of MIDI in your musical creations and optimizing the sonic output of a MIDI file using a basic General MIDI sound module.

▶ Appendix G, MIDI Resources On The Web gives you a list of web sites, which are complimentary to the book's content since you will also find web site addresses throughout the book whenever a reference is made to an existing site.

So there you have it. I hope you will enjoy this book as much as I think you will.

1

The Basics

MIDI, pronounced "MID-ee," is an acronym for Musical Instrument Digital Interface. It is a communication standard that allows musical instruments and computers to talk to each other using a common language. At this point, you might be thinking, "Well, I knew that." If so, great; if not, you have just taken your first step toward understanding what MIDI is all about. Let us now look at how it all started and what the basic principles are behind MIDI.

Here's a summary of what you will learn in this chapter:

▶ Why MIDI was introduced and how it all started.

▶ The different components that make up the MIDI communication protocol.

▶ How MIDI is transmitted.

▶ What type of connectors, cables, and jacks are used to transport the MIDI data.

▶ What the differences are between MIDI In, Out, and Thru (same as Through).

▶ How you can hook devices together using MIDI.

▶ How MIDI can be saved in a standard file format.

▶ What a multi-timbral instrument is.

▶ What MIDI channels are and how they work.

▶ What MIDI busses, MIDI ports, and MIDI patch bays are.

MIDI is a standard, a protocol, a language, and a list of specifications. It identifies not only how information is transmitted but also what transmits this information. Just like AC/DC current identifies the type of electrical current, it also defines how the cables are connected and what type of cables should be used to transmit this current. Another example of this could be a USB connection. It is both a protocol that defines how devices communicate and the type of connectors linking these devices. So MIDI has as many software implementations as it has hardware ones.

A Bit of History

Where to begin? I could start at the very beginning of music, when humans used sticks to create rhythms, and work my way up from there. But, I guess knowing how we got to where we are musically is not the main reason you bought this book. You want to become the MIDI expert, or at least be able to get things working in your musical setup. So with this in mind, we'll start by looking at MIDI from its beginning and find out why and how it evolved from there. Does that seem like a long trip? Well, indulge me a little here, and you might be able to impress your friends with the knowledge you get from these few history pages the next time you're at a party with other musician friends.

Let's skip ahead to the time when synthesizers were introduced—those big monophonic machines that used wires to connect different modules together in order to produce sounds. Eventually, they became polyphonic instruments and later evolved into programmable synthesizers. But yes, there was a time when synthesizers could only play one sound at a time. Where are we? Well, somewhere in the late 1970s. At that time, the main synthesizer manufacturers were ARP, Fairlight, Moog, Oberheim, Roland, Sequential Circuits, Synclavier, and Yamaha. In 1979, the Prophet 5 (see Figure 1.1), built by Sequential Circuits and offering polyphony and programmability, was one of the hottest items you could buy if you had $5,000 to spare.

Figure 1.1
Sequential Circuits,
Prophet 5 synthesizer

At this point in time, just before the Prophet arrived, if you wanted to play a melodic line with the sound coming from two synthesizers made by different manufacturers, you'd have to play them simultaneously with your two hands. This was a nice way to get a rich synth texture, but not very player friendly, since typically both hands would be occupied with a single musical element.

One solution was to only buy synthesizers from a single manufacturer and lock them together using a proprietary protocol or a sequencing machine developed by that same company. Since many manufacturers developed their own analog hardware sequencers, they were all proprietary. These sequencers were nice in the sense that you could record a line and then trigger it in some way, either through a keypad or pedal, but they were still not what musicians wanted. Not to mention the fact that these were step-record sequencers, which means you were limited to entering a series of notes or musical phrases using a very basic step-quantizing method. You had to choose a duration value for a note, play a note to record it, then select either silence or another note to advance, then add another note, and so on. Today, drum machine sequencers still use a similar method of sequencing, but more often than not, it has a limited use, since its editing and real-time functions are not very flexible.

In 1982, during a trade show called NAMM (National Association of Music Merchants), two guys met—one from Roland Corp. (Japan) and one from Sequential Circuits (USA). They started looking at a way to make a communication system that would allow synthesizers to talk to one another. Obviously, these were big companies and each had its own agenda. One wanted a high-end system; the other was thinking low-cost, mass-market production. But one fact remained:

They both agreed to work on this protocol, which at that time was called UMI: Universal Musical Instrument.

Other companies, such as Oberheim and Yamaha, got involved, and after many revisions, in 1983, the MIDI standard was adopted. Not long after that, Sequential Circuits and Roland came out with their first MIDI compatible instrument.

Simultaneously, the personal computer (PC) was emerging as a potential tool for musicians because of its programmability. Roland seized that opportunity and began work on a musical interface device for the IBM PC. Roland saw the PC as being a digital alternative to its analog sequencers, and since this hardware device would allow musical instruments to communicate with IBM PC computers, it was the perfect interface tool to penetrate new markets, since other companies could develop tools that could be used with the interface. Roland figured that if it could take advantage of the fact the PC had no built-in sound chip, it could develop an interface for the PC that would be compatible with the company's entire line of new keyboards. It would then have the upper hand, and musicians would buy their keyboards in droves. Roland decided to build an ISA hardware card that plugged into one of the slots of an AT style IBM PC, to which you could attach a box containing additional circuitry that would serve as the "musical interface" (see Figure 1.2) for the PC. Thus was born the MPU-401 (Musical Processing Unit–Model 401) card that would allow computer users to interface with other MIDI-enabled devices. To this day, the MIDI interfaces built into some sound cards still offer hardware compatibility to the original MPU-401, since it became such a widely used MIDI interface for IBM PC compatible computers.

Figure 1.2
The MPU-401 musical interface box from Roland

Still in 1983, Yamaha released its DX7 synthesizer (see Figure 1.3), which was MIDI compatible. The DX7 was a milestone in synthesizer design because it was the first synth whose sound generation was completely digital. It was extremely successful and became very popular. The fact that MIDI was integrated into the DX7 probably helped the new protocol establish itself as a professional standard.

Figure 1.3
The Yamaha DX7
synthesizer

Roland made the specifications for the MPU-401 card available to other parties, and soon other computer software was being written that supported this standard. By 1985, the Commodore 64, Apple II, and IBM PC could all be adapted for MIDI. One computer, the Atari 512, even had a MIDI interface built in. In 1986, Apple came out with the very popular Macintosh Plus, which quickly became a favorite with musicians because of its GUI. As these computers were now equipped with MIDI capability, many software companies such as Steinberg Research GmbH (now known as Steinberg Media Technologies AG), Twelve Tone Systems (now known as Cakewalk), C-Lab (Emagic), Hybrid Arts, and others, were already producing software sequencers. This was a good thing for musicians and went way beyond Roland's expectation. In fact, software sequencers were much more popular than Roland's hardware sequencers due to their flexibility and wide screen interface.

By this time, Roland had other things to do besides making sure the MIDI specification updates got disseminated to everyone else that supported the format, so all the manufacturers that supported it decided to create an independent organization to provide this service. Thus, the MIDI Manufacturer's Association (MMA) was born. From that point on, manufacturers would rely on their subscription to the MMA to provide them with all the information they needed to implement new specifications in their hardware or software.

At this point in time, no one had thought of a way to save MIDI data to a file for later use or outside of the realtime performance applications, other than proprietary solutions provided by individual software. Up until then, each sequencer used a proprietary file format, which made it impossible to read or write each other's files. It is a company called Opcode, which later provided a software called OMS (Open Music System) for Macintosh users, that offered the MIDI File format specifications to the MMA, opening the road to a common MIDI file format that could be used between software sequencers.

Then, Digidesign came up with the MIDI Time Code (MTC) protocol, which standardized MIDI synchronization between MIDI devices such as hardware and software sequencers, other time code devices using SMPTE (Society of Motion Picture and Television Engineers) through a SMPTE/MIDI converter, and so on. Before this, the only way to synchronize such devices was an often-perilous method involving FSK (Frequency Shift Key) synchronization, which would not necessarily be the same for every device or software. FSK was also strictly a synchronization to TAPE protocol (audio based). It was not meant for machine-machine sync.

Since then, the MMA, in conjunction with the AMEI (Association of Music Electronics Industries, created in 1996 for Japan's manufacturers), has created new standards and recommended practices for the use of MIDI. The MMA performs this through the work of a Technical Standards Board, which supervises working groups dedicated to a wide range of subjects. Some other advances in MIDI protocol pertain to tape machine control through MIDI via a MIDI Machine Control (MMC) protocol, theatrical staging and presentation controls with the MIDI Show Control (MSC) used by lighting engineers, and music delivery with the implementation of General MIDI, Standard MIDI Files (SMF), Downloadable Sounds (DLS), and Extensible Music Format (XMF), all of which will be described in greater detail in this book.

CHAPTER 1

What Is MIDI?

The Musical Instrument Digital Interface (MIDI) allows musicians, sound and lighting engineers, computer enthusiasts, or anybody else for that matter to use multimedia computers and electronic musical instruments to create, listen to, and learn about music by offering a common language that is shared between compatible devices and software. MIDI can be divided into three separate entities: the language it uses, also known as its protocol; the hardware interface it uses to transmit and receive its information (such as connectors and wires); and its distribution formats, such as Standard MIDI Files (SMF). So let's take a closer look at these three aspects of MIDI to better understand how they work together and why MIDI works the way it does, offering you interconnectivity, flexibility, and (in terms of file size) portability.

The Protocol

Fundamentally, MIDI is a music description language in binary form, in which each binary word describes an event of a musical performance. As you saw earlier in this chapter, in the beginning, MIDI was intended for keyboard instruments, so many of its events are keyboard oriented, where the action of pressing a note is like activating an On switch and the release of that note is like turning a switch Off.

Note On, Note Off

When you think about it, each musical instrument makes a sound, which is under the control of a musician. The musician controls when the instrument will start to make sounds—a cellist will pull his or her bow, a bassist will pluck a string, a trumpeter will blow air, and a keyboardist will press a note. Consider this action as the Note On event. The MIDI message itself does not contain the actual sound the instrument makes, but rather the action of playing the note, which note was played, how hard or softly it was played, which program number can be used to play this note back, and, as you will discover later, a moment when a note is played. When a musician stops pulling on the bow, plucking the string, blowing in the trumpet or lifts the finger from the key, the sound stops. With MIDI, when such an action is produced, a Note Off message is sent for that note and the sound stops as well. Figure 1.4 displays the Note On and Off action and its musical equivalent along the bars and beats timeline.

Figure 1.4
MIDI Note On and Note
Off messages

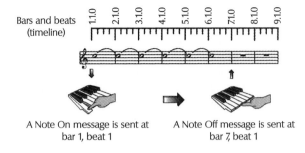

A Note On message is sent at
bar 1, beat 1

A Note Off message is sent at
bar 7, beat 1

In order to identify which note is flicked on or off on the keyboard (or any other device, for that matter), a number is assigned to each note. What about interpretive values, like how hard you strike that note and how hard you press on that note once it's down? MIDI handles all that as well. It sends all this information as binary encoded messages, along with mixing and panning of sounds, controlling parameters that tell various electronic musical instruments which sound to play and even when to make changes in the instrument's setup.

This is the starting point; we will look at how all this information is encoded a little bit later and what you can find in an actual MIDI message.

How MIDI Is Transmitted

One thing you need to remember is that MIDI is sent using a serial transmission protocol rather than a parallel protocol. A parallel transmission, as the name would imply, sends every piece of information in parallel, or simultaneously. The amount of data it can send simultaneously depends on the physical capability of the wire and on the speed at which the devices can send their information. In Figure 1.5, you can send up to four pieces of information simultaneously. By comparison, a CD-compatible digital audio sound needs to send sixteen pieces of information simultaneously (which is why we say it is a 16-bit sound) to reproduce that sound. A serial transmission, on the other hand, sends pieces of information one after the other over its wire. As with the parallel transmission protocol, the amount of information it can transmit depends on the wire and on the speed at which the devices can send information. But since there is only one stream of data in a serial transmission, it can only be as fast as that single stream, whereas a parallel transmission can be as fast as the total number of streams it can send (in Figure 1.5, this is a 4-stream or 4-bit transmission).

Figure 1.5
Parallel versus serial
transmission

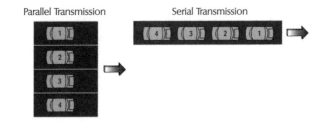

You might ask why MIDI uses a serial transmission rather than a parallel transmission. To answer that question, we have to look back at the time when the protocol was developed. Parallel transmission had some disadvantages that outweighed its advantages and was much more expensive to mass market, since the wires, connectors, and jacks were much more intricate. Serial transmission, on the other hand, was easy to mass-produce, so it was more affordable for the consumer market. It was also fast enough for what manufacturers and potential users had in mind at that point, not to mention more reliable. Things have changed since then, and, in terms of technology, this means faster and better: However, to keep MIDI compatible with all previous devices, the way it is transmitted has not changed since it was introduced.

MIDI sends information at a rate of 31,250 bps (or bits per second). This speed is called baud rate. Since MIDI is transferred using a serial transmission protocol, it sends the information one bit at a time. Every byte in a MIDI message uses 10 bits of data (8 bits for the information and 2 bits for error correction). This means that MIDI sends about 3,906 bytes of data every second (31,250 bps divided by 8 bits to convert into bytes). If you compare that with the 176,400 bytes (or 172.3 kilobytes) transfer rate required for digital audio transmission (playback and recording) in CD audio format, MIDI might seem a bit slow. But since MIDI does not need to transfer as much information as digital audio does, it works well under most circumstances in today's musical environment. In fact, at that speed, you could play up to 500 MIDI notes per second. And even though the information flows in series, rather than in parallel, when playing a complex chord (multiple notes played simultaneously), this will be heard as a chord and not as separate notes because of the relatively high speed at which MIDI information travels through its cables.

The Hardware and Connectors

MIDI information flows through cables, the connectors at each end of the cable, and the jacks into which the connectors go. Physical cables between devices can be as long as fifteen meters (fifty feet). Remember, this is a serial cable; everything is transmitted over one main wire, so the longer the cable is, the longer it takes for the information to get from point A to point B. Another aspect to consider with lengthy cables is that the information loses energy along the way, which causes information degradation, as does any information moving through cables over long distances. This is why cable companies have to put signal amplifiers along the way between the cable company central offices and your house. This loss of energy in MIDI translates into a loss of data, making some MIDI messages unreadable.

MIDI Connector

The MIDI connector itself is a 5-pin DIN jack (see Figure 1.6). You can find the same type of male connector at both ends of a wire, unless you want to extend an existing cable with a special female/male MIDI cable.

Figure 1.6
The MIDI 5-pin DIN jack

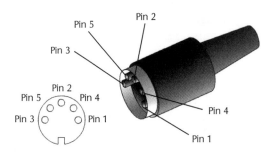

The five pins in the MIDI connector are not all active. As mentioned earlier, MIDI sends information using a serial transmission protocol, so, in reality, only one of the five pins is sending the actual MIDI information. Table 1.1 describes each pin in the MIDI connector and its purpose.

Table 1.1
MIDI Pin description

Pin Number as shown in Figure 1.6	Description
1	Not used; in most MIDI cables, this pin is not even connected to a wire.
2	This is used as electrical shielding (ground). This shielding protects the MIDI cable from transmitting undesirable electrical or radio interference. If only audio cables were all as well shielded as MIDI cables!
3	Like Pin 1, Pin 3 is not used, and in most MIDI cables it is not connected to a wire.
4	This is the actual MIDI data receiver. Information on this cable flows in one direction.
5	This is the actual MIDI data transmitter. As with Pin 4, the information on this cable flows in one direction.

MIDI Jacks

The jacks on instruments, patch bays, or MIDI interfaces are the female version of these connectors. Keyboards usually have three jacks: one labeled In, another labeled Out, and a third labeled Thru (see Figure 1.7) which in the MIDI world means Through. Note that the MIDI Thru connector is usually not found on computer interfaces or MIDI patch bays. The reason for this is explained below.

MIDI information flows in one direction, like an audio cable; it doesn't really matter which side of the wire you plug into your guitar and which side you plug into your amplifier, as the flow of electricity will go from your guitar to the amplifier. MIDI cables are the same. This is because the audio jack on your guitar is an output and the audio jack on your amplifier is an input. Plug your guitar into the headphone output of your amplifier, and all of a sudden, nothing happens. MIDI works the same way.

Figure 1.7
The MIDI connectors on a keyboard or musical instrument—this illustration shows the 3-connector configuration

MIDI Out

The MIDI Out serves as a MIDI output. What comes out of this connector are the MIDI messages (we'll go into what these messages are in a bit) that the device or software generates. It is important to understand that what comes out here is only what comes from the sending or master device. This could be a keyboard, sound module, sequencer, or any other software or hardware transmitting MIDI. Therefore, if you have more than one device in your setup and want to chain them together, you need to use the MIDI Thru (either the physical Thru on your device or a Thru setting inside your software) to echo the information that comes from the MIDI In. The MIDI Out does not send audio information, simply MIDI messages that are interpreted by the receiving MIDI In of another MIDI device. These MIDI messages are digital codes that represent what and how music or events (such as foot pedals being pressed, faders being moved, or program numbers being changed) are being played on the master instrument.

MIDI Outs should always be hooked up to MIDI Ins, no matter what type of setup you have.

MIDI In

The MIDI In serves as a MIDI input. That's where MIDI data comes in and is sent to the hardware or software's processor. Whatever comes in here is processed and can be sent back through the MIDI Thru if you wish to use the MIDI data in another device. The MIDI data basically tells the sound module (for example) to play a certain note at a certain velocity, on a certain channel, using a certain sound in its memory, thus triggering the synthesizer to produce a sound through its audio outputs. The audio output can then be monitored or recorded. But make no mistake: What you are recording or monitoring are the audio outputs, not the MIDI outputs.

MIDI Ins can receive their information from both MIDI Outs, if the previous module in the chain is the master, or MIDI Thru, if the previous module in the chain is echoing the information sent by another master module in a chain.

MIDI Thru

The MIDI Thru serves as an echo of the MIDI In connector port, which means that whatever comes in the MIDI In, goes out to the MIDI Thru, not the MIDI Out. In other words, it repeats the information coming from the MIDI In of this same device. MIDI Thru will not, however, echo information played from its module. For example, anything you play on synthesizer A will be sent out to synthesizer B through its Out jack, not its Thru jack. Synthesizer B will need to use the MIDI Thru to send the information from synthesizer A to synthesizer C, but if you want to send information to synthesizer C that is triggered on synthesizer B, you will need to use the MIDI Out of this synthesizer.

Figure 1.8
How to use MIDI Ins, Outs, and Thrus in a basic keyboard setup

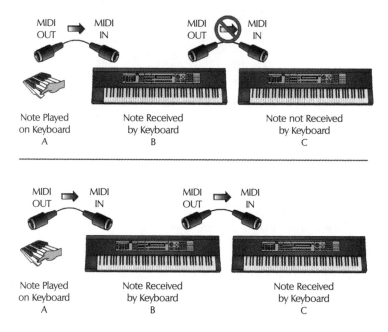

As you can see in Figure 1.8, the note played on keyboard A is sent to keyboard B using the MIDI Out to MIDI In connection, whereas keyboard B in the upper part of the figure will not send the information from keyboard A to keyboard C if it uses the MIDI Out on keyboard B. The proper connection, as shown in the lower portion of this figure, would be to connect the Out of keyboard A to the In of keyboard B, and the Thru of keyboard B to the In of keyboard C. This way, whatever you play on A will be transmitted to both B and C keyboards, using the Thru as a bridge between them.

Daisy Chaining Devices

The method just described, chaining different MIDI devices together, is referred to as "daisy chaining." This will allow you to echo MIDI information from one controller (master) to multiple (slave) devices such as sound modules, for example. You can also use a daisy chain with your computer configuration to send the computer's MIDI output to multiple receiving devices in the absence of a multi-port MIDI interface (an interface with more than one MIDI output on it) or a MIDI patch bay (a MIDI device that works as a MIDI matrix, usually with multiple inputs and outputs) connected to your computer. Although this is an effective way of using more than one MIDI sound module in a simple setup, it has some drawbacks. In theory, you can daisy chain as many devices together as you wish, but, in reality, things are quite different.

Remember that MIDI information travels in series, so the longer it has to travel along different cables and devices, the more potential for delay or data loss. Although the Thru connector does not, in theory, add to the processing time, in practice, messages always go through interface chips that have some minor processing delays. The cumulative effect of daisy chaining does result in measurable and, as the chain is increased, audible delays. A good rule of thumb to observe is to keep your chain as short as possible, not exceeding a three-device chain. If you have many devices to control, a good way to hook them up is by using either a multi-port MIDI interface or a MIDI patch bay, both of which will be discussed later in this chapter.

In a daisy chain, each device responds to its own MIDI channel, so you can use this setup to trigger multiple sounds from different sound modules in a live performance setup. As long as you limit your chain to three devices, the data from the master device (the one you use the MIDI Out on) will send its data to the rest of the devices in that chain. Note that it doesn't really matter if an instrument is active or not in the chain, as its mere presence may introduce loss.

Figure 1.9 displays an example of how MIDI cables are connected between devices in a chain. Note that only the first keyboard (controller or master) uses the MIDI Out to send whatever the keyboard player plays to other devices in this chain. Note that this chain is the same as displayed in the lower portion of Figure 1.8; in this case, however, there is only one keyboard. This type of setup still allows you to trigger sounds from the other devices in the chain, provided that you set all the devices properly in this chain. If you're wondering what needs to be set up, don't worry, we will get into that later.

Figure 1.9
Example of a daisy chain without a computer

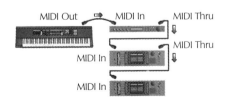

In Figure 1.10, you can see another example of a daisy chain, but this time with a computer at the top of the chain (master). Note that here, the keyboard uses the MIDI Thru to echo the information coming from the computer to other devices in the chain. As mentioned above, computer MIDI interfaces don't normally have MIDI Thrus because they can be programmed within the MIDI application itself to turn the MIDI Out into a MIDI Thru. Using the MIDI Out of the computer will send any MIDI information out to the device that's hooked up to it, just as the previous figure demonstrated. If you look at the keyboard, however, all three MIDI jacks are used. The MIDI In receives the information coming from the computer, the MIDI Thru echoes it out to the rest of the chain, and the MIDI Out sends information that you would play (like an additional musical line) into the computer, allowing you to record it in a sequencer, for example. If you were to use the MIDI Out of the keyboard to feed the rest of the chain, the only thing the other sound modules would receive is the MIDI data coming from this keyboard, not what is coming out of the computer.

Figure 1.10
Example of a daisy
chain with a computer

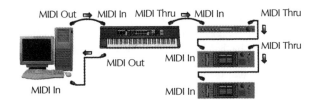

One disadvantage of using daisy chains, besides the practical limit on the number of devices you can hook up to the chain, is that the devices that are past the keyboard in the chain cannot send MIDI data back to the computer to be recorded, such as instrument parameter settings. Since you only have one MIDI In on the computer, it is logical that you use it to receive MIDI notes from the keyboard; therefore, if you wanted to transmit information from other devices, you would need to make manual changes to your wires in order to send pertinent information back to the computer. Using a MIDI patch bay or multi-port MIDI device on your computer would solve this problem quite nicely. But for now, understand that chaining devices together will allow you to control several instruments from one master source, as shown in Figure 1.10. Lastly, any MIDI data sent out by the keyboard above can be echoed through the MIDI Out of the computer back into the keyboard and the other devices in the chain. So in reality, the only true MIDI Out here is the one coming from the keyboard. This might create note doubling, since the keyboard plays the notes as you play them and then plays them again when it receives the echoed data from the computer. We will see later how to prevent this from happening.

The File Formats

So now you know that MIDI data does not contain actual sound, that it travels through cables, that jacks hook up to connectors using a 5-pin DIN, and that you can hook more than one instrument in a chain of devices. But MIDI is also about saving this information for later use. Once you've had time to sleep, you want to be able to listen to your MIDI performance and tweak it a little. That's where files come in handy. There are many different types of files that contain MIDI data. Just look at a file saved in Cubase (a software sequencer) and you will see an extension to this file that is proprietary to this software. The same applies to any other software. This is because software saves everything it needs, and this might include non-MIDI information. But somewhere in that file, MIDI data does find its place.

The basic way to save MIDI to a file is by using a standard called Standard MIDI File format, or SMF for short. An SMF holds all the information needed to reproduce all that MIDI can reproduce; it also has a time stamp on each event so that MIDI sequencers know when to play these events. This time stamp acts like an address on an envelope. A postal worker knows that an envelope goes to a specific address along a specific street. In MIDI, the address is the stamp, the street is the track or song, and the individual addresses or houses are moments in time. The sequencer itself acts as the postal worker, making sure each event is played (or distributed, in the case of the postal worker) at the correct time. Actually, recording MIDI into a sequencer is probably one of the most popular uses of MIDI these days.

MIDI has the advantage of being compact, since you don't record the actual sound when you record MIDI. You record events, just as a database collects information. A database can have links to large content files such as video, audio, or image files, but the actual size of the links, or pointers from within the database, is much smaller than the content they represent. In the same way, MIDI files, though small themselves, can be used to trigger sounds in, for example, a sampler keyboard that might require a lot of space in your sampler's memory. Again, the MIDI files don't contain the actual sample; they act in the same way as the link does in the database. As an example, if you were to record a single four-note chord played over one minute in digital audio using a CD audio format, the end result would be a file using about 10 megabytes, whereas recording the same chord and holding it for a minute in MIDI format would require fewer than 10 kilobytes.

The fact that MIDI does not record audio is perhaps its one disadvantage. When you record the actual audio, you are in full control of the final sound output, whereas with MIDI, the sound output depends on the device or software that is used to reproduce the sound. In the early days of multimedia computers, MIDI was the most popular way of using music in games and applications because it required very little space and was CPU friendly since it didn't require much processing power, just a decent sound card. Today, things have changed a little in this respect, since CD-ROMs and DVDs, combined with increased CPU power and more demanding customers, have made MIDI in games a thing of the past. But the fact remains that MIDI is still a great tool for creating and editing music in both live and studio environments.

MIDI is a binary communication system that is used to transmit music-related information. A MIDI file is a way to save this content to a file on disk for later use. If you were to load a MIDI file into a text editor, you'd find a bunch of nondescript binary codes. You can, however, use a MIDI file disassembler/assembler utility to convert MIDI data into something you could edit. For this, though, you need to understand how everything is encoded. By the end of this book, you'll be able to do so, but for now, remember that MIDI files are usually easier to edit in a sequencer than in disassembler software.

There are three types of Standard MIDI File formats. The following table describes them.

Table 1.2
Standard MIDI File format types explained.

MIDI type	Number of tracks	Contains all MIDI messages	Number of songs, patterns, or musical performance saved in the file
0	1	yes	1
1	1 per channel	yes	1
2	1 per channel	yes	unlimited

Type 0 contains only one song with all the MIDI channels merged into one MIDI track. Type 1 contains only one song as well, but each MIDI channel can be saved on its own track in this song. Finally, Type 2 may contain different songs or patterns, each of them with their own tempo settings, and each pattern or song can save MIDI channels on its own tracks.

Note that when you record your MIDI sequences in a software sequencer, the MIDI files will not be saved in one of those three formats unless you tell the software to do so. Be aware that your software saves more than MIDI information when it saves to file. Saving as an SMF is a good way to make a file cross-platform and cross-software compatible, since SMF format is a standard endorsed by most software developers. SMF can also allow you to save track names (in Type 1 and Type 2 format) to identify the content of each track in your MIDI sequence.

The MIDI Hierarchy

So you have a MIDI In, a MIDI Out, and sometimes a MIDI Thru. What's next? Well, we've seen that MIDI is a series of binary messages sent to translate into musical performances. Chances are, you will want to have more than one musical performance playing at a time. That's where MIDI channels and MIDI ports or busses come into play.

MIDI Channels

A MIDI channel is like a television or radio channel. It is a way for MIDI to isolate information so that a receiving instrument set to a certain channel will filter out all the other information in the transmission, and reproduce or process only the information to which it is tuned. When you are watching channel 3 on your television set, your television set is only processing what is meant for channel 3. This doesn't mean that the rest of the channels aren't there or that the information doesn't enter your television. MIDI channels are the same. When an instrument receives MIDI from its MIDI In (see Figure 1.11), it matches the MIDI data with the appropriate MIDI channel settings in the instrument, playing or reproducing what is set in this instrument as active and ignoring what is set as inactive.

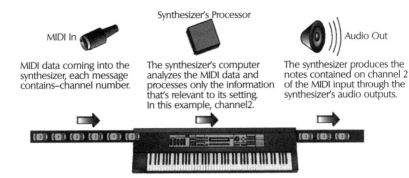

Figure 1.11
How musical
instruments handle
MIDI channels

Synthesizer's Processor

MIDI In

Audio Out

MIDI data coming into the synthesizer, each message contains–channel number.

The synthesizer's computer analyzes the MIDI data and processes only the information that's relevant to its setting. In this example, channel2.

The synthesizer produces the notes contained on channel 2 of the MIDI input through the synthesizer's audio outputs.

CHAPTER 1

MIDI Ports and MIDI Busses

Until now, we have referred to a MIDI connection as a series of cables being hooked up to a physical device's MIDI jacks: MIDI In, Out, and Thru. This set of three jacks can be called a MIDI port or MIDI bus. Most keyboards and sound modules have one MIDI port (a set of MIDI In, Out, and sometimes Thru), and some have more.

Each MIDI port can handle up to sixteen simultaneous MIDI channels, from channel 1 through channel 16. In other words, you can have up to sixteen different instruments playing different MIDI events at the same time. Even if you have only one MIDI device, you still have sixteen MIDI channels per MIDI port.

Some MIDI devices will offer more than one set of MIDI outputs, inputs, and thrus. In most recent devices, this probably means that you will have one MIDI port per MIDI set of connectors (In, Out, and Thru). For example, you might have two MIDI inputs and two MIDI outputs, which would give you two MIDI ports for a total of thirty-two MIDI channels (sixteen per port). However, in older devices, this can also mean that your device allows you to send the same MIDI information over multiple MIDI Outs. To find out if this is the case, you can review your device's documentation and find out if it is a multi-port (or multi-bus) device or simply a multi-output device, which transmits the same sixteen channels over all its outputs. The difference is quite important. On one hand, you have a multi-port device that can transmit on up to sixteen MIDI channels simultaneously on each MIDI port it offers. So if you have four MIDI Out ports, for example, you will have 4×16 channels, or sixty-four simultaneous MIDI channels. On the other hand, you have a single port device with multiple MIDI outputs, all sending the same sixteen channels. Same amount of MIDI outputs, but in the latter case, forty-eight fewer MIDI channels!

Figure 1.12
The different types of
MIDI ports (or busses)

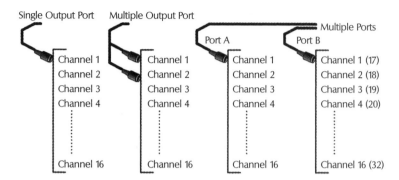

In Figure 1.12, on the left you can see a device with one MIDI Out, offering sixteen MIDI channels through its connection. The second column to the left is a single MIDI port, but one that offers more than one MIDI Out jack. This is useful if you want to send the same information to different instruments but don't want the MIDI chain to be too long. However, it still offers only sixteen MIDI channels. This is the case with some older MIDI patch bays (a matrix offering multiple MIDI inputs and outputs). Finally, the two columns on the right show a device that offers two separate ports, one labeled A and another labeled B, each of which offers sixteen MIDI channels. In this setup, two different instruments can receive different MIDI information on channel 1, provided that you tell the sending (or master) device what information goes where and set up your MIDI connections properly. The numbers in parentheses correspond to the total number of MIDI channels available. Even if you have more than sixteen MIDI channels in your MIDI studio setup, they will always be numbered from 1 to 16. The device sending the MIDI through different ports will identify each set of sixteen channels by giving each port its own name. This name is usually defined by the multi-port MIDI interface itself. That's how, for example, within a sequencer software environment, you can send recorded MIDI events to a device connected to one port rather than another. Imagine that you connect a multi-timbral synthesizer to port A in Figure 1.12 and a sampler to port B in the same figure. You will need to tell your sequencer that the information contained on one track goes to port A, channel 1 and the information contained on another track goes to port B, channel 1. Both devices will receive separate MIDI information, even though they both use the same MIDI channel number.

As you just saw, using multi-timbral instruments allows you to play up to sixteen channels of MIDI data on one single sound module. But what if you have two or three multi-timbral sound modules? Then what? If one sound module uses all sixteen channels, you are left with no other MIDI channels for these additional sound modules. That's when multiple MIDI ports come in handy. Each port offers sixteen channels. Simply multiply the number of available ports by sixteen to get the total number of MIDI channels available in your system.

Using a multiple port or multi-port MIDI device offers another advantage: Since all MIDI data is streamed through a serial transmission protocol, it implies everything is sent in a line, one bit of information after another. The longer this line of data is, the slower the information moves from point A to point B. Take the beginning chord of a symphony, for example, where you might have sixteen instruments playing three notes each. It takes a total of 960 microseconds for MIDI to transmit the note from a struck key to the sound module connected to it. This is so fast that your ear won't hear the delay. Now multiply that short delay of 960 microseconds by sixteen instruments by three notes each (960 × 16 × 3) and you now have 46,080 microseconds between the time the notes are played and the last note is transmitted to the sound module. That's forty-six milliseconds…a very audible delay indeed. Some might argue that if all these instruments play together, you won't feel that delay. I'd say that is completely correct. But nonetheless, if you are going to send a large amount of MIDI data over one single MIDI port, you may end up with what is affectionately called a "MIDI data clog" or "MIDI choking." This is when the data flow breaks down and loss occurs during playback, effectively stopping some instruments from receiving MIDI as they should.

If you were to divide this flow of MIDI information over two or more MIDI ports, making sure each receiving MIDI device is hooked up to its proper MIDI port, you can reduce the possibility of "choking" the MIDI (see Figure 1.13). The information will reach your device quicker, and the device will respond to it in a more natural way since it doesn't have to wait for the information to come in.

Figure 1.13
The difference between sending a high volume of data over a single port and splitting it over multiple ports

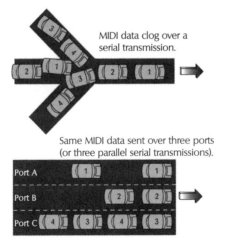

MIDI data clog over a serial transmission.

Same MIDI data sent over three ports (or three parallel serial transmissions).

Port A

Port B

Port C

One Channel, One Sound

No matter how many different sounds you might have in your synthesizer, sampler, or sound module, you can only access one sound at a time per MIDI channel. Now, some synthesizers use names like combis, combos, performances, programs, patches, presets, voices, and what not. When you assign a sound, no matter what the module's manufacturer calls it, and press a key on your controller keyboard, a sound is generated. If you decide that this sound will play on channel 1, then you can only hear that sound on channel 1 until you decide to hear another sound on channel 1. In other words, think of your sixteen channels as a sixteen-member band, where each channel is the equivalent to a separate musician. You've probably seen a big band play at some point in your life, and you might have noticed that some musicians might switch instruments during a show, going from playing the saxophone to playing the flute. The number of musicians in the band doesn't change, but the instruments do. MIDI works the same way. You can have a sound playing on a particular channel and later decide to change that sound during the song. At this point, you might not feel too comfortable with the idea of adding changes along with MIDI, so this is for those of you who have used up all your sixteen MIDI channels and are looking for number seventeen.

Changing a sound while you're playing is just like changing notes. It's as simple as selecting another patch, preset, or program number on your keyboard's control panel. And just as with playing notes, when you change a sound manually on one machine, every machine (device or software) down the chain will respond to this information if they are receiving MIDI from the "master" device. In other words, any change you make in the sound patch number is sent out through MIDI just like any other information. So, any slave device that is set to receive MIDI information from this port's specific channel number will respond by changing as well. Just as you can record MIDI events such as Note On and Note Off, you can also record changes like Patch Changes.

Multi-Timbral Instruments

Most MIDI sound modules, software or hardware, are multi-timbral. This means that one sound module can listen to and play back on sixteen different MIDI channels simultaneously. Each channel the sound module receives can be set to play a different instrument or patch setting. A multi-timbral sound module is like having sixteen different musicians playing sixteen different sounds.

A multi-timbral instrument can isolate MIDI data coming in on any MIDI channel and send it to the proper program to be played through this instrument's audio outputs. Most multi-timbral sound modules can also turn on or turn off a MIDI channel to better control which channel it will process and which ones it will ignore. When a MIDI channel is selected, any MIDI message coming in on that channel will play back the sound you assign to this channel.

Let's say you wish to record and play back a jazz trio made up of a keyboard, bass, and drums. You can assign a channel to each of these instruments, assign a patch to the corresponding MIDI channel, and have the multi-timbral instrument play all three instruments simultaneously (see Figure 1.14).

Figure 1.14
Using multi-timbral
instruments to play back
more than one MIDI
channel at a time

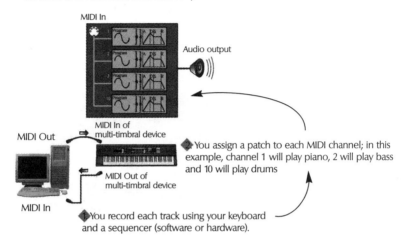

You assign a different MIDI channel to each track in your sequencer. Then you hit play in your sequencer to hear the multi-timbral sound module play the tracks (MIDI chennels) simultaneously.

MIDI In

Audio output

MIDI In of
multi-timbral device

MIDI Out

You assign a patch to each MIDI channel; in this example, channel 1 will play piano, 2 will play bass and 10 will play drums

MIDI Out of
multi-timbral device

MIDI In

You record each track using your keyboard and a sequencer (software or hardware).

In Figure 1.14, the controller keyboard is hooked up to a computer, which acts as a sequencer. Some multi-timbral devices also have built-in sequencers, so the connection to a computer is not a requirement in that case—the built-in sequencer can do the same thing a software sequencer would do in this example, which is to assign each recorded part its own MIDI channel playing a different sound or patch in the sound module.

Each instrument or sound playing in a multi-timbral sound module is often referred to as a "part." In our example, the sound module would play three parts: piano, bass, and drums. A part will respond to all the MIDI messages it receives, including volume, pan, and program settings, for example.

Where each part ends up in terms of audio output depends on the individual sound module's physical audio outputs and its internal software settings. This setting is independent from MIDI, since it refers to how you assign the MIDI channel's audio output on your sound module. In terms of MIDI, there is a good chance that all channels will come from the sound module's MIDI In and will be echoed through its MIDI Thru.

About MIDI Patch Bays

MIDI patch bays in many ways are similar to MIDI ports in that they allow you to effectively connect multiple MIDI devices together to a common port, and in some cases, a MIDI patch bay might also offer multiple ports. However, a MIDI patch bay might only represent one MIDI port in your MIDI studio setup. For example, if you connect all your MIDI devices to a patch bay, there will still only be sixteen MIDI channels available, even though there is more than one set of MIDI Ins and Outs. This is not the case with MIDI ports. By definition, a MIDI port is any device that can handle sixteen MIDI channels. If you can hook up your MIDI patch bay to your computer using a PCI host card or a USB connection, for example, your computer may allow you to address each MIDI set of inputs and outputs as an individual MIDI port. At this point, your MIDI patch bay becomes a multi-port MIDI patch bay.

Figure 1.15
Front and back of a typical singleport MIDI patch bay (with eight Ins and eight Outs)

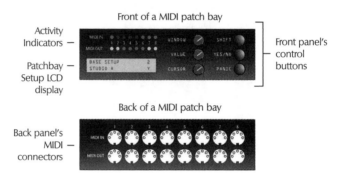

In Figure 1.15, you can see on the back of the patch bay that there are eight inputs and eight outputs. What, no MIDI Thru? Well that's because the patch bay is part hardware, part software. You can plug in up to eight devices—in this example, hooking up the MIDI Out of your devices to the MIDI In of the patch bay and vice versa. Once your connections are made, you can configure the path as you wish, using the front panel controls of the patch bay or even a software interface in some cases.

NOTE
Figure 1.15 does not show any connectors that would allow you to connect your computer to the patch bay other than by using MIDI connectors. However, many patch bays today will allow you to use either parallel or USB connectors to connect to your computer. This would provide you with as many MIDI ports as you have sets of MIDI Ins and Outs on your patch bay. We'll get to that a little bit later.

The patch bay acts as a MIDI matrix, allowing you to decide if you want to send what comes from MIDI In 1 to MIDI Out 4, 5, and 6, for example. On the top part of Figure 1.16, you can see how a signal is taken from MIDI In 3 and sent out only to MIDI Out 2. MIDI In 3 comes from the MIDI Out of that device and MIDI Out 2 is hooked up to the MIDI In of that device. In the lower part of this same figure, the MIDI signal coming from MIDI In 4 is distributed to two devices through MIDI Out 3 and 5. In both examples, the left-hand side displays a matrix point of view and the right-hand side displays how the actual MIDI data flows from the patch bay's MIDI In to MIDI Out. This type of operation in a MIDI patch bay is called MIDI routing. MIDI routing is probably one of the most difficult aspects for beginners to grasp and even for some intermediate users, since making sure your MIDI data flows properly between devices without creating MIDI loops or connections that go nowhere may require some trial and error. But once you understand the principle of MIDI data flow, you will also reduce your troubleshooting time considerably. Until now, the different MIDI setups that were illustrated were quite simple. As we progress, this MIDI routing will get a bit more interesting, especially when a combination of hardware and software settings are involved.

Figure 1.16
Examples showing how you can direct a MIDI stream using a patch bay

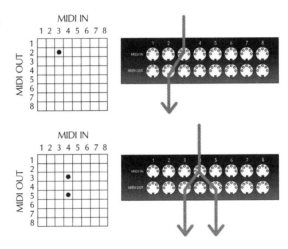

These simple examples show you how sixteen channels of MIDI data can be routed from point A to point B; however, we are still talking about sixteen MIDI channels. If a MIDI patch bay is connected to your computer through a parallel port, serial port, USB, or a type of connection other than a simple MIDI cable, it might support multiple ports as well. For example, the MOTU (Mark Of The Unicorn) MIDI Time Piece AV offers, among other things, a whopping 128 MIDI channels distributed over eight separate MIDI ports (8 ports × 16 channels = 128 MIDI channels).

MIDI patch bays are not only used to route devices; some of them allow you to convert SMPTE time code into MIDI Time Code (this will be discussed later in Chapter 11), save different settings such as MIDI routing configurations, and filter certain types of MIDI messages.

2

Basic MIDI Messages

Before you could learn how to ride a bike, you had to learn how to walk. You started with one step at a time. You had to learn how to control your balance to stand still long enough, and when you felt confident that you could put one foot forward without falling, you did it. This chapter will give you the necessary confidence to take your first step into MIDI messages—your first steps into a world that will help you advance in your creations later. When you understand MIDI messages—when you know why MIDI works, what it can do, and how it does it—you get a glimpse of the possibilities that lie ahead. Here's a summary of what you will learn in this chapter:

► How a MIDI message is structured.

► The difference between types of MIDI messages.

► What these messages contain and what their values represent.

► Which messages are responsible for controlling how your MIDI devices react to MIDI messages.

► How MIDI messages transmit information about a performance, store it, and then reproduce it in time.

► What kind of MIDI messages will allow your device to send and receive information about its parameters.

► How MIDI handles the fact that keyboards don't all have the same number of keys.

MIDI messages are the building blocks of every performance recorded through MIDI. The content of a message is fairly simple. In all MIDI messages, there is a component called a status byte. The status byte is often accompanied by a value that is defined by one or more data bytes. So, a MIDI message can be as short as one byte and can have as many bytes as needed for the values it is transmitting. In most cases, though, MIDI messages will have one or two value bytes attached to it, with the exception of System Exclusive messages.

Status and Data Messages

As seen in the previous chapter, MIDI uses an 8-bit word (1 byte) to transmit its information across a serial transmission. A bit is a switch; it can be on or off, a 1 or a 0. It takes eight switches (bits) to form one byte. For example, your computer needs eight bits to represent the letter "A" in ASCII (American Standard Code for Information Interchange) text. In other words, you read "A," but your computer reads "0100 0001" and understands that if this is supposed to represent a text character, it should display the capital letter "A." An 8-bit word (a word in this case represents the total number of bits needed to represent a character) implies that each message can hold a value from 0 to 255, for a total of 256 different combinations (2 to the power of 8, or 28). These messages are divided into two categories: Status messages and Data messages (see Figure 2.1). In Chapter 1, you learned about MIDI channels and note on/off data. Both pieces of data are part of the Status message.

Figure 2.1
The difference between Status and Data messages

The Status message portion serves to identify the kind of information being sent over MIDI. It tells the receiving device which MIDI channel the event belongs to and what the event is. An event can be a "note on," for example, or a pitch wheel bend, a patch change, or an aftertouch control (this occurs when you bear down on a note after it has been pressed initially).

The Data message portion tells the receiving device what values are associated with the event found in the Status message portion. For example, if you strike a middle C with medium force, the Status message would hold a "note on" event and the Data message would be a note value number of 60 and a velocity level of about 64 (velocity being the strength with which you hit a key).

Status messages use numbers ranging from 128 to 255 (1000 0000 to 1111 1111 in binary numbers) and Data messages use numbers ranging from 0 to 127 (0000 0000 to 0111 1111 in binary numbers). As you might have noticed, in the binary representation of these numbers, the status byte's first digit on the left (the most significant value, also known as Most Significant Bit or MSB) is a one, and in the data byte, this value is zero. This is how the MIDI message recognizes if a byte is a status or data byte message.

NOTE

The concept of Most Significant Bit (MSB) and Least Significant Bit (LSB) is important to understand when trying to grasp MIDI messages.

In any numbering system, the value found on the left always represents a greater number of variables than the values found to their right. For example, in the number 56, 5 represents a multiple of 10, or 5 times 10, and 6 adds only 6 values to this number, changing its value by 6. So 56 is (5×10)+6. If you change the 6 to 7, you only add one to the value of 56, whereas if you add one to the 5, you add ten to the value of 56. Imagine now if you go to a restaurant and the waiter charges you $56 instead of $57. You'd be happy about it, but you'd be even happier if he charged you $47 instead of $57!

In a binary system, when the first bit on the left changes, the change is also more important than when the first bit to the right changes. Therefore, the first bit or byte (when there is more than one byte) to the left is called Most Significant Bit (or Most Significant Byte when a binary word has more than one byte). The bits (or bytes) to the right are called Least Significant Bit (or Least Significant Byte when a binary word has more than one byte).

MIDI uses 8-bit words to transmit its information (2 extra bits that are never displayed as part of the MIDI message but are used for error correction). As stated above, 8 bits can communicate up to 256 different values (2 to the power of $8 = 2 \times 2 \times 2 \times 2 \times 2 \times 2 \times 2 \times 2 = 256$), or 0 to 255. Since MIDI separates its messages into status and data byte messages, it uses the 8th bit (the highest value or Most Significant Bit) to be the toggle bit telling the receiving device that what follows in the word (the remaining 7 bits of information) is status or data information. Thus, when a binary word starts with 1, it is interpreted as a status byte message, and when it starts with a 0, it is interpreted as a data byte message. This use of the 8th bit then limits the range of possible values within MIDI to a 7-bit word, or 128 different values, ranging from 0 to 127. This is why you will notice that values in MIDI, such as MIDI note numbers, for example, are often numbered from 0 to 127.

Here's an example of how this works. Let's say the MIDI device receives the three following values: 200, 127, and 120. It will know that 200 is a status byte because it is between 128 and 255, and that 127 and 120 are the two accompanying data bytes to this status byte because they are between 0 and 127. Here's another example: Let's say the MIDI device receives the three following values: 190, 245, and 98. It will interpret the first number (190) as a status byte, and since the second one is also between 128 and 255, it too will be considered a status byte. However, the last value (98) will be interpreted as the data byte for the number 245's status byte.

MIDI messages are often represented in one of three formats: decimal values, such as 127; binary values, such as 01111111; and hexadecimal, such as 7F. To better understand how to convert binary numbers into decimal or hexadecimal numbers, please refer to "Appendix A: Understanding Binary, Decimal, And Hexadecimal" at the end of this book.

An entire MIDI message can contain up to 3 bytes of information depending on the MIDI function. In Figure 2.2, you can see a binary message with 3 bytes of information. The first byte begins with a 1. This tells the receiving MIDI device that it is a Status message and that the device should expect to receive Data messages subsequently. Note that both the second and third bytes start with 0. In other words, every time a byte starts with a 1, it is considered the locomotive (Status) pulling its cars (Data). The next three bits identify the MIDI function. For a complete list of these functions, refer to Appendix B, in the section called "Expanded Status Bytes List." The remaining 4 bits in the first byte serve to identify the MIDI channel. Since you can define 16 values when you have 4 bits, you will understand that each value corresponds to a MIDI channel and is displayed in table 2.1 below.

In this example, the MIDI function is called Polyphonic Aftertouch (this will be described later in this chapter). This function is applied to a pressed key number, which is identified in the second byte. The amount or level of this function for this specific note number is then determined by the third byte. In this example, the Polyphonic Aftertouch was played at a level of 95.

Figure 2.2
Components of a sample
MIDI message

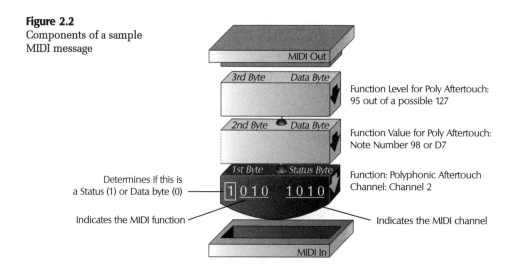

Table 2.1
How MIDI channels are represented in the last 4 bits of the first status byte.

Bits	MIDI Channel	Bits	MIDI Channel	Bits	MIDI Channel	Bits	MIDI Channel
0000	1	0100	5	1000	9	1100	13
0001	2	0101	6	1001	10	1101	14
0010	3	0110	7	1010	11	1110	15
0011	4	0111	8	1011	12	1111	16

MIDI channels work similarly to TV channels: Your musical instrument can receive all the channels but can make only one channel active at a time (in a nonmulti-timbral environment). Just as your TV set receives all the channels through its antenna but can tune into only one channel at a time, determining which channel the message belongs to is an important part of the status byte of a MIDI message. Once the instrument has determined whether or not the message belongs to the channel it is set at, it can process or filter the information accordingly.

If your instrument is multi-timbral, it will retain only the MIDI messages that apply to its active channels. Let's say you have an instrument set to play channels 1 through 5; this instrument will ignore all messages not containing the appropriate bits in the status byte.

All aspects of your musical performance can be represented in a MIDI message. The following sections will identify these aspects and explain how they work and what values are attached to them. To better understand these aspects of MIDI messages, they have been divided into five categories:

▶ Channel Voice Messages are the basic MIDI events representing a musical performance. The most common Channel Voice Messages are Note On and Note Off.

▶ Channel Mode Messages tell devices to send or receive information in a certain way, which is defined by the mode being sent. An example of this would be to turn all sounds off, or all notes off.

▶ System Common Messages are, as the name would suggest, common to all instruments, devices, or software in your MIDI setup. Sequencers use System Common Messages for MIDI time references (through MIDI Time Code), song position, song selection, and tuning.

▶ System Real Time Messages are synchronization commands used by MIDI to control sequences, such as Start and Stop commands imbedded as a MIDI command, along with the MIDI Timing Clock.

▶ System Exclusive Messages are used to send or receive instrument settings such as patch or performance memories. You can also use System Exclusive (SysEx) messages to transfer sample waveforms via MIDI along with other non-music related functions.

You will find a complete list of these messages and their settings in Appendix B.

Channel Voice Messages

This is the backbone of MIDI. Most of what MIDI sends in a live performance are Channel Voice messages. The following section will describe each of those messages so you can understand what is transmitted through MIDI and where to look when editing a MIDI sequence recorded in a MIDI sequencer (sequencers will be discussed in Chapter 8).

CHAPTER 2

Note On

Every time you press on a note, a Note On message is sent. This Note On message contains two pieces of information: the key or note number and the velocity at which the note was pressed. Both of these values can be any value between 0 and 127. In the case of note numbers, you can refer to the section called Note Names And Numbers later in this chapter. As for the velocity, higher values represent harder strokes. This value represents the dynamic value of the note, which is usually musically represented by names such as pianissimo, piano, mezzo piano, mezzo forte, forte, and fortissimo. Note that a velocity of 0 would mean that you don't strike the note, so velocity levels are between 1 and 127 rather than 0 and 127. A zero velocity value represents a Note Off message, which is described in the next section. How hard you have to press a note to get the appropriate dynamic depends on the actual sound itself and the mechanics of your instrument. The following table will give you an idea of the musical equivalent for a range of velocity values when using a standard linear velocity sensitive instrument, which means that the loudness or intensity of the instrument increases at the same rate as the value of the velocity. Note that this loudness or intensity does not affect the actual volume, or level setting for this MIDI instrument, but rather how the note will be played back depending on how it was hit.

Table 2.2
Velocity range explained through corresponding musical intensity indications.

Musical value	Musical Notation	MIDI velocity range
Extremely soft	ppp	1 to 15
Pianissimo (very soft)	pp	16 to 31
Piano (Soft)	p	32 to 47
Mezzo Piano (Softly or moderately soft)	mp	48 to 63
Mezzo Forte (moderate, not too soft, not too hard)	mf	64 to 79
Forte (loud or hard)	f	80 to 95
Fortissimo (very loud or hard)	ff	96 to 111
Extremely loud or Aggressive	fff	112 to 127

Figure 2.3
An example of a Note
On message

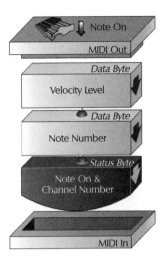

Table 2.3
Different ways to look at the same values found in Figure 2.3: as sequencer MIDI values, binary values, and hexadecimal values.

	Note On & Channel number	Note number	Velocity level
MIDI values	Note On, Ch. 3	60	100
Binary equivalent	1001 0010	0011 1100	0110 0100
Hex equivalent	92	3C	64

In Figure 2.3, you can see an example of the Note On message with the content of its status and data bytes in MIDI values, binary, and hex equivalents.

Most newer keyboards or controllers support velocity levels, but if you have an older model, it might transmit only one velocity level, which is usually set at 64. In this case, it wouldn't matter how hard or soft you hit the key, since it would always be sending a velocity level of 64.

How velocity affects the sound is also determined by the sound itself. Sometimes, hitting the keys with high velocity will make the sound brighter; other times, it will be louder or actually trigger a different sample altogether if your sound module is programmed as such. In other words, the velocity always affects how the sound will react, but not necessarily in the same way for each sound. This is different for the volume level, which always makes a sound louder as the MIDI volume level gets higher.

Note Off

This message is sent when you release a note after striking it. Most devices will use a Note On message with a velocity value of 0 to indicate that the note is off. If your keyboard supports Release Velocity sensing, which detects how fast you release the key once it has been hit, then a Note Off message is sent with its corresponding Release Velocity value. In this case, the Release Velocity value will affect the release envelope of your sound module. This is not implemented on every sound module, so if it is not, the Release Velocity value will act just as a Note On with a velocity at 0, releasing the note and ignoring the speed at which it is released.

Figure 2.4
An example of a Note
Off message

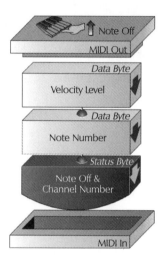

Table 2.4
Different ways to look at the same values found in Figure 2.4 when the keyboard does not support Release Velocity levels: as sequencer MIDI values, binary values, and hexadecimal values.

	Note On & Channel number	**Note number**	**Velocity level**
MIDI values	Note Off, Ch. 3	60	0
Binary equivalent	1000 0010	0011 1100	0000 0000
Hex equivalent	82	3C	00

Table 2.5
Different ways to look at the same values found in Figure 2.4 when the keyboard supports Release Velocity
levels: as sequencer MIDI values, binary values, and hexadecimal values.

	Note On & Channel number	**Note number**	**Velocity level**
MIDI values	Note Off, Ch. 3	60	100
Binary equivalent	1000 0010	0011 1100	0110 0100
Hex equivalent	82	3C	64

In Figure 2.4, you can see the Note Off message as both velocity level set at 0 or as a Release
Velocity level set at 100. Which one will be sent depends on the keyboard controller you use:
If it supports Release Velocity, it will send; if not, it will simply send a velocity level of 0
instead. If your keyboard supports the Release Velocity level parameter, this will affect how
quickly the note will fade once the key is released. On the other hand, if the sound module
receiving this data doesn't support this parameter, it will simply interpret it as a normal
Note Off data (Note On with velocity set at 0).

Channel Pressure or Channel Aftertouch

This function comes into action once you've pressed a key and then decide to press harder
while you're holding the note down. This will, in most cases, add some kind of vibrato-like
modulation to the sound being played. This is similar to a cello player moving his/her finger on
a string while holding it, creating a vibrato on the sustained note. Most controllers (keyboards)
support this type of function; if it doesn't, no channel aftertouch information will be sent. The
harder you press on a key (after the initial key strike), the higher the aftertouch (or channel
pressure) value will be. If you play more than one note, the hardest pressed key will determine
the channel pressure value sent over MIDI.

Figure 2.5
Example of channel
pressure applied to a
2-note harmony

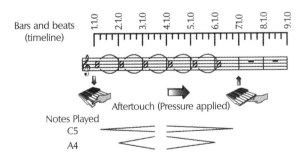

In Figure 2.5, a 2-note harmony is played, but one is being pressed harder than the other. The
resulting channel pressure will always be the higher value. The following table illustrates the
MIDI messages that would be sent.

Table 2.6
The result of Figure 2.5's channel pressure messages sent by a keyboard supporting this function.

Status Byte	Data Byte 1	Data Byte 2	Bar & Beat
Note On, Chan 3	C5	100	1.1.0
Note On, Chan 3	A4	100	1.1.0
Channel Aftertouch, Chan 3	64	none	2.1.0
Channel Aftertouch, Chan 3	127	none	3.3.0
Channel Aftertouch, Chan 3	64	none	4.3.0
Channel Aftertouch, Chan 3	0	none	6.1.0
Note On, Chan 3	C5	0 (Note Off)	7.1.0
Note On, Chan 3	A4	0 (Note Off)	7.1.0

The status byte for a channel pressure or aftertouch message tells the receiving device the name of the function and the channel for this message. The first data byte represents the amount or value for this aftertouch. The second data byte is not used in the channel pressure message. The last column represents the point in time when this event occurs, but it does not represent the actual MIDI message itself, since it is written in bar and beat format. This is just to give you an idea of where to look in the figure.

Polyphonic Key Pressure or Polyphonic Aftertouch

This function is like channel aftertouch but determines the amount of pressure you exercise on a series of keys once they are pressed. The word polyphonic means that each note, or key, can have its own pressure value. This is different from the channel aftertouch or channel key pressure, since each note can have its own pressure level value. So let's say you play a three-note C major chord, and then apply pressure (press harder) on the keys; a series of MIDI messages will be sent out to account for this variation in key pressure, which is also called aftertouch.

Note that not all keyboard controllers or MIDI input devices support aftertouch. If your device does not support this parameter, it will not send polyphonic key pressure messages as you press harder on the keys.

The following table displays a list of MIDI messages that would be sent as a result of the actions illustrated in Figure 2.5. The status byte describes the actual function: In this case, Note On events and Polyphonic Aftertouch (or Polyphonic Key Pressure) and its channel number. The first data byte is used to identify the note number (in this table, the note name is displayed to better relate with the corresponding figure). The second data byte represents the amount of polyphonic aftertouch for that specific note.

Table 2.7
The result of Figure 2.5's Polyphonic Key Pressure messages sent by a keyboard supporting this function.

Status Byte	Data Byte 1	Data Byte 2	Bar & Beat
Note On, Chan 3	C5	100	1.1.0
Note On, Chan 3	A4	100	1.1.0
Polyphonic Key Pressure, Chan 3	C5	32	2.1.0
Polyphonic Key Pressure, Chan 3	A4	64	2.1.0
Polyphonic Key Pressure, Chan 3	C5	78	3.3.0
Polyphonic Key Pressure, Chan 3	A4	127	3.3.0
Polyphonic Key Pressure, Chan 3	C5	32	4.3.0
Polyphonic Key Pressure, Chan 3	A4	64	4.3.0
Polyphonic Key Pressure, Chan 3	C5	0	6.1.0
Polyphonic Key Pressure, Chan 3	A4	0	6.1.0
Note On, Chan 3	C5	0 (Note Off)	7.1.0
Note On, Chan 3	A4	0 (Note Off)	7.1.0

If you compare tables 2.6 and 2.7, you can see the difference between Channel Aftertouch and Polyphonic Key Aftertouch. One offers one level of aftertouch, which it applies to all notes played simultaneously, and the other offers a more precise aftertouch control, assigning each note its own value.

Program Change

Most sound modules and keyboards today have memories in which presets are stored as programs or spaces where you can store your own programs. You can later recall these sounds by selecting the appropriate program number. Some manufacturers might called them presets; others call them programs, instruments, patches, or whatever. When a specific number can access a sound, you can change that sound using a Program Change message. If you have a MIDI device that doesn't contain sounds, like a MIDI-enabled reverb, for example, you can access preset or program numbers stored in the device's memory just as you would with a sound module.

You can access up to 128 sounds using the Program Change function. When sending a Program Change message, the MIDI device associated with that specific MIDI channel will respond by changing the sound or program for this channel. In other words, if you have a multi-timbral device and wish to change the program for the part playing on channel 5, sending a program change for this channel will only affect this part, not the other parts.

Program Change messages contain only one byte of data following the status byte. This data byte holds the program number and the status byte tells the device that this is a program change for a specific MIDI channel, as displayed in Figure 2.6.

Figure 2.6
Program Change MIDI
message

Note that this is different from sound banks: Program numbers identify a specific sound, while sound banks identify a specific set of sounds. To select a specific set of sounds, such as a sound bank, you would use a Sound Bank Control Change described later in this chapter.

On sound modules it became useful to define an ordered and standard set of programs so as to make the playback of MIDI songs more compatible from machine to machine. This would allow you, for example, to set a program change 01, which plays a piano on your sound module, and then have the same program change set a similar piano sound on another sound module rather than a completely different type of sound. This standard set of numbered and named sounds is called General MIDI. We will talk more on this in later chapters.

Also note that even though MIDI channels use values from 0 to 15, they are always displayed as channels 1 to 16 to musicians. Many MIDI devices display their program numbers starting from 1, even if a program number of 0 in a Program Change message selects the first program in the device. However, this approach was never standardized, and some devices use different methods to select a program. For example, some devices require the user to specify a bank of programs and then select one within the bank. Older sound modules might have 2 LEDs, each one having digits allowing numbers from 0 to 9, for example. In this case, to get to program 55, you would need to set your first bank to 5 and then select the program 5. This is different than the Sound Bank Control Change presented above and described later in this chapter. Here, since it is actually an interface issue, which does not allow for more than 9 digits per LED, you would still use a Program Change message to access your specific program number.

Table 2.8
Examples of program number correspondence.

MIDI Program numbers	Device using 3 LEDs with numbers from 0 to 9	Device using 2 LEDs with numbers from 0 to 8	Device using a digital display starting at program 1
0	000	00	1
1	001	01	2
…	…	…	…
8	008	08	9
9	009	10	10
10	010	11	11
…	…	…	…
17	017	18	18
18	018	20	19
Etc.	Etc.	Etc.	Etc.

Pitch Bend Change

Pitch bending can make keyboards more expressive, somewhat like a wind instrument, as when a saxophone player uses inflections in the attack of a sound to accentuate certain melodic lines by bending into a note. Most keyboards today have some kind of pitch bend controller. Some use a wheel, others a joystick. The goal is to be able to slide from one note to another smoothly by bending its pitch up or down. Because the human ear is very sensitive to pitch changes, the pitch bend message contains two data bytes to determine the bend value. Because of this, pitch bend has a resolution of 16,384 steps, which is usually split in 2: 8,192 steps above and below the original pitch. In other words, you can have the following range: minus 8,192 to plus 8,191, with 0 being the original pitch. How much pitch bending this represents depends on the sound module's program setting. The pitch bend wheel range is programmable, so its data bytes values do not determine a range, but rather a percentage over the programmed range. The General MIDI

CHAPTER 2

specification recommends that a pitch bend should have a range of plus or minus 2 half steps, but, in reality, you can program your sound to pitch bend over a full octave if your instrument allows. The Pitch Wheel Range can also be adjusted via an RPN controller message as described below.

Figure 2.7
How pitch bend
messages work

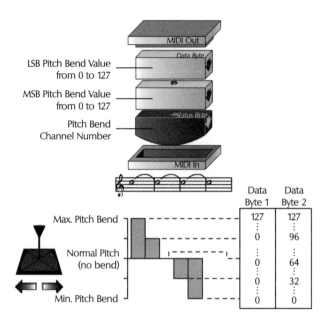

As you can see in Figure 2.7, the center pitch is represented by the MIDI values 0 (data byte 1) and 64 (data byte 2). One step above this would be MIDI values 1 (for data byte 1) and 64 (for data byte 2). One step below the center would be 127 (for data byte 1) and 63 (for data byte 2).

Control Change

Control Changes are a set of a 128 different numbers assigned to different functions. Because there are so many functions to describe, the next chapter is dedicated exclusively to the description of these functions and their corresponding controller numbers. At this point, remember that the first numbers (0 to 119) are reserved for Channel Voice messages and that the control change numbers 120 to 127 are reserved for the next category of MIDI messages: Channel Mode messages.

Channel Mode Messages

MIDI modes affect how the device will respond to incoming MIDI messages and how it will send outgoing messages. The MIDI Specification allows four modes of operation, using two sets of channel mode messages:

▶ Omni On mode—implies that a device can respond to all or any incoming MIDI channel data, regardless of its channel.

▶ Omni Off mode—implies that a device can only respond to its base MIDI channel. The base MIDI channel is the default channel on which the MIDI device is set. This channel can be set directly in the device's preferences. For example, if you set your keyboard to channel 1, it will send and receive information only on this channel in Omni Off mode. Channel 1 in this case will be its base channel. On the other hand, if you have a multi-timbral device, you could send and receive over any MIDI channel. However, in Omni Off mode, the base channel setting will determine which channel will be used to transmit MIDI and which channel it will respond to when receiving MIDI messages. For example, if you set the base channel to 1, any messages which the status byte doesn't identify as being channel 1 would be ignored in this mode.

▶ Poly mode—implies that a device is capable of polyphony and will enable polyphonic playing on any MIDI channel. You have polyphony when you can play more than one note simultaneously (chords) on a given MIDI channel. The number of simultaneous polyphonic voices you can have depends on the device itself, since this is not a MIDI specification, but rather a limitation of the device's design.

▶ Mono mode—implies that a device will not play more than one note at a time on any given channel. However if it is a multi-timbral instrument, it may play two or more notes on two or more separate channels, just not on the same channel.

NOTE
A receiving device will only respond to channel mode messages if they are on the same MIDI channel as their base channel. A device always has a base channel for the purpose of these channel mode messages, even when you are in Omni mode.

These modes can be combined in four ways, which are often referred to as Mode 1, Mode 2, Mode 3, and Mode 4:

▶ Mode 1—Omni On/Poly—In this mode, a device will play MIDI data coming from any MIDI channel and will redirect these channels to the instrument's base channel. It will also play polyphony normally. In other words, voice messages are received from all voice channels and assigned to voices polyphonically. All voices are transmitted on the base channel. This is rarely used because in this mode the receiving device doesn't care which channel the data is from; it will

CHAPTER 2

play back everything. However, if you are playing in a live show and want to layer different instrument sounds coming from different sources, it is a good setting. Otherwise, stay away from this mode.

▶ Mode 2—Omni On/Mono—This mode is similar to the Mode 1, since the receiving device does not discriminate any MIDI channel information. In this case, though, it will only play one note at a time. In other words, voice messages are received from all voice channels, and control only one voice, monophonically. This mode is the rarest one of all since its purpose is quite limited, being that you can't isolate MIDI channels and you can play only one note at a time.

▶ Mode 3—Omni Off/Poly—From the least used (Mode 2) to the most used, this is as common as common gets in today's MIDI world. In this mode, a single channel device (as opposed to a multi-timbral one) will respond to only the MIDI messages set to that device's channel and will ignore all other MIDI messages. In a multi-timbral instrument, the device will respond to all the active channels as separate devices. For example, you could have a sequencer send up to 16 channels of MIDI data to a 16-instrument multi-timbral device, all playing their respective parts. Since it is in Poly mode, each part will play its dedicated polyphony.

▶ Mode 4—Omni Off/Mono—In this case, each active MIDI channel on a receiving device will play only monophonic lines. The base channel determines which will be the active channel on a single timbre instrument, whereas a multi-timbral instrument will treat each MIDI channel as it is internally set up for. In other words, if you have made a MIDI channel active on your device, it will accept and play the MIDI information in monophony. This is not a common mode; however, it can be effective if used with a guitar controller where each string is assigned a MIDI channel and each MIDI channel plays one note at a time.

The channel mode messages are nested in the last eight values of the control change set (control change numbers 120 to 127). So their status byte is identical to a Channel Voice message containing a Control Change function. This subset of control changes is called Channel Mode because they tell the device how to handle data sent or received. It has control over monophonic and polyphonic operations as well as how it handles MIDI channels when receiving a stream of MIDI with multiple channels embedded.

MIDI modes and Local Control messages are described in the following sections. You will find a further discussion on the other Channel Mode messages in Chapter 3. These messages are: All Sound Off, Reset All Controllers, and All Notes Off, which serve to reset parameters to default values (controller 121) or stop Note On messages (controllers 120 and 123).

About Local Control

Keyboard controllers often have sound modules, which contain programmed sounds inside of them. On the other hand, rack-mounted sound modules don't have any keyboard controllers. In fact, you can find many models of synthesizers that offer both keyboard and rackmounted versions of the same model. Keyboards are really two devices in one: a controller device and a sound module device (as shown on the left side of Figure 2.8).

The Local Control message allows you to disconnect the controller part from the sound module part of your keyboard. This message is sent by the control change number 122 (see Chapter 3 for a full description of this controller). When the local control is Off, the MIDI is sent out but the sound module does not produce the sounds triggered by the MIDI input or keyboard part. When the local control is On, the MIDI device produces the sounds at the same time as it is sending the MIDI information to its MIDI output. In both cases, the sound generators or circuitry will receive the MIDI information coming from the MIDI input, regardless of this setting.

Figure 2.8
How local control works

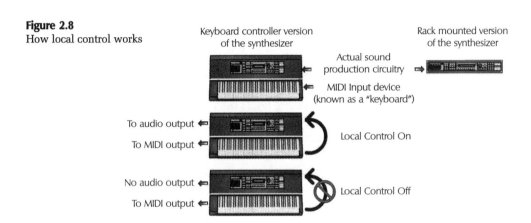

System Common Messages

System Common messages are intended for all channels in a system and enhance the functions of other MIDI commands. They are not related to any specific channel. In most cases, system common messages relate to synchronization features and are used with sequencers since they relate to time positioning, song selection, and tuning features on your MIDI device. Here's a look at these messages.

MIDI Time Code (MTC) Quarter Frame

MIDI Time Code (MTC) will be the subject of a longer discussion in Chapter 11, but suffice to say at this point that the MIDI Time Code message allows music-making devices that contain sequencers to lock up to video making devices that contain SMPTE (Society of Motion Picture and Television Engineers) Time Code. SMPTE is the standard protocol for video synchronization and it works by giving each frame in a filmstrip a specific address. This address looks like a time stamp with hours, minutes, seconds, and frames (sometimes, even sub-frames). It looks something like this: 00:00:00:00, where the first two digit to the left represent hours, then the minutes and so on, just as if you were reading the time of day. In this case, however, each second can be divided into a specific fraction; here, this fraction represent the individual frames.

MTC is basically a MIDI version of this protocol. To use MTC, you will need to have a device that converts the SMPTE into its MTC equivalent, then send this converted signal as MIDI data along a MIDI cable, just like any other MIDI message. Once your sequencer receives this MTC, it can lock to it and play in sync with the video, allowing you to score music, for example, to a video.

The System Common message sends Quarter Frame messages, which handle the basic running of the system. In other words, they tell the sequencer the time-stamp address in hours, minutes, seconds, and frames and which type of time code is being used (if it's PAL, NTSC, drop-frame, non-drop, and so on. This will be explained further in Chapter 5).

Note that MTC is an alternative to another type of synchronization method called MIDI Timing Clock (which is usually referred to as Timing Clock to avoid acronym confusion). Timing Clock is not as precise as MTC, since it does not support any shuttle functions. For example, you can't fast-forward and rewind a video while having a MIDI sequence follow the video as you fast-forward. MTC is meant for video synchronization and refers to a fixed time or absolute reference. Timing Clock is a relative reference: It is relative to the tempo of a sequence, since it subdivides each beat into 24 ticks (ticks are sub-divisions of beats), no matter the tempo of the sequence.

The MTC message contains only one data byte that holds the type of time code and the value for the time address, as shown in Figure 2.9. This message is called Quarter Frame because each message contains a quarter of the information: In the first MIDI message, it gives the hour value, the second represents the minutes, the third represents the seconds, and the fourth gives the frame number. In other words, it takes four MIDI messages (each one containing a status byte and a data byte) to represent a full SMPTE time.

Figure 2.9
The content of a MIDI
Time Code Quarter
Frame message

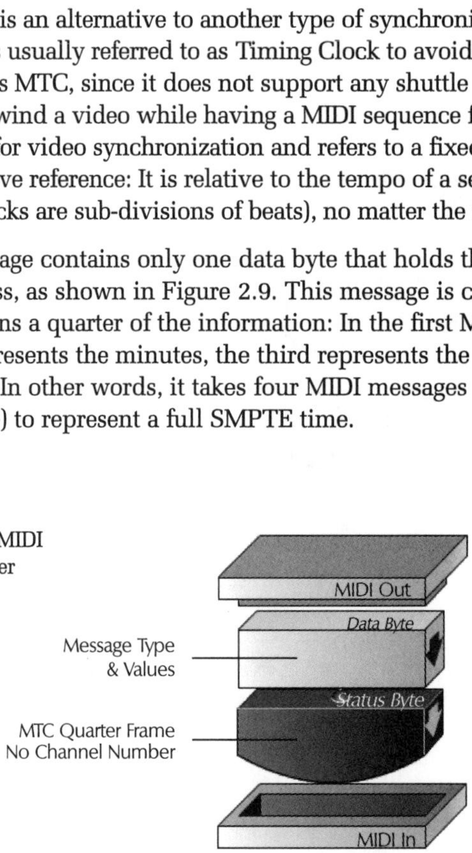

MIDI Out

Data Byte

Message Type
& Values

Status Byte

MTC Quarter Frame
No Channel Number

MIDI In

Song Position Pointer (SPP)

The Song Position Pointer message sets the position of a song in a sequence. Normally, when you work with a sequence, you send a Start command. Every clock-driven instrument will then start playing from the beginning of this sequence to its end, or until you send a Stop command. It then holds its position until you send a Continue command. What the SPP message does is simple: It gives an address to each sixteenth note step in a song, starting with beat 0 at the beginning. SPP messages don't actually tell the sequence to start or stop, but rather tell the devices where to start again once stopped. This sixteenth note step is set every six MIDI Timing Clocks from the start of the sequence. Since there are 24 ticks per beat and the SPP identifies every sixth one, you have an even four SPP addresses per beat, or one SPP address per sixteenth note (24 ticks /6 ticks = 4 times per beat or quarter note = 1 sixteenth note).

To accommodate long songs, two data bytes are used to identify each sixteenth note step. This gives you a total of 14 bits of data to identify each sixteenth note step, or a total of 16,384 sixteenth notes. That's 4,096 beats, or 1,024 bars if you are doing a 4/4 song (four beats of quarter notes per bar). These two data bytes are separated in a Most Significant Byte (MSB) and Least Significant Byte (LSB), as shown in Figure 2.10. As the name suggests, when a value changes in the MSB portion of the message, the increments are greater than in the LSB, even though they all represent sixteenth note steps. Look at the MSB as the integer values and the LSB as the decimal values. You can have as many numbers to the left of a decimal point as you can have to the right, but the ones on the left will always represent greater values than the ones one the right. This principle will be further developed in Chapter 3.

Figure 2.10
The Song Position
Pointer message

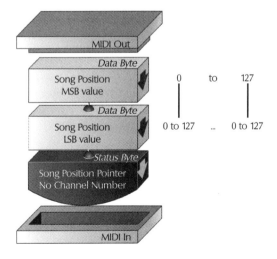

Here's an example of how this works. Let's say you want the sequencer to go to bar 33, second beat in a song that has a 4/4 metric (4 quarter notes or beats per bar). The SPP would point to the 517th sixteenth note step in the sequence ((32 bars×4 beats×4 sixteenth notes) + (1 beats×4 sixteenth notes)) = 516, which is the last sixteenth note of the first beat of the thirty-second bar. The next sixteenth note step would be number 517, and this is our target. This would be represented by the LSB's sixth value (5) and MSB's fifth value (4) ((5 X 1) + (4×128) = 517). This is all done without your knowledge, and, don't worry, you won't have to do the math every time you want to start a sequence.

Once the song position pointer (SPP) message has identified the song's position, the other slaved devices will know where to start once they receive the appropriate command. A device is slaved when a master device sending synchronization information, such as a Song Position Pointer message, controls its transport functions, such as play and stop.

Song Select

Song Select messages allow you to load a song number into a sequencer's memory, and all other connected devices using song memories will load the same song into their memories as well. Imagine, for example, that you have a sequencer in your keyboard and this keyboard is hooked up to a drum machine that holds drum sequences for songs. When you practice your set at home, you can assign the same numbers (or song order) to both the drum machine and keyboard sequencer. When it's time to perform live, all you have to do is send a Song Select message through MIDI and both your keyboard and drum machine load the appropriate song in the set. The Song Select message contains only one data byte, which holds the song number. This also means that you can store up to 128 songs in a set (that's quite a long set; hope you're being paid by the hour, not per night).

Most devices display song numbers starting from 1 instead of from 0. Some devices might even use different labeling systems for songs; for example, Bank A, Number 1 song. However, a Song Select message with song number 0 should always select the first song, just as the first program number on your sound module will always be Program Number 0 in a program change message.

Once the Song Select message is received, it will cue the song at the beginning of the sequence unless a subsequent Song Position Pointer message is sent to this device, telling it to start somewhere else. Songs always default to Song Position 0.

NOTE

For both devices to play properly once their song select has been cued, they should be synchronized using a common MIDI Clock. Otherwise, the sequences might start together but they would quickly drift apart, especially if the tempo setting is different.

Tune Request

This message is mostly used for sound modules that have analog circuitry. Once the device receives this message, it usually initiates a self-tuning operation, which calibrates its oscillators (the actual sound-making portion of the synthesizer) to match up. Older analog synthesizers were known to go out of tune as they warmed up, so during a performance they sometimes would have to be retuned in order to stay in tune with the other instruments, just as you retune a guitar or a bass.

The Tune Request message doesn't contain any data bytes, and its default value is 0. Since digital synthesizers don't go out of tune, this type of message will not be of any use to you if you don't have any analog synthesizers.

End Of Exclusive Message

This message marks the end of a System Exclusive message. It's like the caboose at the end of a train. System Exclusive messages are discussed in the coming paragraphs. However, the end of a System Exclusive (SysEx) message is always identified using this System Common message. End Of Exclusive messages don't have any data bytes and their value defaults to 0.

System Real Time Messages

System Real Time messages control, in real time, all devices in your system, and are channel independent. These messages are used for synchronizing clock-based devices such as sequencers and drum machines, using single status byte messages. If a System Real Time message is not implemented, as in a sound module that doesn't have a built-in sequencer, for example, they are simply ignored.

System Real Time messages are sent at any time at regular intervals, even in between bytes of other messages, to maintain timing precision. Once the system real time passes, the remaining bytes from other messages resume their previous status without any hiccups. In comparison to this, System Common messages such as MIDI Time Code (MTC) are time-based, rather than clock-based. The time is absolute and the clock is relative to the speed of the sequence. Both types of messages serve a similar synchronization purpose; however, realtime messages are music oriented and will serve their purpose when trying to lock two sequences together rather than a sequence and a video, for example. If you take a stick and a rubber band of the same length and draw equally spaced markings on both, you will have lines that will match up. Imagine the stick is a System Common message and the rubber band is a Real Time message. Now, stretch the rubber band. You will notice that the markings on the rubber band no longer match up with the markings on the stick. You will also notice that the spaces separating the marks are still of equal distance in relation to each other. There lies the difference between these two types of synchronizing messages: One is relative to the tempo of a sequence, the other is absolute and will not vary with the tempo of the sequence.

There are six defined System Real Time messages.

CHAPTER 2

Timing Clock

This message is used to synchronize timing across sequencers in a MIDI system. It is sent 24 times per beat (or quarter note), no matter what the tempo of a song (as displayed in Figure 2.11). Look at this as being a ruler with major markings (like inches or centimeters) and minor subdivisions (like fractions of an inch or millimeters). It is simply a way to divide time in an equally spaced format.

When a sequencer is recording MIDI, it starts counting ticks at the beginning of a song, then looks for incoming MIDI events. When other MIDI messages are sent, they are recorded and assigned a tick count so that when it is played back, it will play at the exact same time as it was recorded or later quantized to. This clock can be sent to other devices, and once these devices are set to follow an incoming Timing Clock, they can play back MIDI events in perfect synchronization. Some might debate the accuracy of MIDI timing when compared to digital audio timing, but we'll get back to this later when we will discuss software sequencers that handle both MIDI and audio.

Figure 2.11
A MIDI Clock sends 24 ticks per beat, no matter what the speed or tempo of the sequence might be

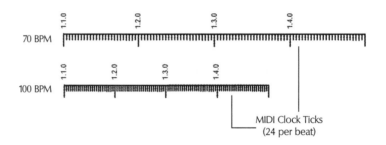

How fast is this timing clock anyway? Well, there are 1,000,000 microseconds in a second. At a speed of 100 BPM (Beat Per Minute), or 100 quarter notes per minute, the sequencer sends 24 ticks per beat for a total of 2,400 ticks in a minute. If there are 1,000,000 microseconds in a second, it means there are 60,000,000 of those in a minute. So 60,000,000/2,400 ticks = 1 tick every 25,000 microseconds, or 1 tick every 25 milliseconds. Now change the tempo to 120 BPM and you have one tick every 20,833 microseconds. So how fast the timing clock is depends on the speed of your sequence. The only constancy in the timing clock is that it subdivides each beat in twenty-four. As mentioned earlier, it is relative to the speed of the sequence being played. So if you look at Figure 2.12, a slave device might receive from a master device a Song Select message to cue a specific song to play, a series of Note On messages when you play a chord, a Foot Controller message when you want to sustain these note on messages, periodic MIDI Clocks in order to keep the playback in sync with the master, a MIDI program change, and, eventually, a MIDI Stop to halt playback.

Figure 2.12
MIDI events as they occur along the MIDI Clock tick timeline—each beat is divided into 24 equally spaced ticks, and the time between each tick is determined by the sequencer's tempo (BPM) value

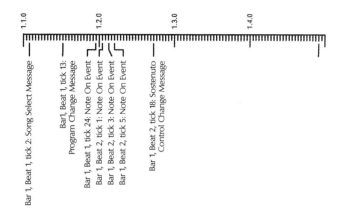

Timing Clock messages do not contain any data bytes and act like pulses, or square waves. Imagine this as being a very fast pulsating metronome, which the sequencer uses to keep track of timing.

Start, Stop, and Continue

These three System Real Time messages allow you to control a sequence of a slave sequencer or drum machine from a master sequencer or drum machine. The Start message tells the sequence to go to Song Position 0, or the beginning of the sequence, and play from there. The Stop message stops the playback of the sequencer, and the Continue message tells the sequencer to continue playing from the point it was last stopped until the end of the song or until you send a Stop command again. When a slave sequencer or drum machine receives these messages, it immediately positions its sequencer at the appropriate location in the timeline. If a Song Position Pointer message precedes the Continue command, the sequencer will then locate the position found in the SPP message and will continue from there. In other words, if you want to start a sequence from anywhere else but the song position 0, you would use the Continue command rather than the Start command, which always starts at the beginning. The Stop command always acts as a pause, leaving the sequence at the position where it receives the Stop command.

If the sequencer is slaved, pressing Start will cause the sequence to go to Song Position 0 and wait for an incoming Timing Clock (from an external MIDI Clock). To stop a sequence and start it again from Song Position 0, you will need to send a Stop message before sending another Start message, or the device will ignore this second Start message.

These three messages do not contain any data bytes. All the MIDI sequencer needs is the status byte telling it what to do: Start, Stop, or Continue.

Active Sensing

MIDI devices are often connected together through MIDI cables. I say often, because you will see later in this book that sometimes these MIDI connections are done virtually inside a computer's software. Now, what would happen if one of your cables got disconnected while you were playing, or in MIDI language, just after you sent a bunch of Note On messages? Well, these Note On messages would get stuck, since the cable carrying the Note Off message isn't connected to the device anymore. Remember, MIDI goes in one direction only, so the sending device (in this case, a sequencer) would not know if the receiving end has received events or not. The receiving device, on the other hand, has no way of knowing if more MIDI data should be coming its way either. So it just holds the notes there until it receives a Note Off event message.

That's where Active Sensing messages come in handy. What this message does is simple, yet very clever. It sends a message to a receiving device. Once this receiving device gets an Active Sensing command, it will expect at least one MIDI event every 300 ms on the MIDI port through which it received this message. If there is no MIDI activity over this MIDI port for 270 ms, then, when Active Sensing is enabled, the sending device will know to send another Active Sensing message to reassure the receiving device that everything is all right and that the connection is not dead. If the receiving device, which is expecting a MIDI event at least once every 300 ms, doesn't receive anything, it then considers this port connection to be dead and sends an All Note Off command to its sound module, effectively killing any stuck notes. It acts in many ways like a carrier signal for a modem; it indicates that the line is still operational.

This is an optional feature that newer devices implement. Many devices don't ever initiate this minimal security feature. To verify if your device supports this feature, you will need to consult your device's MIDI implementation chart.

System Reset

When you turn on a MIDI device, it usually sets itself up using default device parameters. These parameters sometimes vary from one device to the next. Obviously, these parameters can be changed using MIDI messages as you have seen up until now and will continue to discover as you read the rest of the book. The System Reset sends a status byte ordering the receiving devices (all the ones hooked up on the sender's MIDI port, no matter which MIDI channel they are on) to reset their parameters to a nominal state, or as they were when you powered up your device. This is a Real Time message rather than a System Exclusive one because it is more likely that a sequencer will send a System Reset message than a synthesizer. It should be noted that a sending device should not use this message automatically, but it should rather be sent when a musician specifically wants to tell a device to do so. Otherwise, this could lead to a situation where two devices endlessly reset each other. A System Reset message can be useful to bring all the parameters of a MIDI device to its default values. For example, if you've been working on a project and have been tweaking certain parameters on your device to see how these parameters affect the sound, using the System Reset message serves as a one-touch button that brings everything back to the way it was before you started.

Like other System Real Time messages, the System Reset message only contains a status byte.

System Exclusive Messages

Until now, we have discussed messages common to all devices, keyboard, sound modules, and sequencers. No matter which manufacturer built the device, they all share a common language through these commands. As the name "System Exclusive" might suggest, these messages are different from all others. In fact, System Exclusive is used to send some data that is specific to a particular MIDI device. For example, a SysEx message might be used to set the feedback level for an operator in an FM Synthesis device, a dump of its patch memory, sequencer data, or even waveform data. If you consider the last example, it would be useless to send this type of information to a non-waveform based synthesizer. However, most devices will support Pitch Bend, Foot Pedal, Modulation Wheel, and Program Change functions; therefore, they are part of the MIDI standard. In other words, whenever functions are manufacturer dependent, they become part of the SysEx family. That's why this is called System Exclusive: It sends specific information to a specific device, "excluding" the other devices from the conversation.

Every SysEx message starts and ends the same way. However, almost every MIDI device defines the format of its own set of SysEx messages, and a device will understand the values these messages contain if it is being addressed by name. This implies that at the beginning of the SysEx message, there is a manufacturer identification message (Manufacturer ID number) that tells a receiving device, "Hey, I'm talking to you," and a SysEx message ends when it receives an End SysEx Real Time message (or if it receives any other nonsystem realtime message). In between these two status bytes (see Figure 2.13), any number of 7-bit data bytes may be sent (remember that the first bit is always used to identify the status byte). Once the device understands for whom the incoming SysEx is intended, it either ignores it or processes it, depending on the Manufacturer's ID number.

SysEx messages can be used in different ways. Here are a few examples:

▶ When saving a song in a sequencer, you might want to include a series of SysEx messages at the beginning of the sequence that will configure the custom patches you have created for this song. This way, if you change your programs for another song, every time you load this one, your custom settings will be sent back to your specific device, as you saved them in the sequence.

▶ You may also want to send all the parameter settings of a MIDI device into patch editing software (editor/librarian) in order to use your computer's graphical interface to make changes to these parameters, rather than your device's front LCD panel. Once you've edited your parameters and saved them in a file on your computer, you can use a SysEx transfer to send the modified information back to your MIDI device.

▶ You can use SysEx to transmit the patterns from a drum machine to another drum machine, or better yet, to your computer.

Figure 2.13
The construction of a
System Exclusive
(SysEx) message

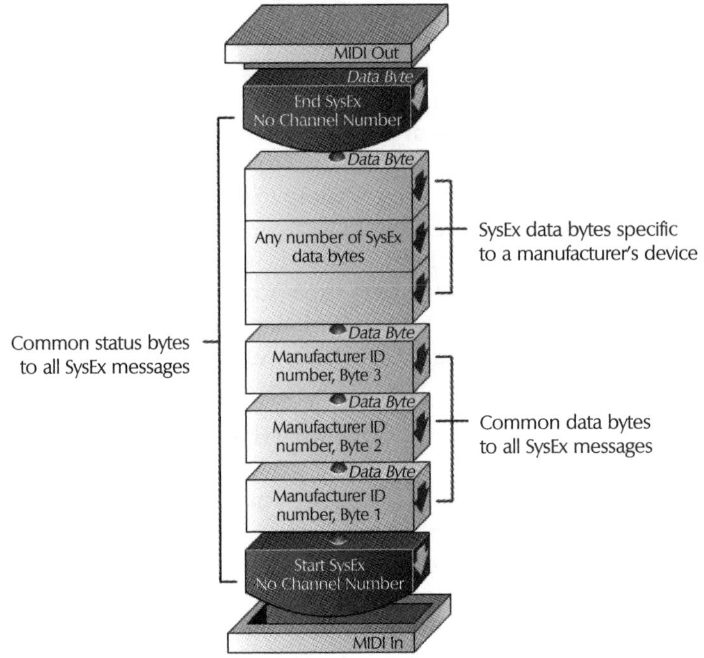

Any company that wishes to can apply for a System Exclusive Manufacturer ID number. It is the MMA's (MIDI Manufacturer's Association) responsibility to assign Manufacturer's ID numbers that are adopted as a standard. You will find a complete list of Manufacturer ID numbers in the Appendix B of this book.

The manufacturer of a product determines the purpose of the remaining data bytes, no matter how many there may be. Usually, what follows the Manufacturer ID number is the Model Number ID as defined by that specific manufacturer. This way, you may have a Korg Triton and a Korg M1 in your MIDI setup and they will both respond to the same Manufacturer ID, but since the model is different, the Triton will know if the rest of the bytes are for it, or for the M1. After this Model ID number, you might find information that will tell the device what the rest of the SysEx message is supposed to do, how many more data bytes the device should expect, and so on. Some manufacturers even have a checksum byte, which is used to check the integrity of the message's transmission. Imagine you're on a tour that brings you by plane into the middle of the Amazon forest. As you get off the plane, your tour guide counts everybody and lets you go off in the wilderness, telling you to be back in an hour. After the hour passes, the tour guide counts the passengers again to make sure everybody made it back. Your tour guide checks to make sure that everyone who came off the plane is back on it; otherwise, the plane won't leave. A checksum byte does a similar process, counting the sum of bytes that pass by and comparing it with a checksum value. If both values match, it accepts the transfer as successful; otherwise, it tells you the transfer failed and waits for further instructions.

As mentioned above, if for some reason a device should receive a MIDI message other than a SysEx data byte, a System Real Time message, or an End SysEx message, it would consider the transfer as being aborted, since such a scenario would indicate an abnormal MIDI condition.

Note Names and Numbers

As a musician, you know that notes are given names. These names might vary depending on the language you speak. For example, in English, notes in a scale are named with letters from A to G, with the most common scale being C (C, D, E, F, G, A, B). Germans have a similar naming system; however, B is replaced with the letter H. In French, this same scale is represented with the following names: C = Do, D = Re, E = Mi, and so on. Between these notes, you have accidental notes, which are half-tones between every note, so you will have C sharp (C#), D sharp (D#), and so on when going upward, and B flat (Bb), A flat (Ab), and so on when going downward. On a piano—and since MIDI was developed with the keyboard in mind many of its references can be made to this instrument—the center of a keyboard is often referred to as middle C. Since all pianos have the same number of keys (88 keys), it's not difficult to find this center C.

Since MIDI is a digital language, numbers have replaced key names. As you might recall, out of the 8 available bits in a message, one is used to indicate whether the byte is a Status message or a Data message. Therefore, with the remaining 7 bits, MIDI can give up to 128 different note values, which it distributes over the whole range of notes.

Figure 2.14
MIDI key numbers over a keyboard range

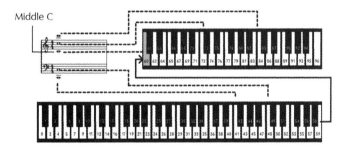

Figure 2.14 shows you how these numbers are distributed over a 96-key keyboard, which are already 12 keys more than any controller keyboard you will find on the market. However, MIDI can expand this range up to 127 (0 to 127 represents 128 values). The middle C in MIDI is always key number 60. So when you play the middle C on your keyboard, the MIDI value sent out is "60."

Because as humans, and as musicians, we are more familiar with note names, references made to MIDI numbers are very rare in both software and hardware interfaces. This is why the note names remain the best way to identify notes. To know which C is being played over a keyboard range, a number is assigned to it so that we know if it's high or low on the keyboard. Now, logic would have it that the lowest C (MIDI value 0 in Figure 2.14) would be considered the C0 octave, then the C above that the C1 octave to differentiate the first octave from the second. The following C would be C2, and so on. Middle C in this case would be C5. But in reality, there are discrepancies on how this is interpreted, depending on the software or hardware you are using. The discrepancy lies in the octave number. Most of the time, middle C is referred to as C4; this would put the lowest C in the MIDI range at octave C-1. In some other cases, as in some software sequencers, middle C is referred to as C3, which would put the lowest C in the MIDI range at octave C-2. In either case, however, C3, C4, or C5 depending on how the hardware or the software handles the note naming, the value for middle C will always be 60, so you need not worry too much about which octave number is attached to the C value if you notice that your keyboard places middle C at C4 and your sequencer software at C3, in terms of MIDI data, it will always be 60. In fact, if you were to play a C major chord on your keyboard, starting on the middle C and doubling the C one octave higher, you would be sending the following numeric values through MIDI: 60, 64, 67, and 72 as MIDI note number values.

As you saw earlier and will see later, these are not the only values you are sending through MIDI. However, note numbers along with Note On or Off values are the basic steppingstones of MIDI, and it should be clear to you by now why this is done.

3
Control Change Messages

Until now, we have discussed only one type of MIDI controller: the keys. Yes, those little black and white rectangles that are laid out in a row. Well, that's just one type of controlling device MIDI offers you. A keyboard is probably the best known, but not the only type of MIDI controller. You can also find on most keyboards devices such as pitch bend wheels, modulation wheels, sustain foot switches, volume foot switches, and joysticks (acting as modulation and pitch bend controllers). Some devices also have breath controllers that allow you to control the sound of the device using your breath. All of these devices have one thing in common: They are meant to give you more control over the expressive elements of a sound module, and, therefore, over your performance. Just like a keyboard, these control devices output MIDI information that can be recorded and played back to reproduce your original performance as precisely as possible. Here's a summary of what you will learn in this chapter:

▶ What control change message are and how they work.

▶ The functions and values associated with each control change message, and how they affect a performance.

▶ The difference between a low-resolution and high-resolution control change message.

▶ Which control change messages are meant as switches.

▶ How channel mode messages work.

What Are Control Change Messages?

As you saw at the end of Chapter 2, when you play a note on a keyboard, MIDI sends a note on message. In this message, two types of information are transmitted: the actual event—in this case, the Note On, and the number value of the actual note you played. This information is divided into the status byte, which identifies the message as being a Note On event, and the data byte that represents the value for this Note On event (the note number). A control change is similar to this as it also uses a status byte to identify the event and one or two data bytes representing the values for this event. Here's an example: Let's say you move the pitch bend wheel. The resulting MIDI message sent needs to identify this event as pitch bend and needs to tell the receiving device the position of this pitch bend. The MIDI message, in other words, always identifies what event or action is being performed and its associated value.

Control change messages are a set of 128 such events or actions that are transmitted through MIDI. Each event is identified by its own number, just like note numbers.

For example, when you move the modulation wheel (mod wheel) on your synthesizer or depress a foot pedal during a performance, a string of MIDI information—a control change message—is sent out that indicates the precise position of that mod wheel or that foot pedal at every instant in time. Just like Note On/Off messages, control change messages can be recorded, and, when combined with the recorded Note On/Off MIDI information, constitute the complete performance information of a given piece as captured by MIDI.

If you have a multi-timbral module, then each of its parts can respond differently to a particular controller number, or even ignore it. As with any other MIDI message, each part assigned to a MIDI channel in a multi-timbral environment usually has its own setting for every controller number, and that part responds only to controller messages on the same channel as that to which the part is assigned. In other words, controller messages only affect the parts in a multi-timbral/multi-channel module for which they are intended, even if other parts are playing at the same time.

You can find in the following table the names of all the control changes. Note that this represents the list of identified control changes as defined by the MIDI specification. However, there is also a provision in this specification for additional controllers that have not yet been defined. These undefined controllers do not figure in this list, since they have no standard function associated with them at the present time.

Table 3.1
List of control change names in alphabetical order.

All notes off	Modulation wheel
All Sound Off	Non-Registered Parameter Number
Balance	Omni mode off (+ all notes off)
Bank Select	Omni mode on (+ all notes off)
Breath control	Pan
Channel Volume (formerly Main Volume)	Poly mode on (incl mono=off +all notes off)
Damper pedal on/off (Sustain)	Poly mode on/off (+ all notes off)
Data Entry	Portamento Control
Effect control 1 & 2	Portamento on/off
Effects 1 to 5	Portamento time
Expression Controller	Registered Parameter Number
Foot controller	Reset All Controllers
General Purpose Controller #1 to #8	Soft pedal on/off
Hold 2	Sound Controller #1 to #10
Local control on/off	Sustenuto on/off

You will find more information on what each controller does and which number is associated with the controller in the control change MIDI message in this chapter.

The Structure of a Control Change Message

As with other MIDI messages, control changes follow a similar message structure. As you can see in Figure 3.1, the status byte tells the receiving MIDI device that what follows is a control change. This is followed by a number corresponding to the actual control change being performed, such as a pitch bend, modulation wheel, or foot pedal. Then comes the value for this control change representing the actual position of the controller. In total, all control messages have three bytes of information. You will see later that some control changes use two sets of control change messages to add a level of precision to the position of the controller. However, the principle of identifying each byte remains the same, no matter how many control messages are sent.

Figure 3.1
The structure of a
control change message

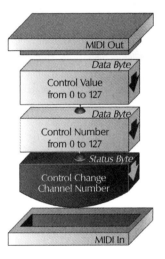

Understanding Controller Numbers

You have read in the previous chapter that MIDI uses 8-bit words in which the first bit to the left identifies each byte as being status or data. This leaves seven bits to represent the control changes. If you do the math, seven bits represent 128 values. So, the first data byte following the control change status byte is a control change number. This identifies which control was used.

Here's a complete list of each available control change represented by the first data byte following a control change status byte:

Table 3.2
List of all control changes (CC) numbers and the function (MIDI event) they represent.

CC Number	Function	CC Number	Function
0	Bank Select	69	Hold 2
1	Modulation wheel	70	Sound Controller 1 (Sound Variation)
2	Breath control	71	Sound Controller 2 (Timbre)
3	Undefined	72	Sound Controller 3 (Release Time)
4	Foot controller	73	Sound Controller 4 (Attack Time)
5	Portamento time	74	Sound Controller 5 (Brightness)
6	Data Entry	75	Sound Controller 6
7	Channel Volume (formerly Main Volume)	76	Sound Controller 7
8	Balance	77	Sound Controller 8
9	Undefined	78	Sound Controller 9
10	Pan	79	Sound Controller 10
11	Expression Controller	80	General Purpose Controller #5
12	Effect control 1	81	General Purpose Controller #6
13	Effect control 2	82	General Purpose Controller #7
14 & 15	Undefined	83	General Purpose Controller #8
16-19	General Purpose Controller #1 to #4	84	Portamento Control
20-31	Undefined	85-90	Undefined
32	Bank Select	91	Effects 1 Depth
33	Modulation wheel	92	Effects 2 Depth
34	Breath control	93	Effects 3 Depth
35	Undefined	94	Effects 4 Depth
36	Foot controller	95	Effects 5 Depth
37	Portamento time	96	Data entry +1
38	Data entry	97	Data entry -1
39	Channel Volume (formerly Main Volume)	98	Non-Registered Parameter Number LSB
40	Balance	99	Non-Registered Parameter Number MSB
41	Undefined	100	Registered Parameter Number LSB
42	Pan	101	Registered Parameter Number MSB
43	Expression Controller	102-119	Undefined
44 & 45	Effect control 1 & 2	120	All Sound Off
46 & 47	Undefined	121	Reset All Controllers
48-51	General Purpose Controller #1 to #4	122	Local control on/off
52-63	Undefined	123	All notes off
64	Damper pedal on/off (Sustain)	124	Omni mode off (+ all notes off)
65	Portamento on/off	125	Omni mode on (+ all notes off)
66	Sustenuto on/off	126	Poly mode on/off (+ all notes off)
67	Soft pedal on/off	127	Poly mode on (incl mono=off +all notes off)

To better understand this list, you can divide control change messages into three categories:

▶ Continuous Controllers: This type of controller sends position information, such as a modulation wheel position or a pitch bend position. Since you will most likely move the modulation wheel to different positions as you record this action, continuous controllers will generate a large number of data to represent these changes as they occur through time. It is therefore named continuous controller since it continuously sends MIDI messages to update the receiving MIDI device on the position of its controller.

▶ Switch Controllers: This type of controller acts as a switch; therefore, it can be on or off. Since the value byte (the second data byte in the control change message) is the same as any other byte, your MIDI device will interpret any values from 0 to 63 as being off and values from 64 to 127 as being on. By default, however, a switch controller will send a value of 0 when off and 127 when on. A sustain foot pedal is a good example of the switch controller in action. When you press the pedal, it is on, and keeps all previous Note On events sustained until it receives a foot pedal off message. It will then release any sustained notes.

▶ Channel mode message controllers: The last set of control change functions is not like the other control changes, but instead resembles channel mode messages, which have been given control change numbers between 120 and 127 (see Table 3.2). They are handled or identified as control changes even if their content (or function) is similar to channel mode messages.

Continuous controller messages can further be divided into two subcategories: low resolution and high resolution. As you might have noticed, two numbers represent some of the controllers. Take controller 0 and 32, which are both used to define the bank select.

In order to keep the structure of control change message identical (one status byte followed by two data bytes, one to represent the control change number and the other to represent its value), some control changes use two messages to identify intermediate values. In other words, some controllers might need more than 127 values to represent positions or variables. Take the bank select, for example. It has two controllers, numbers 0 and 32. This is to accommodate future enhancements in MIDI and larger bank selection numbers. The first controller number, in this case, number 0, is the default controller for bank selections and is supported by all MIDI devices. It allows you to select a bank of programs with values ranging from 0 to 127. This represents a total of 128 different banks. The first controller in this case is considered to be most significant. As for the controller number 32, it can also represent values from 0 to 127, or 128 different values. But in this case, it represents 128 different banks found in one bank of the controller 0. In other words, it represents a subset of values. That's why it is called "least significant." Combining the different values of both controllers, you get 128 times 128 different banks to choose from. This is why it is called high resolution. It offers a greater number of possible values when both controllers are combined, whereas low-resolution controllers have only one controller number assigned to them, and therefore can only represent 128 different values.

This said, most MIDI devices today will ignore any values sent by controllers that represent subsets of values, or Least Significant Byte (LSB) information such as the ones found in the bank select controller number 32.

Figure 3.2 offers a complete look at the control change hierarchy as described above. You will notice that some controller numbers are not represented in this hierarchy. This is because the numbers are not defined by the MIDI specification and cannot be categorized in this structure. Perhaps some of them will be implemented in further MIDI revisions. You will, however, find all control change messages listed in Appendix B.

Figure 3.2
The control change
message hierarchy

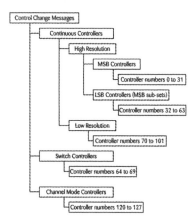

In the sections that follow, you will find a description of each control change and how it controls the sound. Each category and subcategory of control change messages is described in its own section. However, remember that all control change messages are numbered from 0 to 127 and are addressed by the MIDI specification as a set of 128. Their subdivision into categories and subcategories in this chapter is meant for you to better understand their purpose and their explanation, rather than being an actual part of the MIDI specification.

Continuous Control Change Messages

High-Resolution Continuous Controllers

High-resolution and low-resolution continuous controller messages are made up of three bytes. The first byte represents the status byte, which tells the receiving device that this is a control change message. The second byte identifies the actual control change; for example, this is a modulation wheel, bank select, or pan control message. The third byte gives the value for this control change. Where high-resolution control changes differ from their low-resolution counterpart is in their second control number assignment. As discussed earlier, the bank select control change, for example, has two control change numbers referring to this same control change function—number 0 and number 32. Low-resolution control changes have only one control change number. So, for each high-resolution controller, you have two control change numbers assigned: the first, which represents the most significant values or coarse adjustment, and a second, which represents the least significant values or fine adjustment.

This means that high-resolution controllers can have either 128 values, if the MIDI message refers to one control change, or 16,384 values (128 × 128), if both control change numbers referring to the same function are being used. In reality, most of the high-resolution controllers are handled as low-resolution controllers since very few MIDI devices will offer support for controller numbers 32 to 63. What happens when they do is both transparent to the user (you) and the MIDI device receiving the message.

For example, the modulation wheel (controller 1) can have a value of 50 (see Figure 3.3). Then, imagine that a second control change message follows, but now the controller is number 33, which is also a modulation wheel control change message; however, this time, the third byte value represents a fine-tuning of the modulation. So, for every value in controller 1, you have 128 intermediate values.

This is also known as the MSB (Most Significant Byte) and LSB (Least Significant Byte) values, where MSB is the coarse setting and LSB is the fine setting. In our example above, the modulation has a coarse setting of 50; within that coarse setting you can have 128 different values for a total of 16,384 different (7 bits of MSB + 7 bits of LSB = 14 bits = 2 to the power of 14 = 16,384) values for a single control change (see Table 3.3 below).

Figure 3.3
How the MSB and LSB
appear in the MIDI data
stream

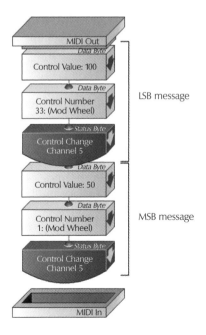

Table 3.3
MSB and LSB value combination table.

MSB values	LSB values	Possible LSB values per MSB value
0	0 to 127	128
1	0 to 127	128
2	0 to 127	128
...	0 to 127	128
127	0 to 127	128
Possible MSB values 128		Possible MSB and LSB combinations (128 X 128) 16,384

Here's how it works:

▶ If your master MIDI device (the one sending the MIDI messages) doesn't support controllers 32 to 63, the subset controllers representing the fine or LSB values for controllers 0 to 31 will never be used or transmitted. If the device receives control change messages for these controllers, they will be ignored.

▶ If your master MIDI device (the one sending the MIDI messages) supports controllers 32 to 63 but the slave MIDI device (the one receiving the MIDI messages) doesn't, the slave will ignore these messages.

▶ If both master and slave MIDI devices support controllers 32 to 63, you will have an increased resolution for this set of control changes. This will enhance each controller by adding 128 fine or LSB values for each one of the 128 coarse or MSB values found in their corresponding control change messages (controllers 0 to 31).

In most cases, the LSB controllers are either not implemented or not used by the devices. The purpose of these higher resolutions is to allow a greater precision over changes made by these controllers. However, using LSB controllers will add a great deal of additional MIDI information in your MIDI data stream, which can clog at the output, especially if you are hooking up multiple devices in a daisy chain rather than using a multi-port MIDI type of connection. The only control you have over the use of these controllers is by not using them if your MIDI device supports them. To find that out, you will need to consult your MIDI device's documentation to see which control change numbers are implemented. On the other hand, if these controllers are implemented and you find this improves the control you have over your performance without slowing the MIDI data flow, their use will be transparent to you in most cases.

Bank Select
Controller 0, coarse or MSB and Controller 32, fine or LSB

Some MIDI devices have more than 128 presets (or patches, instruments, programs, etc). MIDI program change messages only support switching between 128 programs. In order to accommodate more than 128 programs, many devices categorize their programs in banks. For example, let's say a device has 512 programs. It may divide these into 4 banks of 128 programs (as shown in Figure 3.4). The bank select controller (sometimes called bank switch) is used to allow switching between groups of programs. How many programs you have in every bank depends on how your MIDI device assigns them; you can have a maximum of 128 programs in each bank.

For example, if you want program number 129, that would actually be the first program within the second bank (programs and banks always begin with a "0"). Programs 1 to 128 would be numbered, in a MIDI message, as 0 to 127 of bank 0, and program 129 would be numbered program 0 of bank 1. You would send a bank select controller to switch to the second bank and then follow with a program change to select the first program in this bank. A bank select message only affects the MIDI channel that it is assigned to just as a program change. So, you can select a bank for a keyboard on channel 5 without affecting any other MIDI devices on other channels.

Figure 3.4
Comparing the bank select control change message with the program change channel voice message

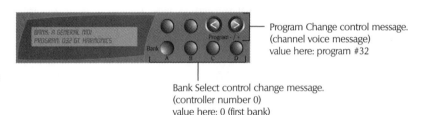

Program Change control message. (channel voice message) value here: program #32

Bank Select control change message. (controller number 0) value here: 0 (first bank)

Controller number 32 is used for fine tuning, meaning that you could have up to 16,384 banks of 128 sounds. However, most sound modules, as mentioned previously, will not use or support this controller since it is rare to find a sound module with that many sounds (it would represent over two million sounds).

Values for both controllers range from 0 to 127.

Modulation Wheel

Controller 1, coarse or MSB and Controller 33, fine or LSB

Sets the modulation wheel (or MOD wheel) to a particular value, which in most cases introduces some sort of vibrato effect. This vibrato effect can be achieved in different ways: through a frequency modulation (changing the pitch with an LFO or Low Frequency Oscillator), for example, or by amplitude modulation (changing the loudness), or a filter modulation.

Controller number 33 adds fine-tuning, or micro amounts of MOD wheel, giving an added resolution to this controller. However, some devices will not support this controller. If that's the case, the messages are simply ignored.

Values for both controllers range from 0 to 127.

Breath Control

Controller 2, coarse or MSB and Controller 34, fine or LSB

This may be used to control a parameter like aftertouch, since breath control is a wind player's version of how to vary pressure so it can be assigned to whatever the musician sets this controller to affect.

As with other controllers supporting MSB and LSB, controller 34 adds more definition to the breath control values. If the device does not support the controller, it will simply ignore its information.

Values for both controllers range from 0 to 127.

Foot Controller

Controller 4, coarse or MSB and Controller 36, fine or LSB

This may be used to control a parameter like aftertouch as well, or whatever the musician sets this controller to affect. This foot pedal is a continuous controller, like a potentiometer or a fader. Think of this as a swell pedal found on B3 organs, where the more you press on the pedal, the louder the sound gets (as suggested in Figure 3.5).

These values are from 0 to 127. However, in a foot switch, values from 0 to 63 are interpreted as being equal to 0 (or as being Off) and values from 64 to 127 are interpreted as being equal to 127 (or as being On). Although in both cases, you may have a foot pedal transmitting values from 0 to 127, in the case of a foot controller, all values are interpreted as individual values. In a foot switch, though, only two value ranges (0 to 63 and 64 to 127) determine the value for this controller, as suggested in Figure 3.5.

Figure 3.5
Foot controller (control change 4 and 36) sends a series of values, whereas some other types of foot-like controllers act as On/Off switches (such as the controller 64, hold pedal)

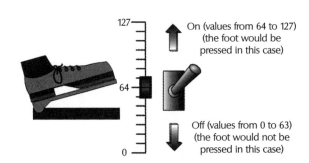

As with other controllers supporting MSB and LSB, controller 34 adds more definition to the breath control values. If the device does not support the controller, it will simply ignore its information.

Values for both controllers range from 0 to 127.

Portamento Time
Controller 5, coarse or MSB and Controller 37, fine or LSB

Portamento is the time it takes for the pitch of one note to slide to a second note's pitch rather than playing this second note's pitch immediately. So, this controller determines the rate (in time) at which portamento slides the pitch between 2 notes.

Controller 37, when supported, adds intermediate values to that rate, making it more precise. If the device does not support the controller, it will simply ignore its information.

Values for both controllers range from 0 to 127.

Data Entry
Controller 6, coarse or MSB and Controller 38, fine or LSB

Data Entry is the value of some Registered Program Number (RPN) or Non-Registered Parameter Number (NRPN). Which parameter is affected depends upon a preceding RPN or NRPN message (which itself identifies the parameter's number). RPN and NRPN are parameters that can be controlled by MIDI but are specific to a MIDI device or not controlled by any other control change messages. For example, the master coarse tuning request message on a multi-timbral MIDI device is an RPN parameter. Using the data entry controller would send a control change value that would be interpreted by the RPN controller as a coarse tuning value if it is used with this RPN.

On some devices, this slider may not be used in conjunction with RPN or NRPN messages. Instead, the musician can set the slider to control a single parameter directly, often a parameter such as what aftertouch can control.

Controller 38, when supported, adds intermediate values. If the device does not support the controller, it will simply ignore its information.

Values for both controllers range from 0 to 127.

Channel Volume
(Formerly known as Main Volume) Controller 7, coarse or MSB and Controller 39, fine or LSB

Channel Volume affects the device's channel or main level, but not its master volume if the device is multi-timbral. If this is the case, then each part has its own volume (this controller), and the master volume of the instrument or device would be found in a SysEx Master Volume message, or take its volume from one of the parts, or be controlled by a general purpose slider controller. The expression controller can also affect the volume level of a channel.

Controller 39 is rarely supported in sound modules, but when supported, it adds intermediate values to the channel volume. If the device does not support the controller, it will simply ignore its information.

Values for both controllers range from 0 to 127.

Balance

Controller 8, coarse or MSB and Controller 40, fine or LSB

If the device has stereo audio outputs, this controller will have an effect on the stereo balance for the corresponding MIDI channel. If it is a multi-timbral device, then each part usually has its own balance.

Typically, balance is used on a channel that has stereo sounds when you wish to adjust the volume of the stereo elements without changing their pan positions, whereas pan is more appropriate for a channel that is strictly a "mono instrument."

Controller 40 is rarely supported in sound modules, but when supported, it adds intermediate values to the balance. If the device does not support the controller, it will simply ignore its information.

Values for both controllers range from 0 to 127. A value of 0 emphasizes the left side in a stereo balance, 64 will center the stereo balance and 127 would emphasize the right side of a stereo balance.

Pan

Controller 10, coarse or MSB and Controller 42, fine or LSB

This determines where, within the stereo field of a stereo audio output device, the sound will be placed. Typically, pan is used on a channel that has mono sounds, but it also affects stereo panning just as well (see balance section above).

Figure 3.6
Comparing the balance control change to the pan control change

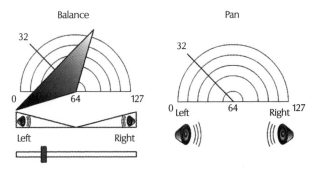

As Figure 3.6 would suggest, when you change the balance of a stereo sound, the weight of the stereo field shifts towards the audio output channel corresponding to the MIDI value. In this case, the value 32 tilts the stereo balance toward the left. In comparison, the pan positions a sound (usually mono) at the same position. If the sound is stereo, the left channel would be slightly louder than the right channel in this example.

Controller 42 is rarely supported in sound modules, but when supported, it adds intermediate values to the pan. If the device does not support the controller, it will simply ignore its information.

Values for both controllers range from 0 to 127. A value of 0 pans the sound hard left in a stereo field, 64 will center the sound, and 127 would pan hard right in a stereo field.

Expression Controller
Controller 11, coarse or MSB and Controller 43, fine or LSB

The expression controller acts as a percentage of the volume controller. Although rarely used since devices don't usually have any knobs, sliders, or buttons assigned to this controller, it can come in handy in certain occasions. This controller divides the current volume into 16,384 steps, acting as an LSB for the volume control, thus adding more "expressive" control over the volume level. You might say, well, the volume controller already has two controllers, taking care of the volume level of a channel. This is true. However, the LSB controller for the volume controller is rarely implemented in MIDI devices, whereas the expression controller is implemented in most of them. For example, you can set several instrument levels using the volume controller, then without changing these relative volume values, change the expression controller as a way to create crescendos or decrescendos while keeping these relative volume levels the same.

Here's a practical example of how this controller can be applied. Let's say you are mixing a piano, bass, and drum sound and have determined that the piano's volume controller should be set at 70, the bass 90, and the drums at 100. Now, let's say you want to increase the volume for these three instruments, but would like to keep the relative balance between them the same. You have three options: You can either calculate manually the value for each instrument by adding a percentage and then rounding up to the closest value, add a fix value to all instruments, or assign the same value to the expression controller for all three instruments.

In Table 3.4, you can see that when you add a value of 32 (out of 128) to the expression controller, all instruments will increase by 25% (0 is 0%, 64 is 50%, and 127 is 100%), bringing the volume of each instrument up by that ratio, therefore keeping the relative balance. However, if you simply add 25 to all instruments, as shown in the table, the end result would upset the relative balance between instruments, as the last row would suggest.

Table 3.4
Practical comparison between the use of volume controllers and expression controllers to maintain the relative balance between different sounds in a MIDI mix.

	Piano	Bass	Drums
Volume level	70	90	100
Expression level with a value of 32, or an increase of 25%	+ 25%	+ 25%	+ 25%
End result	89	113	125
If you add 25 to all the instruments using the volume level	95	115	125
Percentage louder compared to the original value when using volume control	+ 35 %	+ 28%	+ 25 %

If you are using a software sequencer that allows you to use a mixer interface on which you can assign a series of MIDI volume controllers to a group fader, you might not have to use the expression controller at all, since it will be easier to use your software mixing features. Otherwise, using the expression controller as described earlier in the example found in Table 3.4 would be one of the ways you could use the expression controller.

Finally, the expression controller may also be assigned to a foot pedal, just like the foot controller, to control the swelling of the volume by the musician. Since it works on a percentage value of the volume, the expression controller may yield a more subtle effect in volume changes than simply applying volume changes everywhere. The LSB version of this controller (controller number 43) is, however, rarely implemented.

Values for both controllers range between 0 and 127.

Effect Control 1 and 2

Controllers 12 and 13, coarse or MSB and Controllers 44 and 45, fine or LSB

These controllers can be used to control any parameter relating to an effects device such as the reverb decay time for a built-in reverb found in some sound modules. There are separate controllers for setting the volume levels of reverb, chorus, phase shift, and other effects (see controllers 91 to 95).

General Purpose Controllers 1 to 4

Controllers 16 through 19, coarse or MSB and Controllers 48 through 51, fine or LSB

This can be set by musicians to control pretty much anything. They are the equivalent of having 4 additional general-purpose sliders or faders. Note that the general purpose controllers 48 through 51 (the fine or LSB version) are rarely implemented in MIDI devices.

Low Resolution Continuous Controllers

These controllers act exactly the same way as high resolution controllers with the exception that they don't come in pairs, allowing an MSB and LSB version of the same controller. For the most part, they are used to control sound parameters like knobs on a sound module. You can think of these controllers as remote controls in a way, allowing you to control your device from a distance, using control change messages rather than using the onboard physical knob. Which parameters these controllers modify is device dependent, and you will have to consult your device's documentation to know how to implement them.

Low-resolution controllers may come in handy when you want to automate certain parameters of your MIDI device, since you can create a series of control change messages, record them in a sequencer, and then play them back as automation data to control the timbre, attack, or release time of a MIDI device over time.

Sound Controller 1 (Sound Variation)
Controller 70

This will affect the parameters associated with the circuitry that produces the sound, such as the sample rate of a sampler's sound, therefore playing on its pitch. The lower the value, the less the effect, and vice versa, 0 being the minimum and 127 being the maximum.

Sound Controller 2 (Timbre)
Controller 71

As with controller 70, this controller affects sound production parameters. In this case, it adds control to the Voltage Control Filter (VCF) and plays on the envelope's levels. In other words, it controls how the filter shapes the brightness or timbre of the sound over time. The higher the value, the more apparent the effect, 0 being the minimum and 127 being the maximum.

Sound Controller 3 (Release Time)
Controller 72

This controls the VCA's release time envelope. Lower values will make the envelope's release time fade quicker, and higher values will make the envelope's release time longer. The value range for this controller is, as with all other sound controllers, 0 to 127.

Sound Controller 4 (Attack Time)
Controller 73

This controls the VCA's attack time envelope. Lower values will make the envelope's attack time quicker, and higher values will make the envelope's attack time longer, fading in more gradually. The value range for this controller is, as with all other sound controllers, 0 to 127.

Sound Controller 5 (Brightness)
Controller 74

This controls the VCF's cutoff frequency by changing its filter frequency, affecting the overall brightness of the sound. The value range for this controller is, as with all other sound controllers, 0 to 127.

Sound Controllers 6 to 10 (No Default Parameter)
Controllers 75 through 79

These extra five sound controllers can be used to adjust other parameters associated with the sound producing circuitry of a sound module. They are assignable, so they don't modify anything in particular until you assign them to a parameter. The value range for these controllers is, as with all other sound controllers, 0 to 127.

CHAPTER 3

General Purpose Controllers 5 to 8

Controllers 80 through 83

You can assign these general purpose controllers to any On/Off switch you want. They can act as triggers to control a sequencer, for example. Since they are assignable, you will need to associate these controllers with something before you use them. Being switches, values 0 to 63 represent Off and 64 to 127, On.

Portamento Control

Controller 84

This controller sends a MIDI note number to set the starting note of a portamento, which will then be glided in a time set by the portamento time controller to the next Note On message.

When a Note On message is received after a portamento control message, the voice's pitch glides from the key number specified in this message to the new Note On's pitch at the rate set by portamento time (controller number 5), ignoring the current status of portamento on/off (controller number 65). This message only affects the next Note On received on the relevant MIDI channel.

If your device is set to play in poly mode (see description in Chapter 2 under "About MIDI Modes"), receiving a portamento control message does not affect the pitch of any currently playing notes, whether in their sustain or release phase. However, when in mono mode, or if the legato footswitch (controller number 68) is on, a new overlapping note event results in an immediate pitch jump to the note number specified in the portamento control message, and then a glide at the current portamento rate to the note number specified in the new Note On. The value range for this controller is from 0 to 127, which corresponds to note numbers as defined in Appendix B.

Effects Level

Controller 91

This can be used to control the level of effect, such as an integrated reverb or delay, when these are included in your sound module. The value range for these controllers is 0 to 127.

Tremolo Level

Controller 92

This can be used to control the level of a device's tremolo, or vibration. The value range for these controllers is 0 to 127.

Chorus Level

Controller 93

This can be used to control the effect level of a device's chorus. The value range for these controllers is 0 to 127.

Celeste (Detune) Level

Controller 94

This can be used to control the effect level of a device's detune amount, also called celeste. The value range for these controllers is 0 to 127.

Phaser Level

Controller 95

This can be used to control the effect level of a device's phaser amount, which is a form of very slow chorus. The value range for these controllers is 0 to 127.

Data Increment Button

Controller 96

This causes a data button to increase by one its current value. More often, this controller's value is being used to set some RPN and NRPN. It is the preceding RPN or NRPN message that will determine which parameter this switch will affect. This preceding message usually identifies the parameter number itself. Being a switch, values 0 to 63 represent Off and 64 to 127 represent On, which will make the data increment by one. This is slightly different then the usual switch controller, and that's why it is considered a low resolution controller rather than a true switch controller.

Data Decrement Button

Controller 97

Acts like controller 96, except that in this case it decreases the data button's value by one rather than increasing it.

Non-Registered Parameter Number (NRPN)

Controller 98, fine or LSB and Controller 99, coarse or MSB

These controllers will determine which parameter the data button increment (controller 96), data button decrement (controller 97), or data entry controllers (numbers 6 and 38) will affect. Since these two controllers (98 and 99) work as a pair, you can have 16,384 different non-registered parameters. It is up to each manufacturer to determine which parameter number affects which actual device parameter.

An example of NRPN in use is the way a MIDI mixer manufacturer might address specific controllers, giving them functions corresponding to onboard knobs, such as a compressor level if this mixer has an automatable compressor.

Since each device can define a particular NRPN controller number to control anything, it's possible that two devices may interpret the same NRPN number in different manners. Therefore, a device should allow a musician to disable receipt of NRPN, in the event that there is a conflict between the NRPN implementations of two daisy-chained devices. Values for both controllers range from 0 to 127.

It should be mentioned here that the difference between RPN and NRPN is that the former have been adopted, thus registered and approved by the MMA (MIDI Manufacturer Association) and the JMSC (Japan MIDI Standard Committee), whereas the latter have not. This means that a manufacturer might implement some uses for NRPN, but these parameters won't necessarily apply the same way for another manufacturer. You should also know that NRPN controllers and their RPN counterparts (described in the next header) are not controllers you will be using very often, since most manufacturers will use them as a way to send and receive information that in most cases remains transparent to the user.

Registered Parameter Number (RPN)

Controller 100, fine or LSB and Controller 101, coarse or MSB

These controllers work like the ones you just saw (98 and 99), with the exception that they work with RPN (Registered Parameter Numbers) rather than NRPN (Non-Registered Parameter Numbers). Here are the currently registered parameter numbers:

▶ Pitch Bend Range Sensitivity, which sets the number of semi-tones or half steps defined by the MSB of the pitch bend (controller number 6, Data Entry) and the number of cents defined by LSB of the same message (controller number 38, Data Entry).

▶ Master Fine Tuning.

▶ Master Coarse Tuning.

▶ Select Tuning Program.

▶ Select Tuning Bank.

▶ Null Function, used to cancel an RPN or NRPN or to indicate the end of the message.

Switches

Switch type control changes come from controllers that are either On or Off. For that purpose, only two values are needed: 0 indicates Off and 127 indicates On. However, since 7 bits of data are available, most devices will interpret any value less than or equal to 63 as being Off, and all values greater than or equal to 64 as being On.

Damper Pedal (Sustain)

Controller 64

This acts the same way as a sustain pedal on a piano, holding the notes as if they remained pressed until the sustain or damper pedal is released. In other words, it postpones the Note Off event effect. It will also postpone any all notes off controller message (controller number 123). This is different from the foot pedal described earlier (see Figure 3.4) since it is like an on/off switch rather than a foot version of a fader with values ranging from 0 to 127.

Portamento On/Off

Controller 65

This controls the portamento (pitch sliding between two notes). Usually, this controller works with the portamento time controllers (number 5 and 37). If the portamento is off, the portamento time controller will not have any effect.

Sostenuto

Controller 66

This is like the hold pedal controller, except it only sustains notes that are already on when the pedal is pressed, rather than holding all the notes that are played from the moment the pedal is pressed until it is released. When you play new notes after pressing the pedal, they will not be held. In other words, this controller acts as a chord holder for the notes that are on when the pedal is pressed.

Figure 3.7
Example of a sostenuto message

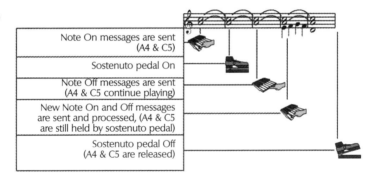

As Figure 3.7 would suggest, a two-note chord is played. Then, the sostenuto pedal is pressed. From this point on, these two notes will be sustained until the sostenuto pedal is released; however, the other notes that are played will not be sustained because they are pressed after the sostenuto pedal's On action.

Soft Pedal

Controller 67

This pedal softens notes by lowering their volume, acting like the center pedal in a three-pedal piano setup. This controller is not necessarily implemented in all devices, as with many others, so you should read your device's manufacturer documentation to find out if and how it implements this controller.

CHAPTER 3

Legato Footswitch

Controller 68

You can use this to skip the attack portion of the VCA's (Voltage Control Amplifier) envelope, which will give you a legato effect between notes. For example, a violin player can play several notes with the bow going in the same direction, which has the effect of softening the attack. This controller enables the keyboard player to do something similar.

Hold 2

Controller 69

This controller will make the played notes take longer to fade out after the release, compared to notes that are played when the pedal is not pressed. Unlike the hold pedal (controller 64), however, it does not sustain permanently the notes until the musician releases the pedal, even if the notes do take a longer time to release. It acts primarily on the VCA's envelope. The Hold 2 controller is an on/off switch.

Channel Mode Messages

Channel mode messages are a subset of control change messages. However, they are not handled as the other control change messages above, since they have a more global affect on a device. And, in most cases, they enable or disable channel-related functions such as MIDI modes, local keyboard control, and the ever so precious "Panic" functions that send a message to a device to release any note on messages in case MIDI gets stuck.

All Sound Off

Controller 120

This controller would cause sound generators to immediately cease all sound, muting all sounding notes that were turned on by received Note On messages, and which haven't yet been turned off by respective Note Off messages. This message is not supposed to mute any notes that the musician is playing on the local keyboard, so if a device can't distinguish between notes played via its MIDI In and notes played on the local keyboard, it should not implement All Sound Off.

The difference between this message and All Notes Off is that this message immediately mutes all sound on the device regardless of whether the Hold Pedal is on, and mutes the sound quickly regardless of any lengthy VCA release times. This controller doesn't use a value range byte, but rather sends a default 0 value when this controller is sent in the MIDI message.

All Controllers Off

Controller 121

The All Controllers Off will reset all controllers to their default states. This means that all switches, such as Sostenuto, are turned off, and all continuous controllers, such as Mod Wheel, are set to minimum positions. The only value for this is 0, since the value byte isn't used.

Local Keyboard (Or Control) On/Off
Controller 122

This controller turns the device's keyboard on or off locally. When a Local Keyboard Off message is sent, the keyboard is disconnected from the device's internal sound generation circuitry, thus sending MIDI information but not producing sounds itself through its audio outputs. So, when the musician presses keys, the device doesn't trigger any of its internal sounds. This is the best way to eliminate loops in the MIDI messages where the sounds would be generated by the musician as he/she plays on the keys, where the sound generation circuitry reproduces what comes in from the MIDI Input and reproduces the same sounds if the same MIDI data coming out of the keyboard devices, and comes back in to this device. Furthermore, if a device is only going to be played remotely via MIDI, then the keyboard may be turned off in order to allow the device to concentrate more on dealing with MIDI messages rather than scanning the keyboard for depressed notes and varying pressure. This controller acts like a switch, with values from 0 to 63 being Off and values from 64 to 127 being On.

In Figure 3.8, you can see two sample setups that would create such a feedback loop if the Local Keyboard is set to On. Let's look at these examples:

1. You play on the keyboard, the notes are sent to the MIDI Out and the sound circuitry produces the sounds through the keyboard's audio outputs.

2. The receiving sequencer (in setup A) or the sound device (in setup B) processes the MIDI information and sends the MIDI back to its MIDI output.

3. The keyboard receives MIDI information from its MIDI input and plays the sounds through its audio output a second time, since they are already playing the same notes when you pressed the keys, thus creating an undesired note doubling effect that usually sounds like a quick flange.

Figure 3.8
Local On/Off message explained in two setup examples

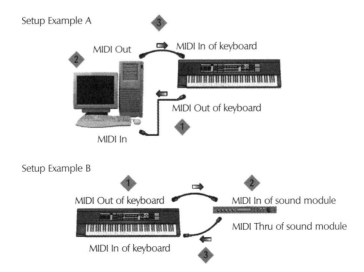

CHAPTER 3

On the other hand, if the Local Keyboard is set to Off, in step 1 of the above example, the keyboard does not produce an audio output, since the MIDI information is ONLY sent to its MIDI output. It will then only process the MIDI information coming from its MIDI input and create the corresponding audio output once.

All Notes Off
Controller 123

Similar to the All Sounds Off (controller 120), this controller turns off all notes that were turned on by received Note On messages, and which haven't yet been turned off by respective Note Off messages unless these notes are being played on the local keyboard by the musician. If a device can't distinguish between notes played via its MIDI In and notes played on the local keyboard, it should not implement All Notes Off. Furthermore, if a device is in Omni On state, it should ignore this message on any channel. What makes this different than the All Sounds Off controller is that if the device's Hold Pedal controller is on, the notes aren't actually released until the Hold Pedal is turned off. See the All Sound Off controller message for turning off the sound of these notes immediately. The only value for this is 0, since the value byte isn't used. This is a softer way of releasing all Note On messages, since it will respect the release stage of any notes that are in their Note On phase.

Omni Mode Off
Controller 124

This sends a message (Omni Off) that has no value byte (default value is 0) and that turns the Omni Mode off. See the discussion in Chapter 2 under "About MIDI Mode." When a device receives an Omni Off message, it should automatically turn off all playing notes.

Omni Mode On
Controller 125

This sends a message (Omni On), which has no value byte (default value is 0) that turns the Omni Mode on. See the discussion in Chapter 2 under "About MIDI Mode." When a device receives an Omni On message, it should automatically turn off all playing notes, just as with the Omni Mode Off.

Monophonic Operation
Controller 126

This controller enables the monophonic operation MIDI mode (Mono On), disabling the polyphonic operation MIDI mode as discussed in Chapter 2.

If Omni is off, this value tells how many MIDI channels the device is expected to respond to in Mono mode. In other words, if Omni is off, this value is used to select a limited set of the 16 MIDI channels (i.e., 1 to 16) to respond to. If Omni is on, this value is ignored completely, and the device only plays one note at a time per active channel in a multi-timbral device. The following paragraphs would then be relevant only if the Omni Off mode was active.

When the value is 0, it tells the device it can receive voice messages on any MIDI channels. However, since this is Mono On, only one voice per channel (monophony) can be reproduced.

If the value is between 1 and 16, that tells the device how many channels can be actively receiving voice messages, the number value defining the number of MIDI channels. A value of 3, for example, would restrict the device from receiving data from more than 3 MIDI channels simultaneously. If it did, they would be ignored.

The base MIDI channel of a device will have an effect on which channel it will respond to when in this mode. For example, if your device is set to channel 2 as the base MIDI channel and the value is set to 3, it will respond to channels 2, 3, and 4 (2 being the base channel and 3-4 completing the set of 3 channels).

Multi-timbral devices operate in a slightly special way. Basically, each part has its own MIDI channel and is usually considered as a separate device, with each part being set to Omni Mode Off and Poly Mode On. Changing the mode to Mono Mode On rather than Poly Mode On would result in a series of monophonic instruments (as many as your devices has multi-timbral parts).

Polyphonic Operation
Controller 127

This enables polyphonic operations (Poly On), thus disabling monophonic operation (Mono On). You can refer to Chapter 2 in the section "About MIDI Mode" to get more details. The value byte isn't used, and defaults to 0. When a device receives a Poly Operation message, it should automatically turn off all playing notes.

4

General MIDI and Standard MIDI Files

Not long after the MIDI 1.0 standard was finalized in the early 1980s, musicians started hooking different manufacturers' MIDI devices together. They quickly realized that the MIDI 1.0 specification had overlooked an important detail: No provision had been made in this standard for a set of standard patches, nor had they ventured into specifications for multi-timbral instruments, since at this point in time, they did not exist. It took almost a decade for the MMA (MIDI Manufacturers Association) and the JMSC (Japan MIDI Standards Committee) to adopt what is known as the General MIDI System Level 1 specification, or GM for short. When adopted in 1991, this specification was designed to provide a minimum level of performance compatibility among MIDI instruments. It has also helped pave the way for MIDI in the growing consumer and multimedia markets that were emerging at the time.

Here's a summary of what you will learn in this chapter:

▶ What General MIDI is and why it was developed.

▶ What a General MIDI sound bank is.

▶ What other aspects of a device are defined by General MIDI.

▶ What a Standard MIDI File is and why it was developed.

▶ What the different types of MIDI files are and how to choose which one to use.

▶ What makes Standard MIDI Files so different from audio files when it comes to distribution over a network.

▶ Why other companies expanded on the General MIDI specification by introducing their own standards.

▶ What the GS Standard is.

▶ What the XG Standard is.

To give you an example of how things were before MIDI, consider this: Let's say you had two synthesizers, an EMU Proteus XR sound module and a Yamaha DX-7 keyboard. You hook both of these devices together and wish to use the keyboard to send patch change messages to the Proteus sound module. The problem you are going to have is that when you send a program change using the DX-7 keyboard, you are sending a program number value and nothing in that number tells the receiving device what kind of sound it should play. It will simply change the program number to the value it receives. If your program number 32 is a bass sound on the DX-7 and you enter that number on this synth, you will have the program number 32 playing on the Proteus, which is probably not a bass sound since it is not a GM module.

In other words, it is difficult to control or embed program changes in a sequencer, save the sequence, and have the sequence play back on another set of MIDI instruments with the appropriate sounds. Compatibility between different systems was hard to achieve because of this, since no two devices had the same list of sounds or had their sounds in the same order.

To address these concerns, Roland proposed an addendum to the MIDI 1.0 specification. This addendum was called "General MIDI" (GM). It added some new requirements to the base MIDI 1.0 specification. These additions did not supplant any parts of the 1.0 specification, and the 1.0 specification is still the base level to which all MIDI devices should adhere. GM has now been adopted as part of the MIDI 2.0 specification.

What Is General MIDI?

To be GM compatible, a GM device such as a keyboard, sound module, sound card, software program, or any other product must meet the General MIDI System Level 1 performance requirements described in the following sections. These requirements must be instantaneous upon demand and should not require additional modification, adjustment, or configuration by the user. This way, a specially prepared score transmitted to the module via MIDI, using a sequencer or MIDI file player, will play back with the correct sounds, regardless of the make and model of the sound module. These recorded sequences can then be distributed as Standard MIDI Files on floppy disks or via other mediums such as the Internet.

It is important to know that General MIDI is a "Recommended Practice" for manufacturers; they do not legally have to comply with it, but since the market usually dictates what should be done by observing what sells, GM has become widespread across most sound-generator manufacturers. So, if you are a game enthusiast or use MIDI files regularly, GM is a must, and chances are you will probably need a GM compatible device. However, if you are a serious music composer, you will feel the need for more sounds than GM provides.

Usually, General MIDI devices are meant for musicians who are not into designing their own sounds, but rather need a sound source they can rely on to hear MIDI files or create MIDI files they can distribute. Since the editing done to a MIDI sound can't be saved to the GM bank directly, you are limited to these 128 programs whenever you want to make sure your song will comply with this standard. For example, inserting a program change number 0 will always result in hearing a piano sound; program change number 26 will always be a jazz guitar, and so on (see Table 4.2 for complete GM program listing). So, GM is not meant for musicians who are looking to put together a MIDI studio, but rather those who wish to distribute or exchange their songs in MIDI format. Every GM device should display the logo found in Figure 4.1 somewhere on the device, or on the packaging if it is software or computer hardware.

Figure 4.1
The General MIDI logo
found on all General
MIDI instruments—
this usually means
that the instrument
complies with all
GM specifications

GENERAL
MIDI

CHAPTER 4

General MIDI Patches

GM's most recognized feature is the defined list of sounds, programs, or patches. However, the GM specification does not specify exactly how a sound should be reproduced. This is still left to the manufacturer's discretion. It is important for a manufacturer to create a sound bank that will provide a good quality sound that adheres to this GM standard. This can result in wide variations in performance and quality from the same song data on different GM sound devices. The creators of this standard felt it was important to allow each manufacturer to have its own ideas when it came to picking the exact timbre for each sound in this set of sounds, as long as they provide an acceptable representation of song data written for GM.

You will find in Table 4.1 a list of different instrument families that are identified in the GM specification. In Table 4.2, you will see a list of sounds with their associated program numbers. All GM devices will have these 128 sounds.

Table 4.1
General MIDI program numbers grouped by instrument categories

Program #	Instrument Category	Program #	Instrument Category
1-8	Piano	65-72	Reed
9-16	Chromatic Percussion	73-80	Pipe
17-24	Organ	81-88	Synth Lead
25-32	Guitar	89-96	Synth Pad
33-40	Bass	97-104	Synth Effects
41-48	Strings	105-112	Ethnic
49-56	Ensemble	113-120	Percussive
57-64	Brass	121-128	Sound Effects

Table 4.2
General MIDI's 128 program names with their associated program numbers, also grouped
by instrument categories

Program #	Instrument	Program #	Instrument
	Pianos		**Organs**
1	Acoustic Grand Piano	17	Drawbar Organ
2	Bright Acoustic Piano	18	Percussive Organ
3	Electric Grand Piano	19	Rock Organ
4	Honky-Tonk Piano	20	Church Organ
5	Electric Piano 1	21	Reed Organ
6	Electric Piano 2	22	Accordion
7	Harpsichord	23	Harmonica
8	Clavinet	24	Tango Accordion
	Chromatic Percussion		**Guitars**
9	Celesta	25	Acoustic Guitar (nylon)
10	Glockenspiel	26	Acoustic Guitar (steel)
11	Music Box	27	Electric Guitar (jazz)
12	Vibraphone	28	Electric Guitar (clean)
13	Marimba	29	Electric Guitar (muted)
14	Xylophone	30	Overdriven Guitar
15	Tubular Bells	31	Distortion Guitar
16	Dulcimer	32	Guitar Harmonics

Program #	Instrument	Program #	Instrument
	Basses		**Brass**
33	Acoustic Bass	57	Trumpet
34	Electric Bass (finger)	58	Trombone
35	Electric Bass (pick)	59	Tuba
36	Fretless Bass	60	Muted Trumpet
37	Slap Bass 1	61	French Horn
38	Slap Bass 2	62	Brass Section
39	Synth Bass 1	63	SynthBrass 1
40	Synth Bass 2	64	SynthBrass 2
	Strings		**Reed**
41	Violin	65	Soprano Sax
42	Viola	66	Alto Sax
43	Cello	67	Tenor Sax
44	Contrabass	68	Baritone Sax
45	Tremolo Strings	69	Oboe
46	Pizzicato Strings	70	English Horn
47	Orchestral Harp	71	Bassoon
48	Timpani	72	Clarinet
Ensemble			**Pipe**
49	String Ensemble 1	73	Piccolo
50	String Ensemble 2	74	Flute
51	SynthStrings 1	75	Recorder
52	SynthStrings 2	76	Pan Flute
53	Choir Aahs	77	Blown Bottle
54	Voice Oohs	78	Skakuhachi
55	Synth Voice	79	Whistle
56	Orchestra Hit	80	Ocarina

Program #	Instrument	Program #	Instrument
	Synth Lead		**Ethnic**
81	Lead 1 (square)	105	Sitar
82	Lead 2 (sawtooth)	106	Banjo
83	Lead 3 (calliope)	107	Shamisen
84	Lead 4 (chiff)	108	Koto
85	Lead 5 (charang)	109	Kalimba
86	Lead 6 (voice)	110	Bagpipe
87	Lead 7 (fifths)	111	Fiddle
88	Lead 8 (bass+lead)	112	Shanai
	Synth Pad		**Percussive**
89	Pad 1 (new age)	113	Tinkle Bell
90	Pad 2 (warm)	114	Agogo
91	Pad 3 (polysynth)	115	Steel Drums
92	Pad 4 (choir)	116	Woodblock
93	Pad 5 (bowed)	117	Taiko Drum
94	Pad 6 (metallic)	118	Melodic Tom
95	Pad 7 (halo)	119	Synth Drum
96	Pad 8 (sweep)	120	Reverse Cymbal
	Synth Effects		**Sound Effects**
97	FX 1 (rain)	121	Guitar Fret Noise
98	FX 2 (soundtrack)	122	Breath Noise
99	FX 3 (crystal)	123	Seashore
100	FX 4 (atmosphere)	124	Bird Tweet
101	FX 5 (brightness)	125	Telephone Ring
102	FX 6 (goblins)	126	Helicopter
103	FX 7 (echoes)	127	Applause
104	FX 8 (sci-fi)	128	Gunshot

Multi-Timbral Capability

To make sure you can hear all parts in a MIDI sequence properly, the GM also provides multi-timbral capability definitions. This means that any GM device should allow you to play and record sixteen MIDI channels simultaneously, with each channel potentially playing a variable number of polyphonic voices. This might be different from one model to another, but a minimum number of polyphonic voices have been set, which is described in the following paragraphs. Each channel can also be set to play a different instrument or program (sound, patch, or timbre, depending on the sound module's convention).

Since MIDI sequences often use percussions or rhythmic parts, MIDI channel 10 in the GM specification is reserved especially for this. In other words, you can't assign a bass sound to this channel, since it will always be dedicated to the percussion sounds as defined above in Table 4.3.

All sixteen MIDI channels are supported. Each channel can play a variable number of voices (polyphony). Each channel can play a different instrument (sound/patch/timbre). Key-based percussion is always on MIDI channel 10.

GM Note Numbers

Note numbers were described in Chapter 2. To make sure the pitch of all GM instruments refer to the same pitch values when it comes to note numbers, the GM specification designates that the A-440 pitch is note number 69 This makes every sound relate to that pitch when a note number is sent through MIDI. In non-GM compatible devices, for example, you might play a melodic part in a high range and would find it was playing an octave higher or lower on another module. This is due to manufacturers that would map middle C on note number 48 or 72, rather than on 60. With GM defining the A-440 (Hz) pitch or the note number 69, middle C will always be note number 60. Obviously, you can change the octave setting for a sound, making it lower or higher. However, the note number in relation to other sounds will be the same, and the default GM sound bank takes that into consideration.

Drum machines were also problematic, since most of the multi-timbral devices came with a built-in set of percussive sounds such as drum kits and percussion. This can be troublesome when recording a percussion part for your song and having it played by another device. Imagine if your bass drum became a tambourine all of a sudden! It could be interesting, but not what you had in mind.

To address this, GM assigns forty-eight common drum sounds to forty-eight specific MIDI note numbers, as shown in Table 4.3. Using channel 10 and these instruments, a composer can safely assume that a drum/percussion part will play the right instruments when played on another GM compatible device. GM drum sounds are not part of the 128 programs defined in the GM sound bank set, but rather an additional set of sounds specific to the number 10 MIDI channel. These sounds are mapped to note numbers on your keyboard in a single special drum map program, which can only be accessed by using MIDI channel 10.

Table 4.3
The GM drum map

MIDI Note #	Drum Sound	Note Name	MIDI Note #	Drum Sound	Note Name
35	Acoustic Bass Drum	B0	59	Ride Cymbal 2	B2
36	Bass Drum 1	C1	60	Hi Bongo	C3
37	Side Stick	C#1	61	Low Bongo	C#3
38	Acoustic Snare	D1	62	Mute Hi Conga	D3
39	Hand Clap	D#1	63	Open Hi Conga	D#3
40	Electric Snare	E1	64	Low Conga	E3
41	Low Floor Tom	F1	65	High Timbale	F3
42	Closed Hi-Hat	F#1	66	Low Timbale	F#3
43	High Floor Tom	G1	67	High Agogo	G3
44	Pedal Hi-Hat	G#1	68	Low Agogo	G#3
45	Low Tom	A1	69	Cabasa	A3
46	Open Hi-Hat	A#1	70	Maracas	A#3
47	Low-Mid Tom	B1	71	Short Whistle	B3
48	Hi-Mid Tom	C2	72	Long Whistle	C4
49	Crash Cymbal 1	C#2	73	Short Guiro	C#4
50	High Tom	D2	74	Long Guiro	D4
51	Ride Cymbal 1	D#2	75	Claves	D#4
52	Chinese Cymbal	E2	76	Hi Wood Block	E4
53	Ride Bell	F2	77	Low Wood Block	F4
54	Tambourine	F#2	78	Mute Cuica	F#4
55	Splash Cymbal	G2	79	Open Cuica	G4
56	Cowbell	G#2	80	Mute Triangle	G#4
57	Crash Cymbal 2	A2	81	Open Triangle	A4
58	Vibraslap	A#2			

GM Polyphony

Again, to ensure that all notes recorded are played, the GM standard also provides for a minimum number of polyphonic voice assignments. Therefore, every GM device needs to allow for a minimum of sixteen voices that can be assigned to any or all MIDI channels simultaneously and eight voices for percussion alone (which are played on channel 10). These twenty-four voices should also be velocity sensitive.

This is the minimum required by the GM standard. However, many devices such as multi-timbral devices offering GM as a separate bank of sounds may offer more than the required minimum number of voices. This is because GM is, after all, a recommended practice, not a standard dictating the maximum number of polyphonic voices a sound module should offer. For example, the Roland JV-1080 is GM compatible, but offers a sixty-four-voice polyphony. Restricting your polyphony to sixteen voices only provides you with a guideline to follow when writing music that will be distributed using GM devices.

 A good example of this would be a MIDI file on your Web page. Since many users don't have fancy synthesizers or sound cards, chances are they will be using a GM synth built into their sound card. Many of them will offer no more than what the GM requires as a minimum. Remember, you have been warned!!!

Other Supported MIDI Messages

Sound banks, note numbers, and channel assignments for percussions and polyphony are not the only parameters defined by General MIDI. As you saw in chapters 2 and 3, a good portion of what MIDI is lies in its functions. Therefore, GM also provides a set of standard channel message supports to ensure that when you insert volume changes in your original song, for example, they will be reproduced properly. Here are the MIDI messages for which every GM device should respond:

> ▶ Control Change 1: Modulation wheel, which is usually hard-wired to control LFO amount, or in other words, the amount of vibrato.
>
> ▶ Control Change 7: Channel Volume.
>
> ▶ Control Change 10: Pan.
>
> ▶ Control Change 11: Expression, which can be assigned to anything, including aftertouch.
>
> ▶ Control Change 64: Sustain.
>
> ▶ Control Change 121: Reset All Controllers (this is actually a Channel Mode Message).
>
> ▶ Control Change 123: All Notes Off (as with the previous, this is a Channel Mode Message as well).
>
> ▶ Registered Parameter Number 0: Pitch Wheel Bend Sensitivity.
>
> ▶ Registered Parameter Number 1: Fine Tuning.
>
> ▶ Registered Parameter Number 2: Coarse Tuning.

Finally, the GM standard has attempted to standardize further by defining a certain number of features. Here's a list of those features:

▶ Every GM module should respond to velocity; however, what the velocity affects in the sound has not been determined. Typically, this affects the VCA level or volume of each note.

▶ The pitch wheel bend range should default to plus or minus 2 semitones (or half steps). This way, you can save pitch bends in a GM file without worrying whether the bend will be going one octave up and down.

▶ GM modules should also respond to channel pressure, which often determines the VCA level or VCO level for vibrato depth. How exactly it responds to the channel pressure is not determined, so you might hear different effects from device to device when using the same sounds in a GM sound bank.

▶ A GM device should provide a MIDI In, Out, and Thru connector; access to a master volume control; and at least two audio outputs (left and right) with an additional headphone connector.

▶ By default, a GM module should power up with all of its channel volume levels at a default value of 90, its controllers and effects should be off, and it should be tuned to the A-440 reference.

Standard MIDI Files (SMF)

You've just seen how the MIDI specifications were enhanced to allow for greater control over instruments through the standardization of some basic features. The most prevalent use of GM, however, is through the sequences it plays. Recording a sequence means that you lay down a certain number of tracks on a software- or hardware-based sequencer and play back these tracks. This is fine if you keep your files at home and are the only one listening to them. But what if you wanted to bring them into another studio, using different software and a different set of sound modules? Well, for the different set of sound modules, you've got GM, right? But what about the sequences?

That's what Standard MIDI Files (SMFs) are for. This is a protocol that you can use to transfer MIDI information from one type of device to another. In most cases, this would be from one MIDI sequencer to another. You could even take a Standard MIDI File and open it in notation software to polish your score if your MIDI sequencer doesn't support any notation outputs.

What is an SMF?

Standard MIDI Files were added to the MIDI specification in 1988 and use a universal language that saves all MIDI notes, velocities, and controller codes as a generic file that may be interpreted by any program that supports this type of file. OK, so you can't open a Standard MIDI File in your graphic software. Most media players such as QuickTime and Windows Media Players, along with all popular sequencers, will allow you to open this type of file, import it into an existing file, or simply create a file and save it, export it as another type of MIDI file, or save your updated version as a Standard MIDI File.

Most of the time, SMF will use the extension .MID at the end of a document to indicate to the applications installed on your computer that this is a Standard MIDI File.

There are three types of SMF files, which were described in Chapter 1, Table 1.2. Type 0 combines all tracks or staves into a single track. Type 1 will save each part (MIDI channel) on a separate track or stave in a score. It will also save the tempo setting and time signature information included in the first track. However, you can only save one song per file with this type. If you want to save patterns, such as drum patterns, the best type of SMF is Type 2. This allows you to not only save your parts on separate tracks, but also save different tempo and time signature settings—one for each track in your file or, as you can see in Figure 4.2, one for each section (Bar 1, Bar 9, and Bar 21). Note that the most common type of file is probably Type 1, since it is more likely than Type 2 to be compatible with every sequencer. Type 2 is more likely to be used as a way to save a series of drum patterns for a drum machine than it is to save an actual song.

Figure 4.2
Standard MIDI File types

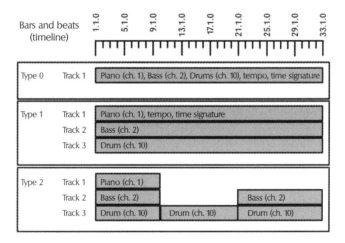

MIDI files don't hold only events such as channel voice messages, channel mode messages, and system messages. They also hold song tempo and tempo changes, time signatures and signature changes, key signatures, text and lyrics, markers, and cue points. Let's not forget time code offsets, which is the time that a song would start at bar 1.1.0 if it were synchronized with a video starting at 09:50:00:00. If you want to start at the first bar of the song, you have to tell the song (through the sequencer sync dialog box) that bar 1.1.0 corresponds to time code 09:50:00:00 rather than time code 00:00:00:00. This is called a time code offset, and it is also saved with your MIDI file.

MIDI files were designed to be generic enough so that any sequencer or MIDI file player could read or write such files without losing the most important data. They are also flexible enough for sequencers to store their own proprietary information into it as extra data. This extra data is organized in such a way that another application won't mistake it for another type of file, but will rather ignore any information it doesn't need and continue loading it into memory.

 Think of it this way: You can type a letter in a text editor, such as Notepad, for instance, or you can type a letter in Word or Word Perfect. Both files will contain text; however, the former contains only text and the latter may also contain formatting, pictures, links, and page layout. MIDI files are similar to ASCII text files in this sense. All the rest of the formatting, pictures, links, and page layout are things that, in comparison to word processors, sequencers will add to a MIDI file in a form that only the sequencer that saved the information will be able to recognize. Instead of text formatting, sequencers save things like automation of control changes that are not supported in MIDI files, or structural information used by the sequencer itself. It does this by inserting a flag byte to indicate certain user settings, like a metronome click, for example. Another application would simply skip this flag byte since it doesn't understand it.

Differences with Audio Files

Why bother with General MIDI if it doesn't allow you to create your own sounds and is limited to 128 sounds from which to choose? As mentioned above, GM is not meant as a creative tool for the working composer/musician, but rather as a way to better distribute MIDI content over a wide network while ensuring a certain level of compatibility and quality throughout different MIDI systems.

GM also opened up markets for the distribution of commercial sequences and karaoke songs. You don't need to know how a sequencer works or how MIDI works to use GM, since it is part of the MIDI specifications of most computers today. So, loading these songs is easily done and, because of its specifications, the makers of these sequences can be sure everybody will hear the songs properly. You can also use ready-made sequences to practice songs without having a band in your living room by simply deactivating the MIDI channel in a GM compliant sequence, thus creating a great educational tool.

With the rise of the Internet's popularity, being able to download music quickly with even the slowest modem has been a major hassle. The GM specification offers a simple, standard way to easily and quickly distribute songs over a network of computers. Let's take a three-minute MIDI file containing J.S. Bach's Prelude & Fugue no.1. The whole content of the file will take up approximately 30 Kb, whereas the same song as a CD-audio quality wav file would take around 31,007 Kb. That's 1,000 times the size of its MIDI equivalent. Even with MP3 compression being very popular, to keep a decent quality, you would still end up with a file around 100 times (about 3,000 Kb) the size of a MIDI file (*.MID). That's because MIDI stores events, as seen in Figure 4.3's top section. These events take very little space, whereas digital audio stores data at a rate of 44,100 samples per second, per channel. It does so in order to be able to reproduce an audio waveform as it was recorded (see bottom half of the same figure).

Figure 4.3
Comparing the content
of a MIDI file and an
audio file

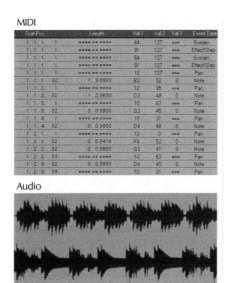

Another difference between MIDI files and audio files is that you can easily change the pitch of a song in a MIDI file if you are using it as a practice tool and wish to adjust the song to your range. With audio, you need specialized software to change the pitch. And, most of the time you have no way of changing only what you need to change, such as pitch sensitive instruments, since changing the pitch of percussive instruments is not desired. Another advantage of MIDI over audio is that you can slow down or speed up the tempo in a MIDI file to fit your needs. If you're working on a solo for a new song your band will be covering, you can slow down the tempo to get all the notes right, then speed it back up when you feel comfortable. With audio, once again, to do this you would need special software or see the pitch change as you play the samples quicker or slower.

However, if you are trying to get a special sound with creative effects or sound design, MIDI files, especially those using GM sound banks, are probably not what you are looking for. Another drawback of MIDI files with GM devices is that, despite recent advances in sound banks, you can't really predict how well the sound module will reproduce your music on someone else's computer. There are still plenty of people running their computers with low quality sound cards with low quality GM sound banks. So, if you want to have full control over the output of your files, you will need to reconsider the use of MIDI files and GM sound banks.

Extending the General MIDI Standard

When GM came out, some companies felt that it didn't go far enough and that it was too limited in terms of sound banks. They also felt that GM didn't offer enough control over sounds themselves through MIDI. So, two of those companies came out with their own versions of General MIDI—both of which offer an extended version of the GM standard. Roland called it the GS Standard and Yamaha called it the XG standard. GS and XG are supersets of the GM standard (see Figure 4.4), offering full backward compatibility with GM and offering more sounds (over 1,000 in some cases) and control over sound parameters. If you don't own any Roland GS compatible or Yamaha XG compatible devices, this will not be relevant to you, since these functions are usually available on Roland or Yamaha gear. However, many sound card manufacturers have adopted these extended parameters in order to allow both GM compatibility and added value to their product. QuickTime, for example, offers a GS sound bank rather than the basic GM sound bank when its MIDI player options are selected.

Figure 4.4
The GS and XG standard are both offering GM compatibility, but propose an additional set of proprietary features

Roland GS Standard

The GS Standard developed by Roland obeys in every way the General MIDI specification and adds many extra controllers and sounds. Some of these controllers use NRPN to give macro control over a synthesizer's parameters, such as the envelope attack and decay rates. It also offers additional sound banks, which includes variations on the GM sound bank and recreations of Roland's famous MT-32 sound module.

The programs in each bank are mapped the same way as a GM instrument patch map would: 128 sounds divided into eight families of sounds. In the GS Standard, if the module receives a request for a bank or program number combination that does not exist, the module will reassign it to the master instrument in that family. So if you use a GS module to create your song, extra information is written in the System Exclusive (SysEx) message to specify that this file contains GS messages. System Exclusive allows MIDI to communicate parameter settings to your MIDI device that are not covered in other MIDI messages. SysEx messages are described in greater detail in Chapter 11. If the GM device doesn't support these extra features, it will simply ignore them and play the sequence as if it was recorded as a GM file. However, a GS module would play the file containing extra GS messages, using its alternative sound banks.

Like GM modules, Roland uses a special logo to identify GS Standard devices, as shown in Figure 4.5.

Figure 4.5
The Roland GS Standard logo certifying that the device is GS compatible

Yamaha XG Standard

As with Roland GS, Yamaha came up with its own version of an enhanced GM, which is, again, a superset of parameters that make any MIDI file developed for GM compatible with an XG device. What Yamaha proposes is a larger number of sound banks, more voice editing capability, integrated effects, and external inputs that will allow you to connect an audio device—such as a guitar, bass, or microphone—and process the sound using the integrated effects.

The XG Standard provides a minimum of 480 sounds instead of the 128 provided with GM, and will allow you to upgrade the device up to two million sounds. It addresses these sounds by using the control change numbers 0 and 32 (Bank Select MSB and LSB controllers), which enables you to choose a program and bank from this large number of sounds. The default set of sounds provided with an XG module is divided into four defined banks and a set of undefined banks for further upgrades. The four banks are as follows:

▶ Melody Voices: the default GM set of sounds and other sounds divided into sound banks.

▶ SFX Voices: a set of sound effects.

▶ SFX Kits: two sets of sound effects, with each effect assigned to a different key on a controller keyboard.

▶ Rhythm Kits: a selection of nine drum kits and percussion (this defaults to channel 10 as with GM. However, with XG you can have rhythm parts on other channels as well).

The XG format also re-interprets some of the control change numbers already assigned to voice editing parameters to allow greater control over the timbre of a sound. For example, the brightness parameter (control change number 74) controls the cutoff frequency in a filter, and some NRPN (Non-Registered Parameter Number found in control changes) numbers are used to control manufacturer specific parameters (Yamaha being the manufacturer in this case). One of the XG efforts has been to give greater realism to sounds by providing control over how a sound reacts to velocity. This is achieved by using velocity sensitive low-pass filters. You see, when you play softly, the sound is often duller, and when you play hard, the sound is often brighter (see Figure 4.6).

Figure 4.6
When a cutoff frequency changes, it affects the brightness of a sound by reducing the amplitude (volume) of the frequencies above the cutoff frequency

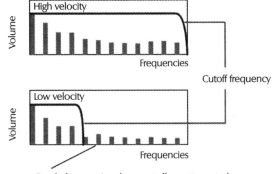

Result: frequencies above cutoff are attenuated

Another feature of the XG Standard is that it offers integrated effects that give you more control over the sound's timbre and presence of your XG compatible MIDI sound module. In other words, these effects are for MIDI sounds, not audio. Among those effects, you will find reverbs (with different room types), choruses, and a minimum of thirty-five different effects combinations such as rotary speaker effects, tremolo, amplifier simulators, and others. Each of these effects can be inserted on a part (voice, or channel) or on the overall mix as a system effect (see Figure 4.7).

Figure 4.7
The routing of effects on an XG device acts in the same way as a mixer—you can assign some effects to all the parts, and others as inserts to add effects to specific MIDI parts

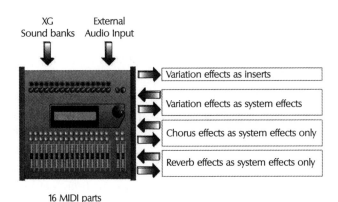

16 MIDI parts

Finally, XG compatible devices also provide audio inputs, which allow users to use their MIDI device as a sound effect processor. Since every XG compatible device works with an integrated digital mixer, you can control the amount of effect you wish to add to an audio source in the same way as you would with a MIDI sound coming from the XG sound bank. You could play a GM version of your favorite song, plug in a microphone, add some reverb on the microphone, and voila! You have your own karaoke machine!

As with GM and GS, XG devices will usually display an XG logo (see Figure 4.8), which tells you if the device adheres to the XG specification.

Figure 4.8
The Yamaha XG logo

5

MIDI Hardware Devices

A musician's ability to recognize the various types of MIDI devices that are available is important for several reasons. First, MIDI devices can be expensive, so buying the device best suited to your needs will save you money. Second, once you've bought these devices, you will want to know how to get them all talking to each other in the most efficient way. Knowing how to do this and making the right choices will help you achieve a successful MIDI studio setup.

Here's a summary of what you will learn in this chapter:

▶ What the different types of sound generators are.

▶ What the different types of MIDI controllers are.

▶ What a patch bay is and how you can use it.

▶ How to optimize a live performance MIDI setup.

▶ How to configure your MIDI studio setup without the use of a computer.

First, we will discuss different MIDI devices that make up a MIDI studio. We initially will focus our attention on hardware rather than software, which will be covered in subsequent chapters. However, the principles shown here are often used in a software environment as well.

Later in the chapter, we will consider some sample MIDI configurations for specific setup situations.

MIDI Devices

MIDI devices come in all shapes, sizes, and forms. They are hardware tools that allow you to control how and when MIDI information is sent from one device to another. Understanding what these devices do and what is available is important when planning your own MIDI setup: deciding which type of sound generator you need, how you can control or send information to these devices using controllers, and how you can integrate these elements into a unit.

Sound Generators

Sound generators are devices that produce sounds. That sounds pretty simple, doesn't it? That's because it is, and furthermore, without them, there would be no point in recording MIDI sequences. You see, among the MIDI devices, sound generators are responsible for the actual sound you hear when you play a MIDI sequence. Unlike digital audio recording, MIDI doesn't record the sound, so sound generators (or sound modules) are necessary to reproduce the audio generated by the MIDI messages you record.

Sound generators come in many shapes and forms, and produce sounds in different ways using different types of technologies to achieve the same goal: generating sounds. When building a MIDI studio, choosing which sound generator you use should play an important part in your planning decisions, since their cost and capability vary widely. One fact remains: The type of sound they generate will directly influence how your music will sound, since every sound module has its own colors and textures. For starters, we are going to take a look at the hardware version of sound generators. We will discuss different virtual sound generators (software-based synthesizers) later in the book (see Chapter 9).

Synthesizers & Sound Modules

Synthesizers create, or synthesize, sounds in an artificial fashion, using different sound elements, such as simple and complex waveforms. Synthesizers produce their sounds through the use of oscillators, voltage-control amplifiers, and filters. Some synthesizers also make use of waveforms—digital samples of real instruments—in combination with oscillators, amplifiers, and filters. Today's synthesizers are capable of generating almost every kind of sound. Synthesizers are usually presented in two forms: as keyboard units or as rack-mounted devices that are often called sound modules. Sounds modules don't have keyboards; instead, they are controlled (i.e., triggered) only via MIDI information sent from a separate keyboard or a computer. Sound modules have the same processing power as a synthesizer with its own keyboard, but they are less expensive than full-blown synthesizers. There are many types of synthesizers on the market. But there are a far greater number of synthesis techniques that synthesizers may use to create sounds than there are synthesizer types. Here are the primary types of synthesizers:

▶ Modular Analog Synthesizer: Earlier types of synthesizers were not like today's synthesizers—they were not built as a single unit device, but rather as individual interconnected boxes that each contained certain types of circuitry (see Figure 5.1). Boxes were connected to one another in order to expand the circuitry's capability. One box contained a signal-creating device, such as a voltage-controlled oscillator (or VCO) or a noise generator; another box might then process the signal from the first box with voltage-controlled filters (VCF) or voltage-controlled amplifiers (VCA). These modules were often huge, and since they were built-in modules (hence the name modular synthesis), they were linked together with patch cables, acting as routing cords. Today, analog modular synthesizers are becoming popular once again because of the warmth and richness of their sound. Some even come with adapter boxes that convert MIDI into Control Voltage (CV), which lets you determine the pitch of a note (see Figure 5.2).

Figure 5.1
The Roland System 700, a perfect example of the early days of modular synthesizers700 (photo courtesy of Kevin Lightner, www.sonicstate.com/synthfool)

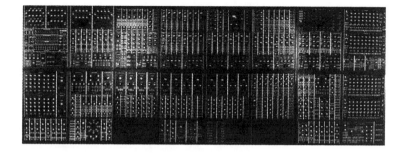

Figure 5.2
The MOTM from Synthesis Technology comes as a kit (each module is an option, including the MIDI to CV converter)— you can find more information on this at www.synthtech.com/motm. Dave Bradley assembled this particular module (www.hotrodmotm.com) using different MOTM modules, just like building a kit car; the MIDI to CV converter appears in the bottom left corner of this module

▶ Self-contained Analog Synthesizer: These synthesizers use the same technology as modular synthesizers, with the exception that they are already prewired—so no need for cables. These synthesizers will generally have an analog-style look to them, with banks of knobs that control oscillators, filters, voltage controls, and other components their front panel. True analog synthesizers are not as common as they used to be, since many of the analog components have been replaced by digital ones, and instead of true analog oscillators (the sound-generating component), synthesizers often use digitized waveforms. But music being what it is, trends have a tendency to reappear, which is why analog-sounding instruments are making a resurgence in music stores everywhere (see Figure 5.3).

Figure 5.3
The Alesis A6
Andromeda is a good
example of true analog
synthesis currently on
the market (picture
courtesy of Alesis,
www.alesis.com)

▶ Digital Synthesizer: In this type of synthesizer, the whole process usually stays in the digital domain. Even their source material is digital (usually digital waveforms reproduced by a sample-playback component inside the device). The end result is that a digital synth can often emulate natural timbres more realistically than its analog counterpart, although some argue that digital synthesizers sound colder or harsher than their analog counterparts. Other digital synthesizers use a strictly digital synthesis method to generate sounds rather than using samples. This is the case with the Yamaha DX-7 (shown in Chapter 1). The Roland D-50, on the other hand, allows users to choose either short PCM samples (see sample-playback synthesizers below) or digitally generated waveforms. A true digital synthesizer is one where all sound generation and manipulation happens in the digital domain, and not simply "digitally controlled" as many self-contained analog synthesizers may be (see above).

▶ Sample-Playback Synthesizer: This is probably the most common type of synthesizer in use today (see Figure 5.4). These synthesizers contain samples stored onboard in ROM chips in the form of PCM (Pulse Code Modulation). Many manufacturers also call these "wavetables." Wavetables may be sampled sounds originating from real instruments or synthesized tones such as sine, square, or sawtooth waves. The wavetables are then processed through various filters and envelopes to give you a whole range of sounds. This type of synthesizer has many advantages: It's versatile, cheap, usually offers a good number of sound banks (programs or presets), has a good number of polyphonic voices, and is easy to use. Many sample-playback synthesizers also include built-in sequencers and effects, which qualifies them as workstations.

Figure 5.4
Two examples of
sample-playback
synthesizers. On top,
you can see the EMU
PK-6 synthesizer with
keyboard controller, and
on the bottom, the EMU
Proteus 2000 rack-
mounted sound module

▶ Physical Modeling Synthesizer: This type of synthesizer emerged in the 90s and is becoming quite a trendsetter. Physical modeling uses software code to produce the sound instead of the usual hardware technique (see Figure 5.5). In other words, it implies that the software code is responsible for the analysis of parameter settings and the subsequent implementation of these settings while generating the actual sound. This type of synthesizer is usually very effective at emulating very complex vibrations, resonance, reflections, and other acoustic phenomena that occur in a real wind or string instrument. You can find this type of synthesizer design in software format as well, since it is so close to the computer in the way it approaches sound.

Figure 5.5
The Yamaha EX5 is an example of a synthesizer that uses physical modeling to produce its sounds

Samplers

Samplers are like sample-based synthesizers, with one very important difference: You can record your own sounds into them to create new programs. In this respect, a sampler is more flexible than its sample-playback counterpart. The disadvantage of a sampler over a sample-playback device is that it is, in general, more expensive and requires greater programming skills since you are the one creating sound banks. On the other hand, many companies specialize in the creation of sound banks for specific models of samplers (such as the Roland S-700 series or the Akai S series sampler, as illustrated in Figure 5.6).

What a sampler typically does is quite simple: It reproduces recorded sounds at a variable frequency that corresponds to the note you play. So, if you've sampled a guitar playing a single note, let's say a G4, you can assign this note to the corresponding G4 key on the keyboard's layout of your sampler. If your sampler does not have a keyboard, then a special key zone mapping window will provide the equivalent of a keyboard where you can place this note. Then, you record another sample on another pitch, let's say a B4 this time, and assign it to that note on your keyboard layout in the sampler's editing window, and so on.

After you've recorded as many samples as you need (usually, this is limited to 128 samples per program or preset), and you've mapped all these sounds to keys on your keyboard, you can play your new guitar program using your keyboard instead of the guitar used for the sampling. This technique is often referred to as multi-sampling, where an instrument is recreated by using multiple samples of its sound over the range of this instrument. This allows for a more realistic result in the end, since the sampler only has to extrapolate the audio sample over a narrow range of keys. In other words, the more samples you have the better the end result will be, especially with acoustic instruments, since our ears are used to hearing these instruments. Furthermore, pitch-shifting a sampled sound over a wide range on a keyboard will result in unnatural artifacts appearing in the sound when played. For example, if you take our original sampled guitar, with its recorded pitch of G4, and play this sample by pressing a G2, the sampler will play the sample at roughly twenty-five percent of its original sampling rate. If you have ever tried this, you will quickly realize that the quality of a sample at 11 KHz is not quite up to par with a sample at 44.1 KHz.

Samplers also use loops in the sound to save on memory used to play back these sounds. Since memory is a big factor in the cost of the instrument, the more memory you use for a sound, the less sounds you will have. Programming loops, at this point, becomes very important if you want to be able to load more than one sound at a time in your sampler.

Just like other synths, samplers offer different types of sound processing features, such as envelopes, filters, frequency oscillators, and others. All these features give you more control over the quality of the sound.

Figure 5.6
The Akai S-6000
sampler—as you can
see, this version of the
device can be rack-
mounted on a 19" rack
and does not contain a
keyboard controller

Because computers have large RAM memories and huge hard disk capability, and because chances are you might already own one, there is a growing number of software developers working hard to bring you a software version of what samplers do. This means you don't necessarily need to buy a sampler to do sampling anymore. However, be aware that using your computer as a sampler implies that a large portion of your RAM will be needed to run the sampler program and that your hard disk will need to be fast enough to read the information on it. This is especially true if you are planning to use a sampler software application simultaneously with a MIDI/audio sequencer for recording and playback.

Drum Machines

This name is usually reserved for synthesizers or sample-playback devices that contain drum or percussion sounds in them. Although some drum machines expand on this definition, the purpose of this type of device is to create drum or percussion tracks. Drum machines often have internal sequencers, allowing you to program drum songs and drum patterns for later use (see Figure 5.7). Instead of using the typical keyboard layout, drum machines will often use buttons, trigger pads, or, in some cases, electronic drum kits to control the sounds they hold. Since drum machines hold mostly drum sounds, the sequences you record in them are limited to playing rhythmic parts.

Figure 5.7
The Boss DR-770
drum machine

Earlier drum machines used analog synthesis to create sounds, but today most drum machines use digital samples. Certain models will even allow you to load sounds into memory so that you can configure your drum machine to play different drum kits. Better drum machines (see Figure 5.10) have touch-sensitive pads so that they can transmit velocity information through MIDI cables as well as Note On messages that correspond to the different pads or controllers triggering the sounds.

Workstations

Workstations are like synthesizers or samplers (sometimes a combination of both), but besides their sound generating abilities they also offer built-in sequencing features that allow you to record MIDI parts on different tracks and play them back using the multi-timbral capability these workstations offer. Think of a workstation as a self-contained music production device (see Figure 5.8). Many workstations also have built-in effects that you can add to the sounds it produces. Finally, a storage device is often provided with workstations so that you can store your sequences when the internal memory is full or when you wish to use these sequences later.

Figure 5.8
The Korg Karma
is an example of a
workstation, which
includes a sample-
playback sound module,
a sequencer, effects,
and various controllers

CHAPTER 5

MIDI Enabling Devices

MIDI enabling devices allow you to create MIDI data. As such, they produce MIDI data that can be played or recorded using other MIDI enabling devices, like a link in a chain. Their main purpose, however, is not to generate sounds that this MIDI data produces. MIDI enabling devices are input devices or interfaces that allow you to modify MIDI data. Some devices included in this section are typical audio related devices, but they all have one thing in common: They respond to MIDI messages. Because of this, you can use these devices in a MIDI setup, and with the help of a sequencer, for example, you can control them using MIDI messages. An example of this would be a MIDI enabled sound effect processor, to which you can send program change messages in order to change a reverb setting, or a MIDI enabled mixer that you can use as a controller to automate your mix, recording every single move you make on the mixer through a series of MIDI messages over different MIDI channels. The possibilities are vast, since the range of MIDI enabling devices is quite wide.

Controller Keyboards

MIDI keyboard controllers are devices that allow you to use a keyboard to trigger MIDI messages, but the controllers don't come with the heavy sound-generating artillery most synthesizers offer. On the other hand, if your synthesizer is mounted to a keyboard and you use this to play or record MIDI into a sequencer, for example, you would probably consider this as a controller keyboard. The point is that any type of keyboard can be used as a controller keyboard; however, some keyboards are manufactured to do just that. Their key action is reminiscent of a piano key action and they will have up to an 88-key keyboard layout. On the other end of the spectrum, you might also find small controller keyboards that hook up to your computer through a USB connection, allowing you to input MIDI data into your software sequencer and generate sound modules. This type of controller usually offers a small keyboard range and no internal sounds. In any case, controller keyboards will rarely offer anything more than a GM compatible sound bank, which is not enough to call them synthesizers because the GM standard offers a very limited sound editing capability.

For a pianist, the best controller keyboards have more realistic piano action (see Figure 5.9), making them more sensitive to every nuance of a performance.

Figure 5.9
The Yamaha P80 is an 88-note controller keyboard with graded hammer action, which provides a more realistic piano action than most regular synthesizers; however, its sound bank is quite limited

Other Types of MIDI Controllers

Keyboards are not the only MIDI controllers. In fact, there is a MIDI controller for almost every instrument family (strings, winds, percussions, in addition to keyboards).

If you are a drummer, and unaccustomed to playing a keyboard, using one to play drum parts will likely be difficult for you. Figure 5.10 shows an alternative. Drum controllers are similar to real drums, with one big difference: They don't make much sound on their own. Each piece of this drum set is nothing more than a velocity sensitive MIDI pad that sends Note On events to a sound module (seen at the left in the picture). Using MIDI language, these events can also be transmitted to an external sequencer to record a performance just as you would with a real drummer. Only in this case, what you record is just the performance's MIDI events, not the sounds coming from the drum kit itself. You could assign any number of sounds to each individual piece in the drum kit later on.

Figure 5.10
The Roland V-Session drum set is a sophisticated drum machine geared for drummers rather than keyboardists

Figure 5.11 shows another example of a percussion-oriented MIDI controller. When hit with a drumstick, each portion of the pad can trigger up to eight different samples coming from a sound module. Both these controllers offer different features that make them more than just note triggers, but the principle behind both of them is the same: to allow a musician to record his/her MIDI performances through an input device.

Figure 5.11
The drumKAT Turbo 2000 from Alternate Mode
(www.alternatemode.com)

CHAPTER 5

Another type of controller is the MIDI guitar. This presents a more complex problem, since guitar strings produce complex vibrations, and quite often the harmonics produced between the strings to create a rich guitar sound can blur the pitch, making it difficult to convert the audio signal into a Note On message with its proper note number. Different techniques have been introduced to solve this problem. One of them is to replace the actual strings with a series of string-like rubber triggers that the guitar player plucks just as he/she would with real strings. The position of the hand on the neck of the guitar and the trigger itself would then convey the proper note number to a MIDI out on the guitar controller. Another technique consists of adding a special kind of converter/pick-up on the guitar (see Figure 5.12) that analyzes the content of the audio to determine the actual pitch of the note.

Figure 5.12
The Ztar Model Z6 (top) and Z6-S (bottom) from Starr Labs (www.starrlabs.com) comes with either rubber strumbars (top) or string triggers (bottom) with pickups

The MIDI wind controller, as shown in Figure 5.13, was designed to be played like a woodwind instrument but sound like anything that could be generated by a sound module. It will allow experienced wind players a great deal of expressive control over sounds generated by sound modules, since it uses different MIDI control change parameters in real time, just as a real woodwind instrument. By translating the player's breath and lip pressure to MIDI data via high-resolution wind and pressure sensors, it can convert air pressure into aftertouch data to modify the tonal quality of the sound. Just as with MIDI drum or guitar controllers, MIDI wind controllers require a certain amount of familiarity with this type of instrument. For example, knowing either saxophone or flute fingering will help your performance.

Figure 5.13
The Yamaha WX5 wind controller (www.yamaha.com)

Another type of MIDI controller, but a nonmusical one this time, consists of devices that offer you tactile control over MIDI parameters such as volume, pan, or any other type of MIDI messages, rather than using a software interface to do so (see Figure 5.14). For example, mixing multiple tracks, using only your mouse to change the volume of several MIDI instruments at once, can be difficult since you can only point and click on one "virtual" fader at a time on a computer screen. Using an "outboard" MIDI control device can provide an economical solution to MIDI automation when working on mixes in collaboration with a MIDI sequencer, since you can record and program (through a software interface) what each physical controller does in your MIDI sequence as another MIDI track. We'll get more into the mixing aspect of MIDI when discussing MIDI sequencers in Chapter 8 and in the section called "MIDI Enabled Mixers" later in this chapter.

Figure 5.14
The FaderMaster Pro from JL Cooper (www.jlcooper.com) allows you to control MIDI parameters by sending MIDI messages to your sequencer

Hardware Sequencers

If you ever wanted to play with an orchestra or a band, but thought it would be too expensive, and figured that a computer would be too big to carry around while you do your thing, hardware sequencers might be just what you were looking for. This said, hardware sequencers are rarely used anymore, since many synthesizers come as workstations, combining the sound-generating capabilities of a synthesizer or sampler with the recording power of a hardware sequencer.

A hardware sequencer is a stand-alone device that allows you to record MIDI performances in two ways: in step recording mode and in realtime mode. The former is similar to the first generation of sequencers, in which a grid of equally spaced events called steps served as a blank slate for your sequence. Take, for example a thirty-two-step sequence. This might correspond to thirty-two sixteenth notes. You play a note on your keyboard to record it into your sequencer, which advances to the next sixteenth note. Some step sequencers will also record this note with its velocity value, while others, in older models, would not. Playing a second note would make the sequencer advance to the third step, and so on. A special key would allow you to advance a step without adding a note to create a silence or create a rhythmic pattern by alternating notes and silences. Note that some step sequencers would even let you record chords when notes are played simultaneously. When you reach the last step in your sequence, you could then play back the sequence at a desired tempo, just as you would play a drum pattern or a music loop.

The real-time sequencer—or simply known as a sequencer, since it is the most widely known form of sequencing today—allows you to record notes using an incoming MIDI stream. The sequencer (see Figure 5.15) usually uses a standard MIDI file format to store MIDI performances; any MIDI message supported by this type of file will be preserved in the MIDI sequence. We'll talk more about how to work with sequencers later in the book.

Figure 5.15
The Roland MC-80
Micro Composer
(www.roland.co.jp/worl
dwide/products/MI/seq
uencers_and_sound_mo
dules/MC-80.html)
is a good example of a
stand-alone hardware
sequencer

MIDI Enabled Mixers

Since multitrack audio technology was introduced, mixing engineers have dealt with the daunting task of handling volume levels, effects, panning, groupings, equalization settings, and an ever growing number of parameters in real-time. Since the majority of us humans have only two hands and ten fingers, there's just so much we can do simultaneously. That's why mixing automation was such a welcomed feature in large mixers: It gave a mixing engineer the ability to record level changes he/she made to a mix during various "practice" passes, so that when it was time to record the final mix, the automation took over and handled all the fader level changes that had been programmed into the mixer. Mixing twenty-four tracks with effects had become manageable—and fun to watch, as the faders moved of their own accord during mixdown. However, motorized faders are not cheap. Eventually, though, luckily for us, MIDI turned out to be the perfect mate for the job.

A MIDI enabled mixer in today's world is a mixer that connects to a MIDI system using MIDI In, Out, and Thru ports, allowing you to send and receive MIDI messages that control different mixer parameters, such as input volume, panning, auxiliary send levels, and so on, thus automating your mix through a series of manufacturer-specific MIDI messages. This doesn't necessarily mean that it uses special messages, but rather assigns different control change numbers or SysEx parameters to control the manufacturer specific parameters. Here's a look at some common MIDI controllable parameters in a typical MIDI enabled mixer:

▶ Program Change messages—can recall entire scenes or mixer setup, just as you would recall a program on a synthesizer or a reverb setting on a multi-processor device. With a single program change, you can recall volume, group, pan, effect, routing, and any other parameter included in a specific mixer device. What exactly it recalls is manufacturer specific, so you might have to consult your mixer's manual to find out how this works.

▶ Control Change parameter controls—allow you to map certain control change messages to certain parameters on your mixer. For example, Control Change number 1, normally used for the modulation wheel, would affect the fader position on the input number 1 on your mixer. Again, this is not a rule, but rather manufacturer specific.

▶ System Exclusive parameter controls—allow you to save as SysEx transmission different parameter settings such as effect, EQ, and dynamic library presets.

▶ System Exclusive bulk dump—allows you to transfer an entire set of memories, settings, and parameters contained in a mixer's memory. Using this type of MIDI transfer, you can save everything your MIDI enabled mixer has in its memory for future use. We will discuss how to do bulk dumps later, in Chapter 11.

▶ MIDI Machine Control—(MMC) is a standard protocol that allows you to control MMC-enabled tape recorders and other devices. In other words, you can control the usual Play, Stop, Rewind, Fast Forward, Record, and Pause buttons directly from assigned keys on your mixer and also save specific locations on a tape and recall these locations later from your mixer.

▶ Local Control—just as with synthesizers and samplers, the control surface of the mixer and the actual values held by parameters inside the mixer are separate. You can set the local control to On or Off when using your mixer in a MIDI setup. This will allow you to record automation into a sequencer, for example, and have the sequencer send the MIDI messages back to the mixer instead of having both the sequencer and the mixer controls trying to control mixer's parameters. This would result in some MIDI data being doubled, causing the mixer to jam or stop responding since the flow of MIDI would become greater than what it can handle.

Many sequencer software developers offer tools that allow users to recreate MIDI devices such as a MIDI mixer inside their software environment. This allows you to place icons representing MIDI enabled controllers and later associate these virtual controllers with their physical counterparts using MIDI messages. Once the icon in your software is programmed to affect a certain parameter in your external device, like a mixer's input volume control, for example, you can control the position of the mixer's fader from the software's interface. This has the advantage of showing you what values have been recorded through MIDI, since most MIDI enabled mixers have very small LCD displays and cannot show all this information simultaneously. In Figure 5.16, you can find an example of this software representation in Tascam's TM-D1000 mixer. The top window shows the Cakewalk version (PC) of the Tascam TM-D1000 mixer, and the lower window shows Emagic's Logic version (Mac) of the same mixer. In most cases, you can search the sequencer's Web site to find out if your mixer setup can be downloaded and used inside your sequencer, or you can create your own mixer setup by building it from scratch using the tools provided by your preferred sequencer software.

Note that it is probably easier to control your mixer directly, since it offers a more tactile environment than a simple mouse. However, these virtual reproductions will allow you to monitor glitches or errors in your mix, and edit later on your recorded MIDI data to repair or change events you think are not right.

For example, if you record some mixer automation using tactile controls (through the actual mixer), but when monitoring, you find that the volume level on one of your inputs seems to be going up and down rapidly, you might not notice this change on the mixer due to the slow response speed of the motorized fader. Or, worse yet, this might simply be a parameter that is hidden away in an LCD screen four layers deep. The software reproduction of your mixer inside the sequencer might offer a clue as to what is being controlled or what has been recorded by mistake. Using this interface to monitor the changes and then using an appropriate MIDI editing window to make the necessary changes will allow you to fix these glitches in a more effective way.

Figure 5.16
The Tascam TM-D1000
(www.tascam.com)
mixer parameters
reproduced in two
sequencer environments

In the same line of ideas, some manufacturers offer control surfaces that look like mixers but are in fact MIDI controllers. This allows you to change mix parameters for example, using a tactile control surface rather than controlling these parameters using your mouse and software interface when connecting the MIDI control surface with your sequencer software.

For example, you could assign a MIDI fader on one of these control surfaces to control the volume level of a channel in your software's mixing window. How much control you have over parameters inside your software environment depends largely on the support your device has from the software developer of the application you are using. Since these control surfaces use programmable parameters, you can assign any control to any type of MIDI messages. In other words, if you can get your sequencer or even sound module to interface with such a device, you can change different parameters in real-time using MIDI to communicate messages back and forth between the control surface and another MIDI application or device. You can find examples of this at the following addresses on the Web:

▶ Kenton Control Freak: http://www.kenton.co.uk

▶ Peavey's MIDI command station PC1600:
http://www.peavey.com/products/amps_mi/midi/

▶ Tascam's US-428 controller under the computer recording section:
http://www.tascam.com/products/

MIDI Enabled Digital Effects

MIDI enabled digital effects are similar to MIDI enabled mixers in that they can be controlled externally via MIDI messages such as control changes and SysEx messages. Here's an example: Let's say you program an external multi-effect processor to suit certain parts of a song, assigning programs 1 through 4 as the presets used by this song. You could, once you programmed these effects, use a MIDI bulk dump to save all the device's parameters with your sequencer file so that when you load your song in the sequencer, your effect's parameter loads with it. Then, by assigning program changes for this device, using a MIDI channel to identify it, you can change the program numbers you've created. Furthermore, you could use the modulation wheel to automate the reverb length of a certain program.

Digital Audio Workstations (DAW)

DAW used to be a simple acronym for identifying proprietary hard disk recording systems. Today, it is still used to identify this type of recording system, but the word proprietary does not necessarily apply. Any hard disk recording system using a sound card or digital audio converters to transform analog signal into digital audio, and then recorded onto a hard disk or tapeless recording system, is now considered a DAW. You can still find the aforementioned type of DAW (see Figure 5.17); however, most of today's DAWs takes a more computer-integrated approach to digital audio hard disk recording. They do so by using an existing sound card's resources combined with the computer's processing power. Finally, computer software provides the user interface that ties all these elements together.

CHAPTER 5

Figure 5.17
The Mackie (www.mackie.com) HDR24/96 is a typical example of a modular hard disk recording system, also known as a DAW, that works as a standalone recording system

Practically every DAW on the market today offers MIDI compatibility, ranging from simple playback control and automation to fully integrated MIDI environments such as the ones offered by sequencers—yes, sequencers. In the past five years, MIDI sequencers have been taking steps toward the digital audio realm, and the lines between pure MIDI sequencing and digital audio recording have blurred tremendously. This is why you could call software that used to be for MIDI sequencing, such as Cakewalk (now known as Sonar), Logic, Performer, and Cubase, the software version of digital audio workstations. Inversely, software that used to be strictly for digital audio recording has made steps towards a greater integration of MIDI functions. To illustrate this, one might point out the efforts that Digidesign's ProTools (shown in Figure 5.18) has made to bring MIDI into what used to be solely a digital audio editing and recording environment.

Figure 5.18
Digidesign's ProTools (www.digidesign.com) software now integrates both digital audio and MIDI tracks

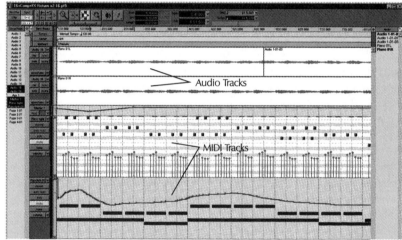

As with other MIDI enabling devices, the DAW allows you to record, play back, and save MIDI events, and, as such, it is part of the MIDI world. However, digital audio workstations could be the subject of an entire book. We will discuss MIDI related functions in later chapters, but you can find more information about digital audio in other fine books at Muska & Lipman's Web site (www.muskalipman.com).

Midi Patch Bays

As mentioned in Chapter 1, MIDI patch bays are in many ways like a MIDI matrix. Here are a few pointers on what you can achieve with such a device:

▶ Use it to simply store different MIDI routing settings in its internal memory for later recall.

▶ Use it as a MIDI Thru or MIDI splitter box—in other words, you can take a signal that comes from one input and send it to multiple outputs on the patch bay. In Figure 5.19 the signal coming from the computer's MIDI Out is received by the patch bay's MIDI In 1 and distributed or split to the patch bay's MIDI Out 2 and 3. Both keyboards will receive the same signal. This is also called routing a signal. In this setup, each MIDI Out on the patch bay becomes a MIDI Thru.

Figure 5.19
The patch bay can act
as a MIDI signal splitter
or Thru box

▶ Use it as a MIDI merge box—this is done by taking the signal from multiple inputs and directing them to a single output. In Figure 5.20, the MIDI signal coming out of both keyboards is sent to the MIDI input of the computer. If both keyboards are sending on different MIDI channels, the computer will record both MIDI channels simultaneously. You could also use this setup to send MTC (MIDI Time Code) from one device to a sequencer while recording MIDI tracks from a controller keyboard simultaneously.

Figure 5.20
The patch bay in this
case acts as a MIDI
signal merger box

▶ Use it as a MIDI Processor—this type of operation can be split further into differen processes: MIDI filtering, MIDI rechannelizing, MIDI transposing, MIDI delay, and MIDI range splitter. In each case, the patch bay receives a MIDI signal, and, depending on the process you decide to apply, the signal will be routed just as mentioned above; i.e., by splitting and/or merging MIDI streams. However, it will also make changes to the MIDI streams as they leave the patch bay's MIDI outputs to reach their destination. Note that some MIDI patch bays do not offer processing functions. Since processing is more expensive to produce due to additional hardware components, cheaper patch bays might not have all of the abovementioned processes available.

CHAPTER 5

Figure 5.21
Using the patch bay in
the middle of a MIDI
studio setup as a MIDI
processor

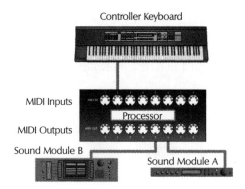

Controller Keyboard

MIDI Inputs

Processor

MIDI Outputs

Sound Module B

Sound Module A

1. MIDI Filtering either filters out certain MIDI messages or changes one type of MIDI message to another, like transforming modulation wheel control messages on channel 1 into aftertouch control messages. Here's an example: In Figure 5.21, the keyboard sends MIDI data to the patch bay's MIDI Input 2. Let's say it is sending over MIDI channel 1 and this MIDI data is routed to the MIDI patch bay's output 6, which is hooked up to sound module A, also set to receive messages on channel 1. You could program the patch bay not to forward any program change messages from MIDI Input 2 to this sound module on MIDI Output 6. This could be useful if you want to be able to change programs on the keyboard but not on sound module A.

2. MIDI Rechannelizing is a fancy term that implies one thing: changing the MIDI channel information from the MIDI data coming in on one or more MIDI inputs of a patch bay. Once again, in Figure 5.21, you could take the MIDI messages from the keyboard (MIDI Input 2) and route it to both MIDI Outputs 5 and 6. Now, you could program the patch bay to transform any MIDI channel 1 information on input 2 going to output 5 to become MIDI channel 2 information for that output and at the same time, remain on channel 1 for the MIDI Output 6 (or sound module A). In other words, the keyboard and sound module A will play on MIDI channel 1, and sound module B will play on channel 2.

3. MIDI Transposing allows you to change the note number of a particular MIDI input on a patch bay, playing on a particular MIDI channel, to be transposed to another note number. If you have a computer running a sequencer, you'll

probably find it easier to do it through there. But if you don't have a software sequencer running, you might find this to be a useful tool when creating lush and thick textures. Once again, send the keyboard's output to both sound modules A and B, but this time, transpose output 5 one octave lower and output 6 one octave higher. If each instrument is set to play on the same MIDI channel, you should have a 3-octave spread just by playing one note on the first keyboard.

4.   MIDI Delay is another useful process if you don't have sequencer software. This feature repeats MIDI messages several times to create a fake echo effect. How you can create this depends on your patch bay, but chances are that the number of times a message is repeated and the velocity at which it will be repeated (in the case of Note On messages) will probably be two of the most common parameters for this processing.

5.   MIDI Range Splitter allows you to determine a note number above which each note will be sent to one output and below which each note will be sent to another output. In our figure above, the keyboard could be sending notes above middle C (note number 60) to sound module A and notes below middle C to sound module B.

Finally, patch bays can do any combinations of the above-mentioned functions as long as your patch bay supports them. To find out if it does, consult your patch bay's documentation.

The Computerless MIDI Setup

So, now that you understand what these devices do, let's see how you can connect them together to get the most out of them. We'll look at different scenarios, since there's more than one way to connect things together, depending on the devices you will be using and the purpose of your setup. For example, a live setup might be different than a studio setup because you need something that is easy to set up and troubleshoot when preparing for a show. You wouldn't want to spend your sound check time finding out why you can't hear all your sounds, right?

We'll first look at some simple setups involving a minimal number of devices, so that you can understand the logic behind them. You will also understand the advantages and disadvantages related to these setups and what to expect from them. For now, as the title suggests, we will look at different setups that don't involve a computer. This will be further discussed in Chapter 6, once we've looked at MIDI interfaces and sound cards.

Obviously, we can't illustrate every possible setup scenario since there are many types of devices that serve different purposes, and the goals you have in mind for your MIDI gear might be different than those of the next reader. Yet, the logic of configuring a computerless MIDI studio remains the same throughout. So read this as a set of suggested setups and make the necessary modifications to fit your own scenario.

Basic Setup

Let's start with a simple three-device setup for a live performance using either one or two controller keyboards. In each example illustrated here, you will have to connect the audio outputs of your devices to a mixer in order to hear the sounds they're making. Audio connections are not shown here, since our purpose is to illustrate MIDI information flow.

Figure 5.22
Simple MIDI setup
for live performance

Out   In   Thru   In

The setup found in Figure 5.22 will allow you to control the second and third device from the first controller in the chain (your controller doesn't have to be a keyboard; it could be a wind, guitar, or drum controller, for example). You can layer sounds from the different sound modules linked to the first controller in order to achieve a thicker sound. If you want all the devices in your chain to respond to the first controller keyboard, they will all have to be set to receive MIDI on the same channel—if the controller keyboard is sending MIDI channel 1 messages, all the other devices will need to respond to this channel.

If you would like to split your controller so that it sends MIDI messages on one channel to one device and another channel to a second device in a chain, you can do this by assigning different zones on your keyboard. To achieve this, however, you will need to have a controller that supports this type of keyboard, or zone split. In that case, you can assign a MIDI channel to each individual zone on your keyboard (see Figure 5.23). Once you have programmed your controller appropriately, you will also need to configure one device to receive messages on one channel and the other device to receive messages on the second channel.

TIP
If one of your sound modules is multi-timbral, you can set it to respond to both channels coming from a split keyboard controller. Enabling both channels on the multi-timbral device will allow this sound module to respond to both channels.

Figure 5.23
Splitting your keyboard,
when this feature is
supported, allows
you to send MIDI
information on
separate channels
simultaneously

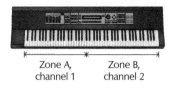

Zone A,   Zone B,
channel 1   channel 2

The disadvantage in setting up MIDI devices in a chain is that you can't hook up too many devices in this chain. The problem is each device may introduce a slight delay or cause errors in the transmission of information, which could lead to errors in the information received by devices later in the chain. If you need to hook up more devices, consider using either a MIDI merge box or a MIDI patch bay. Since this is for a live performance, there's no sequencer involved, so the flow of MIDI information goes in only one direction. In other words, you can't send MIDI from the second or third device back to the first device, since they are not connected in that direction. Connecting the third MIDI Thru connector to the input of the first device might cause a MIDI loop that would once again compromise the integrity of your MIDI information. Remember that your first keyboard is the master, and it alone will be sending information to the second and third devices in the chain; the second keyboard's output is not linked to anything, so it won't be sending MIDI events to the third device. If you wish to have more than one controller keyboard, you will need to use a patch bay or MIDI merge box (see Figure 5.24).

Figure 5.24
Simple MIDI setup
for live performance,
in which two keyboards
can be used as
controllers for a third
sound module or
MIDI device

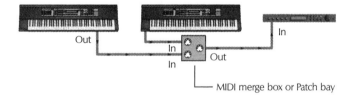

Out

In
In   Out
In

MIDI merge box or Patch bay

In

Using a Hardware Sequencer

When using a hardware sequencer either as an integrated part of your keyboard (workstation) or as a stand-alone unit, chances are you want to send information to this device and use it to send what's recorded back to the devices in the chain. You might also want to hook up a drum machine that holds drum patterns to this sequencer, so the order in which you place your devices will be important.

Figure 5.25
Using a workstation and
a drum machine in a
MIDI setup

As you can see in Figure 5.25, the first device in the chain is a keyboard that acts as a sequencer, since most hardware sequencers today are integrated into a synthesizer or sampler module. This serves as your controller and recorder/playback device. The second unit in the chain is your drum machine. The output of the controller sends control commands such as play, stop, and rewind to the drum machine, so you should set the drum machine to slave to an external MIDI clock. On the other hand, since the output of the drum machine is sent to the controller keyboard/sequencer, you can also set the drum machine as the master time clock and the sequencer as slave. This gives you the flexibility of working on your drum patterns while hearing your MIDI sequence. The MIDI Thru of the drum machine forwards the information arriving from the sequencer to the other sound modules in the chain. In this scenario, the two last devices will not transmit information back to the sequencer. So, if you have SysEx information or bulk dumps that you would like to record into your sequence, you will have to temporarily hook the MIDI out of the appropriate sound module to the MIDI In of the keyboard, unhooking the drum machine from its input.

Since a sequencer allows you to record and play back on multiple channels at once, all multi-timbral devices in this chain will react to their proper MIDI channel, as long as you configure each device in the chain to respond to these MIDI channels. For example, the keyboard could play MIDI channel 1, the drum machine on channel 10, the first sound module could play channels 2 through 9, and the second sound module, channels 11 through 16. This is, of course, if you need all 16 MIDI channels to play simultaneously. Also, remember that two devices can play the same MIDI channel if you wish them to do so.

Using a MIDI Patch Bay

Using a patch bay when you have more than three MIDI devices is useful, especially if you don't have a computer hooked up to your MIDI setup. Since a patch bay allows you to merge different MIDI signals by routing the same signal to multiple outputs, every device in the chain will receive the MIDI events at the same time, rather than have a delay added by a lengthy cable linking all the devices together. When using a MIDI patch bay, it is advisable to turn the local control of the keyboard controller to Off (local Off mode), especially if you send the MIDI Out of this keyboard to the MIDI In of the patch bay, and then send the MIDI Out of the patch bay to the MIDI In of the keyboard. This will avoid MIDI feedback.

Figure 5.26
Linking multiple MIDI
devices to a patch bay,
without using a
computer

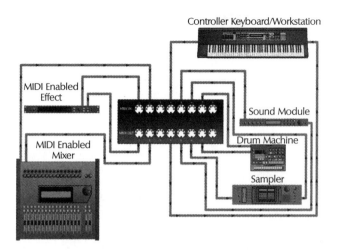

In Figure 5.26, every device's MIDI outputs are connected to the MIDI inputs of the MIDI patch bay, and the MIDI patch bay's outputs are connected to their appropriate device's MIDI inputs. By using this setup, you can create programs within the MIDI patch bay to allow for different types of MIDI flow. Here's an idea of what you could do:

▶ Since the keyboard acts as the controller and sequencer (workstation), the output of this device should be routed to all devices that need to receive MIDI information from the sequencer; in other words, all the devices hooked up to the MIDI patch bay in Figure 5.26. Each receiving device should have its own set of MIDI channel assignments. For example, the keyboard could be channel 1, the sound module (multi-timbral) could be set to channels 2 through 9, the drum machine to channel 10, the sampler to channel 11, the effects processor to channel 12, and the mixer to channel 13. By reserving MIDI channels to specific devices, you will have control over each device individually. In this setup, the master MIDI clock is provided by the keyboard, as it is the only one transmitting MIDI data to other devices. So, the drum machine would have to be set to slave to an external MIDI clock to lock its internal pattern sequencer to the tempo of an incoming sequence. Now that all devices are set to respond to their own MIDI channels, you need to set up the patch bay to take the signal coming from MIDI In 4 (Figure 5.27) to all appropriate MIDI Out (1 through 7 in this case). As mentioned above, if you are routing the keyboard's MIDI output back into its input, you will need to set the keyboard's Local Control to Off; otherwise, you will have MIDI note doubling.

Figure 5.27
Patch bay routing
example 1

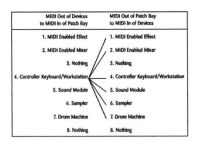

MIDI Out of Devices to MIDI In of Patch Bay	MIDI Out of Patch Bay to MIDI In of Devices
1. MIDI Enabled Effect	1. MIDI Enabled Effect
2. MIDI Enabled Mixer	2. MIDI Enabled Mixer
3. Nothing	3. Nothing
4. Controller Keyboard/Workstation	4. Controller Keyboard/Workstation
5. Sound Module	5. Sound Module
6. Sampler	6. Sampler
7. Drum Machine	7. Drum Machine
8. Nothing	8. Nothing

▶ Continuing the process, let's say you want to be able to send MIDI data back to the keyboard from another device—you could enable the patch bay's MIDI inputs of these devices to be routed back to the keyboard. For example, if you want to record MIDI automation from your mixer into a track on your sequencer (Figure 5.28), you will need to route the MIDI Out of the mixer to the MIDI In (2 in Figure 5.26) of the patch bay, and then route the signal internally so that what comes in to MIDI In 2 goes to MIDI Out 4, as in Figure 5.28.

Figure 5.28
Patch bay routing
example 2

MIDI Out of Devices to MIDI In of Patch Bay	MIDI Out of Patch Bay to MIDI In of Devices
1. MIDI Enabled Effect	1. MIDI Enabled Effect
2. MIDI Enabled Mixer	2. MIDI Enabled Mixer
3. Nothing	3. Nothing
4. Controller Keyboard/Workstation	4. Controller Keyboard/Workstation
5. Sound Module	5. Sound Module
6. Sampler	6. Sampler
7. Drum Machine	7. Drum Machine
8. Nothing	8. Nothing

▶ If you wish to transmit SysEx information from a device—for instance, from a sound module to a keyboard, you can create another setup in the patch bay's memory. It is wise, when doing SysEx transfers between two devices, to establish a direct link between the sender and the receiver. Otherwise, some SysEx data might be lost or cause other devices to lock or reset, especially if you have more than one device made by the same manufacturer. So, in Figure 5.29, you could assign the MIDI signal coming from the MIDI In 5 of the patch bay and send it only to the MIDI Out 4 of the patch bay as well.

Figure 5.29
Patch bay routing
example 3

MIDI Out of Devices to MIDI In of Patch Bay	MIDI Out of Patch Bay to MIDI In of Devices
1. MIDI Enabled Effect	1. MIDI Enabled Effect
2. MIDI Enabled Mixer	2. MIDI Enabled Mixer
3. Nothing	3. Nothing
4. Controller Keyboard/Workstation	4. Controller Keyboard/Workstation
5. Sound Module	5. Sound Module
6. Sampler	6. Sampler
7. Drum Machine	7. Drum Machine
8. Nothing	8. Nothing

6

MIDI and the Computer

Computers today are a big part of MIDI studios, since they offer both versatility and power to the working musician/engineer/producer. For those of you who haven't made the move to add a computer in your MIDI studio, here is your chance to learn the ups and downs of using a computer to make music with MIDI.

Choosing the right equipment for your MIDI needs can be daunting, especially when it comes to computer interfaces and sound cards. Knowing what to look for, understanding the basic components that are available, and how it can be integrated with the rest of your MIDI equipment will help you to make the right choice. Once you've made that choice, you will want to know how to connect the rest of your MIDI devices to your computer and get the MIDI flowing so that you can start recording your performances.

Here's a summary of what you will learn in this chapter:

▶ What a computer MIDI interface is.

▶ What the different kinds of MIDI interfaces are.

▶ How to choose the right MIDI interface for your needs.

▶ What kind of MIDI implementation you can expect from an audio sound card.

▶ How to choose a sound card that is right for your MIDI studio.

▶ What wavetable and FM synthesis are and how they differ from SoundFonts.

▶ Different MIDI connection scenarios to integrate your computer to the rest of your MIDI studio.

▶ What SDS, SMDI, and LTB are.

MIDI Interfaces

A MIDI interface allows you to connect and use your external MIDI devices with your computer, and vice versa, to connect your computer to those same external devices.

MIDI interfaces come in four basic flavors: PCI (internal), USB (Universal Serial Bus), Parallel, and Serial (all three external). Recent technology developments have seen the serial bus on Macintosh computers disappear, so more and more devices use either the PCI or USB protocol to transmit and receive MIDI to the computer. This said, many serial port users, having bought serial port devices for their earlier Macintosh computers, are faced with a difficult decision:

upgrade all their serial port devices to USB or get an adapter that transforms a serial connection into a USB one. If you decide to do this, be prepared to face some bumps along the road, since not all adapter methods are effective at converting the signal properly and MIDI synchronization might be lost in the process.

You can have a simple MIDI In and MIDI Out on a MIDI interface, or multiple MIDI Ins and MIDI Outs on a single MIDI interface, depending on the model itself. The more MIDI Ins and Outs—also called MIDI ports—that you have, the more simultaneous MIDI channels you may have as well, since each MIDI port will support up to 16 MIDI channels. So, an 8-port MIDI interface will give you up to 128 MIDI channels.

You should consider two questions when you get a MIDI interface: What type of MIDI interface best fits my computer, and how many ports do I need on my MIDI interface? The type of MIDI interface you'll need relates to the kind of connector linking the MIDI device to your computer. In order to answer this question, you need to identify which technology is best suited for you and which technology you might already have on your computer. Knowing what's available on your computer might influence your choice of peripherals, since some sound cards already offer MIDI connections and others don't. If yours does, maybe you don't need an additional MIDI interface. The following sections will discuss the different varieties of MIDI interfaces, both external and internal.

Using a Game Port

Many PC-compatible sound cards offer a 15-pin connector for hookup via your joystick connection. This connection can also be used to connect MIDI devices to your computer using a special adapter cable, which offers a male 15-pin connection jack (see Figure 6.1) at one end and a pair of MIDI In/Out at the other end. You can usually still hook up a joystick at the other end of this connector, along with the MIDI connectors.

When such a connector is used, the MPU-401 compatible sound card transmits all 16 channels of information to the computer through a single MIDI port.

Figure 6.1
The 15-pin connector hooks up to a joystick port on your sound card

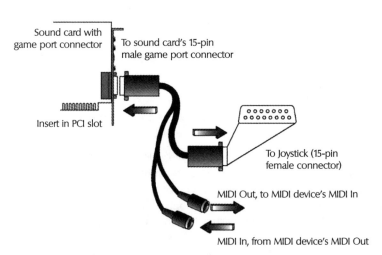

Sound card with game port connector

To sound card's 15-pin male game port connector

Insert in PCI slot

To Joystick (15-pin female connector)

MIDI Out, to MIDI device's MIDI In

MIDI In, from MIDI device's MIDI Out

In the figure below (Figure 6.2), you can see how each pin from the MIDI cables is routed to an individual pin on the 15-pin connector in your sound card's game or joystick port.

Figure 6.2
Computer sound card game port to standard MIDI connector configuration

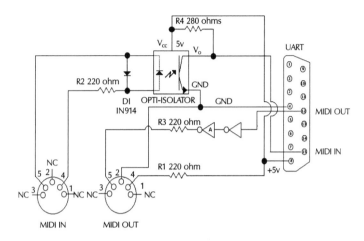

Since this type of connection is integrated to your existing sound card, you don't need to have an extra MIDI interface to connect your computer to MIDI devices, unless you wish to add additional MIDI ports to your system. Also, this type of connector is available on consumer-level products, which means you'll find them most often on sound cards sold in computer stores and music stores. That's because this type of sound card serves as an all-purpose device rather than a semiprofessional or professional sound card. Sound Blaster sound cards, for example, sport this type of adapter.

If you don't have that much money to spend on a MIDI interface, the game port MIDI connection is probably the least expensive solution, since you will kill two birds with one stone: getting a sound card and a MIDI interface at the same time. If the MIDI to 15-pin connector cable is not included with your sound card, you can purchase it separately wherever computer peripherals or computer music products are sold. The drawback with this solution is that you will have only one MIDI port (16 channels) available on your computer. But this doesn't mean that you are out of luck, since many of today's virtual instruments (discussed in Chapter 9) create virtual MIDI ports when they are activated, giving you additional MIDI channels. However, connecting to the external world will be limited to this single port, or 16 channels.

Using a Serial or Parallel Port

Serial and parallel ports, as with USB ports, can be found on the back of your computer. Different platforms offer different types of connectors. For example, the serial port you will find on the back of Macintosh computers is a small rounded connector, and on the back of a PC you will find a flat, multi-pin connector, as shown in Figure 6.3. If you own a Macintosh computer that was made after the first generation of G3, chances are you won't even have this type of connector on your computer. As for PC users, the serial port is rarely used for MIDI, since manufacturers have adopted its game port counterpart as an alternative. This said, there are a variety of MIDI products that support either one of these connectors, and they have proven to be effective in most cases.

Figure 6.3
The Mac 8-pin serial port, the PC 25-pin parallel and 9-pin serial ports

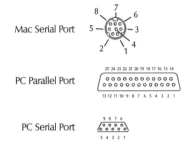

You should note that parallel and serial ports are available on most older computer models but, as we have seen, are completely absent from the newer Macintosh computers and likely will disappear on PC computers as well since newer, more evolved (i.e. faster) technologies are finding their way on the market. There are still many who use these types of connectors to hook MIDI to their computers, but if you are looking for a long-term solution—and do not want to buy new MIDI interfaces when you upgrade your computer in the near future—perhaps you should consider an alternative type of port, such as USB or FireWire.

Owners of peripherals with Mac serial port connectors who just purchased a Blue & White G3 or later model will be happy to know that there are ways to circumvent the lack of serial ports on these computers by adding third-party PCI cards that add serial port connectivity to their Macintosh computers. Unlike USB-to-serial converters, these cards offer a better support for serial port compatibility and work just as if you had a serial port on your computer, which translates into more stable and accurate MIDI timing for your MIDI peripherals. The Stealth serial port from GeeThree (www.geethree.com) is an example of such a device, allowing you to connect any MIDI Interface that uses a serial port connector to your newer Mac computer.

Originally, Macintosh computers had two serial ports (see Figure 6.4) and ran only one application at a time due to a problem with how the baud rate was set for MIDI use. This eventually led to a standard Mac MIDI interface that translated a serial port signal to MIDI by providing a 1MHz clock so that the Mac could divide it down to 31.25 kHz. Programmers at Apple devised many workarounds to deal with this problematic situation. Eventually, due to the demands on serial ports from the growing popularity of the Internet, faxes, and networking, these two ports became oversubscribed, leaving the good people at Apple looking for other ways of connecting peripherals to their computers.

Figure 6.4
The Mac serial ports: printer port (on the left) and modem port (on the right)

In 1999, Apple decided it was time to abandon the serial ports altogether and force everyone to use USB, allowing for a greater number of peripherals to share a common port. This was a good idea for devices like mice and printers, but not so good for serious MIDI users, since USB suffers from a granularity of 1 millisecond. This translates to a very high overhead for small packets of information and a bus shared with other devices. In other words, it's not the ideal situation for external clocks or time code synchronization used with MIDI. Today, developers are hard at work writing code that will allow for stable and precise USB timing in MIDI applications.

In the PC world, things are not so dramatic (yet!). You can still find both parallel and serial ports on most PC motherboards, making them a viable solution for those of you who already have this type of MIDI interface. For those of you wondering if you should go for USB or FireWire, the question is not if this will become an accepted standard in MIDI interface design, but when. You can already find a wide variety of USB MIDI peripherals on the market. However, driver and compatibility issues are still not quite resolved at this time. Sticking with a parallel or serial port MIDI interface might be your best bet for now (see examples of parallel and serial MIDI interfaces for PC computers in Figure 6.5).

Figure 6.5
The MIDIMAN's Portman (www.midiman.com) is an example of a MIDI interface built in both the PC parallel version (left) and the PC serial version (right)

Using a USB Port

USB is a type of connection available on both Macintosh and a PC. With USB-compliant computers and peripherals, you usually just plug the peripheral in and turn it on. The whole process of configuring drivers and telling the operating system (OS) what peripheral it is, is done automatically. You can even change USB peripherals without shutting down or restarting your computer.

USB data travels at a rate of 12 megabits per second (approximately 1,465 Kb/sec). Compared with MIDI, at 3.8 Kb/sec, USB is clearly the faster protocol. However, this is only considered sufficient for medium- to low-speed peripherals in today's computer market. You could also, in theory, connect up to 127 USB devices in a chain. Nevertheless, in practice, this number is more conservative due to the fact that some devices will reserve bandwidth speed over the particular port, making it impossible to add that many devices.

USB device connectors usually sport the icon found in Figure 6.6 to identify this specific type of connection. Take a look at Figure 6.7 to see what a USB connector looks like.

Figure 6.6
The USB icon found
on USB connectors

Figure 6.7
The USB connector
that connects to a USB
port on both Mac and
PC computers

The USB connection is becoming the new standard in both PC and Mac computers, since it offers a cross-platform standard, a plug-and-play approach, and the possibility of hooking up more than one USB device to a single port.

PC's made after 1998 will probably support USB if you are running Windows 98 or Windows 98SE. Windows 95 and Windows NT (4.0) do not support USB; however, Windows 2000 and Windows XP or higher do. Macintosh computers from the Blue & White G3 will also support USB if you have OS 9.04 or higher (USB support was introduced on OS 8.6. However, OS 9.0.4 or higher is recommended).

Once you have determined if your computer supports USB, you may opt for this type of technology (see Figure 6.8).

Figure 6.8
An example of a
USB-to-MIDI interface
from Edirol
(www.edirol.com)

The USB protocol is not without certain problems. USB MIDI interfaces got off to a bad start due to early Macintoshes having only one port and a preliminary driver with a 4ms granularity. The best results required a separate port used only for the MIDI driver and USB Manager 1.3.5 or later. Early iMacs and B/W G3s had a single USB port with a two-connector hub, so the keyboard, mouse, printer, and any other peripherals will be sharing the bus.

Like any new protocol being introduced on the market, software developers are slow to respond to issues of compatibility between certain USB devices and software applications. But this is simply a transition stage and you can probably count on some driver revisions and better integration of USB for MIDI applications in the years, if not months, to come. Many manufacturers have already adopted this type of connection and are working hard to provide support for these interfaces, which, in itself, bodes well for your decision-making process. It is also good to know that most second-generation software (both driver and application software) are more reliable than the first generation. USB is no exception: In the case of Windows XP, many users have experienced problems using USB, since most of the drivers for USB devices are just starting to appear as downloadable updates on manufacturers' sites. This implies that you might want to wait for Microsoft's first service pack before installing Windows XP on your computer if you are not certain your USB peripherals will be supported in this OS, or consult your peripheral's manufacturer's Web site to find out if the device is supported by Windows XP.

Make sure the USB-MIDI interface you purchase or install on your system is stable and compatible with your current system configuration. To find out if it is, simply check the hardware manufacturer's documentation online and any software documentation, as well as discussion forums related to the software you wish to use with this particular interface. Knowing ahead of time how an interface will handle itself on your system might save you some grief.

Multi-Port MIDI Interfaces

Until now, we have discussed different types of connections linking your computer to MIDI devices through stand-alone MIDI interfaces. But in the examples given above, all of these MIDI interfaces have one thing in common: They all have 1 MIDI In and 1 MIDI Out. This is fine if your setup is minimal and you don't need more than 16 MIDI channels to control your external MIDI devices (compared to your internal MIDI devices). However, if you need to have more than 16 MIDI channels, opting for a multi-port MIDI interface might be the way to go.

Most MIDI interfaces offered on the market today can hook up to your computer using one of the connection types mentioned above, and will offer not only multiple MIDI inputs and outputs, but also multiple ports—each additional port giving you 16 MIDI channels. So, if you have a serial, parallel, or USB connection, you can benefit from having 32, 64, 128 or more simultaneous MIDI channels by using a multi-port MIDI interface.

When installing a multi-port MIDI interface on your computer, you will be able to access the different ports through your software MIDI configuration (see Figure 6.9). This is usually done in two basic steps:

1. Installing the software that comes with the device so that your OS can recognize the device and manage it.

2. Activating the MIDI ports through the MIDI setup interface inside your favorite sequencer software, and then assigning a MIDI track to send or receive MIDI information on the desired MIDI port.

Figure 6.9
The MIDIMAN
(www.midiman.com)
USB MIDISport 8X8/s is
an example of a multi-
port MIDI interface,
which also acts as a
MIDI patch bay and
SMPTE/MTC converter

Sound Cards with MIDI Integration

We can't really discuss MIDI interfaces without talking about sound cards, since they are closely related. Some sound cards offer MIDI integration, as we already saw with the use of game ports on sound cards as a way to link your computer to external MIDI peripherals. What will be discussed here are sound cards that offer a bit more than a game port to interface with your external MIDI devices.

The following is a brief overview of audio peripherals and what you should look for in a sound card to meet your needs. But note that since audio is not the main focus of this book, you will probably find more in-depth information in other, more audio-specific books as well as on the Web.

▶ OS Support: It is important that you find a sound card that is supported by your operating system. Before purchasing a sound card, make sure the drivers for your sound card exist and have been tested on the OS you are using. If the driver for the card is still being written, or the manufacturer says it will be available shortly, then it's up to you to decide if you are willing to wait for its arrival. Unfortunately, "shortly" usually means "any time in the year to come, but please buy our product now because it will eventually work. Honest."

▶ Format: Some sound cards may allow you to hook up your portable computer with a PCI slot or PCMCIA connection, while others will use FireWire or USB to communicate with your computer. But most often, sound cards are in PCI format. This means that depending on your needs and computer configuration, one format of sound card will suit you better than another. Find out which format is best for you before deciding on a specific model of sound card. There's no point in getting a FireWire sound card if your computer doesn't support it.

▶ Inputs: There are quite a few kinds of input connectors out there. Most can be separated into two categories—analog and digital. Some cards offer a combination of both, while others offer only one or the other. In the analog variety, the most popular are: mini phone jacks, RCA, unbalanced or balanced inch jack, AES/EBU, or XLR jacks (see Figure 6.10). In terms of digital inputs, the most common types of connectors are SPDIF, ADAT, and TDIF. SPDIF offers a stereo pair of digital input (through a single RCA cable), while the ADAT and TDIF digital inputs offer 8 digital (see Figure 6.11) channels. The advantage of having a multi-input sound card is that you will be able to record different instruments simultaneously on separate inputs. The disadvantage of having a multi-input sound card is that the more inputs you have, the pricier the card will be. This is especially true with high-end connectors to ensure a good quality connection with your audio devices.

Figure 6.10
From top to bottom:
1/4 inch balanced
connector, XLR or
AES/EBU connector,
1/8 inch or mini
connector, RCA
connector

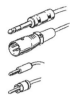

Figure 6.11
Analog and digital
audio connectors as
they might appear on
the back of a sound card
or breakout box

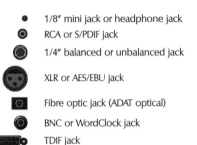

● 1/8″ mini jack or headphone jack

◉ RCA or S/PDIF jack

◎ 1/4″ balanced or unbalanced jack

XLR or AES/EBU jack

Fibre optic jack (ADAT optical)

BNC or WordClock jack

TDIF jack

▶ Outputs: Outputs are similar to inputs in terms of types of connectors. The difference is that these will allow you to send an analog or digital audio signal to an external audio device rather than receive such a signal. Make sure you have good quality connectors if you do not wish to introduce noise into your signal as it is going to an external mixer, recording device, or monitoring system. If you are serious about MIDI (i.e. music or sound), you should avoid sound cards with mini phone jacks (the ones similar to headphone jacks on a Walkman, for example)—they offer poor contacts, are prone to break easily whenever manipulation is involved, and offer a poor overall quality, since they are associated with cheaper sound cards. It is also good to keep the analog-to-digital and digital-to-analog conversions to a minimum, since every time you convert the audio signal, you may introduce errors. So, if you have a digital mixer, having a digital output on your sound card may allow you to interface both devices using a digital audio signal path, which will greatly improve your end result. Some consumer-level sound cards will mark the outputs for surround sound. This is different than regular outputs, since each output is meant to feed a surround sound system in a home entertainment center. However, the concept behind surround sound outputs and sending outputs to a mixer is quite different, and the signal coming out of these outputs will also be different, so just make sure you have the right type of outputs for your needs.

▶ Sample Rate: The sampling rate determines how many samples per second a digital audio signal will use to reproduce the analog sound. The higher the sample rate, the wider your frequency range recorded or reproduced—this will allow you to record or reproduce harmonic content found in the upper frequency range associated with the crispness and sharpness of the sound. Typical sampling rates vary between 44.1, 48, 96, or 192 kHz. Note that higher sampling frequencies require more processing time and faster hard disk speeds.

CHAPTER 6

▶ Bit Depth: The bit depth represents the size of the binary word used to store the amplitude value for a sample. A higher bit depth translates into more precision, a greater signal-to-noise ratio, and a greater dynamic range. Typical bit depths for sound cards may vary between 8, 16, 20, 24, and 32 bits per sample. The larger the binary word, the greater the space needed to store this information, and as with the sampling rate, better quality also means more processing time and more hard disk space (fast hard drives are highly recommended for 24- or 32-bit samples).

▶ Drivers: Since we've already mentioned that it's important for your sound card to be compatible with your OS, you should now consider which types of applications you will be using to create your music. Since some applications are more effective when using a certain type of driver, it is important that your sound card's driver matches these specifications. For example, if you intend to use Tascam's GigaStudio, make sure you have a sound card with a GSIF driver. This type of proprietary driver is optimized to address your sound card, making for a smoother experience when using the software. Another such proprietary driver is the ASIO driver from Steinberg. This type of driver is used to optimize the performance of any application that supports the ASIO protocol, such as Cubase, Nuendo, Logic Audio Reason, and several others. Not having a compatible ASIO driver if you wish to use such software might reduce your sound card's performance. An example of such effects would be apparent when using virtual synthesizers. In such a case, you want your sound card to respond quickly to the notes you play on your MIDI keyboard; not having an ASIO driver would introduce a delay between the time you play a note and the time you hear it. If you've ever tried to play something with this type of delay, you probably understand that this is not a realistic creative environment. So, make sure the proper drivers for your software are available for your sound card.

▶ Multi-Client Capability: In today's MIDI studio and audio-editing studios, computers are carrying an important part of the workload. This implies that quite often you will be running more than one audio/MIDI application simultaneously inside a single computer, especially if you don't have the financial resources to purchase multiple computers to run all your programs in sync. Some software might take over the sound card's control in your computer. Having a multi-client capable driver might allow different software applications to share the sound card's resources rather than to monopolize it, rendering it useless in a second or third application you would like to run simultaneously.

Sound Cards with Synthesizer Integration

Some sound cards may also have a General MIDI sound bank integrated on its board, while others may offer more sophisticated wavetables. However, if you are serious about creating your own music rather than simply using your sound card as a MIDI playing device, you might find that the editing capability and sound quality of those sound modules are not adequate. In general, sound cards that are integrated to your computer system, such as Macintosh or a brand name PC system, will provide such sounds, and the quality and quantity of sounds they provide will vary from system to system.

About GM Sound Bank

As mentioned in Chapter 4, the GM or General MIDI sound bank is a set of 128 sounds that will always have the same names and will sound similar from one GM compatible device to another. If you don't have a GM sound bank synthesizer chip on your sound card, there are different ways of having a GM sound bank saved on your computer to play Standard MIDI Files (*.MID files). QuickTime provides a GS sound set when the MIDI file format support is selected, which gives you access to a virtual GS compatible instrument. Editing this set of instruments, however, is not possible, nor is controlling a QuickTime instrument through a sequencer. In other words, QuickTime provides a sound bank for MIDI file playback purposes only.

As for sound cards that do provide integrated synthesizers, most of them will have GM support (GS support with Roland sound cards or XG support with Yamaha sound cards). That's because these standards are designed primarily for computer file transfers and playback, and are basic features in sound cards that integrate a synthesizer or sound module on their circuit board.

About Wavetable

Wavetables are the main source of sounds for most sound cards with integrated MIDI synthesizers. As you have just seen, GM is the basic sound set for these wavetables. Simply put, wavetable synthesis is similar to sample playback. It uses a series of small digital audio recordings as source material to produce sounds, then these samples are processed by the onboard synthesizer in order to manipulate different parameters of this sound, such as the envelope, the filters, and so on. It usually sounds better than an FM (Frequency Modulation) synthesis sound card, since the origin of the sound is real rather than completely synthesized. Sound cards that use wavetable synthesis are usually more expensive than FM synthesis sound cards; then again, you will quickly appreciate the difference in terms of quality.

Wavetable music synthesis should not be confused with common PCM (Pulse Code Modulation) sample buffer playback. It is similar to it, but extends upon it in at least two ways: First, the waveform lookup table (the actual table of audio sample waveforms) contains samples for not just a single period of a sine function but for a single period of a more general wave shape, such as piano, violin, or brass tone. Second, a mechanism exists for dynamically changing the wave shape as the musical note evolves, thus generating a certain amount of variation in time.

CHAPTER 6

In comparison to this, FM synthesis uses a first digital oscillator as a carrier, which acts as a pitch or frequency generator for the sound. Then, a second oscillator affects this first oscillator to make it modulate through time, creating variations in the sound itself. Usually, an FM synthesizer will use 4 to 6 such modulators and carriers in different combinations called algorithms.

Sound cards that use wavetables will usually have an onboard memory chip on which its samples are saved. Some of these sound cards will even have memory slots allowing you to expand its memory capability and add additional sounds to them as you upgrade it. The larger your wavetable memory, the more sounds you will have. So, if you decide to go with a sound card that offers wavetable synthesis, make sure the memory is expandable or sufficient to house a good sound library. Memory size for sound cards that support wavetable synthesis vary between 2 MB and 64 MB, allowing you to expand your sound sets. The Creative Labs Sound Blaster Live, for example, comes with a 2, 4, or 8 MB sound set, but, depending on system RAM, can be expanded up to 64 MB or more of wavetable synthesis memory.

If you'd like to know more about wavetable synthesis, you can find an article on the Web written by Jim Heckroth at one of the following addresses:

▶ http://kingfisher.cms.shu.ac.uk/midi/mt_tech.htm

▶ http://www.harmony-central.com/MIDI/Doc/tutorial.html#tech

About SoundFonts

SoundFonts are to sound what Type Fonts are to text. They are a way to enhance your musical creations using different sounds that you may add to a SoundFont-compatible sound card just like you can add Type Fonts to your computer's operating system in order to use them in your word processor or desktop publishing software to make a document look good. The main difference between SoundFonts and Wavetables is that you don't use the sound card's memory to load SoundFonts, but the computer's memory instead. So your computer's available memory resources are your only limit to sound set expansion.

In addition, the term "wavetable" is a more generic term used to describe an allotment of sound files one after the other, whereas SoundFonts were developed by Creative Labs and Emu Systems as a wavetable standard used on their sound cards. This allows users to improve the sound quality of their MIDI playback by either loading a better GM wavetable sound-set or adding more sounds to their existing sound library. SoundFonts can be single sounds or complete banks and so can wavetables.

The nice thing about soundfonts is that with software synthesizers, you don't need to have a sound card that supports soundfonts anymore, since some soft synthesizers offer soundfont support and editing capability. Here are some compatible software and hardware products that support soundfonts.

Table 6.1
SoundFont compatibility list

Application	Company	Software/Model	Web site	OS Compatibility
Software Synthesizers	Bismark	BS1	homepage.mac.com/bismark	PC and Mac
	Bitheadz	Unity DS-1	www.bitheadz.com	PC and Mac
	Live Update	LiveSynth Pro	www.livesynth.com	PC
	Seer Systems	SurReal and Reality	www.seersystems.com	PC
	Sonic Syndicate	Orion Pro	www.sonic-syndicate.com	PC
Soundcards	Creative Labs	SoundBlaster Audigy, Live!, PCI, and AWE	www.soundblaster.com	PC and Mac
	TerraTec	EWS Series	www.terratec.com	PC
	Creamware	Power Sampler	www.creamware.com	PC and Mac
MIDI/Audio Sequencers	Cakewalk Software	Cakewalk Pro Audio, SONAR, and SONAR XL	www.cakewalk.com	PC
	Steinberg	Cubase VST	www.steinberg.net	PC and Mac
Editors	Audio Compositor	Audio Compositor	home.att.net/~audiocompositor/	
	Bitheadz	Unity DS-1	www.bitheadz.com	PC and Mac
	Creative Labs	Vienna and SoundFont Manager	www.soundblaster.com /goodies/applications	PC
	SoundFaction	Alive	www.soundfaction.com/alive	PC
	FMJ Software	Awave Studio	www.fmjsoft.com	PC

Different Solutions for Different Needs

Now that you know what is out there in terms of sound cards and MIDI interfaces, you might be wondering what's the best thing for you at this point. Well, that all depends on why you need MIDI in the first place. Or, rather, what you need MIDI to do. So, let's look at different possibilities.

MIDI for Gamers

If playing games is the main purpose behind your purchase of a sound card, don't look too far and don't spend too much money—you'll need the extra cash for game controls, a good video card, and games, of course. Most games today use very little MIDI anymore, since digital audio is so prevalent and computers are much more powerful than they used to be. Game developers have exploited that fact with the addition of realtime audio effects and soundtracks. Because your use of MIDI is minimal, getting a sound card with an integrated synthesizer, preferably one that offers wavetable synthesis, will be sufficient for most of your gaming needs. Such a sound card will also allow you to play back MIDI and audio files. You will most likely find a sound card that will fulfill your needs in any computer store, since this type of application requires typical computer functionality and is offered with most consumer products.

MIDI for Musicians

Chances are you will want two things out of your sound card: quality and connectivity. Factors that might influence your decision:

▶ Quality: Above all else, your first criteria in the selection of a sound card, if you intend to make music, should be the quality of its components: type of connectors, sample rate, and bit depth, of course, but also how the sound card sounds. This is usually determined by the quality of its converters: analog-to-digital (or A/D) for recording, and digital-to-analog (or D/A) for playback. This might seem like an obvious statement, but in the world of technical sheets and specs, we often forget that in the end, it doesn't really matter what the specs say. If the sound card doesn't sound good, no matter how hard you try to sweeten the input, you won't be happy with the result. Talk to friends and professionals, read reviews, and get information before you buy a product and make sure that people using the sound card you've got your eye on are happy customers. If you already have a sound card and are just looking to buy a MIDI interface, then the next point below will be more important to you, since MIDI does not produce any audio output anyway. However, a well-built interface will save you the problem of bad MIDI connections due to manipulation if you need to plug and unplug your devices often.

▶ Compatibility: Since you will be making music with your sound card and MIDI interface, making sure that your device is compatible with the software you will be using is essential. Visit the Web site for the software you will be using and search for tests that have been performed on sound card compatibility issues and reliability under their specific environment. In other words, if you are planning to work with software, make sure the manufacturer recommends the sound card you are also planning to use. This way, you will find out how well the sound card performs with this software. The test the manufacturer runs will ensure you compatibility between the two components. Sometimes, a sound card might perform well in a game environment, but when using virtual synthesizers, it can show its weaknesses more prominently.

▶ MIDI ports: Do you need just one MIDI port, or more? Are 16 channels of MIDI enough for what you wish to do? If you already have a sound card on your computer, does it offer MIDI connectivity? If not, do you want to get a stand-alone MIDI interface, or a sound card with a built-in MIDI port (or ports)? You are the only one who knows the answers to these questions, since you are the only one who knows what you want to do with your computer. Since most mid- to high-end cards don't include MIDI, opting for a separate MIDI interface will probably be your best bet.

▶ Number of audio inputs/outputs: Depending on the type of music you make, the external devices you have, and the software you will be using, how many audio inputs and outputs you need will influence your choice of sound card. Most will offer at least 2 inputs and 2 outputs; however, if recording live musicians in a studio environment using multiple inputs simultaneously is what you wish to do, perhaps a sound card that offers such connectivity is what you should look for. Remember, the more inputs and outputs you have, the more money you can expect to pay for the sound card, especially if the connectors are built with quality parts. If the sound card with multiple inputs and outputs is the same price as another model from a different company with only two ins and outs, chances are the trade-off will be in sound quality (A/D and D/A converters).

▶ Timing and synchronization: If you wish to use a MIDI interface or a sound card with an integrated MIDI port (or ports) and wish to use this in a post-synchronization or cross-platform environment, ensuring the timing of the audio device is accurate could save you a lot of hassle. In audio post-production work, the possibility of using either a SMPTE/MTC converter or word clock is essential to lock two or more devices together in time and to do digital audio transfers between devices. A word clock input allows your sound card to synchronize to an external device using its sampling rate. Inversely, a sound card with a word clock output will allow you to synchronize other devices using this card's sampling rate. A device exhibiting poor synchronization capability will leave you searching for alternatives that are usually more costly than the original cost of your sound card. So, once again, make sure your device supports these features if they are important to you.

Also, due to the density of MTC information, it is often recommended that an entire MIDI Port be dedicated to it, meaning that you would need an interface with a minimum of two ports if you need to synch to MTC and do music MIDI.

▶ Cost: if you are on a tight budget, your choice will be limited, so try to find different sound cards that are in your price range and compare what they offer with your musical needs for the next 12 months. Purchasing a sound card for things you will do two years from now is not a wise decision, since by the time you will be using your sound card to its full capacity, it will have gone down in price and a better, newer model likely will be out anyway. Based on your budget, you can decide if you want to compromise features for quality, or vice versa. Just remember that if music is your thing, maybe cutting down the budget for your video card, or other peripherals, might allow you to purchase a better sound card. And, after all, that's what really counts.

MIDI for Laptop

If you are a laptop user, you might use your MIDI interface or sound card in the same way as if you had a desktop computer. This implies that you might use these peripherals to play games, to simply enjoy music, or to create music. In any case, the paragraphs above will serve you just as well. So, making sure the MIDI or audio device you wish to purchase meets the same criteria when using a laptop as when you are using a desktop is essential. However, using a laptop reduces your choice of peripherals, since you will most likely need a PCMCIA adapter for your audio interface (see Figure 6.12).

Figure 6.12
A PCMCIA laptop adapter for the Layla or Mona sound card from Echo Digital Audio (www.echoaudio.com)

Another option might be through USB devices (see Figure 6.13), since USB is a standard connection on most PC and Mac laptops available today. Using USB to connect might be a more economical solution if you wish only to hook up MIDI peripherals to your laptop, since you won't need an additional adapter card for your USB device, especially if you are happy with the built-in sound card capability of your laptop.

Figure 6.13
The Quattro USB audio interface from MIDIman (www.midiman.com) offers both MIDI and audio connectors through a USB compatible breakout box

MIDI for Macintosh

Macintosh computers have provided audio and MIDI support for a long time and have proven themselves to be very efficient when it comes to handling this type of data. However, with changes made to the MIDI managers working under the Mac OS—OS X, OMS (Open MIDI System developed by Opcode), and FreeMIDI (developed by Mark Of The Unicorn), some MIDI functions are better supported by certain devices than by others. Since the manufacturers that develop these MIDI managers (with the exception of OS X) also develop their own audio hardware, it is not uncommon to see that devices from one company will work better with the MIDI manager developed by the same company. The same principle applies with music software you might be running on your Mac. For example, ProTools from Digidesign, Digital Performer (from Mark Of The Unicorn), and Logic Audio (from eMagic) work with FreeMIDI, and Cubase VST (from Steinberg) works with OMS. So, if you are working with Digital Performer, using a MOTU (Mark Of The Unicorn) sound card will probably be more stable and offer better timing than if you are working with another type of sound card/MIDI interface.

MIDI for Networks

MIDI in itself could be considered as a way to network different devices together, but the idea of networking computers together in order to play different instruments started to interest people when software synthesizers started to arrive in our studios. MIDI in itself doesn't require that much processing power, since it is relatively slow when compared to other forms of communications. For example, the Internet's bandwidth using a 56K modem would be enough to transmit real-time MIDI data, but wouldn't be able to send CD quality digital audio in real-time. Such a digital audio transfer from one computer to another requires communication between the two computers with much broader bandwidth.

When using a network of computers in a MIDI setting, the only advantage you would have here would lie in this network's ability to share the processing of more elaborate functions, such as digital audio processes or software synthesizers running on different computers. This allows each processor to do its portion of the work, sharing "horsepower" resources (in other words, CPU processing time). Since processing is a big part of what the computer has to do when running audio effects within your software environment or software synthesizers, the more processing power you have the better it will be. (As with software synthesizers, you can have software effects such as reverbs, delays, compressors, and others). So, MIDI itself will probably not require you to hook up your computer to a network. However, sharing these processing intensive tasks through a network, having each one running a series of software relating to a MIDI project, may help. In other words, the limit imposed by your computer on the number of virtual or software synthesizers you can run—not to mention virtual samplers that require fast hard disk access and use up a good portion of your RAM—will, on its own, be defined by the sum of its hardware capacity.

Software developers are now developing new ways of handling this problem using networks. Until recently, the only way to lock different slaved computers to a single master computer in a musical or sound application was through time code (SMPTE or MTC) or word clock. The problem with word clock is that it only works with audio transfers and not necessarily with MIDI transfers of virtual synthesizer data.

NOTE

What does sample-accurate mean?

The term sample-accurate usually refers to a synchronization mechanism that occurs between two digital audio signals, where the sampling frequency of one sound card or digital audio device is sent to another sound card or digital audio device to regulate its timing, thus synchronizing the receiving device to the sending device's sampling rate.

Since sampling rates on sound cards occur at a very high speed, usually 44,100 times or more per second, this offers a very reliable and stable synchronizing signal. When two or more devices are locked to a master sampling rate, it is referred to as a sample-accurate synchronization, where every sample in one device corresponds to a sample in another device.

This synchronization is usually transmitted over a special digital audio connection called word clock, or embedded into the existing digital audio cable using the S/PDIF, ADAT, or TDIF format.

This type of synchronization is essential when doing digital audio transfers between two digital audio devices, or it can be used to synchronize transport functions between two devices that support this type of synchronization as well.

This timing resolution far surpasses SMPTE's and MTC's resolution.

Steinberg is one of the companies developing a technology that allows users to lock MIDI timing of different computers in a network with sample-accurate synchronization through a system called the VST System Link, which uses a single channel of a digital audio stream (such as ADAT, TDIF, or S/PDIF) to carry MIDI information over a network of computers, making it possible to run several virtual synthesizers on different machines, all controlled by a single application, thus allowing for shared processing across the entire network. A patch bay software controls the flow of information from one computer and allows for hundreds of MIDI channels to be transmitted over this single digital audio connection. For example, you could use one computer to record audio tracks, a second computer to run virtual synthesizers, and a third computer to process your audio tracks using virtual processing effects (such as reverbs, delays, and compressors). For this system to work, however, you will need compatible ASIO sound cards and software hosts (for now, Cubase SX and Nuendo are the only software supporting this protocol).

Computer-Based MIDI Studio

In Chapter 5, we looked at different ways to connect MIDI devices together. Expanding on these examples, let's next consider how to connect your computer to external MIDI devices using one or more MIDI ports on either your computer's sound card or MIDI interface.

Since getting MIDI in and out of your computer at this point is an important part of setting up your MIDI studio, let's take a look at different ways of doing so, using different studio configurations. Since these examples expand on the setup diagrams in Chapter 5, it is important that you understand the logic behind those examples before looking at the following. If you're unsure, it would be wise to go back and refresh your memory before moving on.

Using a Single MIDI Port Without a Patch Bay

In Figure 6.14, you have an example of a MIDI studio setup using your computer as a sequencer. In the absence of a patch bay, you should connect the MIDI output of your computer to the MIDI input of your controller keyboard, and vice versa (the MIDI output of your keyboard to the MIDI input of the computer). Any other MIDI devices should be connected from the MIDI Thru of the keyboard. In this case, the MIDI Thru of the keyboard feeds the drum machine's MIDI input. If you have more devices to put in the chain, follow this example.

The disadvantage of this configuration is that you will have to connect the MIDI output of a device in the chain to the input of the computer, disconnecting the keyboard temporarily, if you wish to send System Exclusive messages or MIDI information from these devices (drum machine, sound module, or sampler in this figure) to the computer.

Figure 6.14
Hooking up your computer to MIDI devices without a patch bay

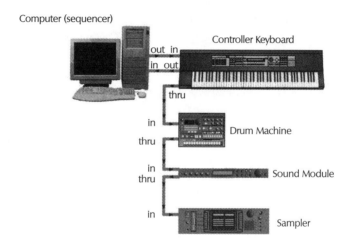

Using a Single MIDI Port with a Patch Bay

When using a patch bay, your computer communicates with this device in the same way all others communicate with it—the output of the device is hooked up to a patch bay's input and the input of the device is hooked up to the patch bay's output. In Figure 6.15, the computer is hooked up to the input and output 3 of the patch bay.

Once your instruments and other MIDI devices are connected, you will need to configure the patch bay appropriately and save your configurations in the patch bay's memory.

If your patch bay is connected to your computer through a PCI adapter card, a USB port or any type of connection other than a simple MIDI port, a software application provided with your

CHAPTER 6

patch bay will enable you to make the configurations easily and save them to memory. This also means that your patch bay will offer as many ports as there are inputs on it.

On the other hand, if your patch bay is connected to your computer through a MIDI cable alone, your MIDI patch bay will transmit and receive only 16 channels of MIDI data, since it is considered to be a single port MIDI device, as shown in Figure 6.15. In this case, you still need to configure your patch bay through a front panel LCD, assigning each input to the proper output or outputs. To take full advantage of the setup shown in Figure 6.15, you can create different settings for different purposes. Here are some examples:

▶ Main Setup: This allows you to use your keyboard to record events into your computer's sequencer and use your computer to echo these events back to the appropriate devices and play back any recorded MIDI messages. This includes sending SysEx messages to configure connected devices.

1. Route the signal that comes from the keyboard to the computer. In this example, PB (Patch Bay) Input 4 to PB Output 3.

2. Route the signal that comes from the computer to every other device in your MIDI setup, excluding the computer itself (to avoid MIDI feedback). In this example, PB Input 3 should be routed to PB outputs 1, 2, 4, 5, 6, and 7.

3. To avoid MIDI doubling in your keyboard, set your keyboard's Local Control to Off.

4. If you have a mixer, as shown in Figure 6.15, you should also route its output to the input of the computer. In this example, PB input 2 to PB output 3. Make sure, as with the keyboard, that the Local Control for your mixer is set to Off; otherwise, it will create a MIDI feedback loop, which can jam your MIDI device.

5. All the other devices' outputs should be left alone (i.e. not routed to an input), so that no unwanted MIDI is sent back to the computer by these devices. That could also create an overflow of MIDI information or cause your MIDI sequencer to record events that were not meant to be recorded. You will need to create another configuration program with a direct link to enable the communication between these devices and the computer.

6. Save this configuration to memory and recall it whenever you need it.

▶ Individual setups for SysEx transmission: Since SysEx messages are complex and usually not transmitted to the sequencer while you are working on a project, you don't need to have the MIDI outputs of these devices connected (in this example, the effects processor, the sound module, the drum machine, and the sampler).

1. Create a patch (configuration program) in your patch bay for each module in your MIDI studio for which you would like to be able to record its SysEx into your computer's sequencer by routing PB (Patch Bay) input to the PB output leading to the computer. Let's take an example from Figure 6.15: Map the PB input 5 (sound module) to the PB output 3 (computer).

2. Make sure no other device is sending MIDI to the computer through patch bay routing. This way, you will be certain that what is recorded in the computer is what you are purposely sending it.

3. Save this configuration to memory and recall it whenever you need it.

▶ Computerless setup: You might want to have a setup that doesn't include the computer. Having a patch bay that you use in both a studio environment and a live show environment would be a good reason for this—considering that you might not want to carry your laptop or computer with you if you don't need it for a live show.

1. As with the previous setups, the idea is to connect the output of your main controller to a patch bay's input.

2. Then connect the output of the patch bay to the MIDI input of your device. You can connect as many devices as your patch bay has MIDI Outs (or MIDI Ins, for that matter) connectors.

3. Route inside the patch bay's interface the PB In to any PB Out you wish to use in your setup.

Figure 6.15
Hooking up your computer to a MIDI patch bay—in this example, the computer has only one MIDI port

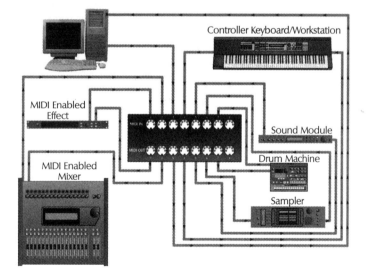

Using Multiple MIDI Ports

A MIDI multiport system is one that offers more than one set of 16 MIDI channels. Each additional MIDI port will give you an additional 16 MIDI channels. There are three ways of obtaining multiple MIDI ports on your computer:

1. Having a multiport MIDI interface, as shown in Figure 6.16, or a sound card that offers more than one MIDI port.

Figure 6.16
The USB MIDISport 2X2 from MIDIman (www.midiman.com) offers 2 MIDI ports labeled Out-A and Out-B in this configuration

2. Having a patch bay that hooks up to your computer with a PCI, USB, or other type of connection. This lets you address each MIDI output as an independent port, as shown in Figure 6.17.

Figure 6.17
The OMS setup window for the MIDI Timepiece AV from MOTU (www.motu.com)—each instrument displayed in this setup could potentially receive 16 channels of MIDI

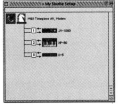

3. Having a virtual MIDI port provided by a software synthesizer, such as VST Instruments (see Figure 6.18) or DX Instrument, or any other virtual type of MIDI communication with a single computer or over a network (such as VST System Link technology discussed earlier in this chapter).

Figure 6.18
In Cubase VST from Steinberg (www.steinberg.net), you can access your virtual MIDI ports through a MIDI track's MIDI output setting—each name in the list could support up to 16 independent MIDI channels

In Figure 6.19, the computer is connected to a MIDI interface with four separate MIDI ports—labeled A, B, C, and D. Each port is connected to a single MIDI instrument or device. This kind of setup will give you a total of 64 MIDI channels. In your sequencer software or MIDI application, select which ports are active and which are not. Then, select which input port (or ports) will receive MIDI, and the MIDI port to which each track your MIDI sequencer should send events. By doing this, you apply a routing scheme inside your computer just as you have seen in a patch bay in a previous section in this chapter.

The advantage of having such a setup is that MIDI data flow is uncluttered, since each connection relays only one MIDI device to the computer, and vice versa, optimizing MIDI performance throughout the system.

Figure 6.19
Example of a parallel connection using a 4-port MIDI interface

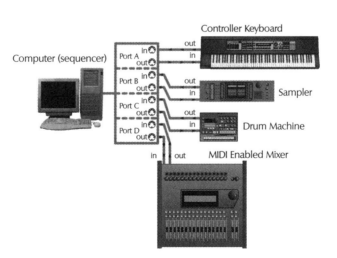

CHAPTER 6

If you have more MIDI devices than available MIDI ports on your computer's MIDI interface, you can always daisy chain some devices together as described earlier in this book. There are no differences between daisy chaining devices that are outside of a computer setup and daisy chaining devices that are connected to a computer. As Figure 6.20 suggests, the keyboard, sampler, and sound modules are connected to the computer's MIDI Port A in a daisy chain. The mixer, however, uses a MIDI port unto itself. This is an advisable practice if you are using a MIDI enabled mixer, since, quite often, the amount of controller data and information sent to and from a mixer can be important, especially during a mixdown process. You wouldn't want your MIDI to start slowing down because of a bottleneck on a MIDI port. Since many MIDI enabled mixers will use several MIDI channels, this type of setup will allow you to take full advantage of all the controls you can have over your mixer, without restricting the number of MIDI channels you can use to control other devices.

Figure 6.20
Example of daisy chain and parallel connections using a 4-port MIDI interface

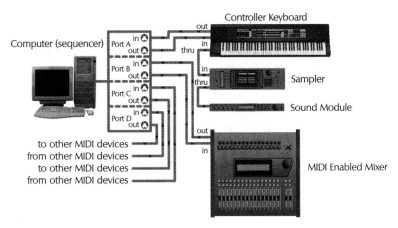

About SDS and SMDI

Hardware samplers are great electronic musical devices because they allow you to load digital audio samples into their memory, edit them, and play MIDI sequences or perform in realtime using these samples. However, their editing capability is often hindered by the fact that they usually offer a very small graphic user interface with a very coarse visual definition. This makes them an awkward editing environment. Your computer, on the other hand, offers a great graphic user interface with software tools that are usually far more sophisticated than the ones available in your sampler. That's why you might want to use your computer to edit samples that will be destined for your sampler.

A sample dump is an extension of the MIDI specification that will allow you to transfer sample data between devices, such as a computer and a sampler, for example. Using MIDI, a sample dump transfers digital audio information back and forth using a protocol called Sampler Dump

Standard (SDS). Since digital audio samples are usually quite large by nature compared to MIDI data, transferring samples to and from a sampler using this method can be quite slow due to the data rate MIDI uses, which is 31,250 Hz baud, or 31,250 bits per second.

As an alternative, if you have an SCSI (Small Computer System Interface) connection on your computer, you might also use the SCSI MIDI Device Interface (SMDI) protocol instead. This protocol uses SCSI to transmit and receive samples to and from a sampler. This protocol is a much more effective way of transmitting digital audio sample data between two devices.

In order to use SMDI or SDS, you will need host software that will allow you to configure the connection between your computer and a sampler. Sonic Foundry's Sound Forge, through its Sampler tools option as shown in Figure 6.21, fills that purpose. You will also need a compatible external sampler and SCSI card if you wish to use the SMDI protocol. If you decide to use SDS, make sure the connection between the sampler and the computer is direct, not daisy chained or filtered in any way.

Figure 6.21
The Sampler
Configuration window
in Sound Forge allows
you to make a
connection with your
sampler through MIDI
or SCSI cables

About LTB (Linear Time Base)

With the growing popularity of virtual or software synthesizers, the need for better MIDI timing within a computer is becoming increasingly important due to the nature of this type of application. Linear Time Base (LTB), which is developed by Steinberg, tries to address this issue by providing a high-speed MIDI timing protocol, offering sample-accurate timing for MIDI communications.

LTB is a MIDI time-stamping technique that bypasses the computer's operating system, in much the same way Steinberg's ASIO drivers do. This allows for a more efficient transfer of information and reduces delays between MIDI events that are played on a keyboard and reproduced by a virtual synthesizer, for example.

LTB is not a new standard, but rather an enhancement to MIDI, and is only supported by a few MIDI devices developed by Steinberg. However, you will be seeing more and more of this type of sample accurate synchronization technology for MIDI in the near future as developers catch on to the importance of having good timing when using software synthesizers in conjunction with hardware synthesizers.

7

MIDI Inside Your Computer

In this chapter, we'll cover the installation of peripherals such as MIDI interfaces and audio sound cards with MIDI support. We'll also cover many optimization techniques to make sure your computer runs as smoothly as possible under audio and MIDI applications.

Integrating such topics into a book about MIDI might seem like overkill, since MIDI in itself does not require that much out of a computer. After all, you could run a MIDI sequencer under a 386-compatible PC, a Mac Plus, an Atari 1040ST, or even a Commodore 64! But the reality of MIDI today is far more complex, as the lines between MIDI and digital audio are blurring with the use of virtual MIDI ports, software synthesizers, and integrated MIDI ports and synthesizers on sound cards.

Don't forget that most MIDI sequencers today are offering ever more digital audio features, taking the traditional MIDI workhouses toward a completely integrated virtual studio environment. Tools like Propellerhead's Reason, for example, which integrates software instruments, as well as digital audio effects processing, mixing environment, MIDI sequencing, and parameter automation, are just a simple reminder of such environments. So, understanding how to configure these peripherals and setting them up properly inside your computer is essential to a successful marriage between your hardware and software.

Here's a summary of what you will learn in this chapter:

▶ How to install a MIDI or audio peripheral in your PC.

▶ How to install a MIDI or audio peripheral in your Macintosh.

▶ The importance of having updated drivers.

▶ What OMS and FreeMIDI are.

▶ How to install drivers (PC and Mac) and system extensions (Mac).

▶ How to optimize your PC for MIDI and audio applications.

▶ How to optimize your Macintosh for MIDI and audio applications.

Installing Your Peripheral

There are three types of peripheral installations:

▶ An external peripheral that is connected to your computer using a single cable such as a USB, serial, parallel, or FireWire connection.

▶ A PCI card that needs to be inserted inside your computer and offers different types of connectors on the back part (or visible portion) of the card.

▶ A PCI card, as with the previous type, but this time, the card is connected to a breakout box, which houses all the connections to your external MIDI and audio devices. This type of PCI card is often referred to as a host card. The breakout box can either sit on your desk or be inserted in a standard 19-inch rack.

Installing a PCI Card

It is highly recommended that you turn off your computer before connecting your external peripherals, such as a MIDI interface, MIDI sync box, or external audio interface. As for the two other types, you should not install any hardware device while the computer is running. So, for good measure, turn off your computer and disconnect its power cable before installing any new device.

Here's how to install a PCI card in your computer:

1. Turn off your computer and disconnect its power cable.

2. Remove the cover from your computer and position it in a way that is easy for you to access the PCI slots on the motherboard.

3. Select the empty PCI slot where you will install your card or host card. Make sure the slot is a PCI slot. PCI slots are distinguishable from ISA slots by being shorter and set back farther from the outside of the computer. If you have a motherboard that was purchased after 2000, chances are you have PCI slots, not ISA slots. For example, newer Macintosh computers have only PCI slots.

4. Before removing the PCI card from its protective anti-static bag, touch the metal power supply case of the computer in order to dissipate any static electricity your body may have accumulated. You might want to avoid working on a synthetic or wool carpet, which are prone to accumulate static electricity.

5. Remove the metal bracket that covers the access hole on the back of the computer. This bracket is typically either fastened to the computer with a single screw or needs to be twisted off. Be careful if twisting, since you could damage motherboard components at the bottom of the bracket.

6. Position the PCI card or host card over the target PCI slot and fit the card loosely over it with the card in the upright position. Press the card gently but firmly downward into the slot until the card is completely and squarely seated in the slot. If the card seems difficult to seat, a slight rocking motion may help.

7. Screw the PCI card's metal bracket down into the screw hole on the back of your computer using the screw you removed in step 5 above.

8. Place the cover back on your computer and place it in its normal position.

NOTE
If your PCI card is a host for a breakout box, it is important that you also connect the host to the breakout box before turning on your computer again.

9. Mount the rack-mount or breakout box unit in your rack, or place it on a desktop in a convenient but secure place.

10. Connect one end of the supplied host cable to the appropriate connector on the rack mount unit, as described by your manufacturer.

11. Connect the other end of the host cable to the appropriate connector on the PCI host card that now resides in your computer.

12. If there are screws on each end to make the connection tighter, make sure they are tightened so that the connecting cable won't become disconnected.

13. Connect the appropriate end of the AC power supply (if your device requires AC power) into the wall outlet to supply standard house current. Plug the other end into the AC power jack behind the rack-mount unit or breakout box.

Preparing Your Connection

If you are going to connect an external device to your computer through a USB, FireWire, Parallel, or Serial cable, you don't need to open your computer up, but you do need to make some necessary verifications in order to establish if the device you are about to install is fully compatible with your system. For example, you will have to make sure you have USB support enabled and running or that you have a serial port available. Also note that while USB and FireWire are hot-swappable interfaces (which implies that they can be plugged in and out while the computer is ON), Serial and Parallel connections generally require the computer to be turned off before connecting anything to these ports.

NOTE

Macintosh computers come equipped with USB already enabled. If you are installing a USB device on a PC, you need to make sure there is a USB port installed and enabled on your computer before continuing with the installation.

From your PC desktop, click Start > Control Panel > Systems > Device Manager. In the Device Manager window (as shown in Figure 7.1), you should find an entry saying "Universal Serial Bus controllers." This should be enabled (see Figure 7.2 to see an installed but disabled device). If the heading does not even exist, it means one of three things: 1) you don't have USB support, 2) you haven't enabled the USB functions in your computer's BIOS, or 3) you don't have any USB devices installed yet on your computer. If you don't have USB support on your computer, you will need to upgrade your operating system to one that supports USB, or upgrade your computer to one that offers USB support.

If your computer supports USB but is not yet enabled, you will need to access your computer's BIOS feature by pressing the Delete key as your computer boots up. In the BIOS feature of your computer, you should locate an option that allows you to enable/disable USB support; if it is set to disabled, change it to enabled, save your settings, and reboot. If it is already enabled, exit the system BIOS without saving, and reboot. Note that you should consult your computer's or motherboard's documentation in order to find out exactly how to enable USB support in your BIOS before making any changes.

If you have made changes to your BIOS, Windows should recognize any USB port present on your computer and it will probably prompt you to enter your Windows installation disk or CD as it installs support for USB on your computer. Simply follow the on-screen instructions and installation process.

Now that you have USB support, you are ready to install your USB device.

Figure 7.1

The System Properties, Device Manager window should display the USB BUS controller if USB is installed on your PC

Figure 7.2
A disabled device
would appear with a red
X over the device as
displayed here for the
Generic USB Hub

If you have a device that connects through a serial port, make sure you have an available serial port on your computer that is not assigned to another peripheral, such as an external modem or serial mouse. On a PC, be sure the serial port is enabled, as shown in Figure 7.3. To access this window, click Start > Settings > Control Panel > System > Device Manager. Then click the "plus sign" next to the Ports (COM & LPT) heading. This should expand the list to display the installed ports. Select one and click the Properties button at the bottom of the Device Manager dialog box. The Communications Port properties dialog box should appear and tell you if the device is enabled or not. If a COM port does not appear at all, you might have to activate it in your computer's BIOS. To activate this port in your BIOS, consult your computer's documentation or consult a computer technician if in doubt.

Figure 7.3
The Device Manager in
Windows allows you to
see if your serial port is
installed and active

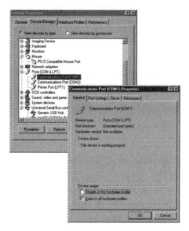

Serial ports are no longer available on Macintosh computers. As mentioned earlier, though, it is possible to add a serial port to your computer if you wish to remain compatible with your MIDI interface using a serial port connection. If your Macintosh does have a serial port, it is recommended that you use the serial port labeled Modem rather than the one labeled Printer, especially if the printer system extension (the Mac's version of a printer driver) is loaded in your operating system. Finally, disconnect any device that might be connected to the Mac's modem port if you wish to install your MIDI interface on this serial port.

CHAPTER 7

After completing these preliminary steps, installing an interface using a simple connection is easy. At this point, you know that your computer supports the type of connection you wish to use; its protocol communication support is installed on your computer so you're ready to install the device's drivers (or system extensions on Macintosh computers). But before you do so, you should:

1. Turn off your computer, even with USB and FireWire devices.
2. Connect the cable to your external device.
3. Connect the other end of your cable to your computer.
4. Gather your installation disk or CD-ROM.
5. Turn on the computer and move on to the next section.

Getting the Right Driver

MIDI application software communicates with MIDI interfaces or sound cards with MIDI interfaces through software known as drivers. A driver is basically a dedicated program that tells your operating system what the device is and how it should interact with it. The driver also gives your MIDI or audio application access to the interface itself, by giving it necessary information on the card itself. Once the application knows how to address the card's properties, it can display this card's options in the setup dialog boxes usually found in the application itself.

For example, once the application knows which card you are using (through the information provided by the driver), you can choose which MIDI port you wish to activate in this application. When you purchase or install a new peripheral, such as a MIDI interface or sound card, you should get a CD-ROM or a diskette with appropriate drivers, or you may be able to download them from the manufacturer's website. In fact, it is recommended that you find out whether the driver provided with your peripheral is the latest version of this driver. If not, it is preferable to download the most recent version of the driver from the manufacturer's website. You can usually find an Internet address for your peripheral included in the documentation that comes with it. You should also know that in some cases, certain revisions of drivers work best with different combinations of environments, such as a specific software version running on a specific operating system. Reading the manufacturer's recommendations, the FAQ's (Frequently Asked Questions), user forums, and newsgroups are a great way to find out this information and make sure you have a combination that works well.

NOTE

In Pre OS X Macintosh operating systems, the term "driver" does not exist; instead, Macintosh refers to "system extensions," which operate in a similar way. Macintosh has adopted the term "driver" in its OS X (version 10). So, to avoid confusion, this book will always refer to "drivers," but be aware that your operating system may still call them "system extensions."

We will look at how to install a driver later in this chapter, since driver installations are OS specific. In other words, you need to install the driver that corresponds to the right device and the right operating system. For example, if you have a MIDI interface X model 1, you should make sure you have the driver for that specific device. Furthermore, if you are running Windows XP or OS X, make sure you have the correct version of this driver. Otherwise, you risk having a device that crashes your computer, doesn't work, prevents other devices from working properly, or simply doesn't work as well as it should. So, as you can see, making sure you have the right stuff is essential.

Most of the time, a text file called "readme" accompanies the driver files. This file usually contains precise installation procedures for your MIDI or audio device and some last minute information about your device that was added after the manufacturer printed the documentation included in its packaging. Take a moment to read this file before starting the installation procedure.

About OMS and FreeMIDI

If you are a Macintosh user and wish to install a multi-port MIDI interface, chances are you will need to install either OMS (Open MIDI System) from Opcode, or FreeMIDI from Mark Of The Unicorn (MOTU). These two applications are different versions of MIDI managers that support multiple MIDI ports and are usually required by many devices and software applications in order to address these multiple MIDI ports. If you only have a single MIDI port, you might not need to install one of these applications; however, they will provide greater control over your MIDI management on Macintosh computers. On the other hand, OS X includes its own MIDI manager, so if you are running this OS, verify with your device's manufacturer documentation to find out how it is implemented in OS X. At the time of the writing of this book, very few MIDI applications were compatible with this new OS from Macintosh.

You can get a copy of both FreeMIDI and OMS at the developers' Web sites: For FreeMIDI, visit www.motu.com, and for OMS, visit www.opcode.com. Before downloading and installing the MIDI manager, consult your device manufacturer's documentation to find out which one works best with your device. Some applications will also only work with one or the other. For example, running Cubase VST on your Mac requires OMS, not FreeMIDI.

Installing both FreeMIDI and OMS is quite simple. Depending on the number of MIDI devices you have, however, it might be a lengthy process the first time through, since you need to configure your MIDI setup before you can use the manager effectively. Once downloaded, unpack or uncompress the file and double-click the installer file. After that, all you have to do is follow on-screen instructions, then restart your computer. Note that most software applications will need OMS to run; however, if you have Performer or Digital Performer, you will need FreeMIDI.

You can run both applications at the same time, but you will need to deactivate system extensions (drivers) from one application to avoid problems.

If you are running a PC, you don't need OMS or FreeMIDI.

CONFIGURING OMS

Here are first-time OMS configuration instructions:

Start by decompressing the OMS file you have downloaded, or locate the Opcode folder on your hard drive. Locate the OMS Applications folder, then OMS Setup. Double click OMS Setup. OMS will inform you that it has not yet been configured. Click OK. Click OK once again in the Create A New Studio Setup dialog box when it appears. If you have not yet installed your MIDI device driver, the OMS driver search will turn up empty. Once you have installed your device and properly configured it, run OMS and look for the OMS Studio Setup. A box will appear asking you to choose the port on which you've attached your MIDI device, as shown in Figure 7.4. Do not choose a port—just click Search. OMS will then begin searching.

Figure 7.4
The OMS Driver
Search dialog box

The OMS Driver Setup shows the installed device in a list when OMS successfully finds the driver. Click OK to let OMS define (shows "Identifying") all the output ports it found on your device.

The OMS MIDI Device Setup dialog box will appear, showing the available output ports with open checkboxes to the left of each port. You will now have to check these open boxes to enable each of the output ports. Click OK.

Next, the My Studio Setup appears with a File Save dialog box over it. You will now need to name and save your new Studio Setup (or use the default name) before you can assign various instruments to the device's outputs and inputs. Assign your various instruments and you are done.

At this point, your MIDI device is ready for use. You may now exit OMS Setup by quitting the application. The rest is up to the configuration within your music software. Generally, this means selecting OMS Compatibility, or Open Music System for your MIDI system setup.

Installing Your Driver Software

Once you've installed your hardware component, enabled the proper communication ports (such as USB or serial), downloaded the proper updated drivers, and installed OMS or FreeMidi if your hardware or software requires it, you are ready to install your peripheral. These instructions are standard steps that you might want to follow to help you understand the process of installing new MIDI-related peripherals on a specific OS running on your computer. However, it is not meant to replace the instructions provided by your device's manufacturer, since there might be some device-specific steps you have to follow.

Installing USB Port Drivers on Windows

When you power up your computer after connecting your device for the first time, the Add New Hardware Wizard window should appear, reporting that it found an unknown device. Depending on the version of Windows you have and the device you are installing, it might automatically identify which manufacturer and model you are attempting to install, especially if you are installing earlier models on a more recent version of Windows, such as Windows XP. If it does not recognize the manufacturer and model of the device, it should ask you to choose a location where it can find the proper files. Simply tell Windows where it can find the latest driver. For example, if it is on the CD provided with the device, specify the path to the CD after loading it in your CD-ROM drive. On the other hand, if you have downloaded the file from the Internet, specify the location of these files on your hard disk.

FILES MAY BE ZIPPED
Some downloadable files are compressed into a single file and need to be expanded into a folder or on a diskette in order for Windows to recognize these files as driver information files. If this is the case, you might have to skip the installation process for now, unpack or uncompress the files to a specific location on your disk, and then proceed to a manual installation of the drivers. This will be explained in following paragraphs.

1. Make sure your installation CD or diskette is in the computer.

2. When the Add New Hardware Wizard reports that it detected an unknown device, click Next.

3. On the next screen, select "Search for the best driver for your device" and click Next.

4. Indicate the path to these files if the computer wasn't able to find them automatically. Select Choose Path, then type in or browse until you locate the appropriate files. In most cases, this will be on your CD drive or in the folder to which you downloaded the files. Click OK when you are finished.

5. On the next screen, Windows should indicate it has searched for the driver files for your device and is now ready to install the driver. Click the Next button to continue. If it tells you the folder does not contain any device definition files, it might be because the path you specified is incorrect or that the file you have downloaded is compressed. Refer to the note above if this is the case.

6. Windows will copy files and then indicate it has finished installing the software. Click the Finish button.

7. Next, you might see Windows indicating that it has found another unknown device and then see it automatically install the software for it, if your device needs it. Simply let Windows install what it needs or repeat these previous steps if necessary.

At this point, the software drivers should be installed on your computer and functional.

In some cases, you might have to manually install a driver on your computer. If this is the case, follow these steps:

1. Click the Start button in the task bar.
2. Click Settings > Control Panel.
3. Click the Add/Remove Hardware icon.
4. Click the Next button on the first Add/Remove Hardware Wizard screen, then select the Add/Troubleshoot a Device item and click Next again.
5. After searching for a new hardware device, you will be shown a screen from which to choose a hardware device; select the Add a New Device item and push the Next button.
6. On the next screen, select "No, I want to select the hardware from a list" and click the Next button.
7. Select "Sound, video, and game controllers" from the hardware type list and click the Next button.
8. Click the Have Disk button.
9. You will be prompted for the location of the manufacturer's driver diskette; browse to or enter the appropriate disk drive specification and folder location and click OK.
10. For Windows 2000/XP users, when the Digital Signature Not Found dialog box pops up, push the Yes button to indicate that you want to continue the installation if you are sure the driver you are installing is the correct driver for your device and operating system.
11. In the Select a Device Driver dialog box, choose the appropriate device from the list and click Next.
12. Click Next to start device driver installation.
13. For Windows 2000/XP users, when the Digital Signature Not Found dialog box pops up again, click the Yes button to indicate that you want to continue the installation.
14. When the files have been copied, click the Finish button in the Completing the Found New Hardware Wizard dialog box.
15. At this point, Windows might need to restart in order for the driver installation to be completed. If this is the case, restart your computer when prompted to do so.

Installing USB Port Drivers on Macintosh

The first time you power up your Macintosh with the newly connected MIDI USB device, you will receive a message saying that an "unknown USB device has been detected." Click OK and proceed with the driver installation. You may also install the drivers first, and then plug in the MIDI device. Just make sure your device is set to function in USB mode if it offers different modes.

For the installation, you will have to insert your CD containing the drivers in the CD-ROM drive, or run the installation directly from a downloaded file from your hard disk. Find the Installer program for your device, double click it, and follow the instructions on screen.

If you are using OMS or FreeMIDI, you will want to turn off AppleTalk, as it is necessary to use the same resources to manage MIDI. Normally, OMS or FreeMIDI should let you know if AppleTalk is on or off and suggest you turn it off. If not, go to the control panel or Chooser under the Apple Menu, select AppleTalk, and turn it off.

Installing Serial Port Drivers on Windows

If you have a MIDI device that uses a serial port to connect to your computer and you need to install it manually, follow the steps below. Note that when you start your computer after connecting your device, Windows should bring you directly to the Add New Hardware Wizard. From that point on, the steps are identical.

1. From the Windows Start menu, select Settings > Control Panel > Add New Hardware.

2. Click the Next button twice. The system will now search for Plug and Play (PnP) hardware.

3. If Windows does find one or more PnP devices, select No; devices on serial ports will never show up as a PnP, so it should not appear in this list. Select Next to continue. Windows then asks if you would like it to search for the new hardware.

4. Select "No, I want to select the hardware from a list" and press the Next button. Windows wants you to select the type of hardware you are installing.

5. Scroll down the list and highlight "Sound, video and game controllers." Then click Next.

6. When the next dialog appears, click the Have Disk button.

7. Insert the driver software CD or diskette in the proper drive and click OK.

8. Type in or browse until you locate the appropriate files. If you have downloaded the files from the Internet, you will have to specify the folder where these files are located.

9. When the next dialog appears, select the proper device and click OK.

10. When the next dialog appears, click Finish. Windows will copy and install the Windows driver files.

From this point on, you might need to do some additional steps depending on the device driver and device you just installed. For additional installation setup information, consult your manufacturer's installation procedure documentation.

Installing Serial Port Drivers on Macintosh

If you have a Macintosh that supports a serial port and its drivers are not currently installed on your system, you will need to install them prior to using this serial port. This might occur if you have added a serial port card on a G3 or G4 computer, for example. Once you have connected your serial port MIDI device to the computer, power up your device and then your computer.

1. Insert the supplied driver software CD or diskette. Have your System Folder open, with the OMS folder accessible.

2. Double click the disk icon when it appears and open the installed device folder for Macintosh. If you downloaded the file from the Internet, open that folder. Once opened, drag the driver icon for your device into the OMS folder.

3. Within your hard drive files, find the Opcode folder. In the Opcode folder, find the OMS Applications folder, then OMS Setup. Double-click OMS Setup.

5. OMS will inform you that it has not yet been configured. Click OK.

6. The Create A New Studio Setup dialog box now appears. Click OK.

7. The OMS Driver Search box asks you to choose the port on which you've attached the installed device (either Modem or Printer). Choose a port and click Search. OMS begins searching.

8. OMS Driver Setup now shows the newly installed device (and the port to which it is attached) in a list when OMS successfully finds the driver. Click OK. [OMS will now define all of the device's output ports. The OMS MIDI Device Setup dialog box will appear, showing the device's available output ports with checkboxes to the left of each port. Make sure that all of these boxes are checked to enable each of the output ports.]

9. Click OK.

10. Next, the My Studio Setup appears with a file save dialog box over it. You will now need to name and save your new Studio Setup before you can assign various instruments to the device's outputs and inputs. Assign your instruments, and you are done. You may now exit OMS Setup by quitting the application.

Optimizing Your Computer for MIDI and Audio

Although MIDI is not a big consumer of computer resources, the use of MIDI-driven software synthesizers might require more from your computer than it can handle. Software synthesizers use your sound card to convert digital sounds it processes into analog signals that you can hear. Sometimes, your software might use samples on your hard drive to produce its sounds. In this respect, then, MIDI can be a big consumer of computer resources. The following tips are meant to help you optimize your system for audio; in other words, software synthesizers and samplers driven by MIDI.

Some of these tips might improve your computer's performance a little and some might improve them a lot. It depends on your system and how it is currently configured. But, before going into the platform-specific optimization tips, here are some general tips that you might want to consider:

▶ Get more RAM. If you intend to use virtual or software synthesizers, the more RAM (Random Access Memory) you have, the smoother your ride will be. Consider 256 MB of RAM as a minimum. If you've noticed that your hard disk is always spinning and your computer is excessively slow, that's a good indication that you might need more RAM, as your computer is using virtual memory—a portion of your hard disk—to compensate for the lack in memory resources. This has two major effects: slowing down your system considerably and putting your hard disk under a lot of stress, which may eventually cause it to experience problems prematurely. But before you go out and buy more RAM, make sure to read some of the optimization tips suggested below—they might solve some of your problems. Also note that all RAM is not created equal and not all motherboards take the same kind of RAM. You should refer to your computer supplier or your manufacturer's documentation to find out how you should go about updating your RAM. Using identical RAM type as the one(s) already installed on your motherboard when upgrading your RAM is a good start, since the easiest way to get unpredictable behaviors from your computer is to mismatch your RAM.

▶ Reduce the quantity of fonts on your system. The more fonts you have, the more memory they take, leaving you less space for audio and MIDI applications.

▶ Defragment your hard disks regularly. Hard disks are like shelves in a grocery store. People come in, grab stuff from shelves, then employees put stuff back at the end of the day, moving misplaced products back to where they belong and cleaning up after the store closes so that the next day everything looks fresh and is easy for you to find. Now imagine if they didn't do that…. Writing on a hard disk, then erasing, then writing again—eventually little bits of information are scattered everywhere on your hard disk, and your computer will have to look all over the disk to gather the information you want and give it to you. This takes time. Making sure you don't have fragments of information spread all across your hard disk is a good habit to get into. Macintosh and Windows both have tools to help you do this effectively. Some recording engineers will use the defragmentation tool on their system after each recording session. Although this is commendable, it might not be necessary in your case. However, defragmenting your hard disks regularly, perhaps once a week, is a good habit to cultivate if you wish a long and prosperous life for your hard disks.

▶ Update. This doesn't mean update your hardware but, rather, getting the latest drivers or system extensions for your peripherals and operating system. This might help solve some conflicts or improve overall performance. On the other hand, "If it ain't broke, don't fix it". If your system works fine the way it is, stick with it. You shouldn't feel the need to update for the sake of updating, but rather to solve issues that may be caused by outdated systems.

Optimizing Your PC

Most of these optimization tips will require that you reboot your computer before they take effect. This said, it might be a good idea to do one optimization at a time, reboot, and witness the effects of this optimization before continuing. If you don't see any changes, bring your system back to the setting it was before you applied these tips. You should always back up your system before optimizing it. If something goes wrong, at least you can go back to how it was rather than losing everything.

If it is possible, it's best to dedicate a computer to audio and MIDI applications only. This means that no other software or hardware peripherals should be connected or installed on this machine. Limiting and controlling what goes in and out will reduce the potential for conflicts, simplify the process of troubleshooting, keep your system resources open for audio/MIDI applications, and avoid all sorts of nasty problems happening while recording. So, leaving games, office applications, and especially Internet-related tools out of your computer will greatly improve your chances of having a healthy audio system.

Reduce Graphics Acceleration

This specifies the amount of acceleration you want for your graphics hardware. Full acceleration is the fastest and is recommended for most computers. If you are using a PCI graphics card, reducing the graphic acceleration might help, however this will not make any noticeable differences if you are using an AGP graphics card. In recent years, it has been found that reducing hardware acceleration in fact puts a heavier load on the CPU and uses up CPU cycles better dedicated to the music applications. Hardware acceleration should only be lowered as a troubleshooting step as it does not typically increase the overall performance of the system. This said, if you use an older PCI graphics card, this tip might apply to you since audio and MIDI applications do not require intense graphic support. You can decrease the hardware acceleration slider as shown in Figure 7.5. If you don't see any changes in your audio and MIDI performance after doing this, such as drops in the audio while the screen is refreshing, set the slider back to full graphics acceleration. To adjust your graphics acceleration rate:

1.   Click the Start button in your task bar.
2.   Select Settings > Control Panel >System > Performance.
3.   In the Performance dialog box, click the Graphics button.
4.   In the Graphics dialog box, drag the slider to the left for no acceleration.
5.   If you find this deteriorates your graphics performance too much, bring it up a notch.
6.   Click the Apply button, then OK.

Figure 7.5
The Advanced Graphics
Settings dialog box

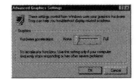

CHAPTER 7

Activate DMA on All IDE Drives

DMA stands for Direct Memory Access, which allows for the transfer of data to and from IDE devices such as your hard disk, without heavy dependence on the CPU, and increases transfer speeds. Activating DMA on your hard disk will improve your hard disk's performance. In theory, enabling DMA increases UltraDMA (hardware interface) hard disk transfer rates to 33.3, 66, 100, or even 133 MB/sec, depending on the hardware your motherboard uses. In practice, speed will increase substantially from the old standard of 16 MB/sec, depending on the capabilities of your drive. Enabling DMA will also reduce the amount of CPU resources required by hard disk transfers by anywhere from 2%-15%. This option is not enabled by default because your hard disk needs to support DMA. So, before proceeding with this optimization, make sure to read your hard disk documentation to find out if DMA transfer is supported. For example, SCSI disks will not support DMA transfers. To activate DMA:

1. Click the Start button in your task bar.
2. Select Settings > Control Panel > System > Device Manager.
3. Click the plus sign next to the disk drive resource entry to expand the list of drives displayed, as shown in Figure 7.6.
4. Select the desired drive and click the Properties button.
5. Make the Settings tab active and check the DMA option box, as shown in Figure 7.7.
6. Click OK twice.

Note that the above is for Win9x/ME; in Windows 2000 and XP, DMA is set at the IDE/ATA controllers section of the Device Manager.

Figure 7.6
The System Properties, Device Manager tab with the disk drive entry expanded—here, you can see one of the selected hard disks

Figure 7.7
Activating the DMA on your hard disk through the hard disk Settings dialog box

Turn Off Auto Insert Notification

The auto-insert notification allows your Win 9x/Me OS to read and recognize any CD-based device inserted in a drive during operation, making its content available to you automatically. For example, if your CD contains a game with an "Autorun" function in its root directory, the CD will launch the application addressed by the Autorun program. If you insert an audio CD, it will automatically load your CD player. This might be useful in most cases, but if you are using sampling CD-ROMs and are constantly loading discs into your CD-ROM drive, it will take system resources away from the audio/MIDI applications by constantly checking the ROM drive for newly inserted discs.

1. Click the Start button in your task bar.

2. Select Settings > Control Panel > System > Device Manager.

3. Click the plus sign next to the CD-ROM drive resource entry to expand the list of drives displayed.

4. Select the appropriate CD-ROM drive and click the Properties button.

5. Make the Settings tab active and uncheck the Auto insert notification option, as shown in Figure 7.8.

6. Click OK twice.

Figure 7.8
Turning off the
Auto insert notification
option in the
CD-ROM drive's
setting dialog box

IRQ settings

PCs use IDs to manage installed devices within a system. Each device is given a number called an IRQ (Interrupt ReQuest) number. The processor addresses each device through its IRQ number. Some PC operating systems' architectures might allow for different devices to share IRQ numbers, as shown in Figure 7.9. Most of the time, this is not a problem. But if your device requires more resources or attention, such as a sound card, it might not like to share its IRQ with another installed device. This might be the case when a sound card shares IRQ numbers with TV capture or tuner cards, graphics cards, SCSI cards, IDE controller, or internal modems.

The easiest way to solve this problem is to turn off your computer and move the audio card to another PCI slot. When you move a PCI card, Windows will scan the PCI busses and will reassign an IRQ number automatically. This might require a few trials before you get an IRQ that won't come into conflict with other devices, but it doesn't require too much technical knowledge of operating systems on your behalf. Avoid using the first PCI slot, since it is usually next to the AGP slot, and having two high throughput cards next to one another is not a good idea. Also, the first PCI slot shares its IRQ with the AGP graphics system.

Figure 7.9
IRQ settings in this system show that the sound card shares its IRQ number (5) with other devices without creating conflicts

If you are not having problems with your peripherals in their current IRQ configurations, don't change anything, since playing with IRQ settings can be tricky. Technical knowledge of the operating system and system hardware is a must when trying to address this type of conflict.

Modify Your VCache Settings

You may or may not have oodles of RAM; however, Windows might be claiming some of it as its own through the VCache setting. VCache, simply put, is a local disk cache in RAM for the most recently requested data from the hard disk. Instead of moving it all back to the hard disk drive, Windows, through the VCache, retains some of the data in this virtual cache for easy and quick access in case it's needed again. Since this information is available through RAM, it greatly increases the speed. This is great if you have enough RAM on your system. If you don't have much to spare, however, VCache will claim an excess of RAM, leading to increased hard disk activity and slowing down your system performance. If you are running Windows 2000 or Windows XP, you should leave these settings alone, since they are well managed by the operating system. Under Windows 9x, the amount of VCache should vary depending on the amount of RAM installed on your system, so read these steps carefully to make the appropriate changes for your system's configuration:

1. Begin by finding your system.ini file. This should be located on your C drive in the Windows folder.
2. Make and save a backup copy of this file in case you wish to revert to its previous state after making the changes.
3. Double-click the system.ini file to open it in your text editor (such as Notepad).
4. Scroll down to where you see the indication [VCache] (as shown in Figure 7.10).
5. Follow the values in Table 7.1, below, and change the MaxFileCache and MinFileCache values.
6. Save the changes you made and exit Notepad or any text editor you used to edit the file.

Figure 7.10
Making changes to
your System.ini file to
optimize the VCache
settings in Notepad

Table 7.1
Optimizing your VCache settings in Windows 98, SE, and ME.

RAM available	MinFileCache Setting	MaxFileCache Setting	Chunksize Setting	NameCache Setting	DirectoryCache Setting	When you are satisfied with the MinFile and MaxFile Cache Settings, you may also enter these values below in the System.ini Comments
16 MB	2048	4096	256	1024	48	You should really get more RAM!
32 MB	2048 or 6144	6144 or 8192	512	2048	48	You can try different settings for the MinFile and MaxFile Cache Settings.
48 MB	3072	10240	512	2048	48	
64 MB	4096	12288	1024	4096	96	
96 MB	8192	20480	2048	4096	96	
128 MB	16384	24576	2048	4096	96	
196 MB	16384	32768	2048	4096	96	With more than 128 MB of RAM, you should limit your MaxFileCache to 70% of the total physical RAM but not exceed 512 MB in the MaxFileCache value.
256 MB	16384	49152	2048	4096	96	
512 MB	32768	98304	2048	4096	96	
1 GB	65536	131072	2048	4096	96	

Hard Disk Cluster Size

When you format your hard disk, you create little boxes (referred to by your computer as "clusters") where information can be stored and used by your computer. Each box has its own address, which the computer keeps a record of in a table of contents. This way, it knows where to look for information when it needs it. The operating system on your computer will create a number of boxes corresponding to three variables: the size of the hard disk you are formatting, the format used, and the size of each box (or cluster).

You can't do anything about the size of your hard disk, but you can choose which format to use and the size of each cluster in this format. If you are using Windows 95, you can only use a format called FAT16 (this is the method the operating system uses to organize files on the disk). On Windows NT, 98, ME, 2000, XP, and above, the most common formats are FAT32 and NTFS (you cannot use NTFS format on Win98 or ME). Cluster sizes can vary between 4 KB to 32 KB (64 KB if you are using a large drive on Windows NT or 2000). Using small clusters may give you more space on your drive because small files will waste less space. For example, a 5 KB file will use two clusters, wasting only 3 KB of space, where the same file on a 32 KB cluster disk will waste 27 KB (see example in Figure 7.11). The flip side of this is that when you are recording large files, such as audio files, your hard disk will need to write information more often, thus slowing down the process overall.

Formatting your hard drive in FAT32 rather than FAT16 format will allow you to use your disk more effectively. By using a program such as Partition Magic from PowerQuest (www.powerquest.com), you can easily convert a FAT16 partition into a FAT32 partition without loosing any information on your disk (i.e. you don't have to reformat your drive completely). Using the same software, you can also determine the optimal cluster size for your drive, as suggested in Figure 7.11. If you are using Windows ME, 2000, or XP, a built-in application will also allow you to convert your disk to FAT32. This said, it always a good idea to back up all your information BEFORE converting your hard disk since there are no guarantees and hiccups might occur during the format conversion process which may cause errors on your disk that will force you to reformat anyway. Better to be safe than sorry.

Figure 7.11
The Resize Clusters dialog box found in Partition Magic—you can access this dialog box when you right-click a drive inside Partition Magic and select Advanced > Resize Clusters

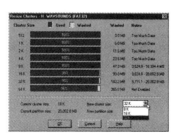

Page Buffer Size

A page buffer stores frequently repeated data in RAM (as opposed to recent accessed data found in the VCache) for faster access when it is required. Having a larger memory buffer storage area will enhance your system's performance by alleviating the need to frequently access the slow hard disk. The default value for this is set at 16 KB, which is represented by the value 4 in your system.ini file. By increasing this value to 32 (or 128 KB) you can reduce bottlenecks in your system. To do this:

1. Begin by finding your system.ini file. This should be located on your C drive in the Windows folder.
2. Make and save a backup copy of this file in case you wish to revert to its previous state after making the changes.
3. Double-click the system.ini file to open it in your text editor (such as Notepad).
4. Scroll down to where you see the indication [386Enh].
5. After the last line in this header, insert the following line—without the quotation marks: "PageBuffers=32" If this line already exists, replace the existing value if it is less than 32.

Disable Unused Ports

If you don't have any USB, serial, or parallel devices hooked up to your computer, you might want to disable these unused ports since, even though they are not being used, they require additional IRQ assignments and unnecessary accessing by the system bus. In some cases, this might be the easiest way to resolve IRQ conflicts. To disable your unused ports, you will need to access your BIOS and disable them from there.

1. Access your system's properties.
2. Select the line displaying the USB serial bus controller.
3. Select any installed component under this heading and click Remove.
4. When all entries have been removed, click Apply, and then OK. At this point you will need to reboot your computer.
5. When your computer reboots, hit the Delete key to access your system's BIOS features.
6. Locate the USB enable/disable function in your BIOS. Once you have located it, disable it.
7. Save your BIOS settings and exit to continue with your system's rebooting process.

Disable Superfluous Startup Items

When Windows boots up, it will activate a variety of programs on startup, such as anti-virus protection, system monitoring, and so on. While some of these items are essential, others will draw resources from your audio/MIDI applications. Culprits include System Agent, Find Fast, Active Desktop, Office Startup, RealPlayer's StartCenter, NetMeeting, Active Movie, Animated cursors and icons, and many others. They may be useful, but they use loads of memory. For example, Norton AntiVirus and Norton Utilities used together may reduce performance by up to 28% depending on your system's resources. To disable these items, do this:

1. From your Desktop, click Start > Run.

2. Type MSCONFIG and click OK.

3. Click the Startup tab.

4. Disable any startup item that you found in the list mentioned above (see Figure 7.12). You will want to leave Windows system items such as System Tray, for example.

5. Click Apply, then OK when done. If you find that you disabled some items you would like to enable again, you can simply run MSCONFIG as you just did once again and add a check next to the desired items in the list.

Figure 7.12
The System Configuration Utility's Startup dialog box— disable Startup items to free up system resources

Screen Savers and Power Management

This is a simple one: Don't use screen savers or power management functions. These features will consume resources at the most inopportune times. As a general rule, try to avoid having anything running in the background that can draw processing power away from your primary objective—recording audio and MIDI. To disable screen savers and power management, right click your desktop and select Properties. Then click the Screen Saver tab and choose None from the dropdown menu (as shown in Figure 7.13). Then in the same page, click the Settings button and select None in every dropdown menu found in that page. When done, click OK twice.

Figure 7.13
Disabling the screen saver

Create a Static Swap File

A swap file or virtual memory was created as a method of extending the limits of installed RAM. When your system becomes low on available memory, Windows can use this virtual memory to buffer the oldest commands to this portion of your hard disk, since a virtual memory is the allocation of hard disk space to this specific task. This effectively allows Windows to temporarily house old information in this virtual memory. The process of juggling commands from virtual memory to active memory is where the name swap file comes from. Windows automatically allocates the amount of hard disk space dedicated to virtual memory, creating a dynamic swap file that grows on demand. This also means that the hard disk space is not dedicated to this file. The advantage of this is that you will have more disk space available for storage. However, as the swap file grows, bits and pieces of it will be scattered across the hard disk, participating in your computer's performance degradation since Windows will be putting data wherever it finds space. This will result in increasing amounts of time and effort from your hard disk in order to retrieve this data. The alternative is to set up a static or permanent swap file. This involves determining a fixed amount of hard disk space that will be reserved for your swap file where overflow information will be stored. The drawback of this optimization is that you will lose the use of this space on your hard disk.

DEFRAGMENTING

It is a good idea to defragment the hard disk where you want to create your static or permanent swap file before creating it. You can do this by using Norton's Speed Disk utility after creating the file if you have this utility, or proceed as follows:

Close all your programs. Switch your screen saver off by selecting Start > Settings > Control Panel > Display > Screen Saver. Then, from the dropdown menu, select None, as shown in Figure 7.13. Click Apply, then OK. Still in the control panel, double-click the System icon. Select the Performance tab, then the Virtual Memory button. Choose the Disable Virtual Memory option in this page. Windows will display a warning that you should ignore at this point and do not reboot. Now, run the disk defragmenter (usually found in Start > Programs > Accessories > System Tools) on all your hard disk, even if it says that your disk is showing 0% fragmentation.

From this point on, continue with the steps below.

To create a static swap file:

1. From your desktop, begin by clicking on Start > Settings > Control Panel > System.

2. In the System Properties dialog box, make the Performance tab active.

3. In the Performance page, click the Virtual Memory button.

4. Select the "Let me specify my own virtual memory" settings option. A good rule of thumb is to set your virtual memory at 2.5 to 3 times the size of your RAM, and it should not exceed 90% of your disk's space (the one where the swap file will be located).

5. Choose the fastest or least-used hard disk (if the fastest one is already overused) on which to create the swap file.

Figure 7.14
Creating a static virtual memory by setting a fixed swap file on one of your hard disks

6. Enter a minimum and maximum value for your swap file. Remember, this depends on your RAM size. In Figure 7.14, the system's RAM is 256 MB, so this value is evaluated at three times the size. You may also see the sidebar for more information on this.

7. Click OK when done.

NOTE
You might find that setting your virtual memory at 2.5 to 3 times the size of your RAM is not sufficient or precise enough. To monitor the use and evaluate the actual amount of space used by virtual memory, you can download a shareware program called Swap Monitor from Flip Tech (www.fliptech.net/swapmon). This utility, once installed, will monitor your swap file usage and keep the results for you. You can then see how big your swap file really needs to be when compared with how your system uses it. You might also want to give yourself a 10%-20% increased margin when setting your swap file size to provide for future applications and system usage. After using this tool, you might learn you don't need as much as 2.5 to 3 times the size of your RAM for your swap file, thus regaining the use of your hard disk space.

CHAPTER 7

Changing the Computer's Role

By default, Windows will set the role of your computer as a desktop computer. This is a safe setting for general Windows-based computers. However, when dealing with demanding hard disk functions such as audio applications, streaming audio data through your system, it might be a good idea to shift some of your system's muscle toward handling these specific needs. By switching the role of your computer from desktop to network server, you allow your computer to focus its attention more toward disk-based operations, which is perfect for these types of applications. To do this:

1. On your desktop, right-click My Computer and choose Properties.

2. Select the Performance tab and then click the File System button.

3. The dialog box defaults on the Hard Disk tab. In this dialog box, select Network Server next to the Typical role of this computer field, as shown in Figure 7.15.

4. Click Apply, then click OK.

Figure 7.15
The File System Properties, Hard Disk dialog box allows you to change the role of your computer

Reducing Read Ahead Optimization

The read ahead function allows your computer to read the information that is coming ahead on your hard disk. Normally, your computer anticipates that you will need this information, since it follows the information you have just retrieved. In most situations, this might be the case, especially with large media files such as audio and video files. However, when you are working in audio/MIDI applications, you might not need to read ahead that much, since you are constantly stopping the playback and changing things as you go along. That's when the read ahead optimization comes in handy. When running digital audio applications that use software samplers, sequencers, and synthesizers, the hard drive needs to go different places quickly, and reading information you don't really need only slows down your system. To do this:

1. Click the Start button in your task bar.

2. Select Settings > Control Panel > System > Performance.

3. In the Performance dialog box, click the File System button.

4. In the File System dialog box, make the Hard Disk tab active.

5. Bring the slider bar for the read ahead optimization to None, as shown in Figure 7.16.

6. Click the Apply button, then OK.

Figure 7.16
The File System
Properties, Hard Disk
dialog box

CHAPTER 7

Disable Write Behind Caching

Normally, your computer will buffer information into a cache memory in order to allow slow hard drives to catch up to fast memory when information is being transferred. This process might help if your hard drive is very slow, but data buffering greatly increases processing delays. By checking the Disable Write Behind Caching, it forces Windows to write data immediately to disk instead, which in turn increases the computer's performance, since the data is not buffered. This is useful when working in an office type application. When recording digital audio files, however, you want your computer to write this information as soon as possible so that you can free up your memory to do other things, like processing the sound. To do this:

1. Click the Start button in your task bar.
2. Select Settings > Control Panel > System > Performance.
3. In the Performance dialog box, click the File System button.
4. In the File System dialog box, make the Troubleshooting tab active.
5. Check the Disable write behind caching for all drives, as shown in Figure 7.17.
6. Click the Apply button, then OK.

Figure 7.17
The File System
Properties,
Troubleshooting
dialog box

Optimizing Your Mac

Although Apple computers are known to be easier to handle than their PC counterpart in terms of peripheral configuration, you still need to take a hand in optimizing your Macintosh for audio and MIDI applications. Avoiding audio pops, dropouts, and clicks due to an overloaded set of system extensions (drivers) or an improperly configured OS is exactly what we are going to look at here.

Create A Minimal Extension Set

A good way to optimize your Mac for audio and MIDI is to reduce the number of active extensions in your system when working with this type of software. You can create a separate set of extensions containing only the extensions necessary to use with your audio and MIDI peripherals and programs. To do this:

1. Open the Extension Manager control panel found under the Apple menu.

2. Select the MacOS Base Set. This might be called MacOS x.xx Base, depending on your OS version.

3. Press the Duplicate Set button in the bottom right corner of the dialog box.

4. Rename the set with a descriptive name such as "Audio," for example.

5. Enable any extensions necessary for your audio and MIDI applications and hardware, such as audio/MIDI sequencers, MIDI interfaces, and audio sound card (Figure 7.18). These extensions might include: FreeMIDI power plug and system extension, OMS, preferred device, MOTU USB driver, ReWire, REX shared library, TimeBandit.shlb, USB floppy enabler, and USB OMSMIDIDriver. This is not a complete list of extensions, but merely a starting point. Just make sure that you read your software and hardware manuals for a complete list of extensions that are required in such a setup.

6. Disable any extensions that do not relate to your audio or MIDI hardware and software and do not play a role in your system's operation.

7. After creating the new extensions set, close the Extensions Manager dialog box.

This new set of extensions should take affect when you reboot your Mac.

Figure 7.18
The Extensions Manager dialog box allows you to activate and deactivate specific extensions that you don't need to use in audio applications and that are not required by your OS

Disable Virtual Memory

Virtual memory may cause performance degradation in Apple computers, as it uses the hard disk rather than using much faster RAM. It is advisable when using audio and MIDI applications to disable it. To do this:

1. In the Apple menu, click the control panel, and then select the Memory item.

2. Under Virtual Memory, select Off (see Figure 7.19). Note that if there is over 995 MB of RAM installed, virtual memory will be disabled.

Figure 7.19
The Memory dialog box in Mac OS lets you turn off the computer's virtual memory

The new virtual memory settings will not take affect until the computer reboots.

Set Disk Cache to Minimum

The settings for the system disk cache can affect performance. In some cases, it may help to set the Memory Control Panel's Disk Cache to 512k or lower, down to the lowest possible value. Higher settings can sometimes cause degraded performance, including audio and synchronization problems.

1. In the Apple menu, click the control panel, and then select the Memory item.

2. Under Disk Cache, select the Custom setting option (Figure 7.20) and then enter 512K in the appropriate box. If you find that your computer doesn't respond well after rebooting, change this value by increments of 512K until its behavior is adequate.

The new disk cache settings will not take effect until the computer reboots.

Figure 7.20
Setting the Disk Cache option to Custom setting allows you to enter a customized value for your disk cache

If you have OMS installed, you probably already know that Opcode recommends not running it with AppleTalk active; however, if you don't have OMS, it is still recommended that you turn this option off while running audio or MIDI applications. It is also a good idea to disconnect any network communication with other computers. This includes Internet communications as well, since these network communications might disrupt or interfere with real-time operations. The control strip can store settings for AppleTalk, File Sharing, Extension Manager, and more. You can use this as an easy way to switch between setups for audio and general purpose computing. To do this:

1.   Click the control strip at the bottom of your screen to expand it.

2.   Locate the AppleTalk icon (shown in Figure 7.21) and select the AppleTalk Inactive option.

Figure 7.21
The Apple expanded control strip lets you quickly change Apple settings

Disable "Deep Sleep"

Deep Sleep is a function that puts your entire Mac in a deep sleep state (hence the name), where not just the monitor and hard disks go to sleep, but everything else as well. Some problems might occur when a PCI device does not support this mode. For example, your Mac might not want to wake up (maybe because it's dreaming of being as popular as a PC, who knows?). In the past, MacOS systems would not attempt to enter this mode if they sensed that one or more of the installed devices did not support deep sleep. With some recent models, this appears to have changed. Support of deep sleep is a function of the PCI controller hardware and cannot be changed. However, there are settings that you can alter that should prevent you from having this problem. To do this:

1.   Open the Energy Saver control panel.

2.   Press the Show Details button or Sleep Setup tab.

3.   Check the box labeled "Separate timing for display sleep" (Figure 7.22).

4.   Also, check the box labeled "Separate timing for hard disk sleep."

5.   Set the times for display and hard disk sleep as desired.

6.   Set the top slider, labeled "Put the system to sleep whenever...", all the way to the right to Never.

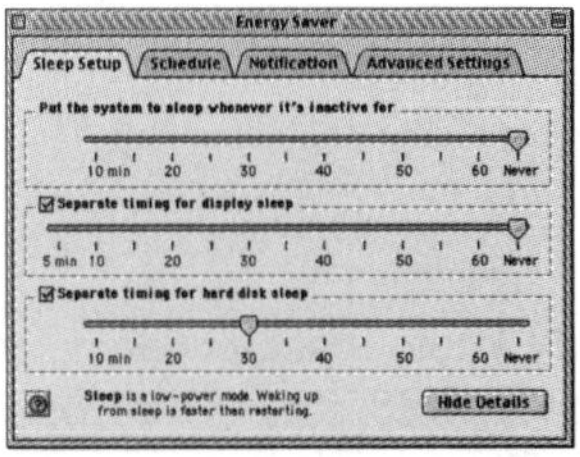

Figure 7.22
The Energy Saver dialog box on a Mac

This will not prevent your display and hard drive from going into sleep mode, but it will prevent your system from going into deep sleep mode.

PCI Card Interaction

Digital audio PCI cards rely on being able to transfer small amounts of data across the PCI bus at regular intervals, several thousand times per second. If other PCI devices, such as video or SCSI cards, tie up the PCI bus for extended periods of time, this may prevent your audio/MIDI PCI card from completing one data transfer before the next is scheduled to begin. If this happens, the audio stream will be corrupted. Some motherboard devices may also share PCI resources, even if they do not use a PCI card. This can also affect the PCI bus as well. Here are a few troubleshooting tips you can follow to prevent this type of problem:

1. Try lowering the colors in your display to thousands rather than millions. You can do this through the control strip.

2. Try swapping the audio PCI with other PCI cards, or simply moving the audio PCI to another PCI slot after turning off your computer. This may improve your performance.

3. For troubleshooting purposes, you may also wish to temporarily disconnect other peripherals, including USB and FireWire devices.

Use Separate PCI Bus On 6-Slot CPUs

If you are experiencing PCI card interaction problems on MacOS systems with two PCI buses (all 6-slot towers, including 9500, 9600, and PowerTower Pro), it is recommended that you distribute cards between the two busses, so that each has the maximum PCI bandwidth available. In particular, try placing the audio PCI card on a separate bus from video (and SCSI) cards.

Beige G3—CD Update

Apple has identified and fixed a problem with certain Beige G3 Macintosh models, in which the CD-ROM could cause long delays in system response while waking up, which may happen when a new CD-ROM is inserted into the drive. These delays may cause crashes with certain digital audio applications. If you have experienced this problem, you can download the G3 CD Update from Apple's Web site (www.apple.com/support/).

CHAPTER 7

8

Sequencing with MIDI

Now, let's take a look at some of the basic functions of the "must have" MIDI application: the sequencer. In this chapter, we'll consider some typical and fundamental operations you can perform with a sequencer. We will also take a look at music notation software, since it often goes hand in hand with MIDI files and sequencers. In fact, many sequencers today offer extensive notation functions that allow you to produce exceptionally good printed music. I remember my days as a student when the jazz bandleader would make an arrangement for the ensemble and ask me to create individual music sheets for each part in the arrangement…if only sequencers had existed back then! I can still see myself scrambling to get those copies out without ending up with ink stains all over my hands.

Here's a summary of what you will learn in this chapter:

> ▶ What sequencers can do for you and what you can do with them.

> ▶ How you can set up your sequencer to record MIDI from one or more MIDI inputs.

> ▶ How you can use punch-ins and punch-outs to record over MIDI.

> ▶ Configuring MIDI tracks to play on different MIDI ports and channels than the one used for recording.

> ▶ What the basic MIDI editing environments found in sequencers are.

> ▶ What other editing capabilities you can expect to find in sequencers.

> ▶ How you can safely save the work you have done in a sequencer.

> ▶ How to use MIDI files to create music sheets.

> ▶ Which musical elements will appear on a music sheet and which ones won't when using a MIDI file to create a music sheet.

> ▶ What to expect when using a scanner and notation software to extract MIDI files from a piece of paper.

This chapter will not discuss specific functions or how-to's in specific software environments, since this is a subject that could fill an entire book itself. So, if you've just purchased sequencer software and wish to use it to its full potential, perhaps getting another book dedicated to your software—one may be available in the Power! series—would be wise. For example, if you're a Cubase user, there's a great book called Cubase Power! (Muska & Lipman) written by yours truly (hint, hint).

What Is a Sequencer?

It might be good at this point to define what a sequencer is—more specifically, a MIDI sequencer. For starters, MIDI sequencers have evolved dramatically in the past twenty years and are now an integral tool for the music-making hobbyist and professional composers and musicians around the world.

A MIDI sequencer is a tool that allows you to record MIDI events and play them back as they were recorded. It also allows you to edit these events using a graphical user interface of some sort, whether via a small LCD on a hardware device or on your computer running sequencing software.

Here are some things you can do with a MIDI sequencer besides just recording, editing, and playing back:

▶ Record MIDI at a slow tempo, then play it back at a different tempo, or change the tempo as it's playing without affecting the sound quality.

▶ Layer different tracks containing different MIDI events assigned to specific MIDI channels so that each track can correspond to its own MIDI channel. This is like having a multi-track recording system, in which each track represents an instrument, or a part of an instrument.

▶ Change or redirect a MIDI channel to a different channel on a sequencer track. This is very convenient when you want to copy something you've recorded on one MIDI channel to another track and change the MIDI channel for this copied track. You end up with two instruments playing the same line you've recorded only once.

▶ You can adjust the performance timing through quantizing, a feature that allows you to align minor imperfections in your rhythmic performance to a predefined meter grid. This grid can represent any metrical subdivision—quarter notes, eighth notes, and so on. This is very useful when you want to make sure all your musical parts are tight, or when you want to give your music a specific feel, like shuffle or swing for example, where the percentage of rhythmic correction varies to give the corresponding feel to this musical part.

▶ You can easily create copies of MIDI events and repeat them over time, making the creation process a cinch, since you don't have to record everything all at once and don't have to replay every part for the length of an entire track. You can simply play a few bars, a chorus, or a verse, then copy that portion and repeat it at another location in time, instantly creating a new chorus or verse, for example.

▶ You can transpose MIDI events without changing the quality of the sound, since all you're doing is adding a value to the Note On values already recorded. Then, when the sequencer plays back, it sends the new Note On values to your MIDI device.

▶ You can convert MIDI events recorded in your sequencer into musical notation and print it so that musicians can read it in a live studio session. How much control you have over the appearance of this musical notation depends on the notation functions built into your sequencer software.

▶ You can create and automate mixes inside the sequencer, using MIDI controls.

MIDI sequencers have slowly integrated audio functions as computers become faster and more powerful. At this point in time, the four major software developers of MIDI sequencer applications—Cakewalk's Sonar, Steinberg's Cubase SX (formerly known as Cubase VST), Emagic's Logic Audio, and MOTU's Digital Performer—all offer full digital audio support. This implies that MIDI sequencers can now handle both MIDI events as well as digital audio files inside the same application.

For example, you can create MIDI tracks and record MIDI events in these tracks and create audio tracks and record digital audio events in these tracks. You can also use software instruments, in some cases, which use MIDI events to trigger the sounds the instruments play, but use the audio sound card to generate the sounds themselves.

In fact, most of the major additions made to these applications in recent versions relate to the treatment and editing capabilities of digital audio and the integration of software instruments, as well as digital audio processing features. This leaves the actual MIDI editing and recording functions pretty much unchanged. This is mostly because MIDI sequencing is pretty much in a matured state, where most of what users wanted to see in these environments already have been integrated in the software.

Does this mean MIDI sequencers are a thing of the past? Not at all, since the addition of software instruments (virtual synthesizers, samplers, and drum machines) as part of the sequencer toolbox gave MIDI a much-needed boost in the past few years. Using the computer as a powerful musical instrument and talking to this instrument through MIDI, just as you would with an external synthesizer, allows you to better control this instrument. For example, you don't have to purchase additional hardware, which can require changes in your studio setup. In other words, you don't have to reconfigure your studio to control this new addition. Also, since your instrument is inside your computer, accessing it is easy because you are already working inside your computer anyway. Finally, you can edit MIDI, which offers a much greater editing capability than does digital audio.

Editing audio is getting easier and easier, but tasks such as pitch change, tempo changes, and even musical content changes are much easier to do with MIDI than with digital audio. Since software instruments are essentially MIDI devices, you have as much control over how it sounds as you have over how it is recorded and edited in your sequencer.

Recording MIDI

Before you can start manipulating MIDI information and digital audio in a sequencer, you need to record it.

Before you can record, you have to make sure your keyboard controller is connected to a MIDI port on your computer and that all your MIDI devices inside and outside of your computer are configured properly. This was discussed in earlier chapters, so by now, I'll assume you are ready to rock! There is perhaps one item that needs to be defined here in terms of MIDI connectivity: You will need to activate the appropriate MIDI inputs and outputs in your sequencer's Setup dialog box (see Figure 8.1). This is a way of telling your sequencer which MIDI port(s) will be receiving the MIDI information you wish to record, and which MIDI port(s) you will use to send playback data to your MIDI devices and software synthesizers.

Figure 8.1
The Cubase VST
(www.steinberg.net)
MIDI System Setup
dialog box allows you to
choose which MIDI
input ports will be used

This is usually done through the MIDI preferences settings inside your sequencer application. Once you've told your software which ports are active and which are not, you can set up your track(s) for MIDI recording.

Setting Up Your Track

A track in a sequencer is like a track on a multi-track recorder. You can use it to record events from one or more MIDI inputs, depending on your MIDI studio setup and the application itself. However you don't need to specify whether a track will be mono or stereo, since MIDI events are neither. What is mono or stereo is the audio output of your MIDI sound module or virtual instrument (synthesizer or sampler). Quite often, to record on a track, you will need to select it or make it active. Let's take a look at how the MIDI signal flows from the input of your computer to the track's output:

1. You play MIDI on your controller: This sends MIDI events to the computer (when it is hooked up to it, obviously). All events will be sent using the MIDI channel assigned on the controller itself. For example, if your keyboard uses MIDI channel 1, all messages entering the application (in this case, the sequencer) will have channel 1 as their channel information.

2. When you activate the MIDI input port inside your sequencer application, you are telling it to enable the sequencer to record the events coming from this port.

3. Then, you need to route the information coming in to the appropriate destination. For example, if you want the events that are played by your keyboard to be sent back to this keyboard, you need to select a MIDI track, and assign its output to correspond to the MIDI port that is hooked up to this keyboard. If you are using a MIDI port called A, then the track should be assigned to send the MIDI events back to MIDI port A. On the other hand, if you would like to send the MIDI coming on port A to another MIDI port, such as a virtual MIDI port created by a software instrument, you can select this as the outgoing MIDI port.

4. Your MIDI events are coming in with MIDI channel 1 as the input channel (in this example), but ultimately, it is the track's MIDI channel assignment that will determine which MIDI channel plays back. So, if you want the events to play on MIDI channel 2, you will need to also select the new channel from the track's

channel setting. This will re-map the events from channel 1 to channel 2 when they come out from MIDI port A (as set in step 3 of this example).

5. Then, the information comes out from MIDI port A on channel 2 and is sent to whatever device is hooked up to this MIDI port. In other words, you can take any signal (MIDI information) coming from any port on any channel and send it to any other port on any other channel.

Figure 8.2
The path taken by a MIDI signal from your MIDI device to a sequencer, and back out to a MIDI device

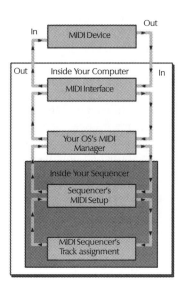

As you can see in Figure 8.2, a MIDI device sends MIDI events to the input of a MIDI interface. Your OS's MIDI manager then makes the link with your software application, forwarding the MIDI events. For your software application to open the door for this information, it needs to be configured properly, as mentioned above. Then, the sequencer's MIDI track assignment will reroute the information accordingly and send the MIDI data back to your MIDI interface, or forward it internally to a virtual MIDI port, such as a software synthesizer.

To find out if you have successfully configured your track, try playing on your keyboard and listen to the result as you hit the notes. If you can hear what's coming out of the desired sound module or virtual instrument, then you have configured your track properly and should be able to record MIDI events on this track.

The control interface for recording in a sequencer is quite simple. Usually, simply pressing the Record button on a control panel, followed by the Play button, should activate the recording process. You might want to configure your sequencer to generate a click track or metronome tick to keep your performance in sync with the bars and beats found in the MIDI sequence.

Recording from Multiple MIDI Sources

Many of you will be using a sequencer in a music creation environment, using a keyboard or single controller device to input your MIDI events into your sequencer. This type of setup is simple and described above. However, you might want to record multiple MIDI sources at once in your MIDI sequencer. This can be done in different ways, depending on your software and its configuration.

Recording from multiple MIDI sources on multiple tracks can be useful when you want to record more than one musician simultaneously, rather than having each musician play one line, record it, and then pass to the next musician. Another use for this application might be for sequencer-to-sequencer transfers, where you want all the tracks from one sequencer to be recorded onto their own tracks in a receiving sequencer. In order to achieve a multi-input or multi-channel recording, you will need to set each sending instrument to a different MIDI channel and activate multiple MIDI tracks for recording in your sequencer, assigning each track to its corresponding MIDI input port and input channel, if this is the case. You might also want to read up on your sequencer's documentation to find out if there are some specific steps you need to take in order to perform this kind of recording operation.

If your sequencer does not allow you to record on multiple tracks at a time, simply assign each instrument its own MIDI channel, if not its own MIDI port, and use editing tools inside your sequencer to extract each MIDI channel recorded onto one track, splitting it into multiple tracks.

Punching In and Out

In the good old days, when you made a mistake while recording, you had to roll back the tape, start the playback, and just before you wanted to record over what sounded bad, you "punched in" the Record button to enable the record function. When you arrived at the point on the tape where you wanted to keep what was there, you "punched out" the record button, reverting to the playback function for that track.

MIDI sequencers also allow you to easily set a "punchin" and a "punchout" time location. This technique is useful when most of a recorded track is good, with the exception of a few bars here and there. Punching in allows you to replace the mistakes without erasing and rerecording the whole track.

In fact, you will find that punching in a MIDI sequencer is particularly simple. That's because you can manipulate MIDI events easily and program your sequencer to punch in at a specific bar and beat, and do the same for the punchout point.

You can also select the MIDI events in an appropriate MIDI editor and delete them. Once deleted, you can record over this track. Since MIDI only records played events, whenever and whatever you play will be recorded at the time and in the track you have selected. Sometimes, however, it might be easier to simply cut out the MIDI events that were bad and add new ones on another MIDI track.

The punch process usually consists of these simple steps:

1. Set your punch-in time. This marks the beginning point at which the existing MIDI events on the track will be replaced by the newly recorded events.

2. Set your punch-out time. This is the point at which the recording will automatically stop on this track.

3. Set a pre-roll and post-roll time. Pre-roll is lead-in time before the punch-in, and post-roll is how long the track will play after the punch-out point. Giving yourself a couple of bars of pre-roll time will allow you to hear the sequence before starting your recording. Note that both the pre- and post-roll functions might not be implemented in your sequencer; read your sequencer's documentation to find out exactly how yours works.

4. Set a loop region. Sometimes you want a portion of a song to loop, or repeat, while recording, so that you can record multiple takes. Each take can be stored on a separate track in your sequencer.

Figure 8.3
The Emagic's
(www.emagic.de) Logic
Audio transport bar
with the cycle mode
and droprecord (punch
in) mode enabled

As you can see in Figure 8.3, Emagic's Logic Audio transport bar has a function that lets you set the punch-in and punch-out times; in this figure, the punch-in is set to bar 3-beat 1 and the punch-out is set to bar 5-beat 1. The cycle mode is also enabled and will loop between bars 1 and 7 (found in the lower right corner of the transport bar).

MIDI Playback Configuration

MIDI sequencers will generally record MIDI events on tracks using the MIDI channel they receive from the input, as mentioned in the "Setting Up Your Track" section above. These MIDI events are then sent to the output port and MIDI channel assigned for the track. So, to properly play back a track, you need to configure this track to send the recorded events to the appropriate MIDI output port and MIDI channel. Take Figure 8.4, for example. In this case, the keyboard sends MIDI events on channel 1, MIDI port A. Let's say you have a sampler hooked up to MIDI port B and want to hear what you recorded on channel 1, played by a sound you loaded on channel 5 of this sampler. You need to assign the output of the MIDI track to MIDI port B, channel 5. You can do this while you are recording, or you can choose to change the playback channel and/or port of the recording later on. This allows you to play back any MIDI information, switching MIDI ports, channels, and even sounds at any point. So, what was originally a piano sound could become a string sound, a clarinet sound, or even a drum sound, simply by changing the MIDI playback configuration of your recorded track.

Figure 8.4
The sequencer's track
setting can change the
track's MIDI output
configuration during
playback

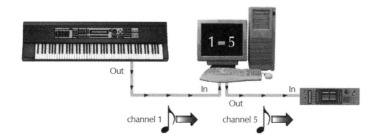

Editing MIDI: Typical Editing Windows

MIDI sequencers give you the ability to edit recorded events in different types of editing windows. Each editing window in a sequencer is designed to emphasize certain types of MIDI events and make its editing easier. So, for example, if you want to create copies of certain sections of your arrangement, you work in one editing window. If you want to tweak a few notes in your string part, you have another window. If you want to add a cowbell and tighten your snare drum, you guessed it, there's an editing window for that as well. So, let's take a look at these windows.

The Main Project Window

In the main project window, you will find a global view of your song or project. This is where you will find all your MIDI and audio tracks laid out in rows on one side of the screen (usually on the lefthand side), and your MIDI events held in boxes on the right. These boxes have different names depending on the application itself, but they usually serve a similar purpose. You can think of them as building blocks containing MIDI or audio events that can be copied, moved, transposed, muted, stretched, or grouped together. Here is a look at the main project window for the five major programs that offer MIDI and audio sequencing, in alphabetical order: Cubase, from Steinberg in Figure 8.5; Digital Performer from Mark Of The Unicorn (MOTU) in Figure 8.6; Logic Audio from Emagic in Figure 8.7; ProTools from Digidesign in Figure 8.8; and Sonar from Cakewalk in Figure 8.9.

Figure 8.5
Cubase SX Project window. Cubase SX is the latest version of Steinberg's Cubase family—it was previously called Cubase VST; Cubase is available on both Mac and PC platforms (www.steinberg.net)

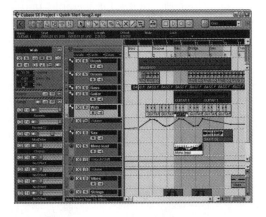

Figure 8.6
Digital Performer main window—Digital Performer is developed by MOTU and is available for Mac platform only (www.motu.com)

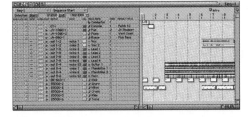

Figure 8.7
Logic Audio Platinum's
main project window—
developed by eMagic,
this software is available
in Mac and PC versions
(www.emagic.de)

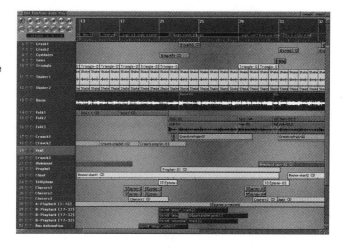

Figure 8.8
ProTools' main editing
area now integrates
MIDI editing as well as
digital audio editing
functions that have
made this software well
known by many studio
owners—ProTools is
developed by Digidesign
(www.digidesign.com)

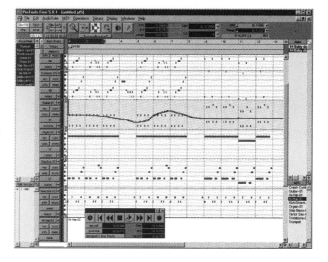

Figure 8.9
Sonar is the latest release from Cakewalk—it was previously called Cakewalk Pro Audio; this software is available only in PC version (www.cakewalk.com)

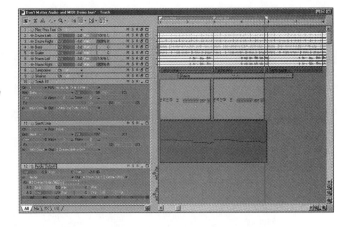

As you can see, the look and feel of these applications might be different, but there are similarities among them. If you break down each application, you can find common areas. These areas are defined in Figure 8.10. Once you understand these common areas, you will be able to quickly find your way around any sequencing application.

Figure 8-10
A video effect is rendered across an entire clip during playback.

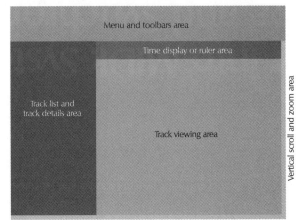

▶ Menu and toolbars area: This is where you will find most of the tools and options available in the software. If the menu is not attached to the project window, it is usually in the top part of the window, which is the case with Digital Performer and Sonar. When you are looking for a function like creating markers, copying events, or inserting a track, menus are usually where you will find what you need. Toolbars are meant as shortcuts to most common tasks, like opening another window, changing the tool you are currently using, and so on.

▶ Track list and track details area: This is where you will find detailed information for each track, such as the name of a track; the type of information contained in a track, such as audio, midi, and automation; and so on. You can also find information that relates to track settings for output assignment, such as MIDI ports, MIDI channels, instrument names used by a MIDI device for this track, and digital audio outputs or inputs used by the software if you are in record mode. You may also switch between different modes for a track, like muting a track, soloing it, or enabling the record-ready state for this track if the software requires it. In some cases, you can even view the track automation in this area. You will want to get familiar with the information displayed in this area because it is crucial to the rest of your sequencer functions.

▶ Time display or ruler area: This is where you will find a horizontal ruler with both the bars and beats of your sequence or the time information for your project. By looking at the ruler, you can quickly spot where you are in the project. You may also find regions and markers in this area as well. Markers are used to identify specific points in your project. You can give the markers a name and quickly navigate between them. Regions are similar to markers in the sense that they serve as reference points; however, they identify a beginning and an end of a section in a project. You can use regions to identify different sections of a song such as a chorus, verse, bridge, and so on.

▶ Track view area: This is where you will find the actual events on each track. An event can usually be one of three things: MIDI data, audio data, or automation data. How these events are called in a sequencer depends on the sequencer itself. But you can think of the blocks represented in a track view area as containers of events. Double-clicking on a container usually opens the associated event type editor window. For example, double-clicking on a MIDI container or clip will open a MIDI editor. On the other hand, if you double-click on an audio clip, or container, it would open an audio editor. You can usually copy these containers, move them around, delete them, and so on. When you do so, you copy, move, or delete any information that pertains to that specific series of events found inside the container. When you record MIDI events, a container is created automatically. If you stop the recording and then start recording again, another container will appear over or merged with the previous container if you were recording over an already recorded series of events. The behavior of the sequencer in this case, whether it replaces or adds to the previous recording, is usually determined by the sequencer's recording options.

▶ Zoom and scroll areas: Moving around in your project, viewing certain details for certain tracks, or going from bar 1 to bar 500 requires that you sometimes change your magnification level to view more information at once, or zoom into a specific detail on screen. The same applies for scrolling. As with any other application, the scroll bars and zoom functions allow you to move your point of view and change your focus within your project. Note that, quite often, you will find quick keyboard shortcuts and even special keyboard combinations to quickly recall a zoom level or a previously stored window setup.

CHAPTER 8

The Piano Roll Editor Window

The piano roll analogy is often used to describe how MIDI works, or what MIDI is. When you think of a piano roll, you imagine a long piece of paper rolled up over a cylinder, with holes punched through the paper along its vertical length. The roll was mounted on a cylinder, which was fixed inside the mechanical piano, and the paper passed through an intricate set of gears to make its way to an empty cylinder. As the player pressed on pedals, the cylinder would start rolling, making the roll move from one cylinder to the next, passing in front of rods that would move as they encountered holes in the paper, thus activating the piano mechanism to play the corresponding note.

The metaphor seems like a good one for describing the MIDI editing environment. The piano roll editing environment is, simply put, a virtual piano roll, where MIDI events appear, passing from right to left—from beginning to end. The lower portion of this environment represents lower notes, and the higher portion, higher notes. In Figure 8.11, you can see a keyboard displayed in the left portion of the window. This represents the MIDI keyboard with its octaves numbered for easy reference. To the right of the keyboard, you can see horizontal rectangles, each one representing a MIDI Note On message. The left edge of these rectangles represents the point in time a note was begun, and the right edge, the point in time when the note was released. The ruler on top identifies the bars and beats when these events occurred, and a grid helps users to quickly tell whether notes are recorded properly according to a rhythmic grid and the note number, as displayed to the left. In this figure, you can also see that each note is color coded to display its velocity value, which is also represented below the piano roll in the display.

Besides a simple Note On message, the piano roll view also displays other information, such as control changes, velocity information, and other selectable MIDI events.

Figure 8.11
Cubase SX's piano roll
MIDI editor with
additional MIDI
controllers displayed in
the lower portion of the
window

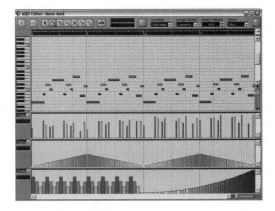

In this type of window, you can edit MIDI events that are part of a container present in the main project window. It is the representation of the contents of this container. You may select an event by clicking on its representation in the piano roll view, move it, copy it, delete it, and change its length, velocity, or any other recorded MIDI parameter for that matter.

Since this type of editing environment represents a good graphical interface, it is the ideal place to edit your MIDI events that are harmonic, melodic, or even rhythmic in nature. As you will see in the next header, drum tracks can be edited in both the piano roll editor and a specific drum editing window.

The Drum Editor Window

MIDI events intended for drum parts, unlike other musical instruments recorded with MIDI, don't normally have length associated with them, since what counts in a drum partition is the attack time. That's why MIDI drums often have their own editing environment. Another particularity with drum tracks is that, although each instrument in a drum kit is mapped to a specific key on the keyboard, these keys do not refer to actual pitch values on a keyboard. That's why in drum editing windows, you will usually find a key name and its associated instrument name rather than the usual keyboard layout on the left hand side, as was the case in the piano roll window. For example, C1 on your keyboard would trigger the kick drum; D1, the snare; E1, the floor tom; and so on. Representing these instruments makes more sense than representing the keyboard used to play these instruments, since C1 in a drum map or drum part, for example, doesn't really play a C1 pitch.

That's why, as shown in Figure 8.12, instead of a keyboard, drum kit specific information is found in the left portion of the window. You can also notice that each MIDI Note On event is represented by a single square in a grid, rather than horizontal rectangles with a length value for sustained notes. This doesn't mean that notes can't be sustained, but rather that it is not pertinent information in the editing environment of a MIDI drum part.

As with the piano roll editor, you can edit MIDI events in this window. The lower portion of the window usually displays other channel voice messages such as velocity or control changes. If your sequencer allows you to define a track as being percussion or drum content rather than simply MIDI content, then chances are, double-clicking on the clips contained on these tracks will open up the drum editing window automatically.

Figure 8.12
The drum editor as found in Digital Performer

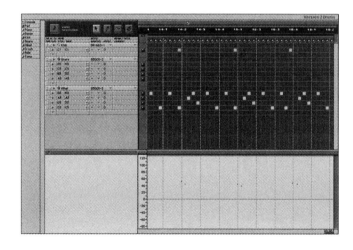

CHAPTER 8

The List Editor Window

The list editor lets you view, in a spreadsheet-like format, all the events that were recorded for a selected track or part in a track. This is not an editing environment where you fine tune melodies or cut and paste notes. You may, however, use this environment to find mistakes or pinpoint the source of problems you can't find in other editors, or if they are present there, not as easily editable. Examples include program changes, aftertouch values, and so on. Since MIDI events appear in a list, you can see them in column form, sorted by the order in which they occur. So, you may have a track that changes its program number every time you start the playback. If this is something you want to fix, the list editor is the place to view and make changes to this type of event. The list editor is a last resort editing environment because it offers a lot of information on each event and is not represented in a music friendly fashion. In other words, you can use this when you are troubleshooting a track or a project and can't find something in other windows, or when you want to add specific information at a specific location on a track and just want to do this by entering its corresponding values in a table, such as the one found in this window. For example, you might want to change the bank select value from 0 to 1 in the list, or change the velocity of a note from 55 to 90, or add a MIDI mode change message that will be sent out to the device connected to the track containing these events.

As you can see in Figure 8.13, each column represents a type of information. In this case, the first column represents the track number, so changing the value in this field for an event would make this event appear in another track rather than in this one. The second and third columns represent timestamps associated with each event (in time and bars and beats formats). The fourth column represents the original MIDI channel that was recorded by the sequencer's MIDI input. The next three columns usually represent MIDI values, and in this case, you can see the note name, its velocity, and length.

Figure 8.13
The list editor, as found in Sonar

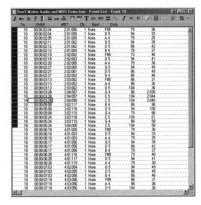

Other Editing Windows

Sequencers offer many other editing environments—some more common than others. Here's a look at some of these other editing windows.

The Score Editor

If you are preparing music for musicians, you will need to create a MIDI recording. Then, using it as the basis for your score layout, you can create individual music sheets for each musician. You could also add notes one by one in notation software, as you will see later, but the information will still remain a MIDI event that you lay out and print, not audio.

As you can see in Figure 8.14, MIDI events become music sheets in the score editor. Obviously, this type of editor will not serve any purpose if you can't read music. But then again, you might use it to learn how to read your own music!

Figure 8.14
Digital Performer's score editor

The Tempo and Meter Editor

MIDI sequencers can also store musical information that can't be recorded by a performer at the same time as he/she is recording a musical part, such as a bass line or keyboard line. Tempo, time signature, or meter changes, for example, need to be included in a MIDI sequencer file, but are not recorded when the performer plays or records a part.

When you play an intro, finish a song, or change the mood anywhere within a song, chances are you might slow down, speed up, or do both. Your song might also start in a 4/4 time signature, later on changing to a 6/8. Unless you have programmed these tempo and meter changes prior to your recording, you will need to add them afterward. This is when a tempo and meter editor come in handy. The ability to add these changes in a sequencer is important because you want your sequencer to follow these changes so that when you add other parts to this recording, they all fall into place at the appropriate bar and beat. The place to do this is usually a special track that controls the playback of all other tracks. What this special track is called depends on the software you are using, but usually it has its own editing environment. In Figure 8.15, the window displays tempos on the left hand side, a graphical representation in the center, and a list display in the right pane. The tools in the upper portion of the window allow you to add or erase information through the graphical display, or simply enter new values, modify, or erase existing ones in the list display.

Figure 8.15
The tempo editor in Sonar

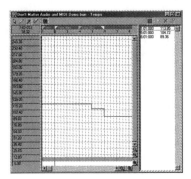

Time signatures are also an important part of MIDI sequences. They represent how the music is organized in bars and beats. For example, a 4/4 time signature means that a bar will be made up of 4 quarter notes, hence the 4/4. The ability to change time signature values in order to reflect the proper bar count in a sequence is crucial. As with the tempo, this also can be found in a control or master track and have its own editing environment.

The Audio Editor

MIDI isn't the only type of data you can record and edit in sequencers. Audio editing is becoming a must-have feature in today's MIDI sequencers. Since audio is very different from MIDI in many ways, editing it is also handled through specific editing environments. Audio editing comes in two basic flavors.

The first type is called nondestructive editing. Nondestructive editing allows you to chop up, move, copy, and edit digital audio without modifying the original digital audio file—hence the name. It works by creating references that identify regions and markers in an audio file, pointing to portions of audio used in your sequencer (see Figure 8.16). These references are kept in a separate file and are needed by your sequencer to properly display the audio segments it uses in its project window. Those segments are what you see represented in the clips in this window. When you delete a clip or segment in the sequencer, you are removing the visual reference to the clip from your project, but not the actual digital audio file on the hard disk. This allows greater flexibility when arranging a song or organizing audio on tracks. It also allows you to reuse certain audio information over and over again without copying the actual audio file over and over.

Figure 8.16
Logic's audio editor is a nondestructive environment that allows you to resize audio segments

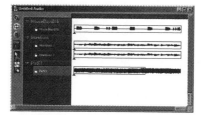

The second type of digital audio editing in sequencers is called destructive editing. In destructive editing, the content of your original digital audio file is modified. This type of editing can serve different purposes. You can remove unnecessary portions of audio data to save disk space, normalize the digital audio recording to get a better output level, and remove noise directly in the file rather than have processing applied in real time. This allows you to save processing power for other essential tasks, or to add tempo and original key information inside your audio file to allow the sequencer to loop this audio file and keep it in sync with the rest of your project's tempo and key (see Figure 8.17).

Figure 8.17
The Sonar Loop construction editor allows you to add slicing markers in an audio file in order for this file to follow the sequencer's tempo—pitch information can also be added to the audio file

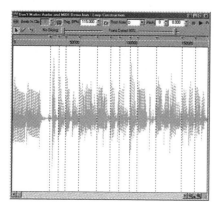

The Pattern Editor

The term sequencer was coined in reference to hardware sequencing devices when this technology was introduced in the early days of synthesizers. At the time, the idea was that a machine could put in sequence a series of notes and then loop that sequence over and over again. Today, sequencers do much more than that, but the concept of looping a sequence is now referred to as pattern sequencing, or step recording. Because the old school sounds and techniques are back in style, so are the old ways of building songs. Today, however, the way software developers go about it is much more sophisticated and much more flexible, since it uses software programs to emulate what hardware devices could do back then. In fact, today you can "sequence" sequences—in other words, create patterns of melodic, harmonic, or rhythmic content that changes over time through pattern sequencing. In Figure 8.18, you will find an example of this. Propellerhead (www.propellerhead.se) developed a product called Reason, which is a self-contained MIDI studio with different virtual synthesizers and an integrated multi-function sequencer. One of those sequencers is called a pattern sequencer. The idea is that you can create patterns that are saved in banks and program numbers. For example, you may have 8 patterns in bank A, 8 patterns in bank B, and so on. Then, in your sequence, you can automate these pattern changes through time, going from pattern D8 to A2 to A3 and to A1 (as shown in the same figure). Each pattern corresponds to its own musical element; in this case, a drum pattern played by the Redrum virtual drum machine inside Reason.

Figure 8.18
Reason's Redrum
pattern sequencer

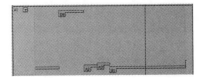

The Controller Editor

MIDI controllers, as you saw in chapters 2 and 3, are plentiful. Some sequencers will display them in the same window as the Note On events through the piano roll editor or in the list editor, as seen above. However, some sequencers will also provide a distinct editing environment in which you can view all the MIDI controllers that have been recorded in your project.

Figure 8.19
Cubase VST's controller
editor

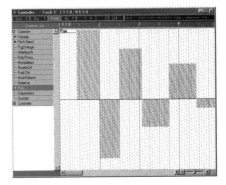

As you can see in Figure 8.19, a list of common MIDI messages and control change MIDI messages appears on the left. The ones that contain recorded values are identified with a dot beside their names, making it easy to see where information has been recorded. In the right portion of the window, a graphical representation of these values allows you to see what was recorded, thus to edit it as well. In this case, the pan controller is displayed.

Saving MIDI Files

As with any other computer application, when you are done working on a project, or after you've worked on it for a while, you have to save it. But saving your project file in the sequencer's default format does not mean saving it as a MIDI file. When you save your file, you are saving all kinds of information that is not MIDI related, such as audio mix automation, effects settings, digital audio files location on audio tracks, and much more. If you want to save your project file as a Standard MIDI File, you need to tell the sequencer application that this is how you want to save it. If you have added audio to your project, the Standard MIDI File will not save it, nor will it save anything that is not supported by the Standard MIDI format.

So why would you want to save as a MIDI file after working in your sequencer? Here are some reasons that might warrant such an operation:

▶ To export this MIDI recording in your music notation software if your sequencer does not have notation options. The MIDI file will hold all the notes and track information that will later be used by your notation software. It will then be able to convert this MIDI data into music sheets.

▶ Cross application and cross platform compatibility: You will be able to take the MIDI tracks of your project into other software that might not support the proprietary file format used by your sequencer. Let's say you prepare your song in your own studio with your synthesizer, saving all your tracks in a sequence, and then exporting the MIDI content to a Standard MIDI File. You can take this MIDI file to another studio and use the equipment they have there, which might sound better than the ones you have at home. Preparing the tracks in your own studio will save you from paying extra studio time, and saving in a Standard MIDI File will allow you to make your work compatible with any sequencer application so you won't have to redo the work.

▶ Preparing a file for the Web: If you are preparing MIDI files for Internet use, you will have to save them in a Standard MIDI format in order for browsers to understand the content of the file and play back its content through the user's sound card, synthesizer, or MIDI player application.

Remember that sequencers will save all the MIDI events, audio events, project settings, automation, loaded virtual instruments, and virtual processing settings (such as reverbs, delays, compressors, and other effects in a file) with the sequencer's extension at the end of the filename. You might not see this extension, depending on your computer's configuration, but it will still be part of the file. It is important that you save your file in this format if you want to be able to retrieve this nonstandard MIDI information later. Most sequencers will not include the digital audio files in this saved project file. However, your project file will contain links to these audio files, so it is important that you remember where the files are or make a copy of them in a safe place. You might want to use a utility in your sequencer to save all the files (including the audio files) used in your project in a single folder on your computer. This will allow you to back up the information on a CD-R, CD-RW, or any other removable media for safekeeping.

TIP

There are two types of computer users: those who have lost information and those who will lose information! This said, making regular backup copies of your work and saving them in a safe location, preferably outside of your working environment, will not only help you retrieve the information in case your computer crashes, but will also provide you with a copy of your work in case something really bad happens to your studio, like a flood, fire, or robbery. We often take these things lightly until something happens, and then we freak out because all our work is gone. Replacing your music is as hard as replacing family pictures; once it is gone, it's just about impossible to get it back. So be wise about this.

Other MIDI Programming Options

Some MIDI sequencers allow you to add to the set of tools provided by the software through a set of customizable functions using a proprietary programming language included in the software. For example, Sonar uses a language called CAL (Cakewalk Application Language). You can use predefined CAL scripts that act like macro commands inside Sonar to do different tasks, such as adding a dominant seventh chord to existing notes on a track, as shown in Figure 8.20. Another tool similar to this is the Interactive Phrase Synthesizer, or IPS, found in Cubase VST, which allows you to generate accompaniment using the MIDI input as source material for its MIDI output.

These tools are meant to extend the possibilities of sequencers and add functionality. Getting to know them might open up new creative possibilities for you.

Figure 8.20

An example of a CAL script—the text beginning with a semicolon at the top of the script tells you what the script that follows will do

```
;; Dominant 7th Chord.cal
;;
;; Treats each note as the root of a dominant 7th chord; creates that chord:
;; For each note event, adds three note events with same time, vel, and dur
;; but a major 3rd, a perfect 5th, and a minor 7th higher.
(do
    (include "need20.cal")  ; Require version 2.0 or higher of CAL

    (ForEachEvent
        (if (== Event.Kind NOTE)
            (do
                (insert Event.Time Event.Chan NOTE (+ Note.Key  4) Note.Vel Note.Dur)
                (insert Event.Time Event.Chan NOTE (+ Note.Key  7) Note.Vel Note.Dur)
                (insert Event.Time Event.Chan NOTE (+ Note.Key 10) Note.Vel Note.Dur)
            )
        )
    )
)
```

Notation: From MIDI to Paper

This next section is for those who know how long it takes to transcribe music to paper by hand and wish there was a better way of doing it—especially if your music calls for a complete band with brass, wind, and string sections.

When you record a musical performance, you might not realize it, but you are doing what musicians have been doing for ages, with one exception: You don't have to write everything down on paper as you work, because the sequencer remembers what you have just played and lets you edit it. This has brought new ways of creating music simply because it makes hearing layers of musical events instantaneous. Fifty years ago, musicians had to understand music harmony, counterpoint, melodic construction, and rhythmic patterns. They had to hear it all in their minds, play the basic elements on their instrument, write it down on paper, and then bring these sheets of handwritten music to musicians in order to actually hear the end result, making last-minute changes once in the studio. This was very time consuming.

Thankfully, you don't have to deal with this anymore. Now, you can record everything inside your sequencer, assign different instruments to tracks, listen to the result, make changes to the parts that don't work well, and when everything is just like you want it, you can convert your MIDI file into musical notation. The fact that you can record your music in a MIDI environment won't make you come up with better ideas, but being able to hear what you wrote does help you to make things better in the long run.

There are two basic software application types that allow you to make the transition between recorded music to musical notation: music notation applications such as Finale (see Figure 8.21) from Coda Music (www.codamusic.com), and sequencer applications that have integrated notation features. Both types of applications will transform MIDI into musical notation, or add musical notation symbols directly onto staves on a score.

Figure 8.21
Finale is a music
notation application
that lets you print out
your music with
publishing-ready quality

Limitations: MIDI to Notation Conversion

Music transcription is like writing a foreign language. It is filled with scripting rules and exceptions. One of these rules relates to the appearance of notes within bars, where each subdivision of a beat has its space and place in this bar. Since music is a mathematical language, making everything fall in where it should rhythmically is very important when writing down this language. Imagine for a second that you needed to speak Russian, Chinese, Greek, or Arabic. Not only would you need to learn how to speak the language and make sentences, you would also have to learn how to write the language using a completely different set of characters.

Now, let's imagine again that your best friend is Chinese. He/she has taught you a few words and you are now able to say a few sentences in this language. That's your first step; now, you may want to write it down. Music notation is just like a foreign language. You can hear it and you can write it down so that other people can read it and play it. When you play a MIDI instrument and record it, it is like learning how to speak a language. When you want to write it down, it is like learning how to write this language. You may be able to do one, but not necessarily the other. This is where notation software can help you. However, as you will see, there are some limitations to what notation software can do on its own.

First of all, as we've seen, if you want to convert your music into sheet music, it has to be in MIDI format. If you've been working with audio loops and samples, you are out of luck—audio files don't convert well into the MIDI files necessary for conversion into musical notation. Some applications attempt to do this, but they work well only on simple monophonic events and are prone to result in more work to fix things than simply transcribing the original part to begin with.

Another such limitation is the difficulty met when trying to convert freely recorded performances into musical notation. When you record a freestyle improvisation using your MIDI keyboard, for example, you are, as suggested previously, speaking the language. If you want to have this printed out, you will also have to know how to write the language and express it as simply as possible, so the tools provided by the notation software can interpret the meaning of your expression as it tries to follow the music scripting rules.

Finally, converting MIDI into music notation is like converting English to French, or vice versa; a software is always limited by its programming, thus it will only interpret what it is programmed to understand. When working with MIDI files, it is important to review the final notation output before printing it. There might be many little details you'll want to correct.

About Musical Notation

Music notation can be broken down into different musical elements. These elements represent different aspects of the music notation, some of which are handled automatically when using a MIDI file to generate the notes for a music score. Others need to be added manually using the tools at your disposal. When you are working on a specific aspect of a score layout, all the related musical elements can be found in one tool palette or one menu. For example, if you want to enter lyrics to a MIDI song file, a lyric tool might be available in a text tool palette or menu, depending on the options available in your software.

The next two headers will discuss both the musical elements that may be imported directly from the MIDI file and other musical notation elements that you will have to add manually. Examples include slurs between notes, special articulation settings, or dynamic indications such as p, mf, f (piano, mezzo forte, forte). Note that with imported elements from MIDI, your software will use default settings in handling the automatic layout. You might want to customize these settings in order to get better results or to match the settings with the type of music you wish to print.

Musical Elements Automatically Imported from MIDI Files

When you convert MIDI events into musical notation, a staff—the place where notes are placed—will be created for each track in your MIDI file. If all your MIDI events are on one track, they will all appear on one staff. To prevent this from happening, make sure to separate each instrument (i.e., give each one its own track) beforehand. You read a staff as you would read text, going from left to right. Most staves use five lines when relating melodic or harmonic content that is meant to be played by a tone-based instrument (i.e. an instrument that plays pitched notes, such as a keyboard, violin, or marimba). Placing notes on a staff's line determines its note value in terms of height in a scale; for example, a C, D# (D sharp), or Bb (B flat). The clef at the beginning of the staff will determine exactly which line corresponds to which note.

Typically, monophonic instruments (capable of playing only one note at a time) will use one staff. Polyphonic instruments (capable of playing two or more notes simultaneously, such as a piano) might use two staves to accommodate notes for this part, since their note range will most likely span across these staves.

A clef tells the musician what each note on a staff represents. For example, in Figure 8.22, the arrow points to a treble clef, telling the musician that the second line from the bottom in the staff represents a G. From that reference point, a musician will know how to read every other note on the staff.

Figure 8.22
Different musical clefs

Clefs will be added automatically to each staff. Your musical notation will attempt to assign a clef corresponding to the note range content of the instrument. However, you might want to change the default assignment for a clef if it makes it difficult to read the notes. In Figure 8.23, both staves are playing an identical bass line, but the top staff uses a treble clef, which was assigned by default. Because the notes are lower than the five lines provided by the staff with this clef, additional lines are added. This makes it difficult to read and a bass player, for example, would not be accustomed to this. That's why it is better to change to a bass clef for this part, as shown in the lower staff of this figure. Notes will appear in the center of the staff, making it easier to read.

Figure 8.23
The top staff shows notes displayed using the treble clef, while the bottom staff shows the same notes displayed with the bass clef

The MIDI events length determines the notes' length values. When playing a part, you might not play precisely on a beat's subdivision, or you might not hold the notes for as long as they should be held. For example, you might anticipate the third beat slightly and might also hold the note for just under a half-note value. But in reality, you would like this to be represented by a half-note occurring on the third beat of this bar. This might not be a bad thing when you want to add feel to your music. However, when converting your performance to music notation, you want to avoid having unnecessary information that would make it harder to read. In Figure 8.24, both staves play the same line, but the top one hasn't been quantized, and no measures were taken to tell the notation software how to optimize the display of events. The lower staff's events have been quantized, and some optimization options were selected to tell the application how to allow for a cleaner display of these MIDI events.

Figure 8.24
The top staff has not been properly quantized; the bottom staff uses a quantizing value that makes it easier to read the actual line

CHAPTER 8

Notes are the graphic representations of your MIDI Note On events. Usually, in a staff, when no notes are played, silences are inserted to tell the musician to count while waiting for new notes to be played. Figure 8.25 shows the most common types of note length values, their musical representation when a note is played, their silence representation when no notes are played, and, in the last column, how many notes of this length are needed to fill a 4/4 bar.

Figure 8.25
Most common note length names with their musical representation, which includes how these values are represented when a note is not played

Length name	Note representation	Silence representation	Number needed to fill a 4/4 bar
Full note	𝅝		1
Half note	𝅗𝅥		2
Quarter note	𝅘𝅥	𝄽	4
Eighth note	𝅘𝅥𝅮	𝄾	8
Sixteenth note	𝅘𝅥𝅯	𝄿	16

A time signature is always added automatically at the beginning of a song, which corresponds to the time signature included in the MIDI file when you saved it. If the time signature changes during the song, a new time signature will be added automatically at the appropriate location.

Time signatures represent the metric division of music. It is usually displayed as a fraction over an integer. The integer represents the value of the beat subdivision and the fraction represents the number of beats in the bar. For example, a 4/4 bar would have four quarter notes per bar, a 6/8 would have six eighth notes per bar, a 2/2 would have two half notes per bar, and so on. This will influence how you count the music and how notes will be divided in bars.

When more than two eighth notes or shorter are played in a row, usually the notation application will create a beam that ties these notes together. This also serves as a way to make it more obvious to see the beat definition when many notes appear in a single bar. This is done automatically, but you can also change the way notes are beamed together, as displayed in Figure 8.26. In the first bar, the first two beats are grouped automatically, but the third and fourth beats are grouped under a single custom beat. In the second bar, the first two beats are separated, whereas the last two are beamed together. This can be used to emphasize certain rhythmical phrases or patterns as you see appropriate.

Figure 8.26
Example of how you can beam different groups of notes together

A key signature indicates the scale or key used in a song or a portion of a song. When a note is played outside this key, an "accidental" note tells the musician that a note doesn't belong to this key. It is important to identify the key at the beginning of each staff for each instrument; otherwise, the notation application might add an unnecessary amount of accidental notes in the staff, making it more difficult to read. In Figure 8.27, the top staff displays a key signature, since this melody is played in the key of F sharp (F#). By adding a key signature, you make the notes easier to read in the staff. Otherwise, you would have to add accidentals, as shown in the lower staff in the same figure. In both cases, the end result remains the same, but these additional accidents are not as easy to read. In some cases, accidentals are unavoidable; however, assigning the right key signature to a staff will minimize the use of them.

Figure 8.27
An example of accidental notes combined with key signatures

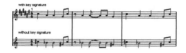

Page and measure or bar numbers are important for musicians because they serve as reference points. For example, when practicing a song, a musician might refer to page 4, bar 22. This helps other musicians to quickly pinpoint the location of a musical event in a part. Usually, this is added automatically by the notation application. You may also add other custom reference points such as section names.

Musical Elements Added Manually

The following elements are part of the musical layout, but are not elements that can be converted from the MIDI events directly because they relate to layout features that are not recorded through MIDI. You will need to consult your notation software documentation in order to use most of these features. Your software, depending on its notation-editing capabilities, might not support some of these elements.

At the beginning of a song, you might have an incomplete bar called a pickup bar that leads in to the first full bar of the song. You will need to tell the notation software how to handle this, since pickup bars are usually not counted in the bar counts. As you can see in Figure 8.28, the first bar is incomplete, showing only three eighth notes out of a possible twelve.

Figure 8.28
An example of a pickup bar at the beginning of a song

When you create your MIDI file, you can set your sequencer to play at a specific tempo setting. However, this tempo setting might not appear by default on a printed page. It is important to tell the musician at what tempo this song should be played. You can add tempo settings at the beginning of the file, as shown in Figure 8.28 at the top of the first staff.

Bar lines are used to define the boundaries of a bar. Normal bar lines are added automatically in your score at the end of each bar. You can, however, use special bar lines that will indicate a change of section or the end of a piece, or tell the musician to go back to a specific bar and repeat the content found between specially marked bars, as displayed in Figure 8.29.

Figure 8.29
Selecting the proper bar
lines will allow you to
tell a musician which
bars should be repeated

You might want to use a nonstandard shape for note heads (Figure 8.30), especially when
representing percussion instruments or spoken words. You can use special note heads included
in your notation application to create this effect manually.

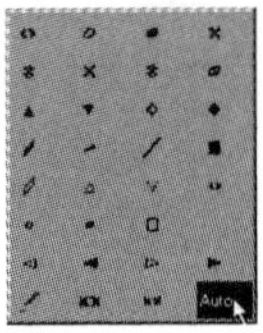

Figure 8.30
Examples of
nonstandard note heads
that you can use to
represent percussion or
to tell a singer, for
example, that the lyrics
associated with these
notes should be
whispered or spoken
rather than sung

Guitar chords, tablatures, and chord names are other aspects of musical writing that you should
incorporate into your score to give additional information to musicians. In fact, if you are
preparing a jazz or improvisational piece, giving a chord structure along with a melodic line and
some rhythmic indications might be all you need (see Figure 8.31).

Figure 8.31
An example of chord
names and guitar
symbols added to a
melodic line

When you play music, you don't always play the notes the same way. Sometimes you hit notes hard, other times, you gently stroke the notes. You might also want to slur between two notes to give it a distinct color. Although this information might be recorded in your MIDI file, it most likely will not translate well into musical notation. Ties, slurs, and other interpretation markings are also useful to give the musician indications on how to play a melodic, rhythmic, or harmonic content. Notation software will usually provide you with tools to add different types of indications, as shown in Figure 8.32.

Figure 8.32
Adding articulation, ties, and slurs to indicate how certain notes should be played

Lyrics are not, by nature, musical events. However, they are part of songs, and as such, can be included on musical sheets. As you can see in Figure 8.33, you can type lyrics below or above your notes and have the text follow the note spacing so that if you add more notes, or more text, the layout will be adjusted appropriately.

Figure 8.33
Adding lyrics to your music

These are only a few aspects of musical notation in relation to MIDI file conversion. You will find that creating scores using MIDI and notation software can be quite engaging. Who knows, you might even want to go into the music publication business once you're done exploring the possibilities these tools offer.

Scanning Musical Scores

Some notation software may provide you with a tool that will convert already written sheet music into MIDI files, although this requires a scanner and a good printed version of the music you wish to scan. This is, by all means, not an exact science. So, the more information besides notes, staves, bar lines, key signature, and clefs there are, the more difficult it will be for the computer. It is as complex to convert a graphic file into MIDI information as it is to scan a graphic file and have software understand what the picture is about.

Score Sequence and Performance Sequence

When creating music using a sequencer, you most likely will work on this music until you get everything just right. This might mean you will spend time recording the perfect interpretation of all your parts, tweaking each one of them until they sound just right to your ears. If you want to create music sheets for musicians, then stop, save your file, make a copy of this file, and rename it. By using the renamed copy of your file, you can now make changes to the MIDI parts that are not well suited for an audio rendering, but are well suited for a musical transcription.

For example, you could quantize all your musical events so that they appear correctly in your score. The idea is to optimize your file for score, not for sound. Since what might sound good to your ears might not be well suited for MIDI notation conversion, it is better to not touch the original version of your MIDI file. When you work in the music notation part of your sequencer or in a notation application, you will end up with a MIDI recording that might not sound as "musical" as your original copy, since it is meant to look better than it sounds. Having a copy of your work will allow you to have the best of both worlds.

9

MIDI Software: A Sound Creation Environment

In the past five years, MIDI has taken somewhat of a back seat to advancements in digital audio. The fact that computers are now capable of handling so much information with such great speed and reliability changed the world of sound creation by integrating big studio technology in small studio setups—and those developments had everyone wondering what would happen with MIDI.

The arrival of software instruments, in my opinion, not only proved that MIDI isn't dead, but has given it a second wind, influencing how musicians around the globe create music. Software instruments are doing this by providing an alternative to MIDI hardware device setups, just as digital audio workstations have given multi-track recording artists the tools they needed to produce better quality material in the comfort of their own home studios.

Getting rid of MIDI hardware altogether is not an option—MIDI sound modules still offer much in the way of processing power, sound quality, and the much-desired tactile surface, which allows you to control its parameters. However, software sound modules offer even more flexibility, and computers are now capable of handling an even greater number of tasks, making them the perfect hosts for these applications.

Here's what you will learn in this chapter:

▶ What software instruments are.

▶ How software instruments integrate into your computer environment.

▶ The difference between plug-ins and stand-alone software instruments.

▶ The best plug-in standard for you.

▶ The advantages and disadvantages of software instruments.

▶ How sound card drivers affect software instrument behaviors.

▶ What virtual MIDI ports are.

▶ How to use a software instrument with your sequencer.

▶ How to automate your software instrument's parameter in your sequencer.

▶ Editor/Librarian: Why you need one.

▶ How to work with an editor/librarian software application.

▶ How you can convert MIDI tracks into audio tracks.

▶ How you can use MIDI to automate your mix using a sequencer.

Software Instruments

There are many types of sound modules—analog and digital synthesizers, samplers, sample playback synthesizers, and drum machines. All of these devices serve a purpose in a MIDI studio. Imagine having the sound creation potential of these machines inside your computer. You can stop imagining now, because that's what software instruments are. With the exception of true analog synthesis, software instruments attempt to emulate the creative power behind these devices. The buttons, knobs, and controls you would find on a real synthesizer are reproduced on your computer screen in great detail in some cases. Other software instrument developers use the fact that they are not tied to a hardware device to push the design envelope one step further, offering very funky looking interfaces. In the end, it all comes down to the sound these software instruments produce, and, in many cases, they will offer you more control over the sound than their hardware counterparts were ever capable of delivering.

So, if you can't afford a $3,000 keyboard, you might just find what you need in a $300 software application!

What Is a Software Instrument?

A software instrument, also called soft synth or virtual instrument, is an application written to emulate a hardware MIDI device. It has the same types of controls as its hardware counterpart (see Figure 9.1), and in some cases, the developers will pitch in a few extra features that are usually not included in the traditional hardware device. In other cases, software instruments approach sound creation in a way that has only been seen in computer environments. So, in this respect, they are a breed of their own.

Figure 9.1
Software instruments offer both realistic recreations of their hardware counterparts and completely new virtual interfaces—these are just some examples of software instruments available today

The idea can be brought down to a simple concept: A software instrument allows you to use your computer's processing power and sound card's digital-to-analog audio converters to emulate synthesizers, samplers, and drum machines.

Currently, there are three flavors of software instruments:

▶ The stand-alone version, which is a software application just like any other, running on its own. It uses your computer's MIDI interface to receive MIDI events, and your computer's sound card as an audio output.

▶ The plug-in version, which comes in different flavors. DirectX, which is supported by Cakewalk through its DXi standard (DirectX Instruments); VST, which is supported by Steinberg and Emagic through their VSTi standard (Virtual Studio Technology Instruments); and HTDM (Host Time Division Multiplexing), which is a format developed by Digidesign (www.digidesign.com) and meant to add software instrument capability to its line of software (ProTools being the most famous one). HTDM is a combination of TDM and RTAS (Real-Time AudioSuite), which gives the ProTools family access to software instruments just as the VST and DirectX standards do. For Digital Performer (from MOTU) users, the MAS (MOTU Audio System) format is supported as well as VST plug-ins if you have the VST Wrapper application, which allows VST plug-ins to be used in Digital Performer. You can find more information on the VST Wrapper at this Web address: www.audioease.com

▶ The proprietary version, which works in specific sequencer host applications, such as Emagic's line of software instruments for Logic Audio Platinum, or even Creamware's (www.creamware.com) selection of software/hardware solutions (see Figure 9.2). Creamware offers software instruments that work only with its sound cards, but can be integrated or controlled by other MIDI sequencers. Contrary to plug-ins and stand-alone versions, proprietary versions require their own hardware. For example, if you don't have a Creamware sound card that supports the software instrument made for it, you won't be able to run the software at all, as it will be looking for a device on your computer that does not exist.

Figure 9.2
Creamware offers a different kind of solution by developing software instruments that use the processing power found on their hardware sound cards rather than using the computer's CPU—this is the Modular 2 software instrument that comes with the Scope sound card

The technology you decide to use will depend on your needs and your current setup. For example, if you are already using Cubase as your sequencer, chances are you will want to continue using the VST standard. On the other hand, nothing prevents you from using any

number of standards in your computer. In fact, Cubase is compatible with DirectX plug-ins; however, it's not compatible with the DXi standard, as it has been developed by a direct competitor (Cakewalk). Also, while the DXi standard is based on the DirectX standard, its implementation inside Cakewalk does not allow it to function inside Cubase or any other sequencer application.

As for proprietary solutions, such as the ones proposed by Creamware, some of them may offer cross-application compatibility. You will, however, need to find out what works and what doesn't before you purchase any software instrument—to avoid getting an application that does not work with your current creative environment.

WHAT IS A PLUG-IN?
A plug-in is a software application that runs within a host application, adding functionality to the application. For example, a software synthesizer plug-in adds the function of a synthesizer to sequencer software; a reverb plug-in adds algorithms with adjustable parameters to create a reverb effect to multi-track hard disk audio recording software. Each host application is compatible with one or more plug-in application standards. On a PC, the most common plug-in standards are DirectX and VST. On a Macintosh computer, the most common plug-in standards are VST and TDM. You install your plug-in application in its own folder or in a folder that is common to all host applications, depending on the plug-in standard. For example, VST plug-ins should be installed in a common folder that all VSTcompatible hosts will share. This will also allow you to share the same plug-in in different host applications without having to install a version of the plug-in in a sub-folder of each application. With DirectX plug-ins, you need to install DirectX support if it is not already installed. Once DirectX support is installed, you install your plug-in in an appropriate folder. As the DirectX plug-in is installed, an entry is made in the DirectX library database found in the DirectX folder. This will allow any host application to recognize a DirectX plug-in installed anywhere on your computer. When you load the host application to memory, it scans the library database to find any compatible plug-ins it can use and loads them in the appropriate plug-in menu inside the application. You can download the latest DirectX support file from this URL: www.microsoft.com/windows/directx.

The advantages of software instruments are plentiful. Here are a few big ones:

▶ Diversity—They can create sounds using a diverse set of controls, which are not limited to the hardware wiring of a real synth. This means that in some applications, you can create your own signal path to create new ways of producing sounds.

▶ Economy—Because everything depends on your computer and not an external device, you don't have to pay for external devices. Program development is not cheap, but when you compare it to the cost of developing and producing an actual synthesizer or sampler, it is clear that a CD in a box will cost less than a 25 Kg keyboard with all its parts.

▶ Flexibility—Software applications, by their nature, are flexible tools. When you want an application to do something, you simply program it. When you work with a hardware sampler, the only upgrades come in the form of a newer model. But flexibility is also about being able to use multiple instances of a software. This means you can load the soft synth more than once in the same song, giving you the equivalent of two or more synthesizers. Have you ever dreamed of having a rack filled with synths to work with? Now it's possible.

Those are the advantages. But you should be aware that software instruments come with some disadvantages as well:

▶ Processing power limitations—A hardware MIDI device provides its own processing power—software instruments do not. Your computer now must handle all required processing power for the application. Not only does your computer have to run your sequencer application, read audio tracks, and record audio tracks to and from your hard disk, it also has to process your software instrument applications. Chances are, the more flexible and powerful those instruments are, the more processor intensive they will be.

▶ Memory limitations—Software synthesizers are loaded in your computer's memory. The more RAM (Random Access Memory) you have, the more applications you will be able to run and the more smoothly they will run. Software samplers might also use your RAM to load a portion of their sounds. If you have limited RAM, you will be limited in the number of sounds you can load simultaneously.

▶ Hard disk speed limitations—When working with software samplers, not only are you using RAM, but you are also using your hard disk as an audio streaming device. If you are running this application along with an audio multi-track or sequencer application, you are putting your hard disk in overdrive, accessing a lot of information simultaneously. Having a fast hard disk will prevent you from getting clicks, pops, crackles, dropouts, and other nasty little side effects. It is recommended that your hard disk be no slower than 7,200 RPM and have an access time averaging around 10 ms or better.

▶ Sound quality—Since your sound card ultimately produces the sound, the quality of its digital-to-analog converters will be an important factor in the quality of the output signal as well. Getting a sound card that sounds good becomes increasingly important as you rely on it more than ever with this type of tool.

Sound Card Drivers and Software Instruments

Since software instruments use your sound card for their audio outputs, you will need a good sound card that provides a low noise output and a good set of well-written drivers. Why are drivers so important when using soft synths? Because how quickly the sound can be generated and converted from digital to analog will make all the difference in the world when playing with the soft synth. In fact, if you don't have a sound card that supports the standards required by these software instruments, or if your sound card doesn't have the proper drivers, you can almost forget about using software instruments altogether. It's that simple.

If you don't have proper drivers, this is what happens: When you play on your keyboard, the MIDI information travels to your sequencer, your sequencer routes the MIDI events to your software instrument, it then processes the information and sends the digital audio information to your operating system. The OS takes the data and forwards it to your sound card's digital-to-analog audio converters. That's when you hear the sound. Most likely, at this point, there is a delay that occurs between the time you pressed on the key and the time you hear the sound. This delay is called latency: the delay between the input and the output.

To avoid latency problems, you need to bypass the operating system, and stream the information directly from the software instrument to the sound card. To do this, you need a specially designed driver. There are a few standards out there that may help:

► The ASIO (Audio Stream Input/Output) and ASIO2 drivers have been developed by Steinberg to optimize the stream of audio information inside your computer. If you use any Steinberg or Emagic software, you should make sure the sound card has an ASIO driver if you want to enjoy your soft synth experience.

► The GSIF (GigaStudio InterFace) driver—developed by Tascam (formerly developed by Nemesys)—as with the ASIO drivers, will greatly improve the stream of digital audio information inside your computer. If you use any Giga products (GigaStudio or GigaSampler), having a sound card with GSIF support will reduce the chances of having bad experiences with software instruments.

► DirectX, WDM (Windows Driver Model), and E-WDM (Enhanced Windows Driver Model) support for any DirectX or (E-)WDM compatible software instrument is essential. This means having the latest driver versions installed on your PC compatible computer. Both drivers are developed around Microsoft technology to provide better data processing and compatibility within the Windows environment.

► The EASI (Enhanced Audio Streaming Interface) driver, developed by Emagic, is similar to Steinberg's ASIO driver in the sense that it optimizes the audio stream by bypassing the OS. Although Emagic supports ASIO and ASIO 2 drivers, if your main working environment is made up of Emagic products, you might want to find a sound card with a driver written in this format.

► Chances are, by the time you read this, there will be a new driver technology out there that provides an even better sound card access for software instruments. Stay alert on this topic by visiting manufacturers' and software developers' Web sites, as well as appropriate newsgroups, since using the best driver technology available to address your sound card will help you get better results from your software instrument.

You can get a sound card compatibility list to find out which sound card supports which standard, and also find out how a particular sound card performs in a specific hardware/software combinations. To get this list, you may visit your sequencer or software instrument's Web site and search for tested sound cards. Here are a few starting points:

▶ If you want to check ASIO and ASIO2 compatible sound cards: http://service.steinberg.net/testbase.nsf

▶ If you want to check which sound cards have been tested by Cakewalk: http://www.cakewalk.com/Tips/audiohw.htm

▶ If you want to check GSIF compatible sound cards: http://www.nemesysmusic.com/support/hardware.html

▶ If you want to check EASI compatible sound cards: http://www.emagic.de/english/support/index.html

Additional MIDI Ports

When you use a software instrument, you are basically loading a virtual synthesizer in your computer. You access this virtual synthesizer or control its functions through its graphical interface. To send MIDI messages to this software instrument, you configure the instrument to receive MIDI messages through your computer's MIDI input port. When you want to use your software instrument in a sequencer environment as a plug-in or as stand-alone software controlled by the sequencer, you need to tell your sequencer application to send MIDI events it receives to this software instrument. That's where virtual MIDI ports come in.

A virtual MIDI port is, for all intents and purposes, identical to a hardware MIDI port. It allows you to send and receive MIDI events over a maximum of sixteen different MIDI channels. It also contains its own name when used inside of a sequencer application. For example, if you are using the GigaStudio sampler, this application will create four virtual MIDI ports in your computer, each of which is given a separate name. You can then decide to make a "virtual" MIDI connection to or from this port by selecting it inside your sequencer, just as you would any other port. The same applies for DXi, VSTi, or any other software instrument. Because the virtual port is, by definition, "virtual," you don't need to make a physical connection. However, you do need to make a virtual connection by assigning the output of a MIDI track to such a port, as discussed in Chapter 8.

Most currently available software instruments create their own MIDI ports when they are loaded, both as stand-alone instruments and as plug-ins. In some cases, a software instrument will create permanent MIDI ports that will stay on your computer even when the instrument is not loaded into memory. For example, when you install GigaStudio or GigaSampler, it creates additional MIDI ports in your Multimedia panel. These ports can be accessed directly from your sequencer when selecting which MIDI Out port to use for a specific track, as shown in Figure 9.3. By selecting this port in your sequencer, you are routing the MIDI messages to the application's MIDI input, as displayed in Figure 9.4. As you can see in this figure, it is the stand-alone software instrument that sends the digital audio information to your sound card's digital to analog converter. This will allow you to monitor your software's audio output.

Figure 9.3
GigaStudio creates four permanent virtual MIDI ports in your system's multimedia configuration

Figure 9.4
Routing of a MIDI signal from its MIDI interface input to a stand-alone software instrument, while passing through a MIDI sequencer

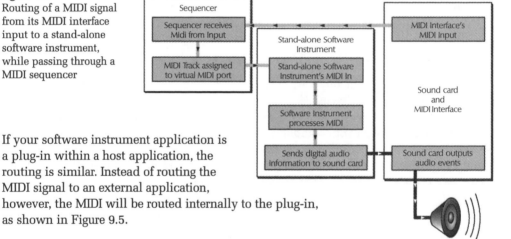

If your software instrument application is a plug-in within a host application, the routing is similar. Instead of routing the MIDI signal to an external application, however, the MIDI will be routed internally to the plug-in, as shown in Figure 9.5.

Figure 9.5
Routing of a MIDI signal from its MIDI interface input to a plug-in software instrument, while passing through a MIDI sequencer

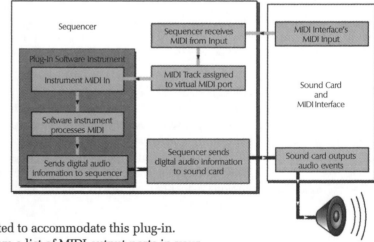

When you load a plug-in software instrument inside a sequencer, a virtual MIDI port is created to accommodate this plug-in. You can then select it from a list of MIDI output ports in your MIDI track, as it will appear there only when the plug-in is loaded.

Stand-alone Software Instruments

Stand-alone software instruments offer working environments that do not require the use of additional software to host the application, so they are not plug-ins to this host application. In other words, you can run the application on its own and trigger the instrument using an external controller keyboard or through a representation of a keyboard on screen. If you want to play it like an instrument, it is advisable to use a controller keyboard.

When you install a stand-alone software instrument, you can configure the application to respond to a MIDI input, just as you would configure your sequencer to respond to incoming MIDI input from one of your MIDI interface's MIDI ports. In all other aspects, it is a software application that works on its own, just like a word processor or graphics editing software.

Inside the application environment, you may use the editing tools that are at your disposal to edit sounds, save sounds, and create sound banks. In Figure 9.6, you can see the Tascam's GigaStudio interface. This application takes sampling to a new level of editing flexibility and overall sampling process, since it allows you to edit sample programs directly in your computer through a graphic interface.

Once your sample programs are saved, you can load them into memory and assign them to specific MIDI channels. After you have configured the application to receive MIDI messages, you can play it just as you would a hardware sampler. GigaStudio also offers a mixing environment that lets you route your samples through effects (the effect can be seen in the lower right corner of this figure), allowing you to further process each sound before it is sent to your sound card's audio output.

Figure 9.6
GigaStudio from Tascam (www.tascam.com) is a stand-alone software sampler—it was the first software sampler to use a hard disk streaming technology to play back samples from a hard disk without loading all the sounds into RAM

CHAPTER 9

If you wish to use this stand-alone sampler application with your favorite sequencer, you can configure GigaStudio to launch your sequencer from its interface (see Figure 9.7). This will allow you to use the sounds loaded in the sampler in your sequencer.

Figure 9.7
You can launch a sequencer, a wave editor, or a sample program editor to create your own sounds from a series of buttons found in the toolbar

Once in your sequencer, you will need to choose the appropriate MIDI port so that the MIDI messages are routed to the sampler application. In this case, the MIDI ports that will appear in your sequencer will be labeled appropriately to identify this application, as shown in Figure 9.8.

Figure 9.8
Selecting the Tascam (Nemesys) GigaStudio MIDI port in your sequencer application

With some stand-alone applications, you will need to launch the sequencer before you can call it from within the other application. Once the sequencer is loaded, you can load the software instrument to activate its virtual ports inside the sequencer. Read the documentation from your sequencer and software instrument to find out exactly how to proceed and in which order the software has to be loaded.

WHAT IS REWIRE?

Rewire is a technology developed by Steinberg and Propellerhead Software. It allows you to connect different software applications together using virtual audio cables. In fact, by activating Rewire channels in the host application, you are patching the virtual audio outputs of another Rewire-compatible software into the host's mixing environment. By allowing the audio to stream between applications, it also provides a sample accurate synchronization between the two applications. Furthermore, you can lock transport controls such as playback, stop, rewind, and record functions from any connected Rewire applications. In other words, when you press Play in one application, all the connected Rewire applications will start playback in sync with the master application's MIDI tempo. Rewire can create up to sixty-four audio channels in your sequencer's mixer window.

Some stand-alone software instruments will offer interconnectivity between applications through internal audio connections made between these applications. Rewire, as described in the previous note, represents one way of connecting a stand-alone software application to a sequencer, in this case Cubase.

Figure 9.9
Reason is a stand-alone application that incorporates a variety of software instruments and a sequencer application bundled together—among those instruments, you will find a synthesizer, two types of samplers, a drum machine, and a variety of effects and other modules to process these instruments

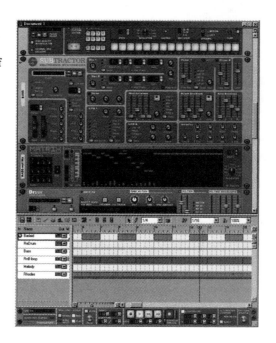

For example, if you are using Cubase with an application developed by Propellerhead (www.propellerheads.se), such as Reason (see Figure 9.9) or Rebirth, you would load Cubase into memory, activate Rewire channels (see bullet 1 in Figure 9.10), and then launch your Rewire-compatible software instrument. In Figure 9.10, you can see that Reason has been loaded and, in bullet 2, the Audio Out of Reason shows that Rewire is active. Therefore, all audio is being patched through Rewire, slaving Reason to the Rewire host. Both Reason and Rebirth are considered stand-alone software instruments, since they run independently from any other software. From this point on, any instrument found in one of the software instrument applications can be triggered and controlled from the sequencer's interface. In bullet 3 of Figure 9.10, all instruments that are loaded in Reason appear as additional MIDI output ports in the MIDI port output selection in Cubase's MIDI track options.

CHAPTER 9

Figure 9.10
Activating Rewire
channels to access
additional software
instruments

Plug-In Software Instruments

A plug-in software instrument can offer the same benefits as a stand-alone version. In fact, many such plug-ins are offered as stand-alone versions as well. However, when using plug-ins, you must install the appropriate plug-in version that corresponds to the host's supported format, as mentioned at the beginning of this chapter. Once you have installed your plug-in software instrument, you are ready to use it as a MIDI-controllable instrument inside your sequencer software.

In Figure 9.11, you can see in the Arrange window of Cubase that the output for the selected track (in reverse highlight) is set to the B4 VST instrument. When pressing on the controller keyboards notes, the MIDI information is passed onto the B4 and keys are pressed on its virtual keyboard, and audio is then transmitted to the software's mixer.

Figure 9.11
Example of a VST
Instrument plug-in and
its MIDI track output
assignment in Cubase

In Cubase, to assign a VST instrument to a track:

1. Select the VST Instrument panel from the Panels menu.
2. In the VST Instrument panel, select an installed VST instrument from the drop-down menu (see Figure 9.12).
3. Select the track you wish to use to control the VST instrument.
4. In the selected track, choose the appropriate MIDI port corresponding to this VST instrument (see Figure 9.13).
5. Now, select a MIDI channel for this instrument.
6. Finally, choose a program number or name from the instrument's program list and start playing.

Figure 9.12
In Cubase, choosing an instrument from the VST instrument's dropdown menu loads this instrument in the computer's memory

Figure 9.13
Assigning the loaded VST instrument's virtual MIDI port to a selected track allows you to route the sequencer's output to this instrument

In Sonar, to assign a DX instrument to a track:

1. Right-click in the track area and create a MIDI track.
2. Right-click again in the track area and create an audio track.
3. Expand both tracks so that you can see their properties.
4. Right-click in the FX section of the audio track and choose the DX Instruments from the context menu, then choose the appropriate DX instrument you wish to use (see Figure 9.14).
5. Now, go back to the MIDI track you just created and choose the DXi's virtual MIDI port from the MIDI output's menu, as shown in Figure 9.15.
6. Choose a MIDI channel for this virtual instrument.
7. Choose a program name or number for the instrument's presets and start playing.

Figure 9.14
In Sonar, the software instrument is assigned to the audio track as an audio FX

Figure 9.15
Assigning the MIDI track to play on the newly created virtual MIDI port corresponding to the DXi instrument

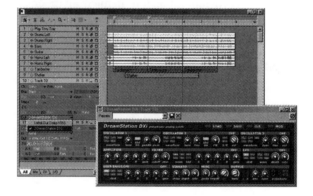

Automating Software Instruments through MIDI

As you know by now, you can control certain parameters of your external MIDI devices through control change MIDI messages. You can automate these changes by recording them inside your sequencer. Stand-alone and plug-in software instruments, like their hardware counterparts, have the same control possibilities. When you use the sequencer's MIDI mixing environment to send different MIDI messages to the hardware or software MIDI device, you are remote-controlling these parameters from the sequencer. In the same way, when you change these parameters from the front end of your instrument (software or hardware), the changes can be recorded in the sequencer and played back in real time. This automation can add more dynamics to your music performance.

How your sequencer handles what you automate depends on the sequencer itself, what you are trying to automate, and how the software instrument, in this case, communicates these changes to your sequencer.

If you are trying to automate common controllers, chances are you can do this through a MIDI mixer in your sequencer or by adding values to the control change area of the piano roll editor in your sequencer. Here's a list of the most common controllers handled and identified within your sequencer:

▶ Channel Voice Messages: velocity, polyphonic key pressure and aftertouch, program changes, and pitch bend.

▶ Channel Voice Messages, Control Changes: modulation, breath controller, foot controller, volume, balance, pan, expression, and sustain.

Since you can use your controller keyboard to automate these common parameters, you will also control these parameters for any instrument assigned to echo the events through the MIDI track's output port setting in your sequencer, provided you have not filtered any of these messages. To verify if these events are filtered from what the sequencer records or not, you can look in your sequencer's MIDI options or preferences. You will find an option corresponding to different filters that are applied to your recording. Un-filter any type of MIDI message you wish to record before starting your automation.

You might also want to automate other parameters in real time through MIDI, such as the cutoff frequency, a resonance filter, or the LFO rate of a software instrument. All these parameters can be, in most cases, automated through your sequencer. However, your software instrument (as well as your hardware device) will use System Exclusive (SysEx) messages to record these parameters to your sequencer in order to automate them later. Here's how to automate parameters in real time:

1. Start by activating your software instrument as described above.

2. Record some MIDI events, such as a melodic line. This is just an example, so you can record whatever type of musical event you want; just keep in mind that you will be automating one or more parameters for this instrument later.

3. Create another MIDI track and choose the same MIDI output port as that used by your software instrument for this track's MIDI output. This is where you will be recording the parameter automation.

4. Make sure, in your sequencer's MIDI options, that you're not filtering System Exclusive messages. In most cases, sequencers filter out System Exclusive messages by default to avoid recording unnecessary messages; however in this case, recording System Exclusive messages is required.

5. Select the empty MIDI track that you created in step 3, and start the record function in your sequencer.

6. Automate the appropriate instrument parameter; for example, changing the amount of resonance, or cutoff value through time. Again, this is just an example.

7. Stop recording when done, rewind, and play what you have just recorded. You should hear the recorded automation and see the graphical representation of the parameter you just recorded move as if you were moving it once again.

When you are done, you can inspect the part you just recorded in a list editor. What you will find are a bunch of SysEx messages corresponding to the values sent by your software instrument as you changed the values on screen.

CHAPTER 9

If your stand-alone software instrument does not send parameter changes to your sequencer, you'll first need to find out whether it supports automation. If it does, you will probably need to map a control change message to a parameter for this instrument. For example, if you want to automate an effect in GigaStudio, you will need to assign a control change number, a MIDI channel, and a MIDI port to this parameter. Once this parameter is set in GigaStudio, sending the corresponding MIDI messages to GigaStudio from your sequencer will automate this parameter, as illustrated in Figure 9.16.

Figure 9.16
Data for Controller #12 recorded in the sequencer is mapped to the room size parameter of the software instrument

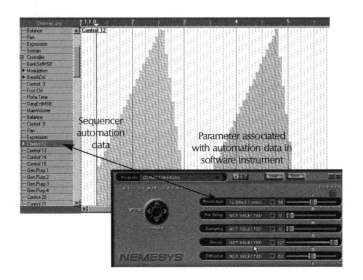

Editors and Librarians

When you are working with MIDI devices such as synthesizers and samplers, editing sounds, saving the ones you like, and recalling banks of sounds are all part of your normal routine. If you are satisfied with the sounds that come with your device and have never edited a sound in it, then this section will not apply to you. On the other hand, if you never did it because you didn't like working with the small LCD on your device, then wait, this section just might put a smile on your face.

There are a great number of synthesizers, samplers, and drum machines out there. Most of them will allow you to control how they sound through a set of parameters, knobs, faders, and buttons. Usually, this is done through pages on your instrument's LCD panel. How much control you have over each sound depends on each device itself. However, computers provide two tools that give you a better grip over what you are editing and also over how you manage these programs.

Editors and librarians do just that. An editor is a software that lets you view the parameters of your MIDI device through a graphic user interface, make changes to the parameters, and save them to a file on your computer. It connects to your MIDI device through a MIDI connection. Once you have configured your editor to send and receive MIDI messages over a specific MIDI port, you can make changes on screen that will affect the connected device.

You communicate through your MIDI connection using SysEx to update the information in your software from the MIDI device, and then use the same SysEx to send the information back to the MIDI device to update your instrument's parameters.

A librarian keeps in a computer file a record of your patch, banks, performances, and other specific information related to your device. When you want to load these sounds, or, more precisely, instructions for how the sounds are to be configured into your synthesizer, you can load the file and transfer the settings to your external device using the MIDI connection between your computer and the device.

Chances are, the editor software will also work as a librarian, allowing you to use one program for editing and storing your sounds. You can even create specific settings for songs, creating a performance in which a set of custom program settings is loaded for your song.

When you load your editor/librarian software for the first time, it will ask you to define which instrument is in your setup, or, more specifically, which instrument you would like to manage using the software. When defining the instruments, you need to make sure your software can communicate with these external devices using MIDI in both directions. This is essential, since SysEx information will be flowing from and to your devices. In Figure 9.17, you can see how each device is connected to the computer through the MIDI interface; these setups are software dependent. Telling the editor/librarian how your studio is configured is the first step in using such a tool.

Figure 9.17
The studio setup window in SoundDiver from Emagic

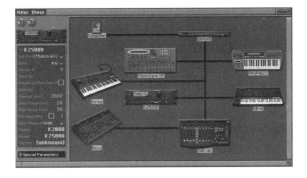

In Figure 9.18, the window on the right displays information for a patch from the Roland JV-1080. All the editable parameters from this device are represented in this scrollable window. When you make changes here, they are sent directly to the instrument, updating the instrument's sound. You can even change the name of a program from your computer's screen and this name will be updated automatically.

You may also use a virtual on-screen keyboard to trigger different notes to audition the changes you make to the MIDI devices parameters.

CHAPTER 9

Figure 9.18
MIDIQuest from
SoundQuest
(www.squest.com)
is an editor/librarian
application

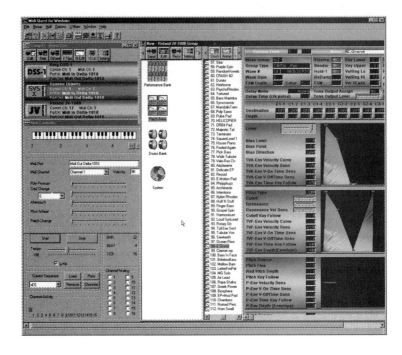

The need for such tools is limited to controlling external hardware devices. In other words, you don't really need an editor/librarian for software instruments, since all the parameters are already inside your computer and are easily accessible. You can see this type of editing environment as an extension of your external MIDI device. This makes it easy to keep these devices in another room even, controlling them from a distance using your computer's MIDI interface to talk with them.

Because this communication is done through SysEx, and every device needs to be configured in your software before you start editing, making changes to one device should not affect any other device. SysEx, after all, is talking to a single device through manufacturer identification codes found in its messages. If SysEx is still a mystery to you and you are not sure you want to start dealing with this right now, don't worry. The messages you send from the editor/librarian's interface will be transparent to you—transparent in the sense that you will change a knob or a value that corresponds to a parameter displayed on screen, not the hexadecimal values that these changes really send to your device.

The only thing that takes a bit of getting used to with these tools is the interface itself. Since there are different kinds of editor/librarians—some are model specific and others offer more universal controls—each company will have its own approach and way of displaying the information on screen. In Figure 9.19, for example, the same Roland JV-1080 appears (see Figure

9.18 to compare) with its editable parameters found in the Patch Edit window. In other words, what you do with the software is similar, but how it gets done might be a bit different, just as with any other MIDI application.

Figure 9.19
The Unisyn
editor/librarian
from MOTU
(www.motu.com)

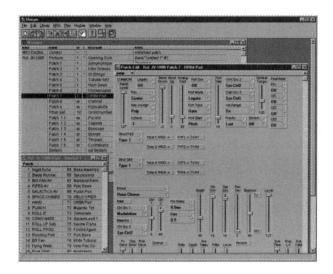

Converting MIDI to Audio

MIDI is not audio. Really? Yes, really. I know this must sound like a stupid statement, but it remains one of the most common misconceptions in audio today. Many people often confuse MIDI and digital audio, and wonder how they make an audio CD from MIDI files. The answer is simple: You have to convert your MIDI into audio beforehand. By now, you probably understand the difference between MIDI and audio because you have been wise and have been reading this book to find out all about MIDI. Congratulations!

How do you convert MIDI into audio? It all depends on the software you are using and what you use to play the MIDI events. There are three possible situations:

1. You are using an external MIDI device with a sequencer.
2. You are using a third party MIDI software synthesizer with a sequencer. This could be software loaded outside of your sequencer but controlled by your sequencer, or a wavetable synthesizer chip on your sound card used to generate sounds triggered by your sequencer.
3. You have software synthesizers loaded as plug-ins inside your software sequencer.

In all three situations, let's assume your sequencer is capable of recording audio while it's playing back MIDI tracks. If not, you will need to have another way to record the audio result of a MIDI performance. In other words, a way of recording the sounds coming through your MIDI device's audio outputs.

Figure 9.20
Converting MIDI
into audio using an
external MIDI device—
in the top portion,
using a mixer,
and in the bottom
portion, without the
use of a mixer

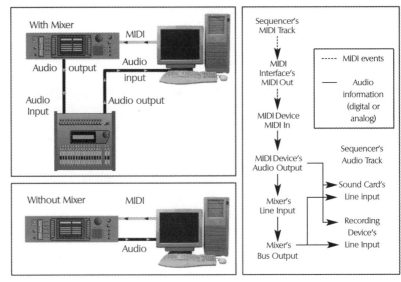

To convert MIDI tracks into an audio track using an external MIDI device (see diagram in Figure 9.20), you must:

1. Start by turning the MIDI metronome off, especially if the same device you are using to record generates this metronome tick.

2. Mute all your audio tracks already created and all the MIDI tracks you don't want to include in the audio file you are about to create.

3. Create an empty audio track, either mono or stereo, depending on the MIDI sound you want to convert.

4. Assign the audio output of your MIDI device to the appropriate audio input on your sound card. If you are using a mixer, make sure your mixer's output is sent to the appropriate recording device.

5A. With mixer: If you are using a mixer that receives the audio signal from the output of your sound card while it is sending the audio signal of your MIDI device you are recording, mute the output of your sound card. Otherwise, you will have a feedback loop. This will occur if the signal coming from the computer's audio output is sent back into its audio input after passing through the mixer.

5B. Without mixer: If you are not using a mixer, connect the audio output of your MIDI device into the audio input of your sound card.

6. Activate or enable the audio track in your sequencer for recording. If you can't record directly into your sequencer, enable your recording device—such as a multi-track recorder or DAT recorder—for recording. In both cases, don't start recording yet.

7. Start playback and monitor the levels of your audio coming into the recording device. This might be your sequencer's audio mixer or your recording device's input indicator. Adjust the levels so that they are always close but under the 0 dB digital limit, without going over it. This will provide the best result.

8. Set appropriate input levels and assure there are no feedback loops. If you notice a feedback somewhere, or a slight phase difference in the sound caused by the monitoring of both the original source of the MIDI device and the audio output of the sound card, mute the output of the sound card to prevent its being recorded back into the audio input.

9. Bring your playback cursor to the beginning of the appropriate part you want to record and start recording the MIDI device's audio output.

10. When done, save the recording and position the newly recorded file, if the sequencer hasn't already done so, at the appropriate location in your project. Usually, this is done automatically. If you have recorded onto another device, such as a DAT recorder, you will need to transfer back into the sequencer, or lock the sequencer through a synchronization function (explained in Chapter 10).

11. Mute the MIDI track you have just recorded and un-mute all the other tracks to hear the result.

12. Repeat this operation for every MIDI track you wish to record as an individual audio track in your sequencer.

To convert MIDI tracks into an audio track using internal MIDI software, you have two possibilities: First, if your software has a built-in recording tool, it might allow you to record the MIDI it receives from your sequencer directly to a digital audio file. This is the case with GigaStudio from Tascam (see Figure 9.21).

Figure 9.21
Tascam's GigaStudio
(www.tascam.com)
allows you to capture its
audio output directly to
a file on your computer

However, if your software does not allow you to capture its audio output directly to hard disk, you will have to proceed exactly as you did with the external MIDI device. However, in this case, instead of sending the MIDI to an external device, you are sending it to another internal MIDI application. The audio output of this internal MIDI synthesizer or sampler software can be recorded internally if you have a full duplex sound card. Full duplex is a term that refers to the sound card's ability to play and record at the same time. If you don't have full duplex capability, you will have to record the audio output of your software synthesizer to an external audio recording device, and then record back into the sequencer.

CHAPTER 9

Finally, if you are using a plug-in virtual synthesizer integrated inside the sequencer application, you will be able to "render" the audio output directly without any conversion. There are two such types of plug-ins: DXi (DirectX Instrument) developed by Cakewalk, or VST (Virtual Studio Technology) Instruments developed by Steinberg (also compatible with Emagic's Logic sequencers). You will have to read your software's documentation to find out exactly how to do this, but here's the principle behind the operation:

The virtual instrument (DXi or VSTi), when loaded, uses your sound card's audio output to generate the sounds they produce. While inside your sequencer, MIDI events played by an external keyboard or a recorded sequence triggers the audio output of the instrument, producing its audio output. When you convert the MIDI data into audio, the sequencer uses a built-in function that renders the audio file internally, taking the notes it has to record from the MIDI information recorded in the associated MIDI track. You can later import the rendered audio tracks and mute the original MIDI tracks in order to mix all the audio content in your project to a final 2-track stereo mix.

Automating Your Mix through MIDI

Using a sequencer to automate your mix is not only easy, but also very versatile. Mixing is part of the final stages of your creative process. Once all the tracks are down, recorded in MIDI or audio depending on your project, you can add life to your creation by placing instruments in their own space, adjusting their levels, panning them, and adding effects.

Creating an audio mix inside your sequencer is usually provided through an audio mixer panel or window in the software itself. MIDI mixing may be done in the same mixing window or a different mixing window. How exactly this is done depends greatly on the software you use. However, when controlling MIDI automation, you are basically sending MIDI messages to your MIDI devices. As you saw earlier in this book, there are specific controller numbers for volume, pan, and other MIDI parameters. Using your sequencer's built-in MIDI mixer gives you a graphic interface to control these parameters and saves changes you make to these values to a special mixing track. You can also embed the automation directly into the actual MIDI track you are mixing simply by adding control changes to the events already recorded on the track.

MIDI-enabled mixers can also be used to add automation to MIDI tracks. In this case, the mixer maps the set of control changes and other MIDI messages to its automatable parameters. Automatable parameters are any parameters that your mixer will let you control, or will use to record automation. For example, moving a fader on your mixer might create a series of volume control messages for the specific fader channel you move. When you record the MIDI events generated by your mixer to a sequencer, you will notice that it does not generate any MIDI note messages, but rather control change messages. When played back, depending on your mixer and its configuration, you might see the fader moving on its own.

Most MIDI enabled and automatable mixers will use more than one MIDI channel to transmit their MIDI data, because they might have many automatable parameters. The volume faders on mixer inputs are a simple example. However, you might also want to control the EQ, the compression level, the solo and mute assignments, recall entire sets, or change integrated effects to a different patch. All these parameters require many MIDI messages, since each parameter needs to be associated with an existing MIDI message. Mixers use proprietary mapping systems, where each MIDI channel and each control change message is assigned a parameter inside the mixer. The exact mapping is pretty complex, and since it is proprietary (each mixer uses its own MIDI event mapping system), all you really need to do is make sure your mixer can send and receive MIDI events.

The bottom line is that you need to make sure that the MIDI channels your mixer uses are not used by any other MIDI devices. This is why it is recommended that a MIDI enabled hardware mixer be assigned to its own MIDI port, providing you have a MIDI port to spare. This will allow you to have a tactile mixing interface that sends MIDI messages to your sequencer and receives these messages from the sequencer during playback.

If you recall correctly (if not, you can always go back to Chapter 2 to refresh your memory), some control change messages have an LSB and an MSB equivalent, giving you a fine and coarse tuning. This is handy when mixing with a MIDI mixer if the mixer uses the fine values. This would mean smooth fades and changes when mixing. Although this is not a common feature in consumer priced mixers, you might find it in high-end devices. In any case, using your mixer's automation capability alongside your MIDI sequencer can definitely be a time saver at mixing time.

10

MIDI Software: A Toolbox Filled With Toys

A number of MIDI applications allow just about anyone to use MIDI in ways that were not possible before the integration of computers into the MIDI world. MIDI players allow a computer user to hear MIDI files through his/her computer sound card's synthesizer chip. MIDI monitors allow a user to monitor MIDI going into or coming out of the computer. These applications represent a new breed of MIDI tools for non musicians.

Other MIDI programs are designed to support special functions not necessarily found in more general MIDI editing software. For example, your sequencer might not provide any MIDI effects, such as MIDI delays or MIDI arpeggios, or you might find a stand-alone utility that converts sample-based sounds from one sampler format to another sampler format handy and useful.

MIDI programmers have also given us new tools to create, edit, convert, and publish our MIDI files on the Web. MIDI, after all, was also meant to link hardware devices through a common communications protocol, right?

Here's a summary of what you will learn in this chapter:

▶ What MIDI players are.

▶ Examples of MIDI utilities and related applications.

▶ Sample format conversion tools.

▶ How to convert digital audio files into SoundFont sound banks so that they can be played just like any other instrument.

▶ Getting applications to share MIDI and audio resources inside your computer.

▶ What the downloadable sound format is and why it was developed.

▶ What the extensible music format is and how you can use it to publish your MIDI files on the Web.

▶ How you can create a single file that contains both MIDI and sound banks for better control over the sound quality on the Web.

▶ How to publish your MIDI files on a Web page.

MIDI Players

A MIDI player is a software application that allows you to play back MIDI files. They exist as Internet browser plug-ins and as stand-alone applications. You can't edit MIDI files with a MIDI player. However, if you don't have a software sequencer, MIDI players will allow you to listen to MIDI files on your computer. MIDI players can, in some cases, include sound banks, which are usually GM, GS, or XG compatible.

For Macintosh users, the easiest way to listen to MIDI files is through either QuickTime or Simple Text. But if you would like to try other options, here's a few:

- ▶ iTunes: www.apple.com/itunes/download
- ▶ Destiny Media Player: www.radiodestiny.com/download/mediaplayer.html
- ▶ Yamaha XG plug-in for your Web browser: www.yamaha-xg.com/midplug/dlmac/dl_mac.html
- ▶ Crescendo plug-in for your Web browser: www.liveupdate.com/FreeDownload.asp

For both Windows and Macintosh users, your OS provides you with some built-in MIDI players, such as Windows Media Player or QuickTime for Macintosh. However, you can also use one of the following alternatives:

- ▶ QuickTime also offers a PC version, which provides you with its own GS sound bank: www.apple.com/apple
- ▶ Yamaha XG plug-in for your Web browser, PC version: www.yamaha-xg.com/midplug/dlwin
- ▶ Winamp is a popular MP3 player (see Figure 10.1), but it also handles MIDI files: www.winamp.com

Figure 10.1
Winamp not only plays audio files, but also supports MIDI files

Utilities

By now, you understand the difference between MIDI and audio. You also know how to convert MIDI into audio. But what about converting audio to MIDI, or converting sound patches used in one sampler software into patches for use in another sampler software? Maybe you're having some MIDI problems and you'd like to monitor the MIDI activity going into or coming out of your computer? How about a tool to organize your MIDI files into a database to find them quickly? These are only a few examples of MIDI utilities that are available. In fact, if there's something you want to do with MIDI, there is probably a software tool available on the Web that will help you do it. One of the great aspects of MIDI is its versatility and its capacity to be easily manipulated.

Let's take a look at some of the software tools that are available to enhance your MIDI experience and make your life easier. These are not the only options you have, but rather an overview of what's available. You will find additional information about software manufacturers in Appendix G, "MIDI Resources on the Web," in this book.

MIDI to Guitar Chords Utility

If your software sequencer doesn't handle guitar chords well, or if its guitar chord detection is limited, there is a little application that might be useful. It recognizes chords and converts them into useful guitar fingering notation so that you can add this fingering information to a score (see Figure 10.2).

Figure 10.2
The MIDI guitar chord finder is a PC freeware available at www.geocities.com/midigtr

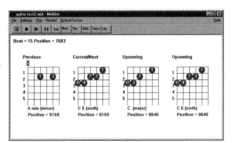

MIDI Message Monitoring

Remember when we were discussing MIDI messages? All those values in status bytes and data bytes? Well, using a MIDI monitor utility allows you to see these messages in action and helps you to understand what's really happening in your MIDI message. For example, Figure 10.3 allows you to monitor MIDI messages in different formats. This might be useful if you are trying to troubleshoot your MIDI setup, searching for filters or modifiers along the way. A modifier is a parameter that is set to transform your MIDI message in some way, and can be found in a MIDI sequencer or a MIDI patch bay, for example. If you are unaware that such a modifier is being applied, you might have varying results, and a MIDI monitor like this one could help you determine if such a modifier is being applied to MIDI messages. You can also use a tool like this to better understand the content of MIDI messages, as it shows you all the values that are passed in the message. In this case, the values H80, H3E, H40, and H00 represent a Note Off on channel 1 for note D3, with a release velocity of 64.

Figure 10.3
The MIDI Monitor window—this PC shareware is available at bcsoft.free.fr; you can download a Mac version of this type of utility from this address: http://rhythm.harmony-central.com/~ftp/softwa re/mac/midi/midimanag eractivity-10.cpt.hqx

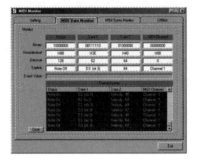

From Digital Audio to MIDI

So, you've created a great guitar line with your guitar and recorded the audio track, but you can't remember what notes you played. You would like to find a way to convert your audio file into MIDI data so that you can play this part on another instrument. This type of conversion is not usually very precise, due to the inherent difficulties of converting polyphonic instruments recorded as audio into MIDI events. However, some software attempts to do just that. You can use this as a starting point, and then work on the MIDI events in a sequencer to extrapolate the rest of the MIDI events needed to reproduce the guitar line, or to print a score of this line using appropriate music notation software.

Figure 10.4
Amazing MIDI's interface lets you convert digital audio into MIDI parts— this PC compatible shareware can be downloaded from: www.pluto.dti.ne.jp/ ~araki/amazingmidi

In Figure 10.4, you can see three file path references appearing in the window. The one in the middle refers to the digital audio input file, which will be used as your source material to be converted into MIDI. To work effectively, this file should contain clear recognizable tones and pitches. In other words, the more instruments and the more reverb or noisy artifacts there are in the audio source material, the less likely you will be satisfied with the resulting MIDI file. This said, you should use an audio editor to remove background noises and possibly normalize the audio content—which boosts the audio signal to its maximum value without clipping. Once you've optimized your audio, you will need a tone file. A tone file is an audio reference with which the software compares the input file. For example, if you've recorded a guitar line as your input file, you might want to also record a single guitar note as a reference. This will increase the software's effectiveness in detecting the actual notes played in the input file. Once both these files are selected, as shown in Figure 10.4, you are ready to start the transcription setup process.

The transcription setup process is used to determine how the audio content should be analyzed. Read the documentation in order to understand what exactly each parameter in this window does. Once you have set the proper parameters for the transcription of digital audio into MIDI, you can proceed to the conversion. What you see at the bottom of this figure is the MIDI result, which can be saved as a MIDI file and imported in your sequencer for further editing. This said, don't expect a perfect match. This is an estimation of what was played, and some notes might appear that were never played. That's why you will need to edit the MIDI events in your sequencer; however, it is a good starting point and may reduce your transcription time when done properly.

Format Conversion Tools

With the popularity and development of sampler software instruments comes a new challenge for MIDI musicians: how to keep using sound programs from your old AKAI S-1000 sampler library in your new GigaStudio, HALion, or Sample Tank software. Thousands of sounds have been programmed in one format or another, and you might also have gathered a good collection of your own sounds, spending many hours tweaking loop points and envelopes and assigning each sample to specific keys to get the end result. In light of all that work, changing your sampler might not seem so appealing after all, particularly if it means having to redo all that work! Rest assured, you won't have to start over from scratch; this is something that software developers have caught up with.

There are already many tools that allow you to convert sounds from one format to another. For example, converting a wave or AIFF file into an MP3 is now easier than ever. However, the challenge when it comes to samplers is the inherent programming that goes into creating an instrument. For example, sampler instruments start with sampled sounds that might be layered across a velocity range. You might have a hard hit snare drum when the MIDI velocity is between 100 and 127, a medium hit snare when the velocity is between 64 and 100, and a low or soft snare hit when the velocity is between 0 and 64. When you play the note to which your snare is assigned on the keyboard, the velocity at which you play will determine which sample is played in the sampler. Then, you might add an envelope to this setting, pan it a bit off center, and so on. Note that you have to assign a good number of samples to different keys on a range of notes in order to have a realistic acoustic instrument. Looping sounds at a specific point in an audio file is also very time consuming, but necessary when programming your sound.

All these elements that go into the creation of a sampled sound need to be reproduced, or translated, from one sampler format to another if you want to be able to use your sample library in a different sampler. That's what format conversion tools are used for.

In Figure 10.5, you can see the Chicken Systems Translator, which allows you to browse the contents of different sampler formats in an Explorer fashion. You can listen to the samples selected before converting them, and you can manage your sounds from this interface.

Figure 10.5
Chicken Systems
Translator
(www.chickensys.com/
translator) converts any
sampler format to any
other sampler format

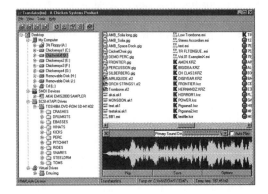

Figure 10.6 shows another example of a sampler format conversion tool that lets you see the structure of each sound as it was originally programmed. Again, converting your sounds will preserve most of the programming information involved in the sound's setup, saving you many hours of programming time. For example, in this figure the sound format used was SoundFont 2.1. This can then be exported to a GigaStudio, Emagic EXS, Pulsar STS, or HALion sampler format, not to mention the usual AKAI S6000 series or plain old MP3.

Figure 10.6
CDxtract
(www.cdxtract.com) is
another conversion tool
for sampler formats—
this is the OSX version

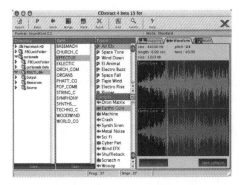

Both these applications will map the proper samples and parameters to their appropriate MIDI note numbers so that, for instance, a C3 sample will correspond to a C3 sample in the converted format.

CHAPTER 10

Samples to SoundFonts

Sometimes, you might want to use individual samples in your computer as a base for a SoundFont set. To use SoundFonts, you will need a compatible sound card, sequencer, or software synthesizer. Once sounds are loaded into your SoundFont-compatible sound card or software instrument, you can use them as you would a sampler—reading samples from the hard disk through this application's interface. Here's an example: With a Sound Blaster AWE64 sound card (a SoundFont-compatible card) and Cubase, you can assign the AWE64's synth as the MIDI track's output. Then, you choose the SoundFont instrument from Cubase's Instrument menu in the Inspector area. This will give you access to the SoundFont banks installed on your sound card.

In order to use SoundFonts with your compatible sound card you will need to make sure the SoundFont Management System provided by your sound card manufacturer is installed on your system. Note that sound cards that support SoundFonts are only developed for PC computers; however, you can use SoundFonts with software instruments that support this format on both platforms. The Unity DS-1 from Bitheadz (www.bitheadz.com) supports SoundFonts (and DLS, as you will see later) and is cross-platform compatible.

Since SoundFonts are organized banks of programs, you should know a little bit about how to create banks from samples. In Figure 10.7, the material for the banks are samples that are recorded on your hard disk or found on a sampling CD. This will be the sound source for the programs you assign in your sequencer. Samples are assigned to individual keys or key ranges. This is called the multi-sample level. Each sample can also be assigned a specific velocity range. If, for example, you wish to have a different sample play when you play harder, you can assign a different sample for higher velocities. Once the multi-samples are mapped to your keyboard, you can assign them to a program and add different playback parameters to them, such as an envelope, a filter, or effects. This mapping of sampled and multi-sampled audio files along with the envelope, filter, and effect settings represent the program itself that you can select from using a program change number. The program and all its settings, including the key mapping and referred samples, will be saved in a SoundFont bank, which is then loaded into your sequencer. Once loaded, you can call a program in a bank.

Figure 10.7
Example of a
SoundFont bank
structure

Program (multi-samples
combined with filters,
envelopes, effects and
modulations)

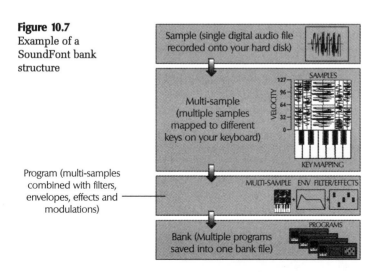

To create such banks, you will need a SoundFont bank editor (see Figure 10.8) to convert digital audio samples into a SoundFont-compatible format.

Figure 10.8
The Unity DS-1 Editor window allows you to create program banks and save them as SoundFonts, and import SoundFonts already made and play them through your sound card as a software instrument

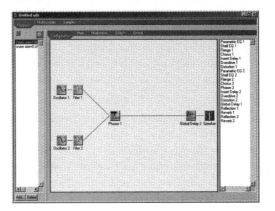

Sharing Resources inside Your Computer

When using MIDI, sharing resources inside your computer usually implies sharing a MIDI port and sound card access. To make sure your resources are spread around adequately, you'll need to plan ahead. Since the main issues at hand are the MIDI ports and how they are used, and the software applications that use the sound card's audio outputs in both audio and MIDI related tasks, knowing what your software requires and the workaround might help you getting over some of these issues. This said, some software is less fussy in terms of shared audio resources, while others might take over your sound card completely, leaving it useless if you load a second application that requires it.

On a PC, you can't get certain software applications to talk to each other internally. For example, if you are running a stand-alone version of a software instrument, Cakewalk's Sonar won't talk to it. By installing a virtual MIDI port, you can create an inter-application communication, or bridge, between applications.

Figure 10.9
Setting up a virtual MIDI port to send MIDI information from one MIDI application to another within your computer

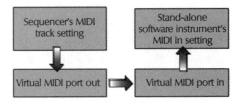

Figure 10.9 shows that configuring one application to send MIDI to another (applications that don't normally share a virtual connection) is quite similar to using software instruments within a single application, or setting up MIDI communication between two applications that are already sharing resources. In this example, you need to set the first application (the one on the left in the figure) to send MIDI to the installed virtual MIDI port's output, and set the second application (the one on the right) to receive MIDI from this virtual MIDI port. Hubi's MIDI Loopback offers such connection. This very small application (it takes 5 KB of memory inside your computer while running) allows you to create up to four additional MIDI ports inside your computer (see Figure 10.10). Once installed, you will find these additional ports in your MIDI setup options. Once activated, you can then send MIDI events through these new ports so that your applications can share the MIDI data (see Figure 10.11). You can download a free copy of this application from the following Web sites:

▶ members.magnet.at/hubwin/midi.html

▶ www.geocities.com/mstella/hmidilb/hmdlpbk.html

Figure 10.10
The Hubi's Loopback port activation window—you can double-click on the port's label to rename it

Figure 10.11
Setting up your application to receive from the newly installed virtual MIDI port

You will find additional information on how to install this application included with the compressed downloaded file.

On a Mac, you can enable inter-software communication of MIDI events through MOTU's FreeMIDI. To activate this function under FreeMIDI, you first need to have this installed on your system. Then, you open FreeMIDI, select the Preferences option in the File menu. In the Preferences window, enable the Inter-application MIDI and click OK. You can then exit FreeMIDI and launch the application that should receive MIDI from your sequencer and select the FreeMIDI input from its MIDI options. You should note that OMS does not support inter-application configuration.

In terms of audio resources, there are two aspects to consider:

1. The capacity your sound card's driver has to share its access between two or more applications. Your sound card needs to have a multi-client driver. This type of driver will allow more than one client (software application) to access its resources at a time. You will need to consult your sound card's manufacturer documentation or Web site to find out if the sound card is multi-client or not. You can also find out what limitations it has in this regard, or tips and tricks on configuring your applications to work well with this sound card.

2. The capacity your software application has to share its access to the sound card resources with others. This means that certain applications will not allow for shared sound card access. It also implies that in some cases, you will need to load a certain application before another. Consult your application documentation to find out what the proper procedures are and what kind of restriction this resource sharing will add to your setup.

Once you have resolved these two issues, there is not much more you can do. If you find that you can't share your sound card resources for one of the reasons mentioned above, you will need to revise your strategy. To avoid this, it is always good to plan ahead: Shop around, ask questions on compatibility and resource sharing issues, check for updated drivers that might improve your sound card's functionality, or get another computer to add overall horsepower to your setup.

MIDI Web Solutions

The Web is a great way to find information and promote your work to others. One of the ways you can do this is by creating a Web site with samples of your work, along with some information about you, your band, or any other information you deem interesting. When it comes to putting your music on the Web, there are two options: posting either audio files or MIDI files.

Posting audio files offers the advantage of assuring your sound quality; it will be the same for every person who visits your Web site. The disadvantage is that the user will have to wait for the file to download to his/her computer in order to listen to it. You could choose to stream your audio content, which diminishes the download time, since streamed audio starts playing as it is being transferred. However, this method requires quite a bit of knowledge and still requires a large bandwidth from the user's perspective in order to avoid dropouts in the sound as it is being downloaded.

The other alternative is MIDI. The advantage of MIDI is that it is usually much smaller than its digital audio counterpart. The disadvantage is that you don't control the final output of the MIDI file on the user's system, and since each system is different, the sound quality (as well as the sounds themselves) might vary widely from system to system. There are options, described below, that may help limit this uncertainty. Among those are downloadable sounds (DLS) and extensible music format (XMF) files.

Once you've decided whether to use audio or MIDI when publishing your music on the Web, you will need to know how to include these files in your Web pages. Here again, you have two options: You can add a link to your file or embed your file in the Web page itself. Both methods are described later in this chapter.

Downloadable Sounds (DLS)

In the past decade, wavetable synthesis has become increasingly prevalent, and so has the need for a standard wavetable-based format that defines musical instruments. Although the GM specification defines a set of 128 instruments, it lacks enough depth and breadth to deliver a truly consistent playback experience across a wide range of platforms. This is due in part to the wide variety of devices used to play these GM sounds. Some GM devices will use FM synthesis or wavetables, while others will use SoundFonts. The result is a wide range of sound quality. The need for a musical instrument standard that allows composers to define exactly how each musical instrument sounds on a wide variety of playback devices is finally met with the downloadable sounds (DLS) format.

When authoring for MIDI, a composer faces two limitations: the limited set of instruments that GM provides, and the lack of consistency in the quality of GM sound banks, ranging from good to outright ridiculous. Other media do not suffer from these problems. For example, a graphic designer or an audio engineer can rely on consistent results on multiple hardware solutions. MIDI, unfortunately, does not offer such consistency, so content developers such as you might opt for digital audio rather than MIDI. However, digital audio is not as flexible and interactive as MIDI, not to mention the additional storage and transmission bandwidth requirements of this medium. These two points are of particular significance on the Web.

DLS (Level 2.1) enables the author to define and create an instrument by combining a recorded waveform or set of waveforms with articulation information. An instrument designed this way can be downloaded onto any hardware device that supports the standard, and then played like any standard MIDI synthesizer. This will give the MIDI author a common playback experience and an unlimited sound palette for both instruments and sound effects, unlike GM. It also offers audio interactivity and MIDI storage compression, unlike digital audio. However, the DLS standard does not contain MIDI events themselves, but rather the instrument definitions (sound banks) needed by a MIDI file to play correctly.

If you look at Figure 10.12, you can see that there are three components required for DLS to work. First, you have the MIDI file, which is the source material that triggers the sounds, just as it would trigger your usual external or software MIDI instruments. It is, for all intents and purposes, a regular SMF file. What is special about it is that it refers to a bank of DLS sounds. It does this by using a DLScompatible software instrument such as Unity DS-1 (www.bitheadz.com) as the instrument that plays your MIDI events.

The DLScompatible instrument or sound bank reader processes the samples found in this bank by applying the DLS architecture to them. This architecture is not uncommon; however, the parameters defined by this architecture must meet a specific DLS standard. In the same figure, you can see how the MIDI fed into the instrument passes through the control logic of the DLScompatible instrument. On the left, envelope generators define the shape of the sound, such as modifying the attack time, decay, sustain, and release times. The information also passes through an LFO to adjust the different pitch of samples to the notes that might be played in your MIDI file. The frequency of the LFO (Low Frequency Oscillator) in this case determines the playback frequency of the sample, not the vibrato or filter sweep frequency as is usually associated with LFOs. This information is combined with the actual samples found in your sound bank and sent to your sound card for audio playback.

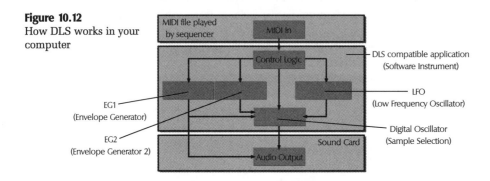

Figure 10.12
How DLS works in your computer

The extended RMID file is a format based on the RIFF (Resource Interchange File Format) developed by Microsoft and used for file types such as WAV and AIFF (Audio Interchange File Format). When used to house MIDI and DLS information, the RMID file contains a single SMF data image, a single DLS data image, plus supplemental data such as a version stamp, copyright notice, and other descriptive information. In this sense, an extended RMID file can be used for portability of music, just like a standard MIDI file, with the exception that authors can define their own instruments rather than using only GM instruments.

To find out more about DLS and RMID, visit the MMA's Web site at www.midi.org.

Extensible Music Format (XMF)

In recent years, the MMA, in conjunction with Beatnik, has developed a new format called eXtensible Music Format (XMF). This file format is actually a meta format—a container file that points to other types of files; in this case, MIDI files, RMF (Rich Media Files), DLS (Downloadable Sample) files, and digital audio files. Its purpose is to serve as a standard format for transmitting MIDI files and sample bank information used by this MIDI file to a MIDI player over the Internet, or between applications that support the XMF standard, just as the RMID described earlier in this chapter.

The concept of an XMF file is similar to other types of metafiles, such as those found with MP3 files (M3U), RealMedia content (RAM—real audio and real video), and Windows Media Format through its WAX metafiles: They all contain links to media file content.

What this means for musicians is that you can create a MIDI file using downloadable sounds (DLS) or GM as your sound banks for this MIDI file, then through the Web or even on cordless communication devices, you can transmit your music using very little bandwidth, since MIDI is small. The quality of the sounds will be guaranteed by the DLS you provide or through the user's pre-downloaded set of DLS.

Here's an example of how this might work. In Figure 10.13, an HTML file on a Web site holds a link to an XMF file. When a user clicks on the link, the XMF file transfers to the user's computer. Remember, the XMF file only contains links to other media files, but since it is small, it loads quickly and prompts the associated plug-in player (such as a QuickTime, Windows Media Player, or other XMF plug-ins you might have on your computer) to load in the user's memory. Once the plug-in is active in the user's memory, this plug-in starts downloading the actual media files referred to in the XMF file.

This is the same process used when creating streaming content on the Web using RealAudio or Windows Media Format. The fact that the metafile itself is small allows the computer to quickly load the player needed to reproduce the content of this XMF file. When it finds links to the media files, it starts downloading them to the computer. When it has downloaded enough information to start playback, it begins to play the content. In the case of XMF files, the content is usually a MIDI file with its associated files: DLS or RMF sound banks.

For example, you could include along with the MIDI file a downloadable sample file, which would contain the custom sound banks you used to create your MIDI file. If the MIDI file only refers to sounds from the GM sound bank through program changes, the XMF player plug-in may use the existing GM sound bank found with your associated player. Or, you can also include your own GM sound bank if you want to make sure the sounds are exactly as you intended them. You may also include production notes in different languages. The XMF file will recognize the user's regional setting and download only the appropriate language for this user. Once these files are downloaded, the MIDI playback will begin. In most cases, this should not be long, since MIDI requires very little space and DLS are, when programmed properly, very space efficient as well.

Figure 10.13
How XMF connects
MIDI files, sounds, and
Web pages together

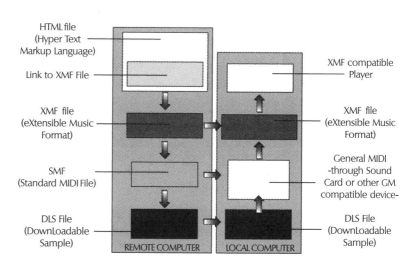

The applications of XMF are still being defined, since this standard has just been accepted by the MMA. At this time, wireless communications and Internet-related MIDI-based applications seem likely to benefit from this standard.

Bundling MIDI Files and Sound Banks for the Web

You can also control the audio quality of your MIDI files on a Web site through the use of a plug-in developed by Beatnik (www.beatnik.com).

Here's how the Beatnik solution works for the end user:

▶ Download the Beatnik player from the Beatnik site for free. This player holds a GM-compatible sound bank of verifiable quality, meaning that anyone using this plug-in will hear exactly the same thing, since the sounds are not system dependent.

▶ Install the player, and you are ready to hear the content created for this plug-in.

Here's how Beatnik works for the content creator:

▶ Download and install the Beatnik player—you'll need it in order to hear your file before you make it available on the Web.

▶ You will also need to purchase the Beatnik RMF editor. This allows you to bundle both your MIDI file and the additional sounds you might be using that are not part of the default set of GM compatible sounds.

▶ Once you have installed the editor, you can import your MIDI files, create instruments that will be used in this file, and export these instruments and MIDI sequences to RMF (Rich Music Format).

▶ You can also create MIDI files in your sequencer and link your sequencer to Beatnik so that it plays the sounds from the Beatnik sound bank. In Figure 10.14, you can see the sample editor window, which allows you to create your source material for your instruments. These instruments can then be assigned to play on different MIDI channels of your song file. The top Player window lets you see the actual MIDI playback of your MIDI file through its assigned sounds.

Figure 10.14
The Beatnik Editor interface allows you to load MIDI files and create your own custom samples to play with this file

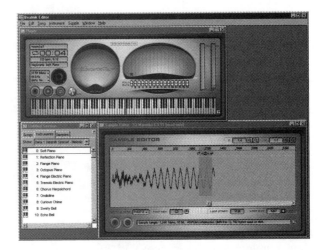

In terms of distribution, the RMF format technology is similar to the XMF file mentioned above in the sense that it can bundle both MIDI and customized sounds into a single file so the creator can take advantage of the high quality sound bank the plug-in provides. The end user needs only to download the customized sounds, which represents a far smaller download time for a great quality experience, since the default sounds (GS sound bank) are already on the user's computer.

With RMF, it is also possible to encrypt the file with your copyright information. Since RMF is a proprietary format, a user can't make copies of your music without your consent, or redistribute your music after changing the copyright information. In other words, the RMF file format protects your material from copyright infringement.

Using MIDI Files in Your Web Pages

As mentioned earlier in this chapter, there are two ways you can include MIDI files in your Web page: by embedding the content into your page, or creating a link to a file inside your HTML page. Both are quite easy to implement.

The first method consists of adding a link to the MIDI file from within your HTML document (Web page). The second method consists of embedding the MIDI file in your page; it will start loading on the user's computer just as a graphic file loads automatically in your browser. The link provides the user with the option of downloading the MIDI file or not, whereas the embedded MIDI file doesn't give the user this option. If your MIDI file is more than 40 KB, you should consider giving the user the option of downloading it. Otherwise, visitors to your Web page will be forced to wait for your file to download before everything appears clearly on the page. There are, however, workarounds to this. For example, adding an embedded file at the bottom of the page rather than at the top will help. This is because Web browsers read HTML and load pages from top to bottom.

Here's the HTML code for adding a link to a MIDI file:

```
<A HREF="MyMIDIFile.MID">Example Of My MIDI Work</A>
```

The opening HTML tag tells the browser that this is the referenced file of a link: <AHREF= " ">. Then, list the name of the actual file you wish to link to—in this example: "MyMIDIfile.MID." The filename must be written between double quotation marks. The text that follows is the text that will appear as the hyper link in your HTML document. Usually, this text will be underlined, unless you program your page otherwise. The last tag indicates the end of the hyper linked text: </A>. If the referenced MIDI file is not in the same folder as your HTML page, you will need to add the relative path to the filename. For example, if your file is in a subfolder called "MIDIFILES," you must add the following information in your file reference description: <A HREF= "MIDIFILES/MyMIDIFile.MID">. Also, note that some Web servers are case sensitive, so making sure you standardize your naming convention will help in avoiding errors.

The other method consists of embedding a MIDI file in your Web page. This method, as mentioned above, will download the file automatically on the user's computer as the page loads. When the file plays, how it looks in your page depends on the player that will load in the user's computer. There isn't much you can do about that, since you can't know for sure what player the user associated with the MIDI file extension. You can, however, provide a link to your favorite MIDI player plug-in in case the user does not have such a MIDI player installed on his/her computer. How it starts playing or how many times it plays are parameters that you can adjust.

Here's the HTML code for adding an embedded MIDI file to a Web page:

```
<EMBED SRC="MyMIDIFile.MID" WIDTH="144" HEIGHT="25" AUTOSTART="TRUE" REPEAT="TRUE">
</EMBED>
```

The HTML tag in this case is <EMBED SRC>. This tag is compatible with both Internet Explorer and Netscape browsers, so you should not have to write different HTML codes for different browsers, as is the case for some HTML tags (such as <BGSOUND>).

The filename represents the file you wish to load automatically in the page's browser. If the file is not in the same folder as the HTML file, you will need to specify the relative path to this file, as explained in the previous link example. The parameters that follow the filename will vary depending on your needs.

The WIDTH and HEIGHT parameters represent pixel values you wish the player to use. The actual look of the player associated with MIDI will vary depending on the user's installed player, which will be invoked by the HTML page. A larger amount will create a larger space for your player to be embedded in, while a width equal to "0" and a height equal to "2" will hide the player from the user's view, making it impossible for the user to use the player's controls. This might be useful if you don't want the user to stop the music.

The AUTOSTART parameter can be set to "TRUE" or "FALSE." If it is set to True, the player will start playing the MIDI file as soon as it is loaded automatically. If it is set to False, the user will have to press the Play button of the player in order to start the playback. Note that if you set your player to be invisible (WIDTH and HEIGHT set to 0 and 2, respectively, as mentioned above), you will have to set the AUTOSTART parameter to True. Otherwise, the user won't know there is a MIDI file there and will not hear anything, nor will it be possible to start the playback.

The REPEAT parameter can be set to "TRUE" or "FALSE." If it is set to True, the player will start playing the MIDI file according to the AUTOSTART parameter's setting, but then will keep on repeating until the user presses the player's Stop button. If it is set to False, the MIDI file will play once and stop when it reaches the end of the file.

The </EMBED> tag marks the end of the embedding information. However, it is not required by your browser in order for the tag to work, unlike the </A> tag in the link. You might find that certain Web page authoring environments, such as FrontPage or Dreamweaver, will report an error in the script if you omit it.

You may combine the linking and embedding methods in the same Web page. Just be sure to set the AUTOSTART parameter to "FALSE," or you might have all the player's instances playing at once, which could cause the page to lock up. Figure 10.15 shows an example of both embedded MIDI files and a linked MIDI file. Note that the player in this case is Beatnik's plug-in. This might be different on your computer, since the MIDI player associated with your browser and OS will influence the layout of the information.

Figure 10.15
HTML sample page as displayed in the browser window

Figure 10.16 displays the sample code used to create this page. You will note in this figure that the text is in lowercase, not in uppercase as in the examples above. HTML code is not case sensitive; however, sticking with one convention will make your life easier when sifting through pages of code. Some HTML editors will color code information as well to help you identify quickly normal text and HTML coding.

Figure 10.16
Sample code that was used to create the page in the previous figure

```
<html>
<head>
<title>Sample Page</title>
<meta http-equiv="Content-Type" content="text/html; charset=iso-8859-1">
</head>
<body bgcolor="#FFFFFF" text="#000000">
    <h1><font face="Arial, Helvetica, sans-serif">My Sample MIDI Page</font></h1>
    <p><font face="Arial, Helvetica, sans-serif">This is a sample song 1, in embedded
    format.</font></p>

<embed src="marimba.mid" autostart="false" width="144" height="60">
</embed>

    <p><font face="Arial, Helvetica, sans-serif">This is a sample song 2, in embedded
    format.</font></p>

        <embed src="marimba2.mid" autostart="false" width="144" height="60"></embed>

    <p><font face="Arial, Helvetica, sans-serif">
    <a href="marimba3.mid">This is a sample song 3, in link format.</a></font></p>
</body>
</html>
```

This is a very simple example using no graphical elements or tables to position your MIDI player and text in the page. However, no matter how complex your pages become, the information needed to actually add a MIDI file, embedded or linked, remains the same.

The examples just given will use any installed MIDI plug-in on a user's computer. If you would like to force the user to use a specific plug-in, though, you will need to add additional code in your page. This is not advisable, since it might deter users from hearing your material—nobody likes to add plug-ins they will use only a few times. However, if you wish to do so, you might consult the documentation on the site that developed the plug-in you want the visitors to use. This would include in most cases a plug-in Class ID parameter, which identifies the plug-in to the browser, and a location from which the user can download the plug-in if the browser doesn't recognize it. In other words, the browser would tell the user that he/she needs to download a plug-in in order to hear the content of this site, and point the user to the proper location from which the plug-in can be downloaded.

Figure 10.17's code demonstrates an example of this with the Crescendo MIDI player plug-in. As you can see, the sample code includes two forms of tags: object and embed. Both of these tags serve the same purpose, but the object tag offers more details for Microsoft products (Internet Explorer). The CODEBASE and PLUGINSPACE parameters will point the user to the proper download page if this plug-in is not already installed on the user's system.

Figure 10.17

Sample code for MIDI plug-in with information for downloading options

```
<html>
<head>
<title>Sample Page</title>
<meta http-equiv="Content-Type" content="text/html; charset=iso-8859-1">
</head>
<body bgcolor="#FFFFFF" text="#000000">
    <h1><font face="Arial, Helvetica, sans-serif">My Sample MIDI Page</font></h1>
    <p><font face="Arial, Helvetica, sans-serif">This is a sample song 1, in embedded
    format.</font></p>

<OBJECT ID=Crescendo
CLASSID="clsid:0FC6BF2B-E16A-11CF-AB2E-0080ADO8A326"
CODEBASE="http://activex.liveupdate.com/controls/cres.cab"
HEIGHT=55 WIDTH=200>
    <PARAM NAME="SONG" VALUE="MyMIDIFile.mid">
    <PARAM NAME="LOOP" VALUE="true">
    <PARAM NAME="NOSAVE" VALUE="true">

<EMBED TYPE="music/crescendo" SONG="MyMIDIFile.mid"
PLUGINSPAGE="http://www.liveupdate.com/dl.html"
LOOP="true" NOSAVE="true" HEIGHT=55 WIDTH=200></EMBED>

</OBJECT>
</body>
</html>
```

11

Deeper into MIDI: System Exclusive and Synchronization

System Exclusive (SysEx) messages and synchronization are probably two of the most misunderstood aspects of the MIDI protocol. Synchronization allows you to lock multiple devices together using time code or MIDI clock, while SysEx is a powerful way to control and automate MIDI device parameters in real time.

SysEx defines and records MIDI events and parameters that are not defined or recorded in other MIDI messages, such as an envelope for a specific sound, or a cutoff frequency in a device's filter. You won't notice SysEx most of the time. But even when you do, you may not see the values that are passed, such as a note number that corresponds to a key on your keyboard, or a velocity value for that key. SysEx passes values in much the same way that values in a control change or a Channel Voice message are passed; what's different is what it affects when it passes these values. In addition, a large portion of SysEx is manufacturer-specific.

Synchronization is not a tool you will use in a typical setup, since your sequencer is, by default, the driving force behind the timing of a song or project. On the other hand, when you work with video, external multi-track recorders, or multiple sequencers, synchronization is essential if you want the timing to remain consistent among the various components. Synchronization is an essential part of music composition for film, since you want to be able to start the video playback and play in sync with the images you see, then rewind, press Play, and listen to what you just recorded.

Here's a summary of what you will learn in this chapter:

- ▶ What SysEx is and what it's for.
- ▶ Why use SysEx.
- ▶ How SysEx messages are constructed.
- ▶ The difference between manufacturer-specific SysEx and universal SysEx messages.
- ▶ How to send and receive SysEx messages.
- ▶ How to record SysEx in your software for later use.
- ▶ Editing SysEx...not! Why?

CHAPTER 11

▶ Synchronization options.

▶ The difference between MIDI clock and time code.

▶ The precision of ASIO 2 synchronization.

▶ What MIDI Machine Control is.

▶ What MIDI Show Control is.

What is SysEx?

SysEx messages fall under two categories: manufacturer specific SysEx messages and universal SysEx messages. In both cases, they transmit information that is not included in any other MIDI messages.

In the case of manufacturer specific messages, SysEx is used to send data that is specific to a particular manufacturer's device, such as a dump of its patch memory, sequencer data, waveform data, or information that is particular to a device. None of these messages are defined in non-SysEx MIDI messages.

In the case of universal SysEx messages, they transmit information to any MIDI device, but like their manufacturer specific counterpart, none of the information they contain is part of the regular non-SysEx MIDI messages. For example, this could be a message telling the receiving device to disable its GM mode, or set its master volume parameter to a specific value. The master volume parameter is different than the channel volume level value, since it affects the general volume level of a multi-timbral device. For example, one multi-timbral device could have channel one's volume set at 64, channel two's volume set at 96, channel three's volume set at 45, and its master volume set at 100. Raising the master level volume for this device to 127 would effectively raise the overall volume level of all the channels at the output of this device, but the actual channel volume level values would remain the same (i.e. 64, 96, and 45).

In other words, SysEx is used to change MIDI device parameters that are not identified or addressed by MIDI messages described earlier in this book. Using SysEx represents the only method of retrieving, sending, or saving these parameter values through a MIDI connection. SysEx messages do not contain any regular MIDI messages.

You could say that SysEx allows you to control how sounds are produced outside the defined MIDI message parameters (such as control change events), while other MIDI events allow you to control what sounds are produced and when to produce them. Here's an example: If you want to change the filter envelope of your sound playing on channel one and you would like to automate this parameter through time, SysEx is the only way you will be able to achieve this. By setting your sequencer to not filter out SysEx messages, you can change the value of this parameter (the filter envelope) on your MIDI device and record it as a series of SysEx MIDI values. When you play it back, the parameter will change through time, just as any other MIDI event—except, in this case, it's called a SysEx MIDI event.

Anatomy Of a SysEx Message

To better understand the beast that is SysEx, let us look at how it is constructed. Hopefully, by the end of this section, you will realize that the beast was only the shadow of a small harmless creature that can easily be tamed. Once you understand what SysEx is about, you will be amazed at how much control you can have over your MIDI device, and realize that this control can easily be translated into new creative musical directions.

A SysEx message can be as small as 10 bytes or as large as 10,000 bytes. Each SysEx message contains eight parts (nine in the case of Roland), each one playing a specific role. These parts are laid out in Table 11.1. In the first column, you will find the part number, sorted in order of its appearance in the SysEx message.

The second column tells how many bytes are used to send this part and whether this part is conveying status or data. Remember that a status byte in a MIDI message identifies to the MIDI device what to do with the following data bytes. You saw that a Note On message, for example, had one status byte that tells the device that this is a Note On for a MIDI specific channel, and that the two following data bytes represented the MIDI note number and the velocity of this note. SysEx messages, in this respect, are identical, as they also contain status and data bytes.

The third column indicates whether this part is defined by the MIDI specification or not. Common implies that the information in this part is common to all devices and all SysEx messages, and is defined by the MIDI specification. An example of this would be manufacturer ID numbers. Although their value is specific to a manufacturer, all manufacturer ID numbers are identified in the MIDI specification. In other words, you will find this information in all MIDI messages, and what the information represents is common to all SysEx messages. Specific implies that the content of this part is specific to a MIDI device or a SysEx message. In other words, this portion of the message contains specific manufacturer-defined values. Looking for a meaning to these values without your manufacturer's documentation would be useless, since the values contained here are meant only for a specific device made by a specific manufacturer. You will need to consult your manufacturer's documentation to find the meaning these values represent for your specific device. This is definitely not something I suggest you do. Sitting down and trying to figure out what value is passed by which parameter and how it is represented in a SysEx message is much more complicated than simply using SysEx in the context of the songwriting process.

The fourth column indicates the content of each part. This content takes the number of bytes indicated in the second column. Finally, the last column to the right describes what each part does.

CHAPTER 11

Table 11.1
SysEx messages parts explained.

Parts	# of bytes (byte type)	Common or specific	Content of byte
1	1 byte (status)	Common	Start SysEx

Description (what this data really means): Tells the device that the following data is a SysEx message

2	1 or 3 bytes (data)	Common	Manufacturer ID number

Description: Identifies the manufacturer to the receiving device. For example, if you have a Korg synth and a Yamaha synth, the Korg synth will ignore the SysEx message when it sees that the manufacturer ID does not correspond to its ID.

3	1 byte (data)	Common	Device ID number

Description: This value is only relevant when you have more than one device from the same manufacturer in a daisy chain. Each device should be set to its own device ID number. This is usually done in your device's system options or system MIDI settings. By having a device ID that identifies each device in your chain, you can address each device with its own set of SysEx messages.

4	1 byte (data)	Common	Model ID number

Description: This identifies the model number of the device. Once again, if you have more than one device from the same manufacturer, the model ID will tell the device if this message applies to it or not. In other words, your Roland JV-1080 will ignore this message if it is identified with the Roland D-50 model ID number.

5	1 byte (data)	Common	Send or receive command

Description: This tells the device if the SysEx message is sending information to it, or requesting information from it. For example, an editor/librarian might be requesting parameter settings from your device. When you edit the settings in the editor, you are sending SysEx to the device to update its parameter to correspond to the changes you made in the software.

6	3 bytes (data)	Specific	Start address

Description: This is the first address on which the SysEx intends to act. The actual meaning of this address is defined in your MIDI device's manual in the address map table (usually found at the end of the manual, since nobody usually pays it much attention). Your device will put the values found in the next part, starting at the value in this part. Let's say you have tickets with numbers on them. Each number corresponds to a specific task. Now, the start address would be like if I were to tell you, "Look at these people in line, walk up to the fifth person, and start giving every one in that line a ticket until you run out of tickets." The fifth person in the lineup represents the start address. In this example, imagine that every person in line represents a parameter in your device. It is from this start address that you will either put values to or retrieve values from, depending on whether you are sending or receiving a SysEx.

7	Variable (data)	Specific	Data values

Description: If part 5 specifies that it is sending a SysEx message to your MIDI device, it will assign the values contained here, starting at the address identified in part 6 to your device. If part 5 specifies that it is receiving (requesting data from your device) a SysEx message from your device, it will retrieve the data contained for the parameter starting at the specified address in part 6. When it is requesting information from your device, this value will correspond to the number of bytes it wants to retrieve. In this case, there will always be 3 data bytes (by default) to identify the length of data it needs to retrieve from your device.

8	1 byte (data)	Roland Only	Roland checksum value

Description: This part is found only in Roland devices and serves as a verification mechanism, using a simple mathematical formula to check the integrity of the SysEx data. This value is compared to the result of the mathematical formula, and if both match, the Roland device will accept the SysEx message as being valid. If the result of the mathematical calculation does not match the content of this byte, it will discard the SysEx message, since it interprets it as being corrupted.

9	1 byte (status)	Common	End SysEx message

Description: Tells the device that the end of the SysEx message has arrived. The device receiving information will then cease to expect SysEx data and the device sending will stop sending information.

CHAPTER 11

Like all MIDI messages, SysEx messages use binary information to communicate its information. The MIDI specification usually represents this information in the form of hexadecimal values rather than in decimal or binary values. You will find in Appendix A, Table A.1 of this book a table with decimal, binary, and hexadecimal equivalences. This should help you to understand the values that are sent; however, the meaning of these values will be explained here. You might also want to take a look at other tables found in this appendix if you feel the need to do so as you are reading this section.

SysEx messages will always start with the F0 value. When the device finds this value in a status byte (such as the one found in part 1 of a SysEx message), it will know that what follows is a SysEx message. All SysEx messages end with the F7 value. F0 represents the Start SysEx message, and F7 represents the End SysEx value. In Table 11.1, F0 is found in part 1, and F7 is found in part 9 (remember that part 8 is found only in Roland devices). Here's an example of a typical SysEx message using a hexadecimal string:

Table 11.2
A SysEx message string, Example 1.

Values sent:	F0	41	10	6A	12	01 00 00 28	06	51	F7
Message part:	1	2	3	4	5	6	7	8	9

In Table 11.2, The message would set the reverb type of a Roland JV-1080 performance to "Delay." Here's how it breaks down:

Table 11.3
Explanation of values found in Example 1.

Part	Value	What this means
1	F0	Status byte's Start SysEx message.
2	41	This is the manufacturer ID number for Roland.
3	10	This is the device ID number that corresponds to the JV-1080 Unit number value, converted into hexadecimal. In this case, the unit would be set to 17. To get the device ID, Roland uses the system common parameter minus one, so 17−1=16; 16 in hexadecimal is 10. This identifies a specific Roland device in a chain if more than one Roland device was daisy chained.
4	6A	This is the model ID number corresponding to the JV-1080. Each device has its own model ID number.
5	12	This is the command ID: Twelve represents a Send command or Dump. If it were 11, it would be a Receive command or Dump Request. There can be other manufacturer-specific commands, such as sequencer dump request or global data dump; however, these will allow your device to send or receive specific sets of values (part 7) for the parameter defined in part 6 of the SysEx message.
6	01 00 00 28	The first set of two values, 01 00, represents the start address for the JV-1080's temporary performance parameters. To find out which address corresponds to which parameter, you will have to look at your device's manual in the parameter base address table found at the end of the documentation. The third value, 00, points to the performance common parameter, telling the JV-1080 that this is not a performance part parameter, but rather a parameter that will affect all parts in a performance, since it is common to all. The last value, 28, refers to the reverb type of this common performance parameter. So, the target for the value found in part 7 is the reverb type for the common temporary

performance parameter. You could call this the start parameter ID address. If more values were sent in part 7, all subsequent values (in part 7) would be inserted from this point on in your device's address map. It goes without saying that this example with these values represents the reverb type for the JV-1080. In another MIDI device, though, these values could represent something completely different.

7	06	This represents the value that will be sent to the reverb type for the common temporary performance of the JV-1080. In this device, 06 represents the Delay.
8	51	This is the Roland checksum byte. The error-checking process uses a checksum formula that is quite simple. In essence, it involves adding all the values of parts 6 and 7 together, converting to decimal, dividing by 128, and subtracting the remainder from 128. In this case: 1+0+0+40 (28 in hexadecimal)+6=47; since 47 is less than 128, you don't need to divide it to get the remainder. Finally, 128−47=81; 81 in hexadecimal is 51. If the values in parts 6 and 7 don't match up to the one in part 8, the SysEx message is discarded. This said, there are as many ways of calculating checksums as there are manufacturers. You shouldn't worry too much about it, since this is always transparent to users anyway.
9	F7	This identifies the end of the SysEx message.

Universal SysEx

As you have just seen, most system exclusive messages are manufacturer specific. However, there is another kind of SysEx, one that's common to all manufacturers, called the universal SysEx message. It is considered a SysEx message because its header and footers are identical to those in the manufacturer-specific SysEx. In other words, it begins and ends with F0 (Start SysEx) and F7 (End SysEx). Universal System Exclusive messages are used for extensions to the MIDI standard. They are not reserved for any particular manufacturer, and may be used by any suitable MIDI device.

Universal SysEx is used for the following types of messages:

▶ To enable or disable GM mode in a GM-compatible sound module. Some devices have built-in GM modules or GM patch sets in addition to non-GM patch sets or non-GM modes of operation. When GM is enabled, it replaces any non-GM patch set or non-GM mode with a GM mode/patch set. This allows a device to have modes or patch sets that go beyond the limits of GM, and yet still have the capability to be switched into a GM-compliant mode when desired.

▶ In a multi-timbral instrument, volume settings for each part are handled by the control change number 7 (volume). However, you can also control the master volume of your device using a universal SysEx message.

▶ Occasionally, a device may want to know what other devices are connected to it. For example, editor/librarian software running on a computer may wish to know what devices are connected to the computer's MIDI port, so that the software can configure itself to accept dumps from those devices. To do so, it may perform an Identity Request by sending this type of SysEx message. In return, the devices will send an Identity Reply message containing information about who they are. Knock, knock. Who's there? It's me Karma, Korg Karma!

▶ MIDI samplers use digital audio waveforms as their audio source. A sub-protocol was implemented within MIDI in which devices can exchange this digital audio waveform data. In other words, it's a protocol that allows the exchange of digital audio data over MIDI cables within the parameters of MIDI. Because of the nature of digital audio, these transfers are usually substantial. The only way to do this is with universal SysEx messages, and so several specific SysEx messages were defined in order to implement Sample Dump Standard (SDS). Many samplers support this protocol. This was discussed earlier in this book (see Chapter 6).

▶ When working with video, you might use MTC (MIDI Time Code) to lock your MIDI sequencer with the videotape playback device. Although MTC quarter frames are system-common messages, a full frame information—meaning a single hour, minute, second, frame, and sub-frame information—can be sent using the universal SysEx message to cue a slave device to a specific point in time. This full frame message sends the complete SMPTE time address in hours, minutes, seconds, and frames in a single message. The slave doesn't actually start running until it starts receiving quarter frame messages. This implies that the slave is stopped when receiving this type of message. During shuttle modes (fast-forward or rewind), the master should not continuously send quarter frame messages, but, rather, send full-frame messages at regular intervals.

There are two categories of universal SysEx messages: real-time and non-real-time. A real-time universal SysEx message occurs at the moment in time it should be sent in order to achieve the desired effect. For example, you might want to send a MIDI Machine Control to start the playback of a tape recorder using a real-time universal SysEx message at the beginning of a song as the sequencer starts playing the sequence. A non-real-time universal SysEx message can occur at any time, and its timing is not critical to the sequence of events. An example of this could be a bulk dump of program settings from your device to your editor/librarian application. You will find more on this in the paragraphs to follow . Every function mentioned in the list above will fall within one of these two categories. This is identified in the first data byte following the SysEx status byte. If you look at Table 11.1, in a manufacturer-specific SysEx message, you would find the manufacturer ID; however, in a universal SysEx, you would find either the value 7E to identify a non-real-time message or 7F to identify a real-time message, since no manufacturer ID is required for universal messages. Let's take a look at each part of a universal SysEx message:

Table 11.4

The content of a universal SysEx message.

Part	Value (or range)	Content	Description
1	F0	SysEx Start (status byte)	This tells the device that the following bytes consist of SysEx information.
2	7E or 7F	Non-real-time or real-time	This tells the device if the universal SysEx is of real-time or non-real-time nature.
3	00 to 7F	Channel	This range of values is meant to identify a device or a channel. Usually, SysEx messages do not have channels; however, it is possible with universal SysEx to specify a channel. This allows a musician to set various devices to ignore certain universal SysEx messages. For example, if the device has a base channel set to 1, it could filter out any universal SysEx messages sent on another channel. This range allows for 128 different channels. However, the last value, 7F, would tell the device to disregard any channel information and respond to any channels.
4	00 to 7F	Sub ID 1	This defines the category of the SysEx's function. For example, when you wish to use the GM mode, the value would be 09. This would activate the GM enable/disable mode. However, whether it is active or not would be defined by a second byte found in part 5. Another example of a sub-ID would be to identify a device control, such as a master volume or a pitch bend. The sub-ID for a device control would be represented by the hex value 04. The specific device control would then be identified in part 5 as well. In some cases, however, only one ID is needed to identify the function, such as when you wish to do a sample dump or a generic handshake between two devices to confirm that the information was sent properly to the right device. You will find a list of all sub-IDs in Table 11.5.
5	00 to 7F	Sub ID 2	This value adds precision to the function defined in part 4 of this message. As mentioned above, this could represent the value set by the GM mode; for example, 00 would be disabled and 01 enabled. It could also identify a device control, such as the master volume or the pitch bend for the device. The actual values for these parameters will be found in the following part.
6	Any value	Data	This part represents the actual data sent by the parameter defined in parts 4 and 5. This could contain any number of bytes. A sample data dump would be quite large, for example. Another example of data could be the MTC full frame SMPTE time code address.
7	F7	End of SysEx	This identifies the end of the SysEx message.

CHAPTER 11

Here's a list of all the defined universal SysEx functions, as found in Sub ID 1 explained in Table 11.4:

Table 11.5
Real-time and non-real-time functions as defined by sub-id1, with their associated hexadecimal values.

Non-real-time Sub ID 1	Function name	Real-time Sub ID 1	Function name
01	Sample dump header	01	MIDI Time Code (MTC) full message and user bit
02	Sample data packet	02	MIDI Show Control
03	Sample dump request	03	Notation information
04	MIDI Time Code (MTC) for cueing purposes	04	Device control
05	Sample dump extensions	05	Real-time MTC cueing
06	General information	06	MIDI Machine Control (MMC) commands
07	File dump	07	MIDI Machine Control (MMC) responses
08	MIDI tuning standard	08	MIDI tuning standard
09	General MIDI		
7B	End of file		
7C	Wait		
7D	Cancel		
7E	NAK (last data packet not received correctly)		
7F	ACK (last data packet received correctly)		

Making a Device Send SysEx

Now that you know what you can find in a SysEx message, how can you make a device send SysEx? Fortunately, that's the easy part. As mentioned previously when discussing patch bay configurations and editor/librarian applications, it is important that a direct MIDI connection between the sender and the receiver be made. You can work with SysEx messages even with devices in a daisy chain. This, however, requires extra precautions, such as assigning a different device ID number for each device in the chain, and making sure that the base MIDI channel is also different. These precautions will help ensure that the MIDI device you meant to communicate with processes only the SysEx messages.

Usually, you will find a function or utility button on the front panel of your MIDI device that allows you to send a bulk dump. This means that you will be sending SysEx messages. From that point, you can choose what kind of information you want to send. For example, you might send user patches, performances, or system settings. If there are no such buttons on your device, there are two workaround solutions:

▶ Get an editor/librarian application that will identify your device, and initiate a SysEx bulk dump request from this application. This will allow your software to receive the appropriate SysEx information from your external MIDI device.

▶ Find out what message to send to the device to make it dump its settings via its MIDI Out. Use the SysEx editor in your sequencer to insert that message in a track. Writing such a SysEx string can be fairly complicated and requires an extensive study of the fine print in the operation manual. So, if in doubt, stick with the first method and get an editor/librarian, as it'll save you a lot of headaches.

Figure 11.1
A bulk dump transfer
of performance banks
in the Roland JV-1080

As you can see in Figure 11.1, the Info section of this dialog box displays the instrument information and the data type of the bulk dump being transferred, along with the device ID number (Comm Ch) and the MIDI ports over which the information is being transferred.

Recording SysEx

There are two reasons you would record SysEx: to save all the values that make up one program, or all programs in the instrument or device so that when you play a song, it remembers the external device's setup. This will allow you to recall the device's parameters, as they were when you saved the song. The next time, when you load the song, you won't have to change anything on your device when you load the song, since the parameters were stored with the sequence using SysEx. This is called a bulk dump.

The second reason would be to store codes that instruct the instrument to change one of its settings, such as the cutoff frequency of a filter, or the decay of a reverb during playback or at the beginning of the song. System Exclusive can be used as a last resort for things that can't be done with regular MIDI messages. This is done through SysEx parameter changes.

Recording a Bulk Dump

Since your MIDI device stores values for its parameter in its memory, changing these values will result in changing the parameters settings as well. Usually, your MIDI device can send all or some of these parameters to your computer or a sequencer using what is called a bulk dump. This action is performed using SysEx messages, as described earlier. You can use a bulk dump to make a copy of your MIDI device's settings, or you can allow editor/librarian software to gather information about your current device settings.

Once your device's SysEx has been dumped into the computer's memory, you can send it back to the device later to reset all the parameters to the way they were when you saved them. If you are using an editor/librarian, you can make changes to these parameters and transmit the changes back to your device. In this case, your computer (through the use of the editor/librarian) becomes a remote control application for your MIDI device.

Most hardware MIDI devices allow you to send a bulk dump of all or some of the device's parameters. Consult your device's documentation. Once you've identified where the bulk dumping function is, and how to proceed, here's what you'll do to record a bulk dump in your sequencer:

1.   Make sure the MIDI Out of your device is connected to the MIDI In of your computer or sequencer.

2.   You might need to disable any SysEx filters from your sequencer's MIDI filter options, as shown in Figure 11.2.

Figure 11.2
The MIDI Filtering option in your sequencer allows you to filter SysEx messages—you need to deactivate this filter option, however, you should leave the Thru option on to avoid creating a SysEx loop

3. Create a MIDI track in your sequencer where you wish to record the SysEx.

4. Click on the Record button in your sequencer to initiate the recording process. Make sure you don't have any other tracks playing at this time, since the SysEx will require a large portion of your MIDI bandwidth. Since you are dumping your device's memory into a MIDI file, it is recommended that you create a MIDI file with just this information.

5. Press the appropriate buttons on your MIDI device to initiate the bulk dump. You might notice during the transmission that your device will display a special message on its LCD screen telling you it's currently transmitting SysEx. When the device is done with its transmission, you should see a message such as "Done" or "Completed."

6. Stop the recording.

7. Save the information.

If you wish to send only certain parameters to your sequencer, you can proceed in a similar way. This would be useful if you would like to change a parameter during playback, like changing the reverb type of your MIDI device's reverb at bar 15, for example. Remember that MIDI is transmitted over a serial cable, meaning that the pieces of information are sent one after the other, not side by side. In the case of SysEx, the entire SysEx message has to be transmitted before the rest of the MIDI messages can resume their course. So if you wish to record SysEx parameter changes as you are playing notes, the more SysEx messages you are sending, the longer it will take for the other events to be transmitted. So, keep your SysEx events as short as possible, or, if you can, make sure not to overload your MIDI port with this type of message. To record parameter changes to your sequencer during playback:

1. Make sure the MIDI Out of your device is connected to the MIDI In of your computer or sequencer.

2. You might need to disable any SysEx filters from your sequencer's MIDI filter options.

3. Create a MIDI track in your sequencer where you wish to record the SysEx.

4. Chances are if you want to update parameters during playback, you probably already have a MIDI track with recorded events. At this point, you'll want to hear this track if you want to update the parameters for the sound used in this track. Make sure this track is not muted.

5. Begin the record process in your MIDI sequencer.

6. Make the changes to your external MIDI device's parameters when it is appropriate in the song.

7. Stop the recording process when done.

8. Rewind and start playback to hear the result. Let's assume the same example: If you've recorded a reverb type change from a plate to a hall reverb, this parameter should now change automatically every time your device receives this SysEx message.

CHAPTER 11

Since you recorded the SysEx events on another track, if you are not satisfied with the result, you can always erase these events and start over without affecting the other types of events recorded for this part. For example, let's say you have a synth line playing on MIDI port A, channel 1, and you want to change the cutoff frequency of the sound used to play this line as it evolves in the song. You would have one track that contains the notes played by the synth and another track that performs the change in the cutoff frequency using SysEx. Erasing the SysEx events will not affect the notes, since they are on separate tracks.

Here are some tips to keep in mind when recording SysEx bulk dumps:

▶ Record just the parameters you need to record. Usually, you can tell your MIDI device what type of bulk dump you wish to perform. This will save space in your sequencer and speed up the SysEx transfer back to your MIDI device. In a live performance, you don't want to have to wait too long between songs for SysEx to be uploaded to your MIDI devices, so keeping things to a minimum is necessary.

▶ If you want your sequencer to send parameter information and patch information to your external MIDI device only before a song starts to play, put the SysEx information before the first bar, if possible, or before the occurrence of MIDI events in your song. This will prevent you from having lags caused by a long SysEx message being sent simultaneously with other MIDI events.

▶ If all you want to do is change the sound settings (program) during playback, you might be better off creating two different programs and using a program change during playback, rather than using a SysEx message. Program changes are more efficient in this case and will take less time to update your external MIDI device. On the other hand, if you want your sound to change dynamically throughout the song—let's say changing the LFO rate when the chorus arrives—you will be better off using SysEx parameter controls for this change.

▶ Avoid sending a SysEx bulk dump from your sequencer to several external MIDI devices simultaneously.

▶ Make sure when you record a bulk dump that you are using the same device ID number as you will be using when sending this bulk dump back to the MIDI device. Otherwise, the device might not accept the SysEx bulk dump.

▶ Certain sequencers will allow you to send a SysEx bulk dump automatically whenever you load a MIDI file. Use this feature to configure your devices appropriately for each song, but keep the previous tips in mind.

Transmitting Bulk Dumps

Once your bulk dump is recorded in your sequencer, you will probably want to send it back to your MIDI device when the time comes to restore the saved information. This is fairly easy to do, since you already know how to do a bulk dump in one direction. Here's how to transmit the information back to your external MIDI device:

1. Connect the MIDI Out of your sequencer to the MIDI In of the external MIDI device.

2. Disable any filters that would prevent your sequencer from playing back the SysEx information.

3. If your MIDI device can deactivate its SysEx reception, make sure this option is disabled. In other words, you want your MIDI device to respond to incoming SysEx information.

4. Solo the track that contains the SysEx data. This might not always be necessary, but it's a good precaution to take, since you might have more than one SysEx data track or other events that will cause the transfer to interrupt abruptly.

5. Play back the data from your sequencer. The display on your external MIDI device should indicate that it is receiving SysEx.

You should take the same precautions when sending SysEx to your MIDI device as you do when your sequencer is receiving SysEx. For example, try not to send more data than required. If all you need to recall is a single program, avoid sending full bulk dumps to your machine. If the bulk dump serves to set up your device for a song, try putting your SysEx in the count-in bars before the actual song starts.

Editing SysEx!?

We've seen what a SysEx message contains and looked at some examples at the beginning of this chapter. If you are a real masochist and really want to edit SysEx manually, you may do so using a SysEx editor if your sequencer provides one. Though it's possible, editing SysEx is not everyone's cup of tea. It requires a profound understanding of your device's parameter map and hexadecimal conversion skills, since each SysEx dump is usually made up of many strings of SysEx messages. In other words, it's best to leave the handling of SysEx messages to your software applications, such as sequencers and editor/librarians.

CHAPTER 11

MIDI Synchronizing Options

MIDI, as you know by now, serves as a communication mechanism between two MIDI compatible devices. It also serves as a synchronization tool between different time-based devices. This could be a sequencer and a drum machine, two sequencers, a sequencer and a video playback device, or even a sequencer and a multi-track tape recorder with intelligent MIDI capability. In this last example, the tape recorder would control the playback of your sequencer through time code (SMPTE converted into MTC), and then your sequencer would send playback control commands to this device through MIDI. This is called MIDI Machine Control (MMC). A more recent addition to MIDI synchronization has been the development of ASIO 2 and other such drivers, which allow you to synchronize effects to the MIDI tempo. For example, you can use a delay effect in which each occurrence of the delay will be in sync with sixteenth notes in your sequence. If you change the tempo of your song, your delay stays in sync. This is useful, since traditionally if you wanted this type of effect, you'd have to manually calculate delay times and then recalculate them if you changed the tempo setting.

Before we take an in-depth look at synchronization, it is important to understand the different types of synchronization, its terminology, and basic concepts. The idea behind synchronization is that there will always be a master/slave relation between the source of the synchronization and the recipient of this source. There can be only one master, but there can be many slaves to this master. There are three basic synchronizing methods here: time code, MIDI clock, and word clock.

Time Code

Time code is an electronic signal used to identify a precise location on time-based media such as audio, videotape, or digital systems that support time code. This location represents a time address in hours, minutes, seconds, frames (some more advanced synchronization devices will even display the usually hidden sub-frame information). The electronic signal is sent along with the media to allow other devices to synchronize with this signal. A locking mechanism in the receiving device is used to make sure the time location of the sending device is matched by the time location of the receiving device's time location.

For example, a videotape could contain time code information that is sent to a sequencer in order for the sequencer to lock and follow the video's time location. Imagine that a postal worker delivering mail is the locking mechanism, the houses on the street are location addresses on the time code, and the letters have matching addresses. The postal worker reads the letters and makes sure they get to the correct address, just as a synchronizing device will compare the time code from a source and a destination, bring the two (or more) devices into simultaneous operation, and make sure the correct things are happening at the same time. This time code is also known as SMPTE (Society of Motion Picture and Television Engineers) and it comes in three flavors:

- ▶ MTC (MIDI Time Code) is the MIDI version of SMPTE time code and is normally used to synchronize audio or video devices to MIDI devices such as sequencers.

- ▶ VITC (Vertical Interval Time Code) is normally used by video machines to send or receive synchronization information to and from any type of VITC-compatible device. VITC may be recorded as part of the video signal in an unused line, which is part of the vertical interval. It has the advantage of being readable when the playback video deck is paused.

▶ LTC (Longitudinal Time Code) is also used to synchronize video machines. Unlike VITC, however, it is also used to synchronize audio-only information, such as a transfer between a tape recorder and a sequencer. LTC usually takes the form of an audio signal that is recorded on one of the tracks of the tape. Since LTC is an audio signal, it is silent if the tape is not moving.

Each one of these time codes uses an hours:minutes:seconds:frames format.

WHAT ARE FRAME RATES?

As the name implies, a frame rate is the number of frames a film or video signal displays in one second. Locking frame rates with MIDI through MTC might seem challenging at first, but once you understand which frame rate your video project uses, you'll figure it out fast.

The acronym for frame rate is "fps" for Frames Per Second.

There are different frame rates depending on what you are working with:

▶ 24 fps—This is used by motion picture film. You will likely not encounter this medium, since chances are you do not have a film projector hooked up to your computer running Cubase to synchronize sound.

▶ 25 fps—This refers to the PAL (Phase Alternate Line) video standard used mostly in Asia and SECAM/EBU (Sequential Color And Memory/European Broadcast Union) video standard used mostly in Europe. If you live in those areas, this is the format your VCR uses. A single frame in this format is made up of 625 horizontal lines.

▶ 29.97 fps—Also known as 29.97 Non-Drop. This refers to the NTSC (National Television Standards Committee) video standard used mostly in North America. If you live in this area, this is the format your VCR uses. A single frame in this format is made up of 525 horizontal lines. On some devices using only two digits to represent the time code format, you might see this time code represented as 30 fps. However, you should not think of it as the actual 30 fps time code, which represents the NTSC black and white standard. This latter format is quite rare, and unless there is another way used by your time code reader to identify properly the difference between 29.97 Non-Drop and 29.97 Drop Frame, when it is written "30," you may assume it refers to 29.97 Non-Drop.

▶ 29.97 fps DF—Also known as 29.97 Drop Frame (hence the DF at the end). This can also be referred to as 30 DF on older video time code machines. This is probably the trickiest time code of all to understand since there is a lot of confusion about the drop frame. In order to accommodate the extra information needed for color when this format was first introduced, the black and white's 30 fps was slowed to 29.97 fps for color. Though this is probably not an issue for you, in broadcast, the small difference between real time (also known as the wall or house clock) and the time registered on the video can be problematic. Over a period of one SMPTE hour the video will be 3.6 seconds or 108 extra frames longer in relation to the wall clock. To overcome this discrepancy, drop frames are used. This is calculated as follows: Every frame 00 and 01 are dropped for each minute change, except for minutes with 0's (like 00, 10, 20, 30, 40, and 50). Therefore, two frames skipped every minute is 120 frames per hour, except for the minutes ending with zero, so 120 − 12 = 108 frames. Setting your frame rate to 29.97 DF when it's not—in other words, if it's 29.97 (Non-Drop)—will cause your synchronization to be off by 3.6 seconds per hour.

▶ 30 fps—This format was used with the first black and white NTSC standard. It is still used sometimes in music or sound applications where no video reference is required.

▶ 30 fps DF—This is not a standard time code protocol and usually refers to older time code devices that were unable to display the decimal points when the 29.97 Drop Frame time code was used. Try to avoid this time code frame rate setting when synchronizing to video, since it might introduce errors in your synchronization. SMPTE does not support this time code anyway.

As stated above, in any synchronization situation, there is always a master/slave relation. The master's time code controls any slaved device set to follow it. When you want to synchronize different devices, you need to set the sending device as the master and the receiving devices as slaves in order for these devices to follow the master's timing.

Sequencers have special synchronization options that allow you to set up your software to either control other connected devices or slave to an incoming time code or synchronization clock. In order for synchronization to occur, you need to make sure that the following components are set up properly:

▶ Physical connections: This will vary depending on the type of synchronization you are using. For example, if you are using MIDI clock, you will need to connect the master and slaves using a MIDI connection. Since your master is sending the MIDI clock, the MIDI Out of the master should be connected to the MIDI In of the slave device(s). On the other hand, if you are using a SMPTE time code such as an VITC or LTC, you will need to convert this to MTC (in most cases) in order for your sequencer to recognize the time, since most sequencers are MTC compatible.

▶ Master/slave relations: You will then need to configure your sequencer to a master or slave position. This will allow this sequencer to either send out synchronization information or wait for it to arrive on a designated MIDI port or other synchronization connection.

▶ Sync format: Telling the software which type of time code you are using is important if you want it to stay synchronized. Choosing one of the aforementioned time codes in your sync dialog box will ensure this.

▶ Point of entry: Setting up the software to expect time code on such and such a port will tell your sequencer where to look for a synchronization signal. For example, if you were using a multi-port MIDI interface with a built-in SMPTE-to-MTC converter, you would select the appropriate port on the interface that corresponds to your incoming sync signal. If you are sending MTC to another device, you must also want to configure to which port you want to send MTC information.

MIDI Clock

MIDI clock is a tempo-based synchronization signal used to synchronize two or more MIDI devices together with beats-per-minute (BPM) for a guide track. This is different than time code, since it does not refer to a real-time address (hours:minutes:seconds:frames). MIDI clock sends 24 evenly spaced MIDI clocks per quarter note. So, at a speed of 60 BPM, it sends 1,440 MIDI clocks per minute (one every 41.67 millisecond), whereas at a speed of 120 BPM, it will send double that amount (one every 20.83 millisecond). Because it is tempo-based, the MIDI clock rate changes to follow the tempo of the master tempo source. You don't have to do anything when changing the tempo; the MIDI clock rate will follow automatically.

When a master sends a MIDI clock signal, it sends a MIDI Start message to tell its slave to start playing a sequence at the speed or tempo set in the master's sequence. When the master sends a MIDI End message, it tells the slave to stop playing a sequence. Up until this point, all the slave can do is start and stop playing MIDI when it receives these messages. If you want to tell the slave sequence where to start, the MIDI clock has to send what is called a Song Position Pointer message. This is a system common MIDI message and was discussed in Chapter 2. For example, if you want to lock a software sequencer to a hardware sequencer, the song position pointer message tells the slave device (the software sequencer) the location of the master device's song position (the hardware sequencer). It uses the MIDI data to count the position where the MIDI Start message is in relation to the master. The Song Position Pointer message would tell the software sequencer the bar and beat position of the hardware sequence.

Using MIDI clock should be reserved for use between MIDI devices only, not for audio or video. Since it's a tempo-based system, it is not well suited for use with audio or video. While MIDI clock keeps a good synchronization between similar MIDI devices, audio requires a much greater precision. Video, on the other hand, works with time-based events, which do not translate well when you change the tempo's BPM speed.

Another type of MIDI-related synchronization is MIDI Machine Control (MMC). The MMC protocol uses System Exclusive messages over a MIDI cable to remotely control hard disk recording systems and other machines used for record or playback. Many MIDI-enabled devices support this protocol, which is described later on in this chapter.

CHAPTER 11

MIDI Time Code (MTC)

MTC messages are an alternative to using MIDI clocks and Song Position Pointer messages (telling a device where it is in relation to a song). MTC is essentially SMPTE (time based) mutated for transmission over MIDI.

On a soundtrack of a movie, there are six categories of sounds: music, sound effects, room tones or ambiances, Foley, ADR (Automatic Dialog Replacement), and, last (but probably the most important), dialog. All of these categories, with the exception of music, refer to nonmusical time references, such as seconds and frames rather than bars and beats. As you could imagine, a car explosion doesn't really have to be on bar 5, beat 2, but rather at 45 seconds and 3 frames past the scene's beginning. Referring to time this way is called absolute time referencing, and it is the way these nonmusical elements are referred to when working on a film/video project. In contrast, musical elements are often referred to as relative music based time location. They are relative to a bar and beat, however, changing the tempo of the song will change when in absolute time.

This said, if you are working on music for a film or video project, you will have to deal with both relative and absolute time references. That is because the film itself sends time code information that represents the absolute time, and your MIDI sequencer will work in relative time against this absolute time reference.

ASIO 2.0

Steinberg developed a cross-platform, multi-channel audio transfer protocol called ASIO (Audio Stream Input/Output). Many manufacturers of audio/MIDI hardware and software are adopting this protocol. It allows software to have access to the multi-channel capabilities of a wide range of sound cards. It also expands on the basic capabilities of a standard sound card, allowing you to use more than two audio channels at once. For example, by using a sound card with eight inputs and eight outputs, you could record on these eight inputs simultaneously and also play back on the eight outputs simultaneously.

The ASIO 2.0 specification defines the interface that manufacturers of professional sound cards must use to create an ASIO driver for their hardware. The driver allows the host application (audio/MIDI) to see all of the inputs and outputs available on the sound card. This allows the users to record more than two tracks simultaneously. This is not a very radical departure from other types of drivers. However, ASIO 2 shines by providing the user with a way to bypass the operating system and making the link between the audio card and the host application more efficient. This translates into smaller delays between the input of a sound card and its output. A long delay would make it very difficult to record audio and monitor what you're playing through headphones as you are playing other recorded tracks in your project. This delay is called latency, and ASIO drivers reduce this latency factor to very small amounts; in some cases, as low as 1 millisecond. When playing with software instruments, the shorter the delay between the time you press on a MIDI note on your keyboard and the time you hear the actual note generated by the instrument, the better or more realistic the feel of playing a real instrument will be.

With ASIO 2.0 drivers comes a new feature called ASIO Positioning Protocol. This is a technology that ensures that audio in the host application (such as Cubase) is in sample accurate sync with external devices. Sample accurate implies that for each sample being sent out, there will be a corresponding sample received. In other words, imagine a time code with as many time location addresses as your project's sampling rate. This is part of the ASIO 2.0 feature specification. In order to take advantage of the ASIO positioning protocol, your audio hardware must have an ASIO 2.0 driver written for it. It can read an external word clock, which is a digital clock provided by the sample rate of an external device, and lock to it. This will give you a sync that is accurate to one-forty four thousandths of a second, or approximately 0.02 milliseconds. To find out if you can use ASIO drivers, you will need a compatible host application and a sound card that offers ASIO support. You will have to consult your software and hardware documentation to find out if they do. Currently, Steinberg, Emagic, and Propellerhead's software products support ASIO.

MIDI Machine Control (MMC)

MIDI Machine Control (MMC) was added to the MIDI protocol in 1992, and serves as a transport control mechanism between various machine types. At the time it was developed, it was thought that MMC could be used to connect different transport controls between audio tape recorders, video, CD players and recorders, and other digital audio recording systems. However, in today's practical applications, MMC is used as a way to control the transport controls of an audio tape recorder or digital audio multi-track using your sequencer.

MMC allows you to send MIDI to a device, giving it commands such as play, stop, rewind, go to a specific location, punch-in, and punch-out on a specific track. Although MMC is quite extensive with its 100-page-long official documentation, its use in the music world has not been extended to its full potential. This is because the market has adopted a more integrated approach, using computers as a way to record audio rather than an external analog tape recorder, while external digital audio multi-track recorders use other technologies to lock up to other devices such as time code and word clock sync.

In order to make use of MMC, in a setup where you are using a multi-track tape recorder and a sequencer, you would need to have a time code (SMPTE) track sending time code to a SMPTE/MTC converter (see Figure 11.3). Then, you would send the converted MTC to your sequencer so that your sequencer can stay in sync with the multi-track recorder. Both devices are also connected through MIDI cables. It is the multi-track that controls the sequencer's timing, not vice versa. The sequencer, in return, can transmit MMC messages through its MIDI connection with the multi-track, which is equipped with a MIDI interface. These MMC messages will tell the multi-track to rewind, fast-forward, and so on. When you hit Play in the sequencer, it tells the multi-track to go to the position from where playback in the sequencer begins. When the multi-track reaches this position, it starts playing the tape back. Once it starts playing, it then sends time code to the sequencer, to which it then syncs.

Figure 11.3
The time code, once
converted to MTC, sends
the synchronization
signal to the sequencer,
while the MIDI,
through MMC, sends
the transport controls
from the sequencer to
the tape recorder

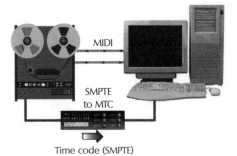

Time code (SMPTE)

MIDI Show Control (MSC)

MIDI Show Control (MSC) is intended to provide MIDI control of lighting and other theater equipment such as smoke machines, elevators, and lighting automation of a play (see Figure 11.4). It can also be used at amusement parks and other similar venues for synchronizing purposes, as well as for controlling various equipment via MIDI remote control.

MSC differs from anything else within MIDI since, first of all, the chances of a lighting MSC setup and a MIDI music setup being hooked together are remote at best. One of the reasons for this is that there are very rigorous safety protocols built into MSC due to the safety hazard that automating a light or an elevator movement implies. These safety protocols are not implemented in music-oriented MIDI. Imagine for a second that a crane starts moving as someone is on it; this could be a bit more catastrophic than if you send the wrong control change to your MIDI device, for example. In short, if you wish to use MIDI and MSC together, you can synchronize them using MTC, MIDI clock sync, or time code when you need to have lighting controlled by musical events that occur in time. However, hooking both setups together would probably be counterproductive, since MIDI messages tend to lose their effectiveness when a large number of devices are receiving and sending information simultaneously. This is why it is suggested to use multiple MIDI ports rather than daisy chaining multiple MIDI devices together. For the same reason, it is more efficient to separate the two systems, since they do not control the same type of equipment and their purpose is different. It just happens that the communication system they use is derived from the same protocol: MIDI.

Figure 11.4
The LCEdit+ is a
software that is used
with hardware
components, which
allow you to control a
lighting setup—this
software goes with the
LanBox-LC hardware
interface (www.cds.nl/)

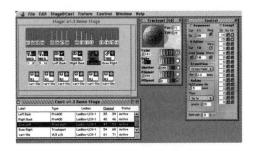

Appendix A
Understanding Binary, Decimal, and Hexadecimal

Since MIDI is a binary "language," understanding how to convert binary numbers to decimal values is sometimes important. This is especially true if you are trying to find out why a MIDI file has errors, or simply to understand how the MIDI language works. MIDI is also expressed in hexadecimal values because of its simple two-digit approach, which is sufficient to express all the values included in the MIDI specification. Because it is most likely expressed in hex, chances are, if you want to edit a specific value in a SysEx message, converting hex to its decimal value can become a handy tool.

This said, you don't need to know how to use hex or how to convert it to use MIDI. This protocol is meant to be pretty transparent, and the values that are passed through a MIDI connection are usually converted into something easy to understand once in your sequencer, for example. But since many examples and descriptions of how MIDI works refer to hex values, this appendix will give you the necessary tools to make the conversion an easier one.

So without further ado, let's take the plunge into the wonderful world of the MIDI numbering system.

Decimal Numbering System

In our day-to-day lives, we count and number of things based on the decimal system. It is so named because it is based on 10 values, which can be combined to give us every possible combination of numerical values. These 10 values are 0, 1, 2, 3, 4, 5, 6, 7, 8, and 9. Adding a second digit in front of the first one, so 10 follows 9, forms the next value in this series. This added digit represents multiples of 10; therefore, $(1 \times 10) + 0 = 10$. With two digits, you can express values of up to 99. After this, you need to add a third digit in front, which represents multiples of 100 (or 10×10). The pattern repeats when you reach 999—a fourth digit is added, which represents multiples of 1,000 (or $10 \times 10 \times 10$), and so on. So, the value 4,568 can be interpreted as $(4 \times 1000) + (5 \times 100) + (6 \times 10) + (8 \times 1)$, all of which are multiples of 10 because this is how the "decimal" system works. The decimal numbering system is referred to as "base 10" because of this.

Binary Numbering System

Computers use a different numbering system, called the binary system. It is so named because it is based on values of 2, which can be combined to give us every possible combination of numerical values. The two binary values are 0 and 1.

The binary system makes great sense in the computing environment, where the two binary values of 0 and 1 can correspond to the on and off states of an electrical switch. Counting simple switches is a relatively straightforward task for a computer. If you have only one digit in your system, you can have two different values (0 or 1). For this reason, the binary system is also referred to as "base 2." When you want to represent a value higher than 1, you need to add another digit in front of it, which will allow you to have 4 different values: 0, 1, 10, 11 (00 and 01 are the same as 0 and 1).

To have more than four different values, you can add a third digit in front, which will give you eight values: 0, 1, 10, 11, 100, 101, 110, 111. Notice that every time you add a digit, it multiplies the possible values by the base value. So, one digit is 2, two digits is $(2 \times 2 = 4)$, three digits is $(2 \times 2 \times 2 = 8)$, and so on, just like in the decimal (base 10) numbering system. So, the value 255 in decimal is represented by 1111 1111 in binary, the value 17 in decimal is represented by 1 0001, and so on.

Hexadecimal Numbering System

The Hexadecimal numbering system uses sixteen different values, which are a combination of the first ten decimal values and letters from A to F to represent values 11 through 16: 0, 1, 2, 3, 4, 5, 6, 7, 8, 9, A (10), B (11), C (12), D (13), E (14), and F (15). Because hexadecimal numbering uses sixteen values, every subsequent digit added in front of the first adds a multiple of sixteen (because this is a "base 16" numbering system). So, after F would come 10, 11, and so on, until FF. In fact, you express 256 different values when using only two digits in this system $(16 \times 16 = 256)$. We look at hexadecimal values because, although MIDI uses binary language, binary is more difficult to calculate because of the high number of digits it uses. If you take the same examples given above, the value 255 in decimal becomes 1111 1111 in binary and FF in hexadecimal, which is much shorter than its binary representation. Imagine trying to represent the value 65,535 in decimal; this would take sixteen characters, while its hexadecimal value is represented by only four— FF FF. Since MIDI messages are sent over a binary system, converting these binary numbers into hex values makes it easier to understand their meaning due to the smaller number of characters hex uses to represent these messages. You will also find that most MIDI documentation does not refer to binary values, but rather to hexadecimal representation, and here lies the real reason why understanding this numbering system is important.

In table A.1, you can compare decimal, binary, and hexadecimal numbering values:

Table A.1
Equivalents between decimal, binary, and hexadecimal numbering.

Decimal	Binary	Hexadecimal	Decimal	Binary	Hexadecimal
0	00000000	00	27	00011011	1B
1	00000001	01	28	00011100	1C
2	00000010	02	29	00011101	1D
3	00000011	03	30	00011110	1E
4	00000100	04	31	00011111	1F
5	00000101	05	32	00100000	20
6	00000110	06	33	00100001	21
7	00000111	07	34	00100010	22
8	00001000	08	35	00100011	23
9	00001001	09	36	00100100	24
10	00001010	0A	37	00100101	25
11	00001011	0B	38	00100110	26
12	00001100	0C	39	00100111	27
13	00001101	0D	40	00101000	28
14	00001110	0E	41	00101001	29
15	00001111	0F	42	00101010	2A
16	00010000	10	43	00101011	2B
17	00010001	11	44	00101100	2C
18	00010010	12	45	00101101	2D
19	00010011	13	46	00101110	2E
20	00010100	14	47	00101111	2F
21	00010101	15	48	00110000	30
22	00010110	16	49	00110001	31
23	00010111	17	50	00110010	32
24	00011000	18	51	00110011	33
25	00011001	19	52	00110100	34
26	00011010	1A	53	00110101	35

Decimal	Binary	Hexadecimal	Decimal	Binary	Hexadecimal
54	00110110	36	84	01010100	54
55	00110111	37	85	01010101	55
56	00111000	38	86	01010110	56
57	00111001	39	87	01010111	57
58	00111010	3A	88	01011000	58
59	00111011	3B	89	01011001	59
60	00111100	3C	90	01011010	5A
61	00111101	3D	91	01011011	5B
62	00111110	3E	92	01011100	5C
63	00111111	3F	93	01011101	5D
64	01000000	40	94	01011110	5E
65	01000001	41	95	01011111	5F
66	01000010	42	96	01100000	60
67	01000011	43	97	01100001	61
68	01000100	44	98	01100010	62
69	01000101	45	99	01100011	63
70	01000110	46	100	01100100	64
71	01000111	47	101	01100101	65
72	01001000	48	102	01100110	66
73	01001001	49	103	01100111	67
74	01001010	4A	104	01101000	68
75	01001011	4B	105	01101001	69
76	01001100	4C	106	01101010	6A
77	01001101	4D	107	01101011	6B
78	01001110	4E	108	01101100	6C
79	01001111	4F	109	01101101	6D
80	01010000	50	110	01101110	6E
81	01010001	51	111	01101111	6F
82	01010010	52	112	01110000	70
83	01010011	53	113	01110001	71

Decimal	Binary	Hexadecimal	Decimal	Binary	Hexadecimal
114	01110010	72	144	10010000	90
115	01110011	73	145	10010001	91
116	01110100	74	146	10010010	92
117	01110101	75	147	10010011	93
118	01110110	76	148	10010100	94
119	01110111	77	149	10010101	95
120	01111000	78	150	10010110	96
121	01111001	79	151	10010111	97
122	01111010	7A	152	10011000	98
123	01111011	7B	153	10011001	99
124	01111100	7C	154	10011010	9A
125	01111101	7D	155	10011011	9B
126	01111110	7E	156	10011100	9C
127	01111111	7F	157	10011101	9D
128	10000000	80	158	10011110	9E
129	10000001	81	159	10011111	9F
130	10000010	82	160	10100000	A0
131	10000011	83	161	10100001	A1
132	10000100	84	162	10100010	A2
133	10000101	85	163	10100011	A3
134	10000110	86	164	10100100	A4
135	10000111	87	165	10100101	A5
136	10001000	88	166	10100110	A6
137	10001001	89	167	10100111	A7
138	10001010	8A	168	10101000	A8
139	10001011	8B	169	10101001	A9
140	10001100	8C	170	10101010	AA
141	10001101	8D	171	10101011	AB
142	10001110	8E	172	10101100	AC
143	10001111	8F	173	10101101	AD

Decimal	Binary	Hexadecimal	Decimal	Binary	Hexadecimal
174	10101110	AE	204	11001100	CC
175	10101111	AF	205	11001101	CD
176	10110000	B0	206	11001110	CE
177	10110001	B1	207	11001111	CF
178	10110010	B2	208	11010000	D0
179	10110011	B3	209	11010001	D1
180	10110100	B4	210	11010010	D2
181	10110101	B5	211	11010011	D3
182	10110110	B6	212	11010100	D4
183	10110111	B7	213	11010101	D5
184	10111000	B8	214	11010110	D6
185	10111001	B9	215	11010111	D7
186	10111010	BA	216	11011000	D8
187	10111011	BB	217	11011001	D9
188	10111100	BC	218	11011010	DA
189	10111101	BD	219	11011011	DB
190	10111110	BE	220	11011100	DC
191	10111111	BF	221	11011101	DD
192	11000000	C0	222	11011110	DE
193	11000001	C1	223	11011111	DF
194	11000010	C2	224	11100000	E0
195	11000011	C3	225	11100001	E1
196	11000100	C4	226	11100010	E2
197	11000101	C5	227	11100011	E3
198	11000110	C6	228	11100100	E4
199	11000111	C7	229	11100101	E5
200	11001000	C8	230	11100110	E6
201	11001001	C9	231	11100111	E7
202	11001010	CA	232	11101000	E8
203	11001011	CB	233	11101001	E9

Decimal	Binary	Hexadecimal
234	11101010	EA
235	11101011	EB
236	11101100	EC
237	11101101	ED
238	11101110	EE
239	11101111	EF
240	11110000	F0
241	11110001	F1
242	11110010	F2
243	11110011	F3
244	11110100	F4
245	11110101	F5
246	11110110	F6
247	11110111	F7
248	11111000	F8
249	11111001	F9
250	11111010	FA
251	11111011	FB
252	11111100	FC
253	11111101	FD
254	11111110	FE
255	11111111	FF

Converting Values

The following table displays the number of values that can be displayed when using different numbering systems. The first row indicates the number of digits in the number, and the first column on the left displays the numbering system used. As you can see, the hexadecimal system displays a greater number of values with the fewest number of digits. And, as you can already notice, displaying the decimal value 256 takes three digits in decimals, but will take eight digits in binary (1111 1111) and two digits in hexadecimal (FF).

APPENDIX A

Table A.2
Possible values in a numbering system displayed by digit increments.

Digits :	8	7	6	5	4	3	2	1
Decimal	100,000,000	10,000,000	1,000,000	100,000	10,000	1,000	100	10
Binary	256	128	64	32	16	8	4	2
Hex	4,294,967,296	268,435,456	16,777,216	1,048,576	65,536	4,096	256	16

The above table can also be used as a reference point when converting values from one format to another. As you can see in this table, you can express a far greater number of values using hexadecimal numbering than with decimal or binary numbering systems. Here are a couple of examples of how this works.

First, let's take the value 11010110 in binary. How can you find out what value this has in decimal or hex?

To convert a binary value into a decimal value, you multiply each digit by its multiple, starting with 1 for the smallest value (digit number 1), then 2, then 4, then 8, and so on, as shown in Table A.3

Table A.3
Converting a binary value into a decimal value.

Digit's Multiple	128	64	32	16	8	4	2	1
Binary Value	1	1	0	1	0	1	1	0
Total	128	64	0	16	0	4	2	0

You then add up the totals: 128 + 64 + 0 + 16 + 0 + 4 + 2 + 0 = 214. So 11010110 is the binary equivalent of 214 in decimal.

To convert this same binary value (11010110) into a hexadecimal value, the process is similar, but you need to divide each cluster of four digits into two separate calculations. Why divide it in two? Because it takes four binary digits to represent as many values as one hexadecimal digit (sixteen values). The first four digits of the binary word will give you the second hexadecimal digit, and the last four digits in the binary word will give you the first hex digit, as shown in table A.4.

Table A.4
Converting a binary value into a hexadecimal value.

Digit's Multiple	8	4	2	1	8	4	2	1
Binary Value	1	1	0	1	0	1	1	0
Total in Decimal	8	4	0	1	0	4	2	0

If you add up the first four digits, you get 13 as a decimal value, or D in hex. The next set of four digits added up gives you a total of 6 in decimal values or 6 in hex. So, the hex equivalent to 11010110 in binary and 214 in decimals is D6.

To reverse this calculation, you can multiply the digits in a hex value to extrapolate their decimal equivalent as follows: $D6 = (D \times 16) + (6 \times 1) = (13 \times 16) + (6 \times 1) = (208 + 6) = 214$.

If you have a three-digit hex number, for example, you would multiply this third digit by 256, the fourth digit by 4,096, and so on, as table A.2 suggests.

The choice is yours here. You can try to understand what eight binary digits represent, since every MIDI message comes in 8-bit words, or you can simply use a set of two hex digits representing the same value. Here's an example of this conversion as it applies to a MIDI message:

Table A.5
A single MIDI message displayed in binary, hex, decimal, and its MIDI equivalent for the musician.

Type of Byte	Status Byte	Data Byte	Data Byte
In Binary	10010111	00111100	01101110
In Hex	97	3C	6E
In Decimal	151	60	110
What it means in MIDI:	Channel 8 Note On	Middle C (number 60)	Velocity of 110 out of 127

Appendix B
MIDI 1.0 Specification

The following tables represent the MMA's (MIDI Manufacturers Association) 1995 update of the MIDI 1.0 specification, which defines the MIDI protocol. You should use this appendix as a reference guide and a summary of the information explained in chapters 2 and 3.

Expanded Status Bytes List

In the following tables, you will find a list for each category of status bytes found in a MIDI message. Remember that each MIDI message starts with a status byte and is then followed by its appropriate number of data bytes. This section lists all possible status byte values sorted in binary order and what they represent.

Table B.1
Expanded status bytes list for the Note Off function.

STATUS BYTE					DATA BYTES	
1st Byte Value: Binary	1st Byte Value: Hex	1st Byte Value: Dec	Note Off Function		2nd Byte	3rd Byte
10000000	80	128	Chan 1		Note Number (0-127)	Note Velocity (0-127)
10000001	81	129	Chan 2		"	"
10000010	82	130	Chan 3		"	"
10000011	83	131	Chan 4		"	"
10000100	84	132	Chan 5		"	"
10000101	85	133	Chan 6		"	"
10000110	86	134	Chan 7		"	"
10000111	87	135	Chan 8		"	"
10001000	88	136	Chan 9		"	"

10001001	89	137	Chan 10	"	"
10001010	8A	138	Chan 11	"	"
10001011	8B	139	Chan 12	"	"
10001100	8C	140	Chan 13	"	"
10001101	8D	141	Chan 14	"	"
10001110	8E	142	Chan 15	"	"
10001111	8F	143	Chan 16	"	"

Table B.2
Expanded status bytes list for the Note On function.

STATUS BYTE				DATA BYTES	
1st Byte Value: Binary	1st Byte Value: Hex	1st Byte Value: Dec	Note On Function	2nd Byte	3rd Byte
10010000	90	144	Chan 1	Note Number (0-127)	Note Velocity (0-127)
10010001	91	145	Chan 2	"	"
10010010	92	146	Chan 3	"	"
10010011	93	147	Chan 4	"	"
10010100	94	148	Chan 5	"	"
10010101	95	149	Chan 6	"	"
10010110	96	150	Chan 7	"	"
10010111	97	151	Chan 8	"	"
10011000	98	152	Chan 9	"	"
10011001	99	153	Chan 10	"	"
10011010	9A	154	Chan 11	"	"
10011011	9B	155	Chan 12	"	"
10011100	9C	156	Chan 13	"	"
10011101	9D	157	Chan 14	"	"
10011110	9E	158	Chan 15	"	"
10011111	9F	159	Chan 16	"	"

Table B.3
Expanded status bytes list for the polyphonic aftertouch function.

| STATUS BYTE | | | | DATA BYTES | |
1st Byte Value: Binary	1st Byte Value: Hex	1st Byte Value: Dec	Polyphonic Aftertouch Function	2nd Byte	3rd Byte
10100000	A0	160	Chan 1	Note Number (0-127)	Aftertouch amount (0-127)
10100001	A1	161	Chan 2	"	"
10100010	A2	162	Chan 3	"	"
10100011	A3	163	Chan 4	"	"
10100100	A4	164	Chan 5	"	"
10100101	A5	165	Chan 6	"	"
10100110	A6	166	Chan 7	"	"
10100111	A7	167	Chan 8	"	"
10101000	A8	168	Chan 9	"	"
10101001	A9	169	Chan 10	"	"
10101010	AA	170	Chan 11	"	"
10101011	AB	171	Chan 12	"	"
10101100	AC	172	Chan 13	"	"
10101101	AD	173	Chan 14	"	"
10101110	AE	174	Chan 15	"	"
10101111	AF	175	Chan 16	"	"

APPENDIX B

Table B.4
Expanded status bytes list for control change and channel mode messages.

STATUS BYTE				DATA BYTES	
1st Byte Value: Binary	1st Byte Value: Hex	1st Byte Value: Dec	Control / Mode Change Function	2nd Byte	3rd Byte
10110000	B0	176	Chan 1	See Table B.10	See Table B.10
10110001	B1	177	Chan 2	"	"
10110010	B2	178	Chan 3	"	"
10110011	B3	179	Chan 4	"	"
10110100	B4	180	Chan 5	"	"
10110101	B5	181	Chan 6	"	"
10110110	B6	182	Chan 7	"	"
10110111	B7	183	Chan 8	"	"
10111000	B8	184	Chan 9	"	"
10111001	B9	185	Chan 10	"	"
10111010	BA	186	Chan 11	"	"
10111011	BB	187	Chan 12	"	"
10111100	BC	188	Chan 13	"	"
10111101	BD	189	Chan 14	"	"
10111110	BE	190	Chan 15	"	"
10111111	BF	191	Chan 16	"	"

Table B.5
Expanded status bytes list for the program change function.

| STATUS BYTE | | | | DATA BYTES | |
1st Byte Value: Binary	1st Byte Value: Hex	1st Byte Value: Dec	Program Change Function	2nd Byte	3rd Byte
11000000	C0	192	Chan 1	Program # (0-127)	NONE
11000001	C1	193	Chan 2	"	"
11000010	C2	194	Chan 3	"	"
11000011	C3	195	Chan 4	"	"
11000100	C4	196	Chan 5	"	"
11000101	C5	197	Chan 6	"	"
11000110	C6	198	Chan 7	"	"
11000111	C7	199	Chan 8	"	"
11001000	C8	200	Chan 9	"	"
11001001	C9	201	Chan 10	"	"
11001010	CA	202	Chan 11	"	"
11001011	CB	203	Chan 12	"	"
11001100	CC	204	Chan 13	"	"
11001101	CD	205	Chan 14	"	"
11001110	CE	206	Chan 15	"	"
11001111	CF	207	Chan 16	"	"

Table B.6
Expanded status bytes list for the channel aftertouch function.

| STATUS BYTE | | | | DATA BYTES | |
1st Byte Value: Binary	1st Byte Value: Hex	1st Byte Value: Dec	Channel Aftertouch Function	2nd Byte	3rd Byte
11010000	D0	208	Chan 1	Aftertouch amount (0-127)	NONE
11010001	D1	209	Chan 2	"	"
11010010	D2	210	Chan 3	"	"
11010011	D3	211	Chan 4	"	"
11010100	D4	212	Chan 5	"	"
11010101	D5	213	Chan 6	"	"
11010110	D6	214	Chan 7	"	"
11010111	D7	215	Chan 8	"	"
11011000	D8	216	Chan 9	"	"
11011001	D9	217	Chan 10	"	"
11011010	DA	218	Chan 11	"	"
11011011	DB	219	Chan 12	"	"
11011100	DC	220	Chan 13	"	"
11011101	DD	221	Chan 14	"	"
11011110	DE	222	Chan 15	"	"
11011111	DF	223	Chan 16	"	"

Table B.7
Expanded status bytes list for the pitch wheel control function.

| STATUS BYTE | | | | DATA BYTES | |
1st Byte Value: Binary	1st Byte Value: Hex	1st Byte Value: Dec	Channel Aftertouch Function	2nd Byte	3rd Byte
11100000	E0	224	Chan 1	Pitch wheel LSB (0-127)	Pitch wheel MSB (0-127)
11100001	E1	225	Chan 2	"	"
11100010	E2	226	Chan 3	"	"
11100011	E3	227	Chan 4	"	"
11100100	E4	228	Chan 5	"	"
11100101	E5	229	Chan 6	"	"
11100110	E6	230	Chan 7	"	"
11100111	E7	231	Chan 8	"	"
11101000	E8	232	Chan 9	"	"
11101001	E9	233	Chan 10	"	"
11101010	EA	234	Chan 11	"	"
11101011	EB	235	Chan 12	"	"
11101100	EC	236	Chan 13	"	"
11101101	ED	237	Chan 14	"	"
11101110	EE	238	Chan 15	"	"
11101111	EF	239	Chan 16	"	"

Table B.8
Expanded status bytes list for the system common, realtime, and exclusive functions

STATUS BYTE				DATA BYTES	
1st Byte Value: Binary	1st Byte Value: Hex	1st Byte Value: Dec	Channel Aftertouch Function	2nd Byte	3rd Byte
11110000	F0	240	System Exclusive	Actual SysEx message	Actual SysEx message
11110001	F1	241	MIDI Time Code Qtr. Frame	Actual time address	Actual time address
11110010	F2	242	Song Position Pointer	LSB	MSB
11110011	F3	243	Song Select (Song #)	(0-127)	NONE
11110100	F4	244	Undefined	N/A	N/A
11110101	F5	245	Undefined	N/A	N/A
11110110	F6	246	Tune request	NONE	NONE
11110111	F7	247	End of SysEx (EOX)	"	"
11111000	F8	248	Timing clock	"	"
11111001	F9	249	Undefined	"	"
11111010	FA	250	Start	"	"
11111011	FB	251	Continue	"	"
11111100	FC	252	Stop	"	"
11111101	FD	253	Undefined	"	"
11111110	FE	254	Active Sensing	"	"
11111111	FF	255	System Reset	"	"

MIDI Note Numbers

The following table lists all the MIDI notes and their corresponding note numbers according to the MIDI specification.

Table B.9
MIDI note numbers.

Octave #	C	C#	D	D#	E	F	F#	G	G#	A	A#	B
–1	0	1	2	3	4	5	6	7	8	9	10	11
0	12	13	14	15	16	17	18	19	20	21	22	23
1	24	25	26	27	28	29	30	31	32	33	34	35
2	36	37	38	39	40	41	42	43	44	45	46	47
3	48	49	50	51	52	53	54	55	56	57	58	59
4	60	61	62	63	64	65	66	67	68	69	70	71
5	72	73	74	75	76	77	78	79	80	81	82	83
6	84	85	86	87	88	89	90	91	92	93	94	95
7	96	97	98	99	100	101	102	103	104	105	106	107
8	108	109	110	111	112	113	114	115	116	117	118	119
9	120	121	122	123	124	125	126	127				

Controller Messages (Data Bytes)

The following table is a summary of controller messages in numerical (binary) order. This table is intended as a quick reference to all controller and channel mode messages. Since all control change messages contain the same first status byte (identifying it as a control change event), this table only represents the second and third byte of each message.

Note that in this table, the abbreviation MSB refers to Most Significant Byte, and LSB to Least Significant Byte.

Table B.10
Control change and channel mode messages (status bytes 176-191)

2nd Byte Value: Binary	2nd Byte Value: Hex	2nd Byte Value: Dec	Function	3rd Byte Value	3rd Byte Use
0000000	0	0	Bank Select	0-127	MSB
0000001	1	1	Modulation wheel	0-127	MSB
0000010	2	2	Breath control	0-127	MSB
0000011	3	3	Undefined	0-127	MSB
0000100	4	4	Foot controller	0-127	MSB
0000101	5	5	Portamento time	0-127	MSB
0000110	6	6	Data Entry	0-127	MSB
0000111	7	7	Channel Volume (formerly Main Volume)	0-127	MSB
0001000	8	8	Balance	0-127	MSB
0001001	9	9	Undefined	0-127	MSB
0001010	0A	10	Pan	0-127	MSB
0001011	0B	11	Expression Controller	0-127	MSB
0001100	0C	12	Effect control 1	0-127	MSB
0001101	0D	13	Effect control 2	0-127	MSB
0001110	0E	14	Undefined	0-127	MSB
0001111	0F	15	Undefined	0-127	MSB
0010000	10	16	General Purpose Controller #1	0-127	MSB
0010001	11	17	General Purpose Controller #2	0-127	MSB

0010010	12	18	General Purpose Controller #3	0-127	MSB
0010011	13	19	General Purpose Controller #4	0-127	MSB
0010100	14	20	Undefined	0-127	MSB
0010101	15	21	Undefined	0-127	MSB
0010110	16	22	Undefined	0-127	MSB
0010111	17	23	Undefined	0-127	MSB
0011000	18	24	Undefined	0-127	MSB
0011001	19	25	Undefined	0-127	MSB
0011010	1A	26	Undefined	0-127	MSB
0011011	1B	27	Undefined	0-127	MSB
0011100	1C	28	Undefined	0-127	MSB
0011101	1D	29	Undefined	0-127	MSB
0011110	1E	30	Undefined	0-127	MSB
0011111	1F	31	Undefined	0-127	MSB
0100000	20	32	Bank Select	0-127	LSB
0100001	21	33	Modulation wheel	0-127	LSB
0100010	22	34	Breath control	0-127	LSB
0100011	23	35	Undefined	0-127	LSB
0100100	24	36	Foot controller	0-127	LSB
0100101	25	37	Portamento time	0-127	LSB
0100110	26	38	Data entry	0-127	LSB
0100111	27	39	Channel Volume (formerly Main Volume)	0-127	LSB
0101000	28	40	Balance	0-127	LSB
0101001	29	41	Undefined	0-127	LSB
0101010	2A	42	Pan	0-127	LSB
0101011	2B	43	Expression Controller	0-127	LSB
0101100	2C	44	Effect control 1	0-127	LSB
0101101	2D	45	Effect control 2	0-127	LSB
0101110	2E	46	Undefined	0-127	LSB

0101111	2F	47	Undefined	0-127	LSB
0110000	30	48	General Purpose Controller #1	0-127	LSB
0110001	31	49	General Purpose Controller #2	0-127	LSB
0110010	32	50	General Purpose Controller #3	0-127	LSB
0110011	33	51	General Purpose Controller #4	0-127	LSB
0110100	34	52	Undefined	0-127	LSB
0110101	35	53	Undefined	0-127	LSB
0110110	36	54	Undefined	0-127	LSB
0110111	37	55	Undefined	0-127	LSB
0111000	38	56	Undefined	0-127	LSB
0111001	39	57	Undefined	0-127	LSB
0111010	3A	58	Undefined	0-127	LSB
0111011	3B	59	Undefined	0-127	LSB
0111100	3C	60	Undefined	0-127	LSB
0111101	3D	61	Undefined	0-127	LSB
0111110	3E	62	Undefined	0-127	LSB
0111111	3F	63	Undefined	0-127	LSB
1000000	40	64	Damper pedal on/off (Sustain)	<63=off	>64=on
1000001	41	65	Portamento on/off	<63=off	>64=on
1000010	42	66	Sustenuto on/off	<63=off	>64=on
1000011	43	67	Soft pedal on/off	<63=off	>64=on
1000100	44	68	Legato Footswitch	<63=off	>64=on
1000101	45	69	Hold 2	<63=off	>64=on
1000110	46	70	Sound Controller 1 (Sound Variation)	0-127	LSB
1000111	47	71	Sound Controller 2 (Timbre)	0-127	LSB
1001000	48	72	Sound Controller 3 (Release Time)	0-127	LSB
1001001	49	73	Sound Controller 4 (Attack Time)	0-127	LSB
1001010	4A	74	Sound Controller 5 (Brightness)	0-127	LSB
1001011	4B	75	Sound Controller 6	0-127	LSB
1001100	4C	76	Sound Controller 7	0-127	LSB

1001101	4D	77	Sound Controller 8	0-127	LSB
1001110	4E	78	Sound Controller 9	0-127	LSB
1001111	4F	79	Sound Controller 10	0-127	LSB
1010000	50	80	General Purpose Controller #5	0-127	LSB
1010001	51	81	General Purpose Controller #6	0-127	LSB
1010010	52	82	General Purpose Controller #7	0-127	LSB
1010011	53	83	General Purpose Controller #8	0-127	LSB
1010100	54	84	Portamento Control	0-127	Source Note
1010101	55	85	Undefined	0-127	LSB
1010110	56	86	Undefined	0-127	LSB
1010111	57	87	Undefined	0-127	LSB
1011000	58	88	Undefined	0-127	LSB
1011001	59	89	Undefined	0-127	LSB
1011010	5A	90	Undefined	0-127	LSB
1011011	5B	91	Effects 1 Depth	0-127	LSB
1011100	5C	92	Effects 2 Depth	0-127	LSB
1011101	5D	93	Effects 3 Depth	0-127	LSB
1011110	5E	94	Effects 4 Depth	0-127	LSB
1011111	5F	95	Effects 5 Depth	0-127	LSB
1100000	60	96	Data entry +1	N/A	N/A
1100001	61	97	Data entry −1	N/A	N/A
1100010	62	98	Non-Registered Parameter Number LSB	0-127	LSB
1100011	63	99	Non-Registered Parameter Number MSB	0-127	MSB
1100100	64	100	Registered Parameter Number LSB	0-127	LSB
1100101	65	101	Registered Parameter Number MSB	0-127	MSB
1100110	66	102	Undefined	N/A	N/A
1100111	67	103	Undefined	N/A	N/A
1101000	68	104	Undefined	N/A	N/A
1101001	69	105	Undefined	N/A	N/A

APPENDIX B

1101010	6A	106	Undefined	N/A	N/A
1101011	6B	107	Undefined	N/A	N/A
1101100	6C	108	Undefined	N/A	N/A
1101101	6D	109	Undefined	N/A	N/A
1101110	6E	110	Undefined	N/A	N/A
1101111	6F	111	Undefined	N/A	N/A
1110000	70	112	Undefined	N/A	N/A
1110001	71	113	Undefined	N/A	N/A
1110010	72	114	Undefined	N/A	N/A
1110011	73	115	Undefined	N/A	N/A
1110100	74	116	Undefined	N/A	N/A
1110101	75	117	Undefined	N/A	N/A
1110110	76	118	Undefined	N/A	N/A
1110111	77	119	Undefined	N/A	N/A
1111000	78	120	All Sound Off	0	0
1111001	79	121	Reset All Controllers	0	0
1111010	7A	122	Local control on/off	0=off	127=on
1111011	7B	123	All notes off	0	0
1111100	7C	124	Omni mode off (+ all notes off)	0	0
1111101	7D	125	Omni mode on (+ all notes off)	0	0
1111110	7E	126	Poly mode on/off (+ all notes off)	N/A	N/A
1111111	7F	127	Poly mode on (incl. mono=off +all notes off)	0	0

MIDI Messages

The following tables are a summary of the channel voice messages, mode messages, system common messages, and system real-time messages.

Here's a legend of values you will find in the tables under this section. Each value in this legend represents a series of variables grouped under one value. For example, cccc is used below to represent the channel numbers in a message, but since there can be sixteen different MIDI channels, each "c" represents a bit that will be replaced by its corresponding MIDI channel value in the binary word. In other words, a Note Off event always begins with 1000 and is followed by its channel number, which can be any value between 0000 and 1111, corresponding to the sixteen MIDI channels. The number of times a character is repeated in the legend represents the number of bits that can change depending on the value it represents. That's why the note number is represented in this legend by seven "n" letters, since there can be 128 different note numbers.

▶ cccc: represents the channel number.

▶ nnnnnnn: represents the note number.

▶ vvvvvvv: represents the velocity value.

▶ #######: represents the control change number.

▶ VVVVVVV: represents the value for the control change.

▶ ppppppp: represents the program number value.

▶ PPPPPPP: represents the pressure value.

▶ mmmmmmm: represents the Most Significant Bit value.

▶ lllllll: represents the Least Significant Bit value.

▶ iiiiiii: represents the manufacturer ID number.

▶ ddddddd: represents SysEx data values.

▶ sssssss: represents the song selection value.

Table B.11
Summary of channel voice messages.

Status Byte	Data (2nd Byte)	Data (3rd Byte)	Description
1000cccc	0nnnnnnn	0vvvvvvv	Note Off event: This message is sent when a note is released (ended)
1001cccc	0nnnnnnn	0vvvvvvv	Note On event: This message is sent when a note is depressed (started).
1010cccc	0nnnnnnn	0vvvvvvv	Polyphonic Key Pressure (Aftertouch): This message is sent when the pressure (velocity) of a previously triggered note changes.
1011cccc	0#######	0VVVVVVV	Control Change: This message is sent when a controller value changes. Controllers include devices such as pedals and levers. Certain controller numbers are reserved for specific purposes. See Channel Mode Messages.
1100cccc	0ppppppp		Program Change: This message is sent when the patch number changes.

| 1101cccc | 0PPPPPPP | | Channel Pressure (Aftertouch): This message is sent when the channel pressure changes. Some velocity-sensing keyboards do not support polyphonic aftertouch. Use this message to send the single greatest velocity (of all the current depressed keys). |
| 1110cccc | 0lllllll | 0mmmmmmm | Pitch Wheel Change: This message is sent to indicate a change in the pitch wheel. The pitch wheel is measured by a 14-bit value. Center (no pitch change) is 2000H. Sensitivity is a function of the transmitter. |

Table B.12
Channel mode messages (See also control change in table B.11)

Status Byte	Data (2nd Byte)	Data (3rd Byte)	Description
1011cccc	0#######	0VVVVVVV	Channel Mode Messages: This is the same code as the Control Change (Table B.11), but implements Mode control by using reserved controller numbers. The numbers are:
1011cccc	01111010	00000000	Local Control Off: When Local Control is Off, all devices on a given channel will respond only to data received over MIDI. Played data, etc., will be ignored. 2nd Data byte = 122, 3rd Data byte at 0 = Local Control Off
1011cccc	01111010	01111111	Local Control On: This restores the functions of the normal controllers. 2nd Data byte = 122, 3rd Data byte at 127 = Local Control On
1011cccc	01111011	00000000	All Notes Off: When an All Notes Off is received, all oscillators will turn off. 2nd Data byte = 123, 0 = causes All Notes Off (See text for description of actual mode commands.)
1011cccc	01111100	00000000	Omni Mode Off: 2nd Data byte = 124, 0 = causes All Notes Off
1011cccc	01111101	00000000	Omni Mode On: 2nd Data byte = 125, 0 = causes All Notes Off

1011cccc	01111110	00000000	Mono Mode On (Poly Off): This is where M is the number of channels: 2nd Data byte = 126, v = M (also causes All Notes Off)
1011cccc	01111111	00000000	Poly Mode On (Mono Off): 2nd Data byte = 127, 0 = also causes All Notes Off

Table B.13
System common messages

Status Byte	Data (2nd Byte)	Data (3rd Byte)	Description
11110000	0iiiiiii	0ddddddd	System Exclusive: This message makes up for all that MIDI doesn't support. If the synthesizer recognizes the I.D. code as its own, it will listen to the rest of the message (ddddddd). Otherwise, the message will be ignored. System Exclusive is used to send bulk dumps such as patch parameters and other non-spec data. (Note: real-time messages may be interleaved ONLY with a System Exclusive.)
...	...	0ddddddd	11110111
11110001			Undefined.
11110010	0lllllll	0mmmmmmm	Song Position Pointer: This is an internal 14-bit register that holds the number of MIDI beats (1 beat= six MIDI clocks) from the start of the song.
11110011	0sssssss		Song Select: The Song Select specifies which sequence or song is to be played.
11110100			Undefined.
11110101			Undefined.
11110110			Tune Request: Upon receiving a Tune Request, all analog synthesizers should tune their oscillators.
11110111			End of Exclusive: Used to terminate a System Exclusive dump (see above).

Table B.14
System real-time messages

Status Byte	Data (2nd Byte)	Data (3rd Byte)	Description
11111000			Timing Clock: Sent 24 times per quarter note when synchronization is required (see text below).
11111001			Undefined.
11111010			Start: Start the current sequence playing. (This message will be followed with timing clocks).
11111011 was stopped.			Continue: Continue at the point the sequence
11111100			Stop: Stop the current sequence.
11111101			Undefined.
11111110			Active Sensing: Use of this message is optional. When initially sent, the receiver will expect to receive another Active Sensing message each 300 ms (max), or it will be assume that the connection has been terminated. At termination, the receiver will turn off all voices and return to normal (non-active sensing) operation.
11111111			Reset: Reset all receivers in the system to power-up status. This should be used sparingly, preferably under manual control. In particular, it should not be sent on power-up.

System Exclusive Messages

Table B.15
System exclusive single byte manufacturer ID numbers (North American Manufacturer's Group)

Byte 1	Manufacturer's name
01H	Sequential Circuits
02H	IDP

03H	Voyetra/Octave-Plateau
04H	Moog
05H	Passport Designs
06H	Lexicon
07H	Kurzweil
08H	Fender
09H	Gulbransen
0AH	AKG Acoustics
0BH	Voyce Music
0CH	Waveframe Corp
0DH	ADA Signal Processors
0EH	Garfield Electronics
0FH	Ensoniq
10H	Oberheim
11H	Apple Computer
12H	Grey Matter Response
13H	Digidesign
14H	Palm Tree Instruments
15H	JL Cooper
16H	Lowery
17H	Adams-Smith
18H	Emu Systems
19H	Harmony Systems
1AH	ART
1BH	Baldwin
1CH	Eventide
1DH	Inventronics
1FH	Clarity

Table B.16

System exclusive single byte manufacturer ID numbers (European Manufacturer's Group)

Byte 1	Manufacturer's name
20H	Passac
21H	SIEL (Italy)
22H	Syntaxe (UK)
24H	Hohner (Germany)
25H	Twister
26H	Solton
27H	Jellinghaus MS (Germany)
28H	Southworth Music Systems
29H	PPG (Germany)
2AH	JEN
2BH	SSL Limited (UK)
2CH	Audio Veritrieb-P. Struven
2FH	Elka/General Music
30H	Dynacord
33H	Clavia Digital Instruments
34H	Audio Architecture
35H	GeneralMusic Corp.
39H	Soundcraft Electronics
3BH	Wersi
3CH	Avab Electronik Ab (Sweden)
3DH	Digigram
3EH	Waldorf Electronics GmbH
3FH	Quasimidi

Table B.17
System sxclusive single byte manufacturer ID numbers (Japanese Manufacturer's Group)

Byte 1	Manufacturer's name
40H	Kawai
41H	Roland
42H	Korg
43H	Yamaha
44H	Casio
46H	Kamiya Studio
47H	Akai
48H	Victor Company of Japan Limited
49H	Mesosha
4AH	Hoshino Gakki
4BH	Fujitsu Elect
4CH	Sony Corporation
4DH	Nisshin Onpa
4EH	TEAC
50H	Matsushita Electronic
51H	Fostex Corporation
52H	Zoom Corporation
53H	Midori Electronics
54H	Matsushita Communication Industrial
55H	Suzuki Musical Inst. Mfg.
56H	Fuji Sound Corporation Ltd
57H	Acoustic Technical Laboratory, Inc.
5CH	Seekers Co., Ltd

Table B.18
System exclusive multibyte manufacturer ID numbers (North American Manufacturer's Group)

Byte 1	Byte 2	Byte 3	Manufacturer's name	Byte 1	Byte 2	Byte 3	Manufacturer's name
00H	00H	01H	Warner New Media	00H	00H	3EH	NSI Corporation
00H	00H	04H	Silicon Graphics	00H	00H	3FH	Ad Lib, Inc.
00H	00H	07H	Digital Music Corp.	00H	00H	40H	Richmond Sound Design
00H	00H	08H	IOTA Systems	00H	00H	41H	Microsoft
00H	00H	09H	New England Digital	00H	00H	42H	The Software Toolworks (Anne Graham)
00H	00H	0AH	Artisyn	00H	00H	43H	RJMG/Niche
00H	00H	0BH	IVL Technologies	00H	00H	44H	Intone
00H	00H	0CH	Southern Music Systems	00H	00H	47H	GT Electronics/ Groove Tubes
00H	00H	0EH	Lake Butler Sound Company	00H	00H	4FH	InterMIDI, Inc.
00H	00H	10H	Alesis	00H	00H	55H	Lone Wolf
00H	00H	11H	DOD Electronics	00H	00H	64H	Musonix
00H	00H	14H	Studer-Editech	00H	01H	05H	MIDIman
00H	00H	15H	Jeff Tripp/Perfect Fretworks	00H	01H	06H	PreSonus
00H	00H	16H	KAT	00H	01H	08H	Topaz Enterprises
00H	00H	17H	Opcode	00H	01H	09h	Cast Lighting
00H	00H	18H	Rane Corp.	00H	01H	0AH	Microsoft Consumer Division
00H	00H	19H	Spatial Sound/ Anadi Inc.	00H	01H	0CH	Fast Forward Designs
00H	00H	1AH	KMX (Ken Yprilla)	00H	01H	0DH	Headspace (Igor's Labs)
00H	00H	1BH	Allen & Heath Brenell	00H	01H	0EH	Van Koevering Company

00H	00H	1CH	360 System	00H	01H	0FH	Altech Systems
00H	00H	1DH	Spectrum Design and Development	00H	01H	10H	S & S Research
00H	00H	1EH	Marquis Musi	00H	01H	11H	VLSI Technology
00H	00H	1FH	Zeta Systems	00H	01H	12H	Chromatic Research
00H	00H	20H	Axxes (Brian Parsonett)	00H	01H	13H	Sapphire
00H	00H	21H	Orban	00H	01H	14H	IDRC
00H	00H	24H	KTI	00H	01H	15H	Justonic Tuning
00H	00H	25H	Breakaway Technologies	00H	01H	16H	TorComp Research Inc
00H	00H	26H	CAE	00H	01H	17H	Newtek Inc
00H	00H	29H	Rocktron Corp.	00H	01H	18H	Sound Sculpture
00H	00H	2AH	PianoDisc	00H	01H	19H	Walker Technical
00H	00H	2BH	Cannon Research Group	00H	01H	1AH	PAVO
00H	00H	2DH	Rogers Instrument Corp.	00H	01H	1BH	InVision Interactive
00H	00H	2EH	Blue Sky Logic	00H	01H	1CH	T-Square Design
00H	00H	2FH	Encore Electronics	00H	01H	1DH	Nemesys Music Technology
00H	00H	30H	Uptown	00H	01H	1EH	DBX Professional
00H	00H	31H	Voce	00H	01H	1FH	Syndyne Corporation
00H	00H	32H	CTI Audio Inc.	00H	01H	20H	Bitheadz
00H	00H	33H	S&S Research	00H	01H	21H	Cakewalk Music Software
00H	00H	34H	Broderbund Software, Inc.	00H	01H	22H	Staccato Systems
00H	00H	35H	Allen Organ Co.	00H	01H	23H	National Semiconductor
00H	00H	37H	Music Quest	00H	01H	24H	Boom Theory / Adinolfi Alternative Percussion

00H	00H	38H	APHEX	00H	01H	25H	Virtual DSP Corporation
00H	00H	39H	Gallien Krueger	00H	01H	26H	Antares Systems
00H	00H	3AH	IBM	00H	01H	27H	Angel Software
00H	00H	3CH	Hotz Instruments Technologies	00H	01H	28H	St Louis Music
00H	00H	3DH	ETA Lighting	00H	01H	29H	Lyrrus dba G-VOX

Table B.19
System exclusive multibyte manufacturer ID numbers (European Manufacturer's Group)

Byte 1	Byte 2	Byte 3	Manufacturer's name	Byte 1	Byte 2	Byte 3	Manufacturer's name
00H	20H	00H	Dream	00H	20H	15H	ADB
00H	20H	01H	Strand Lighting	00H	20H	16H	Jim Marshall Products Ltd
00H	20H	02H	Amek Systems, Ltd.	00H	20H	17H	DDA
00H	20H	04H	Dr. Böhm/Musican International	00H	20H	1FH	TC Electronics
00H	20H	06H	Trident Audio	00H	20H	2FH	LG Semiconductor
00H	20H	07H	Real World Studio	00H	20H	30H	TESI
00H	20H	09H	Yes Technology	00H	20H	31H	EMAGIC
00H	20H	0AH	Audiomatica	00H	20H	32H	Behringer
00H	20H	0BH	Bontempi/Farfisa	00H	20H	33H	Access
00H	20H	0CH	F.B.T. Elettronica	00H	20H	34H	Synoptic
00H	20H	0EH	LA Audio (Larking Audio)	00H	20H	35H	Hanmesoft
00H	20H	0FH	Zero 88 Lighting Limited	00H	20H	36H	Terratec Electronic
00H	20H	10H	Micon Audio Electronics GmbH	00H	20H	37H	Proel SpA
00H	20H	11H	Forefront Technology	00H	20H	38H	IBK MIDI
00H	20H	13H	Kenton Electronics				

Appendix C
The Standard MIDI File Format

This appendix is meant for those of you who would like to understand how a Standard MIDI File saves recorded MIDI events into a file format and then reproduces this content through MIDI sequencer applications. You do not need to read through this if you want to use only SMF, since most of what is explained here is done automatically by your sequencer application anyway. If, on the other hand, you are curious to know how MIDI is recorded into a file and are the type of person who needs to know everything, this appendix was meant just for you. This is, after all, a book called MIDI Power! So dig in. On the other hand, if this does not describe your personality, you can skip this appendix.

The Standard MIDI File (SMF) format was designed to record and play back musical performances through a MIDI sequencer. This format saves MIDI messages and a time stamp associated with each message. The time stamp represents clock durations; in other words, how many clock pulses to wait before playing the event. Here's a look at what an SMF contains:

▶ MIDI messages: all types of messages, including SysEx.

▶ Time stamps for each message.

▶ Tempo settings for the song.

▶ Pulse Per Quarter Note (PPQN) resolution information or resolution expressed in time code format (SMPTE).

▶ Time signatures for the song.

▶ Key signatures for each track.

▶ Track names: A track is usually associated with a musical part. For example, a bass track represents a bass part.

▶ Pattern names: A pattern represents all parts or tracks in a song, or all parts for a portion of a song. For example, you could have many patterns representing different beats, just as a drum machine saves patterns in memory banks.

The information contained in an SMF represents the common elements that all sequencer applications will understand. The SMF format also supports sequencer proprietary information. This allows sequencers to save additional information to the file without making it unreadable by other sequencers. It works a bit like the manufacturer ID number in a SysEx message. In this case, however, the sequencer ID is attached to parts of the information that are sequencer specific and can be found anywhere in the file, not just at the beginning of the file as manufacturer ID numbers are. For example, a sequencer can save a file with the metronome clock set to On by attaching specific information to the SMF. Another sequencer will simply ignore this information if it doesn't understand it. In other words, SMF can always be backward-compatible because of these ID messages. If the application doesn't understand them, it simply skips them. These ID messages are sent in what is called a MIDI chunk.

SMF is most often used in sequencer applications. But it can also be used in other MIDI applications such as editor/librarian applications, since SMF can hold SysEx information that can store or load instrument settings used by these latter applications. The most common application of SMF, though, is to record and play back MIDI songs in a MIDI sequencer application.

MIDI Chunks

A MIDI chunk is a group of related bytes MIDI uses to save or transmit information to and from an SMF. It is the building block of MIDI files and is comparable in structure to a MIDI message, in the sense that it is made up of a status byte and followed by a series of data bytes. Each chunk can contain many bytes of information, depending on its content. There are two types of chunks: header chunks and track chunks. Both have a similar structure but serve different purposes. The header chunk is found only once, at the beginning of the SMF. It defines the information that follows as a MIDI file. There will always be only one header chunk in a MIDI file, since its only purpose is to define the MIDI file itself.

This could be compared to the SysEx's Start SysEx message. Following the header chunk are a series of variable length track chunks that contain MIDI messages found in the MIDI file's tracks. A track in a MIDI file represents the same thing as a track in a sequencer. So, if you have ten tracks in your sequencer and you save it as a MIDI file format, this file will contain ten track chunks under its header chunk. Each track chunk is structured as follows:

▶ Four bytes that define what type of chunk this is; those four bytes are called the chunk ID. This will be referred to as the MThd chunk (MIDI Track, header chunk) or MTrk chunk (MIDI Track, track chunk). These four bytes will represent ASCII characters, as opposed to binary values. ASCII stands for American Standard Code for Information Interchange. Computers can only understand numbers, so an ASCII code is the numerical representation of a character such as "a" or "@" or an action of some sort. So in hex, this could be either 4D 54 68 64, which represent the four letters M, T, h, and d in ASCII; or 4D 54 72 6B, which represent the four letters M, T, r, k.

▶ Four bytes (32-binary bits in this case, not ASCII) that represent the total length of the chunk's data portion. This excludes the 8 bytes needed to identify the chunk's type and length. In other words, it tells the receiving device how long the information that follows this header will be.

▶ The data holds a variable amount of binary bytes, which represents information specific to the chunk type (MThd or MTrk). This will be explained below.

In Figure C.1, you can see a typical chunk structure in a standard MIDI file. This represents the meta-structure of the MIDI file, where chunks are defined as being either MThd or MTrk, and their respective data length. It also shows what type of data appears for each type of chunk.

Figure C.1
The SMF chunk
structure

CHUNKS		
TYPE 4 bytes (ascii)	TYPE 4 bytes (32-bit binary)	DATA variable bit length (binary data)

MIDI File
| MThd | 6 | FORMAT | TRACKS | DIVISION |
| MTrk | length | delta time | events | |

MThd Chunk

There will be only one MThd chunk per MIDI file since this identifies the format of the MIDI file, the number of tracks it holds, and how it is divided in terms of time base or clock base. Since each event in a MIDI file occurs in time, the header chunk defines how much time it should wait between each event. This time base or clock base represents the default value that applies throughout the file. In other words, it uses this value as a time grid value that will serve as a reference to align all the events found in the file. A MThd chunk will always hold six data bytes of information (see Figure C.2):

▶ 2 bytes for the format

▶ 2 bytes for the number of tracks. When the MIDI format 0 is used, this will always be set to 1, otherwise, it can be any number of tracks found in your MIDI sequence or pattern.

▶ 2 bytes for the division, which defines the default unit of delta-time for this MIDI file. A delta-time can be either the number of time units in each quarter note or the frame rate and ticks for each frame. What type of time metering system it uses (MIDI clock or SMPTE time) depends on the setting used when the file is saved or the setting used by the device using the MIDI file.

Figure C.2
The content of an MThd
chunk (header chunk)

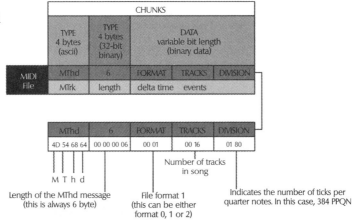

In a MIDI file, an event's time precedes the data bytes that make up that event itself. In other words, the bytes that make up the event's time-stamp come first. A given event's time-stamp is referenced from the previous event. For example, if the first event occurs 8 clocks after the start of play, then its delta-time is 08. If the next event occurs simultaneously with that first event, its time is 00. So, a delta-time is the duration (in clocks) between an event and the preceding event. A delta-time is stored as a variable length quantity set of bytes. A variable length quantity is a method MIDI uses to optimize the information needed to transmit values in a MIDI file.

Format

The two format bytes indicate the file format of this SMF. File format is designated by one of three values that corresponds to the MIDI formats discussed earlier in this book:

> ▶ MIDI format 0 contains one single track containing MIDI data on possibly all sixteen MIDI channels.

> ▶ MIDI format 1 contains one or more simultaneous tracks starting at an assumed position of zero. Each track can hold one or more MIDI channels. The sum of these tracks is considered as one sequence or pattern. The first track of a format 1 file is special, and is also known as the tempo map. It should contain all meta-events such as time signatures, tempo settings, and so on. This is probably the most common MIDI format.

> ▶ MIDI format 2 contains one or more sequentially independent single-track patterns. If your sequencer separates its MIDI data into different blocks of memory but plays only one block at a time, then it will read or write this type. In this case, each block is considered as a different sequence or pattern. Drum machine patterns are a good example of this pattern sequence use.

Division

The last two bytes in the MThd chunk indicate how many pulses, or clocks per quarter note (referred to as PPQN) resolution, the timestamps are based upon. For example, if your sequencer resolution is set to 384 PPQN, as shown in Figure C.3, the value in hexadecimal for this field would be 01 80. This is referred to as the deltatime. In other words, a timestamp called deltatime occurs at intervals determined by the PPQN value and saved with the file.

Figure C.3
The system resolution
for this sequence is set
at 384 PPQN

This division value, as shown in Figure C.2, can also represent SMPTE values rather than PPQN as discussed in the previous paragraph. This will be the case when the first byte is one of the four following values: –24, –25, –29 (for the 29.97 dropframe standard), –30 (for the 29.97 nondrop standard), which correspond to the four SMPTE standard frame rates.

If bit 15 (when counting from right to left from 0 to 15, for a total of 16 bits) is a 0 (in binary), then it means the division represents ticks per quarter note. If it is a 1, then bits 0 to 7 represent the number of deltatime units per SMTPE frame and bits 8 to 14 represent the SMPTE frame rate mentioned above.

Here are tables representing the possible values found for this division:

Table C.2
Samples of typical PPQN values converted into hex value found in the MThd division data field.

HEX	PPQN
00 60	96
00 C0	192
01 80	384
07 80	1920

Table C.3
SMPTE values expressed in the MThd division data field (bits 8 to 14) to identify the frame rate.

HEX	Value	Description	Binary
E2	–30	29.97 frames per second (nondrop)	(11) 1110 0010
E3	–29	29,97 frames per second (drop frame)	(11) 1110 0011
E7	–25	25 frames per second	(11) 1110 0111
E8	–24	24 frames per second	(11) 1110 1000

NOTE

Two extra bits (in parenthesis) are required to identify the negative values, which explains why in Table C.3 10 bits are used to display the negative value. Also, the hex value FF FF FF FF would precede the current hex values in this table (for example: FF FF FF FF E2), otherwise E2 represents the decimal value 226, not –30.

Table C.4
Ticks per frame resolution values expressed in the MThd division data field (bits 0 to7) when using SMPTE format.

HEX	Value	Description	Binary
04	4	MIDI Time Code (MTC) resolution (or ticks per frame)	00000100
08	8	SMPTE bit resolution (or ticks per frame)	00001000
0A	10	SMPTE bit resolution (or ticks per frame)	00001010
28	40	Millisecond resolution when combined with 25 fps SMPTE	00101000
50	80	SMPTE bit resolution (or ticks per frame)	01010000
64	100	SMPTE bit resolution (or ticks per frame)	01100100

NOTE

By combining the SMPTE frame rate of 25 fps (frames-per-second) with the resolution of 40 subframes per frame, as seen in Table C.4, you get 1000 subframes per second. This represents exactly 1 millisecond per subframe, which is why each deltatime increment in this case is equivalent to 1 millisecond (or 1000 microseconds).

MTrk Chunk

The MThd chunk is usually followed by a series of MTrk chunks. Any other types of chunks would be proprietary and would be ignored by a device reading the MIDI file if it does not recognize it. In other words, if the MThd chunk is followed by something other than an MTrk chunk, all devices with the exception of the device for which this chunk type was meant will ignore it.

Like the MThd chunk, the MTrk chunk contains three parts: the type, which identifies it as being an MTrk chunk; the length, which represents the total number of bits it contains in its data portion; and the data itself. The data for an MTrk chunk contains all of the MIDI event data and timing bytes for these MIDI events, along with non-MIDI data for one track. You can have as many MTrk chunks as there are tracks in your MIDI file, as defined in the MThd chunk's tracks field mentioned above. For example, if the MThd chunk indicates that this is a format 0 MIDI file with one MIDI track, there will be only one MTrk chunk following the MThd chunk. On the other hand, if this is a format 1 MIDI file and it has sixteen tracks, the MThd chunk should be followed by at least sixteen MTrk chunks (see Figure C.4).

Figure C.4
The MTrk chunk and its different types of events

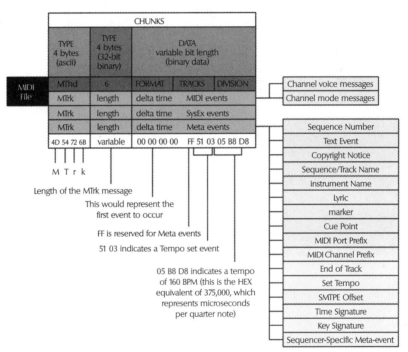

In a single MTrk chunk, you can have three types of events:

> ▶ MIDI events: This is the core of the MIDI file, since it represents all channel voice messages and channel mode messages as defined in this book. Running status (see note) is applicable within MIDI files. Running status is cancelled by any SysEx or meta event.

> ▶ SysEx events: These can be both manufacturer specific and universal system exclusive event messages that are saved in a MIDI file.

> ▶ Meta data events: These are used for things like track names, lyrics, and cue-points, which don't result in MIDI messages being sent, but are still useful components of a MIDI file.

WHAT IS A RUNNING STATUS?

Since many messages share the same status byte information, a running status means that all subsequent MIDI messages that are sent with the same status byte information will omit this similar status byte from the message and only transmit the data bytes.

Here's an example: Let's say a musician plays a 3-note chord (C3-E3-G3) over channel 1. If you look at the left message in Figure C.5, this is what you would get. Each status byte is identical and adds redundant information to the MIDI message. However, a running status, as found on the right of this figure, shows that the status byte is only found at the beginning of the set of MIDI events that carries the same status byte. When a running status occurs, no additional information is added to the MIDI message or string of messages, but, rather, the sequencer will omit saving the redundant information in its MIDI stream. Similarly, MIDI devices will understand that a running status is in effect when receiving only a series of data bytes. For this to work, certain rules apply:

▶ A running status can only be used as long as the same status byte still applies, as shown in Figure C.5. It will stay active until a new status byte is received; in other words, there are no time limits to running status bytes.

▶ It only applies to channel voice and channel mode messages. Furthermore, it is not affected by system real-time messages.

▶ Any SysEx or system common message as well as a device power on will cancel the running status. If a running status is cancelled, subsequent data bytes are ignored until the next status byte arrives.

Using a running status will reduce the MIDI data needed to communicate information, thus making the communication more efficient. This is particularly important when large amounts of data are transmitted over a single MIDI port. Sequencers and MIDI files will usually use a running status.

Figure C.5
Comparing normal
MIDI messages without
running status bytes
(on the left) with the
same MIDI message
with a running status
byte (on the right)

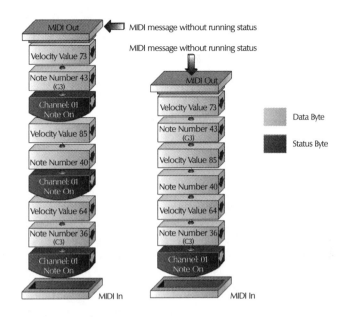

MIDI Events

MIDI events such as channel voice and channel common messages are transmitted/saved in the same way they are transmitted through MIDI, with the exception that they have a deltatime stamp attached to each of them. So, if we look at the example in Figure C.5, the MIDI data would contain the subsequent information in the MTrk chunk data field. Note that the deltatime is equal to zero because all events are played simultaneously, rather than one after the other. Therefore, there are no delays between each event.

Table C.5
Content of the MTrk data field for a C major chord MIDI event with running status.

Deltatime (in variable-length quantity)	Status byte	Status value in Hex	First data byte	Hex value	Second data byte	Hex value
00	Note On, Channel 1	90	Note number	24	64	40
00	(running status)	N/A	Note number	28	85	55
00	(running status)	N/A	Note number	2B	73	49

The complete MTrk data in hex format for this event would look like this:

▶ 4D 54 72 6B 0A 00 90 24 40 00 28 55 00 73 49

In the example above, the values in italic represent the chunk's type, the value in bold represents the length of the data field, the underlined values represent the deltatime values, and the normal text represents the MIDI events themselves.

SysEx Events

The only difference with SysEx sent over MIDI in real time and SysEx found in an SMF is the addition of the deltatime value after the Start SysEx status byte. For example, if you had this SysEx message sent in real time:

▶ F0 41 10 6A 12 01 00 00 28 06 51 F7

It would look like this in an SMF (notice the second value, which represents the deltatime in variable length quantity format):

▶ F0 07 41 10 6A 12 01 00 00 28 06 51 F7

Meta Events

Meta data events are used to store special non-MIDI related information that is relevant to a standard MIDI file. All Meta events begin with the reserved status byte value FF, which identifies it appropriately as a Meta event. This is followed by the type's identification byte and acts like a second status byte, since it defines the values that follow it. Following the identification is the data's length value in variable length quantity format, which includes only the actual length of the data for this event, not the type and the length byte itself.

Meta events are not mandatory unless otherwise specified, and certain sequencers might not support some Meta events. In this case, they would simply be ignored. You can also find more than one Meta event per MTrk chunk. When this happens, Meta events are separated by their respective deltatime value to indicate the time at which they should occur following the previous event. This implies that MIDI events and Meta events can coexist in the same MTrk chunk.

There are sixteen defined Meta event types that can hold information such as track names, MIDI port information, time signatures, tempo settings, and so on. The next sections detail these.

Sequence number

▶ When: This is an optional event that must occur before any non-zero deltatime events and before any MIDI events of a MTrk chunk.

▶ Common identifying value: FF 00 02

▶ Number of data bytes: 2 bytes

▶ Complete message representation in hex: FF 00 02 XX XX, where XX are variable value bytes.

▶ Represents: In a MIDI file format 0 or 1, this event is placed in the first MTrk chunk and represents the sequence number. If there were several MIDI files, this would represent the song collection's number; in other words, each file would contain its own sequence number. There can only be one sequence number for the whole file. In a MIDI file format 2, this number represents each pattern or MTrk chunk. If the XX XX value is omitted in the SMF, then the first MTrk chunk is the first pattern. There can be one sequence number per MTrk chunk.

Text event

▶ When: This is an optional Meta event, but usually this is found at the beginning of an MTrk chunk.

▶ Common identifying value: FF 01

▶ Number of data bytes: Variable

▶ Complete message representation in hex: FF 01 LL LL XX XX XX…, where LL represents the length of this event in byte and XX represents the actual text in 8-bit ASCII or 8-bit binary format. The length is expressed in variable length quantity format and can use as many bytes as it needs.

▶ Represents: Any amount of text for any purpose, such as adding comments on the song, MIDI setup instructions.

Copyright

▶ When: This is an optional Meta event, but usually is found at the beginning of an MTrk chunk.

▶ Common identifying value: FF 02

▶ Number of data bytes: Variable

▶ Complete message representation in hex: FF 02 LL LL XX XX XX…, where LL represents the length of this event in byte and XX represents the actual text in 8-bit ASCII or 8-bit binary format. The length is expressed in variable length quantity format and can use as many bytes as it needs.

▶ Represents: A copyright text message.

Sequence/track name

▶ When: This is an optional Meta event, but usually this is found at the beginning of an MTrk chunk.

▶ Common identifying value: FF 03

▶ Number of data bytes: Variable

▶ Complete message representation in hex: FF 03 LL LL XX XX XX…, where LL represents the length of this event in byte and XX represents the actual text in 8-bit ASCII or 8-bit binary format. The length is expressed in variable length quantity format and can use as many bytes as it needs.

▶ Represents: The text representing the name of the sequence or track.

APPENDIX C

Instrument

▶ When: This is an optional Meta event, but usually is found at the beginning of an MTrk chunk.

▶ Common identifying value: FF 04

▶ Number of data bytes: Variable

▶ Complete message representation in hex: FF 04 LL LL XX XX XX…, where LL represents the length of this event in byte and XX represents the actual text in 8-bit ASCII or 8-bit binary format. The length is expressed in variable length quantity format and can use as many bytes as it needs.

▶ Represents: The name of a track as found in most sequencers. This could represent the actual instrument's name, or something else, since you could have a track playing a guitar instrument, but choose to call this track "Rhythm Guit." Usually, the actual instruments are set by the MIDI device's program change event within the MTrk chunk if these program changes have been saved with the MIDI file. This is especially true when it comes to GM sound module program changes. This is a visual aid to identify a track.

Lyric

▶ When: This is an optional Meta event and can occur anywhere in the MTrk chunk.

▶ Common identifying value: FF 05

▶ Number of data bytes: Variable

▶ Complete message representation in hex: FF 05 LL LL XX XX XX…, where LL represents the length of this event in byte and XX represents the actual text in 8-bit ASCII or 8-bit binary format. The length is expressed in variable length quantity format and can use as many bytes as it needs.

▶ Represents: Text for a song's lyrics, which occurs on a given beat. A single lyric Meta event should contain only one syllable.

Marker

▶ When: This is an optional Meta event and can occur anywhere in the MTrk chunk.

▶ Common identifying value: FF 06

▶ Number of data bytes: Variable

▶ Complete message representation in hex: FF 06 LL LL XX XX XX…, where LL represents the length of this event in byte and XX represents the actual text in 8-bit ASCII or 8-bit binary format. The length is expressed in variable length quantity format and can use as many bytes as it needs.

▶ Represents: Text that represents a marker occurring on a given beat. Marker events might be used to denote a loop start and loop end (i.e. where the sequence loops back to a previous event).

Cue point

▶ When: This is an optional Meta event and can occur anywhere in the MTrk chunk.

▶ Common identifying value: FF 07

▶ Number of data bytes: Variable

▶ Complete message representation in hex: FF 07 LL LL XX XX XX…, where LL represents the length of this event in byte and XX represents the actual text in 8-bit ASCII or 8-bit binary format. The length is expressed in variable length quantity format and can use as many bytes as it needs.

▶ Represents: Text representing a cue point that occurs on a given beat. A cue point might be used to denote where an audio file or sampled sound starts playing. The text in this case would represent the file's name.

MIDI channel

▶ When: This is an optional Meta event, but usually this is found at the beginning of an MTrk chunk before any Meta event but after the sequence number Meta event.

▶ Common identifying value: FF 20 01

▶ Number of data bytes: 1 byte

▶ Complete message representation in hex: FF 20 01 XX, where XX represents the MIDI channel. A value of 0 represents the first MIDI channel.

▶ Represents: Since MIDI file format 0 saves all parts in one track—therefore one MTrk chunk—you can assign a MIDI channel Meta data to associate a channel with subsequent Meta events or MIDI voice messages, since both would be in the same track. For example, you could have the rhythm guitar playing on MIDI channel 1 and the melodic guitar playing on MIDI channel 2, therefore naming these two parts through the instrument Meta event and then assigning a MIDI channel to these parts. It is also possible to have more than one MIDI channel event in a given track, if that track needs to associate various events with various channels.

MIDI port

▶ When: This is an optional Meta event, but usually is found at the beginning of an MTrk chunk before any MIDI events.

▶ Common identifying value: FF 21 01

▶ Number of data bytes: 1 byte

▶ Complete message representation in hex: FF 21 01 XX, where XX represents the MIDI port number. A value of 0 represents the first MIDI port in the system.

▶ Represents: This is used to identify a specific MIDI port on your system, while saving a MIDI file. This allows you to use more than sixteen MIDI channels (sixteen per port).

APPENDIX C

End of track

▶ When: This is not an optional Meta event and it should be found at the end of every MTrk chunk in a MIDI file.

▶ Common identifying value: FF 2F 00

▶ Number of data bytes: none

▶ Complete message representation in hex: FF 2F 00

▶ Represents: This is used to identify the end of an MTrk chunk. There will be only one end of each track Meta event per MTrk chunk.

Tempo

▶ When: This is an optional Meta event and can occur anywhere in the MTrk chunk. If there are no Tempo Meta events in the MTrk chunk, the default tempo setting assumed will be 120 BPM.

▶ Common identifying value: FF 51 03

▶ Number of data bytes: 3 bytes

▶ Complete message representation in hex: FF 51 03 XX XX XX, where XX represents the value in microseconds per quarter note of the tempo; in other words, how long each quarter note in the sequencer will be.

▶ Represents: Indicates a tempo change in microsecond per quarter note format. For example, a tempo of 160 BPM would be converted into microseconds (375,000 microseconds), then into hex (05 B8 D8). This represents the amount of microseconds for each quarter note.

SMPTE offset

▶ When: This is an optional Meta event. If the file is in MIDI format 1, it should be stored with the tempo map in the first MTrk chunk and will have no meaning in any other MTrk chunk. It also has to appear, when it does, at the beginning of the MTrk chunk, before any MIDI events.

▶ Common identifying value: FF 54 05

▶ Number of data bytes: 5 bytes

▶ Complete message representation in hex: FF 54 05 HH MM SS FF BB, where HH represents the hour value of the SMPTE, MM the minute value, SS the second value, FF the frame value, and BB the subframe value in one-hundredths frame division, even if MThd division setting specifies a different subframe division setting.

▶ Represents: This is the SMPTE start time in hour, minute, second, frame, and subframe format for the MTrk chunk. A SMPTE offset refers to the SMPTE time at which the sequence should start. For example, you might have an SMPTE offset at 09:59:45:00:00, which implies that bar one, beat one of the MIDI file will only start when it receives this SMPTE (converted into MTC) time stamp.

Time signature

▶ When: This is an optional Meta event and can occur anywhere in the MTrk chunk. If there are no time signature Meta events in the MTrk chunk, the default time signature setting assumed will be 4/4.

▶ Common identifying value: FF 58 04

▶ Number of data bytes: 4 bytes

▶ Complete message representation in hex: FF 54 05 NN DD MM CC, where NN represents the numerator value of the time signature. DD represents the denominator value and is a negative power of two, where 2 is equal to a quarter note, 3 to an eighth note, and so on. MM represents the number of MIDI clocks in a metronome click, and CC represents the number of notated thirty-second notes in a MIDI quarter note (or the 24 MIDI clocks). The standard is usually eight since there are normally eight thirty-second notes per quarter note.

▶ Represents: This allows a program to relate what MIDI thinks of as a quarter note, or if it is something different. For example, if you have a 4/4 time signature, the event would read as follows: (FF 58 04) 04 02 18 08, where the first 04 represents four values defined by the next DD byte, 02 (which represents quarter notes, or 2 to the power of 2 is equal to 4). This means that there are four quarter notes per bar. 18 in hex is 24 in decimal, which implies that there are twenty-four MIDI clocks in one quarter note, and 08 means that there are eight thirty-second notes per quarter note. Here's another example: If you have a 9/8 time signature, the event would read as follows: (FF 58 04) 09 03 24 08, where the first 09 represents how many values there will be defined by the denominator byte, 03 in this case (2 to the power of 3 is equal to 8). Each dotted quarter note value holds thirty-six MIDI clocks (twenty-four in Hex) and there are eight thirty-second notes per quarter note (by default).

Key signature

▶ When: This is an optional Meta event and can occur anywhere in the MTrk chunk.

▶ Common identifying value: FF 59 02

▶ Number of data bytes: 2 bytes

▶ Complete message representation in hex: FF 59 02 AA MM, where AA represents the number of accidents in the key signature. A value of minus seven would mean seven flats, minus six would mean six flats, and so on. Zero would represent the key of C (no flats and default key if Meta event is not present). Positive values represent the number of sharps, up to seven sharps. The MM value represents the key mode. A value of zero represents a major mode and one a minor mode.

▶ Represents: This allows you to set a particular key signature to an MTrk chunk.

Proprietary event

▶ When: This is an optional Meta event and can occur anywhere in the MTrk chunk.

▶ Common identifying value: FF 7F

▶ Number of data bytes: variable

▶ Complete message representation in hex: FF 7F LL LL XX XX, where LL represents the length of this event in byte and XX represents the actual text in 8-bit ASCII or 8-bit binary format. The length is expressed in variable length quantity format and can use as many bytes as it needs.

▶ Represents: A program to store proprietary data can use this. The first bytes should be a unique ID, which identifies the program using these proprietary events, or to some other program that might recognize it. A four ASCII character ID is recommended for this.

Appendix D
Understanding Timing Concepts

As a musician, you are probably familiar with the concept of beats per minute (or BPM) when working with sequences. This usually determines the speed at which the song will play. However, sequencers use other timing mechanisms, such as sequence resolution, which determines the precision of each quarter note. Then, there are the synchronization concepts inherent to any type of work where two or more devices need to be locked together. This is the case with MIDI clock, mainly used to synchronize two or more MIDI devices, and SMPTE, which is used when working with video or time-based projects.

Since MIDI files save information regarding these timing concepts, it might be useful to understand how they can relate to one another. This might help you to identify problems that might occur with timing or synchronization.

Beats Per Minute (BPM)

Since this is probably the most common way to express the speed of a musical project, let's start here. BPM expresses the tempo of a song by defining how many quarter notes are found in each minute. MIDI files, however, use the opposite of this to express timing. BPM expresses the number of quarter notes per time, whereas MIDI files use time per quarter notes. This makes it easier to specify more precise tempo divisions than with BPM.

A quarter note always refers to a single beat, no matter what the tempo is or the time signature division. This value is not the most precise way to count information in the computer or sequencer world, however, since a beat may be shorter in some cases and longer in others, depending on both the time signature and tempo setting of the song. It's also possible that both of these values might change along the way in the song.

For a musician, a tempo of 60 BPM means that there will be 60 evenly spaced beats in every minute. This determines the speed of the song. To convert this tempo into a MIDI File format's tempo, using the three bytes of data in the MThd chunk, you need to convert the value of a quarter note into the number of microseconds each quarter note takes to play back.

One microsecond is the equivalent of one one-millionth of a second (1/1,000,000). So, in one minute, there are 60,000,000 microseconds. If you want to know how many microseconds each quarter note lasts, you need to divide 60,000,000 by the BPM value. For example, at 60 BPM,

60,000,000 / 60 = 1,000,000 microseconds (in hex: 0F 42 40), or 1 second, since 60 BPM is the equivalent of one beat every second. At a tempo of 160 BPM, 60,000,000 / 160 = 375,000 microseconds (in hex: 05 B8 D8) for each beat or quarter note. Another more precise application of this would be with a finer resolution tempo, such as 120.56 BPM, which would be 497,677 microseconds to the quarter note. By using time per quarter note instead of quarter notes per time, a greater resolution is provided, without the use of fractions.

Later, if you need to lock MIDI with time code, using the time per quarter note will become increasingly useful, since SMPTE also uses a time scale, based on hours, minutes, seconds, and frames. Having a reference to time will help resolve the differences between BPM and SMPTE.

Pulses Per Quarter Note (PPQN)

Sequencers use an internal timing resolution to synchronize events known as Pulse Per Quarter Note (PPQN). This division is also called "ticks." In other words, a tick is the smallest unit in your sequencer's resolution. Your sequencer will then use the PPQN resolution to represent the location in time of a MIDI event, rather than using a microsecond value. For example, you might see that an event occurs at 1.1.48. This implies that an event occurred at bar one, beat one and a half, if the sequencer's PPQN or resolution is set to 96 PPQN, where 48 represents the eighth note value. Today's sequencers typically offer much higher PPQN resolution, going from 96 PPQN to 1920 PPQN. Sequencers using such a high resolution will usually subdivide each beat into sixteenth notes, adding the PPQN after this. For example, 1.1.48 would then become 1.1.2.0000, where the value two represents the second sixteenth note value.

Using the BPM's microsecond value, you can then determine how long each pulse in a PPQN resolution lasts. Do this by dividing the value of microsecond per quarter note by the PPQN value. For example, each pulse (or tick) in a song playing at 160 BPM with a 96 PPQN resolution would last 3,906.25 microseconds.

Here's the formula:

▶ (microseconds per minute) divided by (beats per minute) = 60,000,000 / 160 = 375,000 microseconds per quarter note.

▶ (microseconds per quarter note) divided by (pulses per quarter note) = 375,000 / 96 = 3,906.25 microseconds per pulse.

In other words, to have a resolution of 96 PPQN at a tempo of 160 BPM, each pulse will last 3,906.25 microseconds, or 3.9025 milliseconds, or 0.0039062 seconds.

Both BPM and PPQN values are independent of each other, since you can change the sequencer's resolution without affecting its BPM setting. However, a higher resolution will yield a greater precision in the timing of MIDI events in relation to the performance itself. With more precision in resolution, you get more accurate MIDI timing in your recording of a MIDI performance. And that's where all the subtleties of interpretation come into play.

A faster BPM will result in shorter pulse times, and a slower BPM will result in longer pulse times.

MIDI Clock

The MIDI clock, as mentioned earlier, serves mostly to keep two MIDI playback devices in sync by generating a MIDI clock signal every one twenty-fourth of quarter note. In other words, you always have 24 MIDI clocks per quarter note. This clock is tempo dependant, as with the PPQN resolution. However, it is far less precise than its PPQN counterpart, since it divides each quarter note into only 24 values. This value is interpreted as a tempo-based timing clock.

To relate a MIDI clock with the tempo's microsecond value, you need to divide the quarter note's microsecond value by the number of MIDI clock it holds, which is always set to 24. Keeping our previous example of 160 BPM, where each quarter note lasts 375,000 microseconds, you would divide this value by 24. Here's the formula to do this:

▶ (microseconds per minute) divided by (beats per minute) = 60,000,000 / 160 = 375,000 microseconds per quarter note.

▶ (microseconds per quarter note) divided by (MIDI clock per quarter note) = 375,000 / 24 = 15,625 microseconds per MIDI clock tick.

In relation to the PPQN, if you are using a resolution of 1920 PPQN, each MIDI clock will represent 80 PPQN clocks. At 96 PPQN, each MIDI clock will represent 4 PPQN.

SMPTE

SMPTE keeps track of time, not tempo. It is a time-based synchronizing mechanism rather than a tempo-based mechanism, such as BPM, PPQN, and MIDI clock. There are four types of SMPTE time codes: 24 frames per seconds, 25 frames per seconds, 29 frames per second (which is actually 29.97 frames per second with drop frame; see Chapter 11 for more details), and 30 frames per second (which is actually 29.97 frames per second without drop frame). Further subdivision of time breaks up each one of these frames into subframes.

To better understand the concept of time-based timing in relation to tempo-based timing, compare audio to MIDI. For example, if you look at Figure D.1, you will notice on the left side that a series of notes are played at 127 BPM. At this speed, the entire series of events, or entire bar, fits into 1.89 seconds. The audio event also plays at the same beat and also fits into 1.89 seconds. However, if you change the tempo to 60 BPM, the MIDI events within the same bar will take 4 seconds to play, whereas the audio file still plays within 1.89 seconds. This is one example of how relative tempo timing differs from absolute timebased timing.

Figure D.1
Comparing MIDI and
audio events

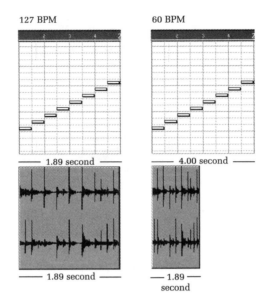

Furthermore, if you look at Figure D.2, you will find the SMPTE time line at the bottom. This represents time in hours, minutes, seconds, and frames (no subframes are included in this example). In the center of the figure, you can see the first frame of a scene, which starts at the SMPTE time stamp of 01:00:04:00 (or one hour, four seconds). At the top, you can also see two tempo timelines. The one right above the video frame is set to play at 120 BPM, while the timeline above that is set to play at 60 BPM. Notice that if the song plays at 120 BPM, the bar and beat location corresponding to the first frame in the video is bar 3, beat 1. On the other hand, if the sequence plays at 60 BPM, the same first frame will correspond to bar 2, beat 1.

If you consider the end of the frame to be the end of the video sequence, then at 120 BPM, the video sequence will play over eight complete bars, whereas if the MIDI file plays at 60 BPM, the same video will play over four bars.

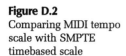

Figure D.2
Comparing MIDI tempo
scale with SMPTE
timebased scale

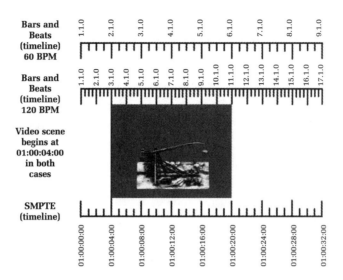

In order for a MIDI file to lock to a time code such as SMPTE, the microsecond-measuring units are once again invoked.

Many MIDI devices will use an MTC-converted SMPTE time code to synchronize with video players, for example. In other words, the SMPTE is converted into a format that is supported by MIDI files, such as MTC. Internally, your sequence will still have to keep a PPQN resolution and a BPM tempo. By converting the passing of subframes and frames into microseconds, you can find a match for each pulse. Let's take an easy example to illustrate this. If you have a frame rate of 25 fps (frames per second) and 40 sfps (subframes per second), you would have a total of 1,000 subframes in one second. Each subframe would last 1 millisecond, or 1,000 microseconds (1,000 microseconds = 1 millisecond, 1,000 milliseconds = 1 second).

Let's go back to our example of a sequence playing at 160 BPM with a 96 PPQN resolution. We had found that each quarter note takes 375,000 microseconds. If you divide this by 1,000 subframes, you will end up with the value representing the number of subframes actually fitting into one quarter note. So 375,000 / 1,000 = 375 subframes per quarter note. Now, since you have 96 pulses in each quarter note, you need to divide the number of subframes per quarter note in order to have completed the circle back to the value in milliseconds of subframes. In this case: 375 subframes / 96 PPQN = 3.90625 subframes will pass in every pulse. Since this value is in milliseconds, multiplying it by 1,000 should give you the exact same microsecond per pulse value, which is 3,906.25 at this speed and PPQN resolution.

APPENDIX D

Formulas

Here is a recap of these and other useful formulas:

▶ Getting the microseconds per beat value (MSPB): 60,000,000 / BPM

▶ Getting the microseconds per pulse value (MSPP): MSPB / PPQN

▶ Getting the microseconds per clock value (MSPC): MSPB / 24

▶ Extracting the BPM from the MSPB value: 60,000,000 / MSPB

▶ Getting the number of PPQN per MIDI clock: PPQN / 24

▶ Getting the number of subframes per quarter note (SFPQN): MSPB / (frames per second × subframes per second)

▶ Getting the number of subframes per pulse (SFPP): SFPQN / PPQN

▶ Getting the amount of microseconds per subframe (MSPSF): 1,000,000 × frames × subframes

▶ Getting the number of microseconds per pulse (MSPP) using frames and subframes: (SFPQN/PPQN) × frames per second × subframes per second

Appendix E
The MIDI Troubleshooting Checklist

If you find yourself perplexed or facing a problem you just can't seem to resolve, this appendix offers a checklist of questions and procedures that can help. Usually, things get complicated when we don't know where to start, and then we circle around the problem, sometimes never finding a solution. These questions may help you find something you overlooked in your setup—perhaps the one missing piece that's causing your current trouble.

Each section covers a specific type of problem. You should read each question and be in a position to verify it if it applies to you or if you can say "yes" to the question. If you can't answer the question, or realize that in order to say yes you need to make a change to your setup, then make the change and try again. If the problem hasn't been solved, continue reading until you reach the end of the list. If, following a change, you find it solved your problem, then stop reading and start working on your project.

I Can't Hear Any Sound

When trying to access sounds from a MIDI keyboard controller:

- ▶ Is the device supposed to generate sounds?
- ▶ Is the volume turned up high enough?
- ▶ Is your audio output connected to a sound-monitoring device such as an amplifier and speakers or a pair of headphones? If so, are those powered up and ready to receive the audio signal? Is the level on those devices set so that you can hear something?
- ▶ Is your keyboard's Local MIDI setting set to the "On" position? If not, change it.
- ▶ If your keyboard is a sampler, perhaps you need to load sounds into its memory before continuing. Are there any sounds currently loaded into your memory?
- ▶ Are you in the device's "Play" mode? Some devices, such as workstations, will have different modes, and some of them will not allow you to hear the sounds as you play unless you are in the proper mode.

When trying to access sounds from a sound module while triggering events from a controller keyboard:

▶ Make sure you've checked the previous list of questions before you continue.

▶ Is the MIDI Out of your keyboard connected to the MIDI In of your sound module?

▶ Are you sure the MIDI cable is securely connected at both ends? Has this MIDI cable been tested in a successful setup before? Sometimes, we assume the problem is with the way things are connected. Though that's often the case, faulty MIDI cables may also be the cause of bad MIDI transmissions.

▶ Is your controller keyboard sending MIDI events over the same MIDI channel as set in the sound module?

▶ Are there any intermediary devices between the MIDI device sending the information and the one receiving it? If so, are the MIDI connections appropriate for this setup (MIDI Out of device 1 to MIDI In of device 2, then MIDI Thru of device 2 to MIDI In of device 3, and so on)?

When sending MIDI from a controller keyboard to a MIDI sequencer:

▶ Make sure you've checked the two previous lists of questions before you continue. It is always easier to troubleshoot a problem when you've got the bases covered. The previous questions help ensure that everything outside of your computer setup is hooked up properly and is functional.

▶ Is your keyboard's MIDI Out connected to the computer's MIDI In? If there's a device between the controller and the computer, is the MIDI connection set up properly?

▶ Is the MIDI interface to which your keyboard hooks up to installed properly on your computer? In other words, have you been able to send MIDI successfully using this MIDI interface? If you are not certain, verify that your MIDI interface is installed and functional before continuing.

▶ If you are using a Mac, is either FreeMIDI or OMS installed on your computer? This is especially important in two instances: If you are not running on OSX, and if you are using a multi-port MIDI interface.

▶ Did you configure your software to receive from the proper MIDI input port?

▶ Did you set the MIDI track to play on the proper MIDI channel? In other words, does the track MIDI channel assignment correspond to the device's MIDI channel, and is this MIDI channel active on your MIDI device?

▶ Multi-timbral MIDI devices can set parts to play certain MIDI channels and not others. You can also set a multi-timbral device to respond—or not—to a specific MIDI channel. Are you sure your MIDI device is set to respond to the channel setting in your sequencer's track?

▶ Is your MIDI sequencer at least receiving MIDI from its input? Most MIDI sequencers have a MIDI activity display that lets you see if a signal is received or not. If you don't see any activity from the MIDI input monitor window, you might want to go back and verify the previous links in your chain (by making sure you've checked the previous questions in this appendix).

▶ If there is MIDI activity entering the MIDI sequencer but nothing happens at this point, try re-routing the MIDI coming into your sequencer to another device or another MIDI channel to see if your MIDI output is working. Are other instruments (software or hardware) responding to MIDI events being sent by your keyboard controller?

▶ Have you looked at your MIDI configurations inside your software application to find out if it is not filtering a specific type of MIDI event? Usually, SysEx events are filtered, which, unless you are doing SysEx transfers, is fine.

▶ If you are trying to access the built-in sounds on your sound card, you will need to use a sequencer or other type of MIDI application to connect the MIDI In of your computer to the sound card's onboard synthesizer. In other words, your sound card's MIDI input will not automatically receive the MIDI from this input unless you "echo" it back to the sound module on this sound card; you do this through a MIDI Thru switch found in a MIDI application such as a sequencer.

When sending MIDI from one software to another inside your computer:

▶ Have you connected both applications through a virtual MIDI port that would allow these two applications to exchange MIDI messages?

▶ Does your sound card have multi-client support? In some cases, when software takes over the control of the sound card, any other application that attempts to access the sound card will be denied access. If this second application is a software instrument, chances are you won't hear anything. Consult your sound card and software documentation to find out how to deal with this issue.

I Have a MIDI Feedback Loop

A MIDI feedback loop occurs when a MIDI message is sent back to the device that initially sent it and plays again, then sends it back into the same MIDI cable and…well, you get the point. It's a loop and it's nasty. To avoid loops, here's what you can do:

▶ Use the MIDI Out connector only on the device you will be using as a controller. Typically, if you are using a keyboard and some sound modules, use the MIDI Thru from all the other devices if they are used in a chain.

▶ Unless your keyboard is used on its own or in a live setup without a patch bay or a computer, you should make a habit of setting it to Local Off mode in order to prevent it from playing its own sounds twice. Normally, in a computer setup or in a patch bay setup, you can set the output of the computer or patch bay to send MIDI messages back to the keyboard. That way, you can hear the audio result of these MIDI messages.

▶ Avoid configurations in which all the outputs of all MIDI devices are connected to all inputs of all MIDI devices when using a MIDI patch bay or a multi-port MIDI interface. This type of setting will surely be susceptible to MIDI feedback loops. Create different settings for different needs.

▶ You might also want to check some typical MIDI setups found earlier in this book to figure out the best way to hook up your equipment.

▶ A virtual MIDI port might cause a MIDI feedback loop between two applications. Make sure the virtual MIDI doesn't echo the MIDI messages back to the source of the MIDI events being sent.

I'm Having MIDI Sync Problems

Synchronizing two MIDI devices together can be a bit tricky. In some cases, especially when older MIDI devices are part of your setup, the MIDI sync capabilities might be limited. However, understanding the basic principle of synchronization will help you establish a successful sync between two devices.

This basic principle reads as follows: There should be only one master sending its synchronizing signal to one or more other devices. Once you've got this down, all you need to figure out is what kind of sync this device can output and how to set every other device in the chain to lock to this signal.

Following are some common sync options.

When using MIDI clock to sync two MIDI devices such as a drum machine and a MIDI sequencer:

▶ Make sure the master device is set to send the sync signal.

▶ Make sure the MIDI connection between the two devices is set appropriately, both in terms of hardware connection (through MIDI cables) and through software setup (assigning a specific MIDI port through which you are sending the MIDI clock, and a MIDI port through which you are receiving a MIDI clock).

▶ Set the receiving device to slave to the external MIDI clock.

▶ Make sure the type of sync signal, in this case a MIDI clock, is the same on both devices. Having one device set to receive a MIDI clock while the master is sending an MTC will not work.

When using MTC to sync two MIDI devices or a MIDI device to a video playback device:

▶ Most video playback devices with time code on them will not have MIDI Time Code (MTC), but rather SMPTE time code. To use SMPTE with a sequencer, for example, you will need to convert it to MTC first, so you will need to have an SMPTE-to-MTC converter somewhere in your setup.

▶ Once you've determined that you do indeed have an SMPTE-to-MTC converter, you will need to set this converter to send out the MTC signal it converted from the SMPTE master to any other device it should control. Sending a converted SMPTE-to-MTC time code to a slave device implies that you will control the MIDI playback from the video playback. Make sure your MIDI device is set to receive (or slave to) the MTC.

▶ Set your synchronization options properly in your receiving device. If you are transmitting 24 fps time code, then this device should be set accordingly.

▶ Make sure your device—your sequencer, for example—is also looking for a sync signal on the correct MIDI port. Then, activate the sync option in your application to start only when it is locked with the incoming MTC signal.

▶ If you are using two MIDI devices and one generates MTC while the other slaves to it, make sure, once again, that the master/slave relationship is observed and that all MIDI ports used to transmit and receive the MTC signal are configured properly in the appropriate setup windows.

Appendix F
MIDI Arrangements: Tips & Tricks

Working with sequencers is a great way to create and edit your music. Getting around in your sequencer's environment is one thing, but knowing how to get the best results from it depends greatly on the sequencer application you will be using. However, there are some tricks that can help you get more out of your musical arrangement. Remember: The tools you are using to create music will not necessarily make your music better. How you write and arrange your music, however, will make all the difference.

This appendix will focus on ideas for making your MIDI sequences sound better, no matter which sequencer application you are using. After all, a sequencer is only a tool that lets you organize and edit your musical ideas; it won't make the music for you.

Getting a Thicker Sound

To many ears, getting a thicker sound often means adding musical parts. While this can be a good way to add more depth to your musical arrangement, it might also lead to an overcrowded and muddled arrangement, where the important musical parts get lost in a sea of notes and rhythmic patterns.

Quite often, the desire for a thicker sounding arrangement comes from the fact that the sounds used in the current arrangement are not thick enough to convey the depth you had hoped for. This is often the case when using low quality sound modules or GM sound banks alone. The following tips will help you thicken your sound without adding musical parts to your arrangement.

Doubling Parts

Sometimes, all your part needs is a bigger sound. To achieve this using a GM device, you can create a copy of a part onto another track and assign it a second, similar patch. For example, try using two piano sounds or two string ensemble sounds.

Once you've doubled your part, you can pan the first hard left and the second hard right. The drawback to this technique is that you will now be using twice as many voices in your sound module. In other words, if you were playing a three-note harmony part in which each note uses two voices in your sound module, instead of taking up six voices it will now take up twelve. If your sound module is limited to twenty-four voices, you will need to make sure not to use too many doubled parts. An alternative is to bounce completed MIDI parts to audio, if your sequencer supports both audio and MIDI sequencing.

In Figure F.1, you can see that the events playing on both tracks are the same, but they play on different MIDI channels. Furthermore, one track is panned hard left and the other (the one selected in the figure) is panned hard right (found to the left of the pointer in the figure).

Figure F.1
The same part is copied onto another track, playing simultaneously, but with a different patch

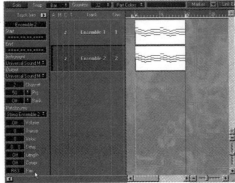

Adding Delay

To increase the effect of the previous technique, you can add a very slight delay between the two tracks by shifting all the events in one track forward or backward a couple of ticks. You may want to use the instrument with the more noticeable attack as the original, and the instrument with the less noticeable attack as the delayed part. Don't add too much delay, or you will hear both instruments as separate entities, and that will only muddy your arrangement.

If your sequencer uses a quantization grid when you are editing the events, make sure this grid is turned off. Otherwise, you will not be able to move over these events in small increments. You should also make sure that you select all the events in a part before using this method, to avoid having some notes farther apart than others.

This technique basically simulates what happens in the real world when more than one musician plays the same part, as when twenty violinists play the same notes. These twenty players will play in sync, but there will always be very small variations in their attack time. These variations blur the attack a bit, making it sound thicker.

In Figure F.2, you can see the same part played on two channels and displayed in a single piano roll editing window. Here, the first part plays on the beat and appears in a lighter shade. The second part, played on another channel, appears on top with a darker shade. As you can see, the delay between the two parts is very small, making the attack difference barely noticeable.

Figure F.2
The delayed notes
appear in a darker shade
over the original part
that's in a lighter
shade—you can notice
this mostly at the bar 5
mark

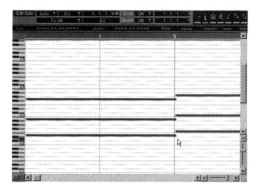

Detuning

You may also want to slightly detune a set of doubled parts. For example, by setting the first
part a few cents off, using either the finetune parameter on your device or adding one pitch
bend event at the beginning of each track (see Figure F.3), you can increase the width of the
sound. For a better result, you should tune one instrument sharp and the second instrument flat
by the same amount, so that the ear centers the end pitch, as it should be. Note that you should
use this in conjunction with the doubling part technique, in which a musical part is doubled up
on two different MIDI channels and panned hard left and hard right.

Figure F.3
The left window shows
that the instrument's
pitch bend level is set
down, while the right
window shows the
pitch bend level is up,
creating a slight detune
effect

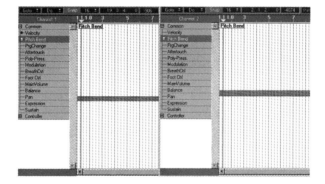

Orchestrate

One of the philosophies behind orchestration is to double an existing musical line at a different
pitch or different volume level using different instruments, rather than making every instrument
in the orchestra play a different musical part. For example, the flute might play a line and the
piccolo might double that line one octave higher (see Figure F.4). The flute and piccolo have a
similar timbre. They do differ slightly, though, and while the intensity of the doubled line will
not change tremendously, its overall effect will sound different than if the flute were to play the
line on its own.

You can apply this principle as well, even if you are not using orchestral instruments in your arrangement. This is done by doubling a musical line and transposing this line one octave higher or lower. Doing this will add emphasis to the line, drawing more attention to it. In other words, use this technique only when appropriate; otherwise, attention will be drawn away from more important parts.

Figure F.4
Example of a doubled melodic part—the first staff played by the piccolo doubles the flute one octave (12 half-steps or semi-tones) higher

You may also want to try doubling a third (three half-steps above for a minor third or four half-steps for a major third) or a perfect fifth (seven half-steps above or five half-steps below) to get a different color altogether.

When you double a line like this, you will want to adjust the volume level of the secondary part in order to make it sound farther away, so that the primary line sounds different—as opposed to simply hearing two parts playing the same line.

Large Voicing

When you lay out a harmonic progression using a piano or guitar, you might be using one hand with closed voicing, in which every note in the chord is not far from the other one. This is a good way to get the idea of where the chords should go harmonically. It is easier to play a chord progression when all notes are close by rather than when each note in the chord is far apart from the other note in the same chord, not to mention moving your fingers to other notes as the chords change. However, when adding instruments, such as harmonic pads, to your song, you might get a bigger bang for your buck if you space out the voicing a bit. While still using the same number of voices, large chords will fill the space better than small chords (see Figure F.5).

Figure F.5
The upper staff displays a close voicing harmonic progression, while the lower staff displays a wider version of the same chord progression.

Quantizing De-Humanizes

Quantizing is a technique often used with sequencers to tighten the rhythm of MIDI events in a musical part and to correct slightly sloppy playing. This technique places the notes you play on a grid of pre-established note values, such as quarter notes, eighth notes, or sixteenth notes, for example. As you record, any MIDI Note On event that's not entirely accurate—in light of the quantization value you have chosen—will be moved to the closest grid line defined by the quantization value in effect in Figure F.6.

Figure F.6
An example of MIDI events, before quantization (above) and after quantization (below)

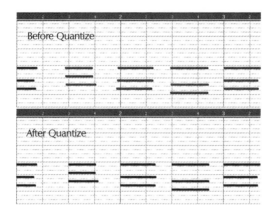

Although it is useful to quantize MIDI events to improve the rhythmic integrity of your musical performance, quantizing can also remove some of the feeling from your performance. Sequencer software applications now offer different quantization options that allow you to control the degree of quantization and may also affect more then just the note's position in the timeline. For example, it may affect the velocity level of notes that are played within this timeline. When using these tools to adjust your timing, you should always listen to the result and try not to remove all the subtle variations in rhythm you played when recording. When the sequencer offers a control over the amount of quantization, start with small changes, increasing slightly this amount until you are satisfied with the result without removing the human element from the performance.

MIDI Effects

With the prevalence of software instruments, MIDI instruments are more and more compatible with audio processing, since they use the computer's sound card to generate their sounds. Therefore, they are often treated as audio events and benefit from the effects processing available for any other digital audio event. However, since the musical parts are recorded using MIDI, they are also considered MIDI events and you can edit them as such in MIDI editors. In short, you get the flexibility of MIDI in terms of editing, and the flexibility of digital audio in terms of processing. This allows for overall greater flexibility and also greater control over the types of effects you can achieve with MIDI sound modules.

Another addition to sequencers has been the implementation of integrated MIDI effects, which allow you to create variations on the MIDI events recorded, both in real-time and playback modes. Figure F.7 shows an example of such a MIDI effect. Here, you can create instant arpeggios using musical events recorded on a track, or by playing real-time MIDI events through the MIDI effects module.

Figure F.7
The MIDI Arpeggio module in Cubase VST allows you to create instant arpeggio lines from a MIDI input

The techniques described below are, however, ways to accomplish certain MIDI effects without the use of software instruments or integrated MIDI effects. If you have a tool that offers a similar result, you will probably find it easier to simply use it. On the other hand, if your sequencer doesn't offer MIDI effects, here's how you can achieve a simulated echo using MIDI, and a simulated auto-pan effect using control change messages.

MIDI Echoes

Adding an echo to a MIDI part might add a nice color to your overall music. This type of echo consists of repeating the note, notes, or pattern of a musical part at a specific interval a number of times, and each time it repeats, the velocity goes down a bit.

If you look at Figure F.8, you will find an example of a simple repeating pattern. In Figure F.9, you can see that this pattern is now more complex, since the same pattern has been copied over four times, and each time, the velocity level has been reduced by a quarter as well. The last repetition, in this case, plays at the quarter velocity of its first occurrence. This, in effect, creates the impression of an echo; however, no external processing is involved. It's only a repetition of the first set of MIDI notes that will give the illusion of echoes being played.

Figure F.8
Original musical pattern
used to create an echo
effect

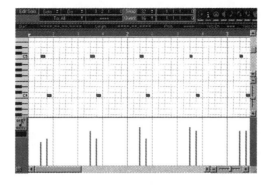

Figure F.9
The original pattern is
repeated, each time with
a lower velocity value,
creating an echo effect

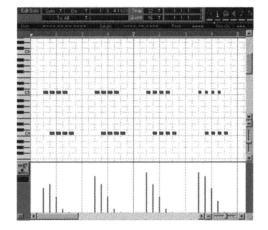

Here's how to create a MIDI echo effect without the aid of a special sequencing tool designed for the purpose:

1. Start by recording your original musical part. Long, sustained notes do not work as well as short notes in creating this effect, since you will be repeating the notes over, cutting sustained notes anyway.

2. Copy the MIDI part to another MIDI track below. If you want the echo to repeat three times, copy the same part on three separate tracks.

3. Make sure each track is playing on the same MIDI port, MIDI channel, and instrument.

4A. If your sequencer offers control over the playback of your MIDI events, such as a velocity control, this will make things easier. If that's the case, all you need to do is set the velocity value for each track at a value lower than the preceding track. For example, the first track contains your original data, so you leave it alone. Set the velocity of the second track about 25% lower than that of the first track. Continue like this for each copied part, reducing each time by about 25% in this case, since you have three repetitions. In terms of values, it might look like this:

The first track equals no change in velocity, the second track is –32 less than the first track, the third track is –64 less than the first track, and the fourth track is –96 less than the first track.

4B. If your sequencer does not support velocity control over tracks, you may edit the velocity controller in the appropriate editing window in order to make each repetition a bit softer than the preceding one.

5. Now that you have adjusted the velocity for each repetition, you will need to move each part in time. To do this, open the appropriate editing window (usually the piano roll type will do well for this) for the first copy (not the original recorded part).

6. Activate your quantization grid in this window to make sure your events will snap to the desired value. If you want your echo to follow at intervals of sixteenth notes, set your grid to snap to sixteenth notes.

7. Select all your events in the editing window for this first copy and move the events one-sixteenth note to the right (later in time). I'm using the sixteenth note as an example; you may want to use another value to determine the spacing of your echo. It's up to you.

8. Repeat steps 5 through 7 for the remaining copies of the original part, moving each copy one value more to the right. In this case, one sixteenth note every time.

9. Listen to the result once you are done and make adjustments as you see fit.

You may want to merge all the parts into a single part when you are done, having all copies appear on one track. To do this, you will need to consult your sequencer's documentation to find out how it handles multiple overlapping parts on a single track.

Rotating Pan

Another MIDI effect that can add movement to your song—without adding musical elements—involves panning a rhythmic pattern using the controller number 10, which controls the panning. There are many ways to do this depending on the sequencer you use; the easiest way would be to add pan automation through a MIDI mixer inside your sequencer. If your sequencer does not support MIDI automation mixes, you can add control change values in one of the edit windows, as shown in Figure F.10.

Figure F.10
Example of a MIDI
panning effect

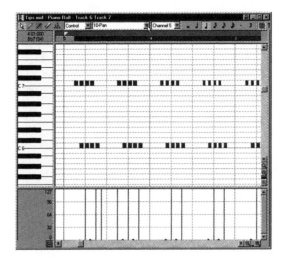

The idea in using this effect is to create motion, so rapidly changing the pan from a hard right to a hard left position (MIDI values 127 and 0) will be more effective than gradually panning from left to right. Panning a sound after its Note On message has been sent will likely not take effect until the next Note On message is received.

Appendix G
MIDI Resources on the Web

This appendix is not a complete listing of all MIDI resources on the Web. As you could imagine, doing a search on any search engine using the key word "MIDI" would result in millions of possible pages. But I have chosen a few selected links that should help you get started and complement the information you found in this book.

Happy surfing!

Tips and Tutorials

Another MIDI Tutorial, http://www.borg.com/~jglatt/tutr/miditutr.htm
Additional information about MIDI and related topics.

Cubase.net, http://www.cubase.net/
This site offers discussion forums, news, and tutorials for Cubase users.

Eddie's Home, http://www.2writers.com/eddie/midiIndex.htm
This guy has written a couple of interesting MIDI-related articles from a user's point of view. Worth the detour.

Exploring MIDI,
http://nuinfo.nwu.edu/musicschool/links/projects/midi/expmidiindex.html
A series of tutorials and information pages on MIDI and audio-related topics.

Hinton Instruments, http://www.hinton.demon.co.uk/mac/macmidi.html
This page offers additional optimization tips for your Macintosh.

Mac Beat, http://www.macbeat.com/tech.html
This page offers additional optimization tips for your Macintosh.

MIDI Basics, http://www.midiworld.com/basics.htm
Additional information about MIDI and related topics.

MIDI OX, http://www.midiox.com/index.htm
The FAQ section of this site has interesting information about MIDI, SMPTE, and SysEx.

MIDI Tutorial, http://kingfisher.cms.shu.ac.uk/midi/main_p.htm

Additional information about MIDI and wavetable synthesis.

SoundFonts, http://www.soundfonts.com/

Information about SoundFonts and related topics.

Tascam, http://www.tascam.com/support/faq/pc_optimize/index.php

This page offers additional tips to optimize your PC.

Directories and Listings

Digital Experience, http://www.digitalexperience.com/cards.html

Has a pretty good list of sound cards and their properties, including prices, connectors, types, OS, and so on.

Epinions, http://www.epinions.com/inst-Topics-All-Keyboards_MIDI

This site offers reviews and user comments on audio and MIDI gear.

Harmony Central, http://www.harmony-central.com/

Offers a wealth of MIDI- and audio-related information.

MIDI.com, http://www.midi.com/

This site offers mostly MIDI file searches and discussion forums on MIDI, as well as some interesting links.

MIDI Farm, http://www.midifarm.com/

A good place to get industry related news, MIDI files, and MIDI information.

Music Software, http://www.hitsquad.com/smm/

This site contains links to downloadable MIDI- and audio-related software for Windows, Macintosh, Linux, BeOs, and Atari.

PC Sound Card Technical Benchmark, http://www.pcavtech.com/soundcards/

This site contains the results of a test on different sound cards, rating their qualities.

Planet MIDI, http://www.planetz.net/midi/

Yet another site that offers plenty of good MIDI resources and MIDI files.

Synth Zone, http://www.synthzone.com/

This site offers many links and information on sound module manufacturers, as well as on software developers.

Online Magazines

Computer Music, http://www.computermusic.co.uk/main.asp
This site contains loads of information, tutorials, reviews, and forums.

M2CMag, http://www.mc2mag.com/
Self proclaimed as the music players network, this site offers a wealth of MIDI and audio information.

StreamWorks Audio, http://www.streamworksaudio.com/
Online magazine for music enthusiasts.

Associations

MIDI Manufacturers Association, http://www.midi.org/
To get the lowdown on the latest MIDI developments.

Association of Music Electronics Industries, http://www.amei.or.jp/index_e.html
This is the Japanese counterpart to the MMA.

Hardware Manufacturers

Aardvark, http://www.aardvark-pro.com/pc_audio.html
Sound card manufacturer.

Apple, http://www.apple.com/creative/music/midi/
This page offers information on audio and MIDI peripherals for Macintosh computers.

AudioTrak, http://www.audiotrak.net/eng/index.html
Sound card manufacturer.

Creamware, http://www.creamware.de/en/Home/default.asp
Sound card developers.

Digidesign, http://www.digidesign.com/
Sound card and other audio-related device manufacturer. Digidesign also developed the ProTools software.

Echo, http://www.echoaudio.com/
Sound card manufacturer.

Edirol, http://www.edirol.com/
Audio-related device manufacturer.

APPENDIX G

GeeThree, *http://www.geethree.com/*
PCI serial port manufacturer for Macintosh computer users.

JLCooper, *http://www.jlcooper.com/*
Developers of MIDI and audio controllers, as well as some audio-related devices.

KAT, *http://www.alternatemode.com/*
The makers of drum pad controllers.

Korg, *http://www.korg.com/*
Makers of audio and MIDI devices.

Mackie, *http://www.mackie.com/default.asp*
Makers of audio sound reinforcement devices.

MIDIMAN, *http://www.midiman.com/*
Makers of sound cards and other computer-related sound and MIDI interfaces.

MOTU, *http://www.motu.com/*
Makers of sound cards and other computer-related sound and MIDI interfaces and software (such as FreeMIDI and Digital Performer).

Roland, *http://www.rolandus.com/*
Makers of audio and MIDI devices.

StarrLabs, *http://www.starrlabs.com/*
Makers of guitar controllers.

Yamaha, *http://www.yamaha.com/*
Makers of audio and MIDI devices.

Software Developers

Cakewalk, *http://www.cakewalk.com/*
MIDI and audio software developers.

CDXtract, *http://www.cdxtract.com/*
Software for sample format conversion. Very useful if you use samplers and software instruments.

Coda Music, *http://www.codamusic.com/coda/*
MIDI software developers (notation application).

Emagic, *http://www.emagic.de/english/news/index.html*
MIDI and audio software developers.

Native Instruments, *http://www.native-instruments.com/*

Developers of many software instruments available in different formats.

Nemesys (Tascam), *http://www.nemesysmusic.com/*

Developers of GigaStudio sampling software application. You will also find a list of tested sound cards on this site.

Propellerheads, *http://www.propellerheads.se/*

MIDI and audio software developers.

Sonic Foundry, *http://www.sonicfoundry.com/*

Audio software developers.

Steinberg, *http://www.steinberg.net*

MIDI and audio software developers.

Index

D

Index

Index

Index

S

T

U

V

W

X

Index